MUSLIMS AND CHRISTIANS ON THE EMMAUS ROAD

J. Dudley Woodberry
Editor

MARC
919 West Huntington Drive, Monrovia, California, USA 91016

Woodberry, J. Dudley, **editor**

Muslims and Christians on the Emmaus Road

Contributing authors and editors:

Adeyemo, Tokumboh	Antablin, Florence	Chapman, Colin
Chastain, Warren	Conn, Harvie	Cragg, Kenneth
Douglas, Robert	al Ghazali, Hasan	Green, Denis
Hiebert, Paul	Huffard Evertt	Malek, Sobhi
Marantika, Chris	Mensah, Muhammadou	Parshall, Phil
Register, Ray	Shenk, David	Smith, D.
Stacey, Vivienne	Standish, Alberta	Uddin, Rafique
Vander Werff, Lyle	Wilson, J. Christy, Jr.	Woodberry, J. Dudley

Olson, David, editorial consultant

Muslims and Christians on the Emmaus Road has been selected and adapted in large part from the papers presented at the conference centered on Islamic-Christian themes under the sponsorship of the Lausanne Committee for World Evangelization in July of 1987 in Zeist, Netherlands. Publication has been in close cooperation with the Strategic Planning Committee of LCWE.

ISBN 0-912552-65-4

Printed in the United States of America. Body type: Palatino 13 pts., reduced photographically 25%. Typesetting/pagination: Microsoft Word 3.02 by International Development Services, Arcadia. Printing and binding: Book Crafters, Chelsea, MI. Cover art: Walt Edler Graphics, Monrovia, CA.

MARC Publications
Missions Advanced Research & Communications Center, Monrovia, CA
A Division of World Vision International
919 W. Huntington Drive, Monrovia, CA 91016
Telephone: (818) 303-8811

Dedicated to

Mary Belle Varker, M.D.

a companion and helper on every road since my boyhood
and faithful to the heavenly vision

CONTRIBUTING AUTHORS

Tokumboh Adeyemo
General Secretary, Association of Evangelicals in Africa and Madagascar, Nairobi, Kenya, and a former Muslim.

Florence Antablin
Former Instructor in art history, University of California, Fresno. Service in Lebanon and Saudi Arabia.

Colin Chapman
Lecturer in the Study of Mission and the Study of Religion at Trinity College, Bristol, England. Service in Egypt and Lebanon.

Warren Chastain
Director of Strategy and Special Projects, Zwemer Institute of Islamic Studies, Pasadena, CA. Service in Thailand and Indonesia.

Harvie Conn
Professor of Missions and Director of the Urban Missions Program, Westminster Theological Seminary, Philadelphia, PA. Service in Korea.

Kenneth Cragg
Assistant Bishop of Wakefield, England. Former Assistant Bishop in Jerusalem Archbishopric, based in Cairo, and Professor in Lebanon, Nigeria, the United States, and England.

Robert Douglas
Director, Zwemer Institute of Islamic Studies, Pasadena, CA. Service in the Middle East.

Hasan al-Ghazali
A Middle Eastern businessman working in a Middle Eastern country.

Denis Green
Director of Training and Research, Asia Pacific Christian Mission, Auckland, New Zealand. Service in Indonesia.

Paul Hiebert
Professor of Anthropology and South Asian Studies, School of World Mission, Fuller Theological Seminary, Pasadena, CA. Service in India.

Evertt Huffard
Associate Dean, the Harding Graduate School of Religion, Memphis, TN. Service in Jerusalem and Nazareth.

Sobhi Malek
Egyptian directing North African radio ministry and Bible correspondence courses with the Assemblies of God in Malaga, Spain.

Chris Marantika
President, Evangelical Theological Seminary of Indonesia, Yokjakarta, and Indonesian Area Dean of the Asia Graduate School of Theology.

Muhammadou Mensah
Pseudonym for development workers from Africa, the Middle East, and Central and South East Asia.

Phil Parshall
Director, Asian Research Center, Manila. Service in Bangladesh and the Philippines.

Ray Register
Southern Baptist Representative in Nazareth and the Arab villages of Galilee.

David Shenk
Director, Eastern Mennonite Board of Missions and Charities, Salunga, PA. Service in Somalia.

D. Smith
Missionary in a Middle Eastern country.

Vivienne Stacey
InterServ worker in Pakistan, the Gulf, and North Africa.

Alberta Standish
Working with Muslim women in California. Service in the Middle East.

Rafique Uddin
A Muslim believer in South Asia.

Lyle Vander Werff
Professor of Religion, Northwestern College, Orange City, IA. Service in Kuwait.

J. Christy Wilson, Jr.
Professor of Missions and Evangelism and Dean of the Chapel, Gordon-Conwell Theological Seminary, South Hamilton, MA. Service in Afghanistan.

J. Dudley Woodberry
Assistant Professor of Islamic Studies, School of World Mission, Fuller Theological Seminary, Pasadena, CA. Service in Lebanon, Pakistan, Afghanistan, and Saudi Arabia.

CONTENTS

OLD FORMS AND NEW MEANINGS: "Known...in the breaking of the bread"

SPIRITUAL EMPOWERING: "Clothed with power from on high"

RESOURCES FOR UNDERSTANDING: "He opened their minds to understand"

FOLLOWING ANCIENT FOOTPRINTS

As a pilgrimage, it was a short one.

It began in Jerusalem, where two god-fearing men found their faith faltering. Disappointed and despondent at a turn of events they could not understand, they decided to seek the comfort of familiar surroundings in their home town of Emmaus.

Seven miles—but then an unrecognized Teacher came up to them and discussed their problem. In no time, it seemed, they were in Emmaus, their destination. And they could not bear to end what had been such an exciting and revealing conversation.

"Please stay with us," the two begged of the unrecognized Stranger, "and let us go on talking."

It was in the breaking of bread at the supper table when the veil was finally lifted. Just as he disappeared from before them, they were startled to realize that their Companion had been none other than Jesus Christ, the resurrected Messiah.

The pilgrimage ends as the two men rush back to Jerusalem. There, doubts are resolved, faith is affirmed, commitment is offered and power received for extending the Kingdom of God and of his Christ to all the earth.

As we review their familiar story, we are struck by its contemporary quality. Two Middle Eastern men walking dispiritedly along the dusty road to Emmaus, discussing the controversy over a man who had recently been executed. The environment, their facial features, and even their clothing are remarkably similar to those of many Muslim people in current times. Today, countless Muslims literally walk along the same road. And hundreds of years after Cleopas and his friend had their discussion on the way to Emmaus, Muslims echo their conversation about the man who died on a cross.

As the original travelers turned away from Jerusalem, so the later ones turn their focus of worship (*qibla*) away from that city. Both see Jesus as "a prophet mighty in deed and word" but cannot reconcile his messiahship with a crucifixion. Like the earlier ones, the later wayfarers recognize the prophets but are "slow of heart to believe all that the prophets have spoken" and "their eyes were [are] kept from recognizing him" as he really is.

Jesus, who walked beside and conversed with his Middle Eastern friends so many years ago, is our example today as we walk behind with our Muslim companions. He "drew near and went with them," asked them questions, then "interpreted to them in all the Scriptures the things concerning himself." This story of a revealing encounter with Jesus Christ lends itself as a natural vehicle for reflection on crucial issues in witness to Muslims. We use it to provide a framework for this book.

It is our prayer that those who join the dialogue through these pages will also have their eyes opened by the Unrecognized Companion.

As I come to the end of the road in the preparation of this manuscript, there are many I must thank for walking with me. First, Edward R. Dayton and Bradford Smith of the Lausanne Committee for World Evangelization, invited me to start down the road to direct their Muslim program and publications, with David Montague and the Zwemer Institute for Muslim Studies under the direction of Robert Douglas providing the administration. David ably handled the organization and administration of the conference at which most of these and many other papers were presented and discussed, and William Mottinger tirelessly entered the papers into the word processor.

World Vision and the Lausanne Committee for World Evangelization have also contributed purses to help meet expenses along the road. During the final miles, companions from MARC have helped prepare the text for publication. Dayton Roberts, Betty Clark and Mitali Perkins have overseen the process. Special thanks go to David Olson who has gone over all the manuscripts to make sure they communicate to lay-persons and has added marginal summaries. My own secretary Jone Bosch, has entered some of the final material into the word processor.

Finally, my gratitude goes to my life companion, Roberta, and our children John, Corinne, Robert and David who have supported and enlivened my walk on this and many another dusty road.

Advent, 1988   J. Dudley Woodberry
Pasadena   Editor

The Emmaus Story in the Bible

That very day two of them were going to a village named Emmaus, about seven miles from Jerusalem, and talking with each other about all these things that had happened. While they were talking and discussing together, Jesus himself drew near and went with them. But their eyes were kept from recognizing him.

And he said to them, "What is this conversation which you are holding with each other as you walk?"

And they stood still, looking sad. Then one of them, named Cleopas, answered him, "Are you the only visitor to Jerusalem who does not know the things that have happened there in these days?"

And he said to them, "What things?"

And they said to him, "Concerning Jesus of Nazareth, who was a prophet mighty in deed and word before God and all the people, and how our chief priests and rulers delivered him up to be condemned to death, and crucified him. But we had hoped that he was the one to redeem Israel. Yes, and besides all this, it is now the third day since this happened. Moreover, some women of our company amazed us. They were at the tomb early in the morning but did not find his body; and they came back saying that they had even seen a vision of angels, who said that he was alive. Some of those who were with us went to the tomb, and found it just as the women had said; but him they did not see."

And he said to them, "O foolish men, and slow of heart to believe all that the prophets have spoken! Was it not necessary that the Christ should suffer these things and enter into his glory?" And beginning with Moses and all the Prophets, he interpreted to them in all the Scriptures the things concerning himself.

So they drew near to the village to which they were going. He appeared to be going further, but they constrained him, saying, "Stay with us, for it is toward evening and the day is now far spent." So he went in to stay with them.

When he was at table with them, he took the bread and blessed, and broke it, and gave it to them. And their eyes were opened and they recognized him; and he vanished out of their sight. They said to each other, "Did not our hearts burn within us while he talked to us on the road, while he opened to us the Scriptures?"

And they rose that same hour and returned to Jerusalem; and they found the Eleven gathered together and those who were with them, who said, "The Lord has risen indeed, and has appeared to Simon!" Then they told what had happened on the road, and how he was known them in the breaking of the bread.

—Luke 24:13–35 RSV

GOING TO EMMAUS

Originally the unifying theme for this book (and the conference behind it) was found in a prayer uttered near this Emmaus road about 2000 years earlier by the father of Jews, Christians, and Muslims: "that Ishmael might live before thee" (Gen. 17:18). Yet this reference, though part of our common heritage, called to mind rejections and hostilities which this volume does not reflect because the need for open dialogue is now so great and so timely. Consequently, the chapters are clustered around Luke's account of the discussions along the Emmaus Road.

Following Ancient Footprints : Overview

The two disciples and Jesus talked about many things to which the account in Luke 24 merely alluded. Likewise the conference in Zeist, Holland, where most of the papers which became chapters of this book were first read, included many things that publication costs have barred from this collection—area studies, other crucial issues and interaction by participants, many from the Third World and representing every area of the Muslim world. These papers provide an overview of these conversations, the issues they identified, and some of the conclusions they reached.

"What is this conversation . . . as you walk?": Varieties of People

Cleopas and his friend were discussing the events of the day when Jesus drew near, walked with them, and asked questions (vss. 15, 17, 19). Any meaningful dialogue with Muslims needs to start by walking with them, listening to them, and asking them questions. In this section we look at the religious and political trends in the Muslim world from fundamentalism to agnosticism. Then we seek to understand the animistic substrata of much Muslim faith and practice, the uneasy alliance it has with ideal Islam, and its implications for witness. Finally, we look at major social trends—especially urbanization and poverty—and the holistic Christian response for which they call.

"He interpreted . . . in all the Scriptures": Scriptural Perspectives

The two travelers to Emmaus started where Muslims start—"Jesus...was a prophet mighty in deed and word" (vs. 19). And they stumbled on the same event—his crucifixion (vs. 20). Thus "beginning with Moses and the prophets," in which both groups of travelers believe, "he interpreted to them in all the Scripture the things concerning himself" (vs. 27). Since the eyes of the subsequent wayfarers like those of the former have been "kept from recognizing him" (vs. 16), we too need to search the Scriptures with Muslims looking over our shoulders. Temple Gairdner of Cairo said at the Pan-Anglican Congress in England in 1908:

> Who shall gauge the debt we may have to confess to Islam if... [it] prove finally to have compelled us to explore unknown depths of the riches of the revelation of the Triune God?

This section seeks to rethink the Gospel for a Muslim audience. It starts with the common theme of God's desire to reveal and follows that desire beyond revealing his will to revealing himself. Then it moves to Muslim and Christian diagnoses of the human condition. Traditionally, Muslims have started from the premise that human nature is good or neutral, requiring no transformation such as a "new birth." These people, therefore, revisit Muslim sources from the Quran to Khomeini to show an awareness that the human predicament is far graver than traditionally recognized. Does this not then suggest the need for the more radical solution found in the gospel?

Next there is the recognition that certain themes such as love and sin, which strike a responsive note in Western Christians, do not vibrate to the same extent in Eastern Muslims. Other biblical themes such as the honor of God, which Western Christians filter out of their understanding and presentation of the gospel, find a more responsive ear with Eastern Muslims. For this reason we seek to interpret the gospel in terms which are seen as more relevant to a Muslim audience. Finally we turn to the witness of worship. As Muslims often express their faith through the recitation of the names of God, Christians are given a suggested model for expressing their faith by the recitation of the biblical witness to Christ, whom Muslims also recognize as "a prophet mighty in deed and word" (vs. 19).

"Their eyes were opened": Forms of Witness

Prior to the disciples' journey to Emmaus, women had born witness to the resurrection of Jesus, "but these words seemed to them as idle talk" (vs. 10-11). Likewise the subsequent Muslims reject the witness to that resurrection by rejecting its antecedent crucifixion. Even when the disciples saw Jesus, "their eyes were kept from recognizing him" (vs. 16), as Muslims have since failed to recognize all he claimed to be. Yet, after the scripture and then their eyes were opened (vss. 27,31), they returned to Jerusalem and bore witness to what had happened (vss. 33, 35)—a witness Jesus confirmed by his presence (vss. 36, 39). The center of attention (*qibla*) had returned to Jerusalem, but Jesus turned outward again with the words:

> ...repentance and forgiveness of sins should be preached in his name to all nations, beginning from Jerusalem. You are witnesses of these things (vss. 47-48).

In this section a number of effective witnesses tell how they share their faith—from discussing in coffee houses to using the natural web of communication through relatives and friends. As women were the first disciples to witness and bear witness of the Risen Lord, so special attention is given to sharing faith among women in their natural context and when they are in foreign contexts.

"Known . . . in the breaking of the bread": Old Forms and New Meanings

Jesus was incarnated into a culture. As was culturally appropriate, he "appeared to be going further" when he and his companions approached Emmaus (vs. 28). In keeping with their cultural reflex, "they constrained him, saying, 'Stay with us, for it is toward evening'" (vs. 29). Then he took bread—the common means of bonding with others—as he had three nights before at the Last Supper, and revealed through it his identity as the Suffering Messiah. An old form took on a new meaning.

The first study in this section looks at the Hebrew Christians addressed in the Epistle to the Hebrews, who retained Jewish forms of worship and may have given the appearance of remaining within Judaism. Since these forms are similar to Muslim forms, biblical guidelines are drawn for Muslim contextualization. Next an attempt is made to start identifying lessons from recent attempts at contextualization among Muslims. Then a Muslim follower of Christ gives the principles that he and similar brothers and sisters are following in a Muslim country and which God has blessed with a phenomenal ingathering of new believers. Finally, we look at those architectural forms that have been used to express and house adoration by Muslim and Christian alike. They have been freely borrowed and returned and still lend themselves undiminished to manifest and embrace worship in spirit and in truth.

"Clothed with power from on high": Spiritual Empowering

The disciples were told to "stay in the city until you are clothed with power from on high" (vs. 49). Christ "blessed them" (vs. 50), and they responded by being "continually in the temple blessing God" (vs. 53). Previously in the analysis of Folk Muslims, the centrality of power in their world view was demonstrated. Here we move from an understanding of power to practical guidelines for being channels of God's power in exorcism and healing, concerns especially of Folk Muslims. Then we turn for biblical models to guide our praying and finally to experiences of the fruit of prayer for Muslims.

"He opened their minds to understand": Resources for Understanding

In the story of the Emmaus Road, Jesus "opened their minds to understand the Scriptures, and said to them, 'Thus it is written...'" (vss. 45-46). This section seeks to identify the resources of places and literature along the way that might better introduce us to our Muslim companions in travel and be used by our Divine Companion to open our minds to understand the scriptures, that we together might recall "Did not our hearts burn within us while he talked with us on the road, while he opened to us the Scriptures?" (vs. 32).

CHAPTER ONE

CONVERSATIONS ALONG THE WAY

David W. Shenk

We, as concerned Christians from every section of the Muslim World, convened in Holland in the summer of 1987, by invitation of the Lausanne Committee for World Evangelization to consider critical issues in Christian witness among Muslims. Our reflection together involved four dimensions:

- prayer, worship and Biblical study

- critical reflection on related theological issues

- reports and analyses of the status of witness and church formation in selected regions of the world

- practical approaches to Muslim evangelism derived from our Biblical and theological reflection and contemporary experience.

Confession and Commitment

As the people of the Book, we stand upon that which God has revealed in the Biblical Scriptures. It is for that reason that we believe in one God only, the creator and sustainer of the universe. In his great love for all people, he reaches out to us, inviting us to repent of our sinfulness, and to become his own covenant people.

We confess that in Jesus the Messiah, we have met the one in whom God has fully and definitively revealed himself, the only Lord and Savior of humankind. We rejoice in the presence of the Spirit of God, who is working throughout the world, seeking and calling people to righteousness and to the knowledge of God, who is revealed in the Messiah—the way, the truth and the life. It is this reality which compels us to be present, to witness, to serve, to invite, to pray, to wait, in anticipation that all Muslim people will have the opportunity to discover in Jesus the Messiah forgiveness of sin and the fruit of salvation, both now and eternally.

We expect that those who believe will become members of redeemed communities which will be authentic signs of the Kingdom of God. We believe this vision and commitment is in harmony with the will of God who desires that all peoples may hear the Gospel and experience salvation through repentance and faith in Jesus the Messiah.

Significant Themes

The pre-conference planning included a wide-ranging survey of persons involved in witness among Muslims to ascertain their perceptions of critical issues. From these responses, six major themes were identified:

— Culture and contextualization
— Folk Islam and power encounter
— Evangelism and conversion
— National and international mission
— Urbanization and poverty
— Research and training

Each day focused on one theme. Our days included in-depth Bible study, theological reflection, regional stories and reports and practical implications.

The central theme of the conference was proclaimed in the keynote opening address: "That Ishmael might live before Thee." This theme helped to provide the conferees with the reminder that both Muslim and Christian communities profess to be the faith descendants of Abraham.

Abraham struggled with the question: How is God's promise, how is his Kingdom, to be fulfilled?

We remember that God promised to give Abraham descendants, how his patience was tested and he had a son by Hagar. This act of Abraham reveals the profound depth and agony of the question: Does the promise of God need the assistance of human striving, or is the vulnerability of obedience all that God desires in order that we might receive the fulfillment of the promise of salvation?

Muslims and Christians face the same issues as they meet one another in faith conversations. Is the Kingdom of God established through the instruments of power used at Medina, or does the Kingdom break through in the vulnerability of the cross? Is political power an effective way of establishing God's will on earth, or is God's mission extended through suffering redemptive servanthood? Is the community of faith sustained through the instruments of law or by the gift of grace? Is the community of the people of God created through Gospel, that is, the grace of our Lord Jesus Christ; or through Islam, that is, the divine mercy of revealed guidance?

These issues are not just present when Muslims and Christians meet one another; they are in the soul of every human, and in the spirit of everyone who desires to live by the faith of Abraham. Is the promise of God, the gift of grace, the vulnerability of suffering love as revealed in Jesus really sufficient to establish and fulfill God's will on earth? "Yes!" is the witness of the Bible and the faithful of God with his Church.

Biblical Reflection

Our Biblical studies looked at six dimensions of Christian relations with Muslims.

1. We considered the meaning of the Abrahamic prayer, "O that Ishmael might live in thy sight!" (Gen. 17:15). We reviewed all the Biblical references to Ishmael.

We also looked at Quranic and other data concerning the relationship of Islam and the Arabs to Ishmael. It is in Medina that Ishmael acquired special significance for Muslims for it is through him that they perceive the legitimization of the *ummah*as the community of faith which is in continuity with Abraham.

It is in Jesus the Messiah that the new community of redeemed people is formed which supersedes not only the *ummah*, but all other communities (Ac. 4:23-31).

2. We searched the Bible as we sought for an appropriate Christian response to the Islamic perception of God. The Bible affirms some Muslim perceptions of God, yet we only experience and know God as Father through Jesus the Messiah.

Too often Christians exaggerate only the evil among Muslims, and fail to recognize much that is true and good. We deplore expressions of evil and the demonic wherever these are evident, whether among Muslims or Christians.

3. We listened to the Apostle Paul sharing Christ in ancient Athens (Ac. 17:16-34). Just as Paul built upon indications of truth in Athenian tradition, so we also, in witness among Muslims, need to hear and understand the truth which is already present, as we also give witness that salvation is found in Jesus crucified and risen.

4. We discovered parallels and also differences between the prophet Jeremiah and the Quranic perceptions of prophethood. We found that a full understanding of the ministry of the Biblical prophets may serve as a bridge for Muslims to understand Jesus, for they do accept him as a prophet.

5. We reviewed the meaning of the term, Son of God, in the Old Testament, where it refers to the people of the covenant, or the king as a representative of the people. Jesus claims to be the Son of God; this certainly does not refer to a physical sonship, but rather indicates the nature of his ministry, his personhood and his special relationship to God. Jesus as the incarnation of the Word of God helps us understand the meaning of Son. In the Synoptic Gospels the Word of Jesus performs the work of God and reveals the truth of God. This fact is further clarified in John, where Jesus is described as the one in whom the Word became flesh.

6. We were deeply touched as we considered the costliness of unconditional love.

In the Quran God loves, forgives and is merciful, but these gifts to humankind do not affect God himself. God loves only those who do right; his forgiveness is inscrutable.

Yet in the Gospel God demonstrates his unexpected love and forgiveness at great personal cost. "God demonstrates his own love for us in this: while we were still sinners, Christ died for us" (Rom. 5:8).

Significant Theological Considerations

In one way or another, all our theological deliberations related to his central question: How should Christians faithfully express and communicate the Gospel of the Kingdom of our Lord Jesus Christ? We explored four issues central to this overall commitment.

Contemporary Trends in Islam

There are voices of theological reflection within Islam today which are raising questions about the relationship between political power and the faith community. Too often the instruments of political power corrupt. Perhaps the Medina model of the integration of political, military and faith communities was only appropriate under the leadership of the prophet, and subsequent expressions of Islamic faithfulness would be best exemplified in situations where the state is secular.

Other voices reflect on the role of suffering within the faith experience. Perhaps the faithful *ummah* should anticipate experiences of suffering in a world which ignores the will of God. Even Muhammad suffered for thirteen years in Mecca.

Although these voices are noteworthy, they are nevertheless heard only on the outer edges, the margins of Islamic theology. The mainstream of theological reflection continues to perceive the triumphalism of Medina as normative for authentic Islam. However, although Medina is the model community for most Muslim theologians, there is also a persistent secularizing stream within Islam which seeks pragmatic rather than strictly religious solutions to the crisis presented by modernity.

Of even greater significance is the quest by many Muslims for a sustaining spirituality for times like these. That search is expressed in many areas of modern life, including the inward crisis of faith, Islam in relation to the state and the role of religion in society. In a sense all of Islam responds to these issues from a "fundamentalist" perspective, for the doctrine of *tanzil* means for the Muslim that the sent-down Quran is the unalterable given for all of life's questions.

On the other hand some modernist theologians search for new meanings within the Quranic framework which are relevant to modernity. Could it be that this search will also lead some to consider the Gospel?

Contextualization

Modern missiology has often stressed the need for the emergent church to take root in the local society; this is to say that the church needs to become indigenous.

Contextualization is a still broader concept expressing relevance not only to the cultural but to all the other variables in the society as well, while it also judges aspects of them. To what extent are Christians in a Muslim culture free to develop and initiate cultural patterns and usages in worship from within the surrounding Muslim communities and from an older Christian past?

We turned to the Biblical book of Hebrews to learn from the Jewish Christian experience in contextualization. These contextualized Jewish Christians were in danger of being reabsorbed into Judaism, and so they were encouraged to make their stand for Christ more evident. Our discussion focused on several cautions which included:

1. Muslims sometimes perceive of a contextual commitment, especially in worship, as being devious, a sort of fifth column within the heart of the Islamic *ummah*, an attempt to seduce people unawares into a Christian trap.

2. A commitment to contextualization may sever the emerging believing community from the symbols of relationship with the universal church. This relationship is vitally important to a minority community struggling for identity and security. The traditional churches and the emerging church in a Muslim context need to develop a relationship which helps to inform both the traditional and the new Christian communities of the essence of the church as the body of Christ, which is both local and universal, both ancient and new.

3. Contextual symbols and practices may sometimes communicate meaning inimical to the essence of the Gospel, as for example, praying towards a geographical locus such as Jerusalem, or a regular prayer ritual which communicates a legalism similar to that of Islam. Contextualization may lead to forms of syncretism which betray the Gospel.

4. In many situations modernizing trends among Muslims will lead the emerging congregation to seek a worship style which symbolizes freedom from the traditional Muslim forms. For example, they may choose to stand for prayer rather than prostrate, or to sit on chairs rather than on the floor, or for men and women to worship together. In this case, the quest for modernity will determine the form in which contextualization is expressed.

Nevertheless, we believe that the nature of the Gospel itself requires a commitment to the principle of contextualization. This, for example, is one reason why the church in mission has always striven to translate the Bible into the languages of peoples. We believe it is the will of God that the body of Christ become authentically present in every culture and that the Gospel be interpreted with clarity and relevance among every people. It is right for Muslims who have believed in Jesus the Messiah to worship with idioms and forms which express the incarnational presence of the Gospel in their culture.

A good test of the appropriateness of particular expressions of contextualization is this question: Does the surrounding Muslim community perceive that the new Christian congregation is a new creation, or only a modified expression of the *ummah*? Our theological consideration of contextualization was informed by examples of practical experience. In fact, we shared in our own "contextual" worship, where the Gospel was expressed in Muslim worship forms. Some of us wept as we bowed with faces to the floor confessing Jesus the Messiah our Lord and Savior. We listened to stories of emergent Christian communities in Muslim societies who are expressing a contextual lifestyle, worship ritual and theology. In several locations, contextualized church planting is developing momentum as a people group movement! Yet even these movements are not without suffering; perhaps this is especially so because a contextualized Christian fellowship is disturbingly present and relevant. Such a church is indeed "in but not of the world" (Jn. 17:14-19).

Folk Islam

Folk Islamic societies have accepted traditional cosmologies which perceive of the Creator at the apex of the power hierarchy with lesser intermediary spiritual powers permeating natural phenomena. Modern medicines, medicinal herbs or the use of traditional Muslim medical science for cures of illness are often interwoven with Quranic prayers for healing. Many Muslims wear Quranic and other talismans to ward off evil forces. In this manner they seek *tawiz* the protection of God, the all-powerful and merciful. Spirit experts are called upon to exorcise demons from the possessed.

Strictly secular or psychological approaches to demon possession or cures for diseases do not really connect with the Islamic world view and the folk perceptions of reality. The occult therefore often intermingles with prayer and medical science. Yet spiritism and occult practices seem to intermingle with fear. Often the "cure" for demon possession is actually accompanied by a proliferation of the "disease."

A relevant Christian witness needs to include spiritual power encounter through the power of our crucified and risen Lord Jesus Christ. The church must express and communicate the Messiah as the one who is triumphant over all demons and who is indeed the great physician. The demons need to be cajoled and entreated by the Muslim spirit experts, but in the name of the Messiah the demons tremble and obey. The touch of healing power in the name of Jesus the Messiah is good news indeed, even when modern or traditional medicines are applied.

What symbols are appropriate to express security in the healing and protecting power of Christ? When do symbols become superstition or magical? When Christian symbols are used, it is important to teach the real meaning of the symbol. Confession of sin, prayer by the elders, the laying on hands and anointing with oil for healing are Biblical and contextual within folk Islam.

However, it is also important to recognize that the powers of evil are in human institutions and structures as well as the spirit world. Human structures, including those of the *ummah*, present major obstacles to the Gospel. Furthermore, power encounter with persons or structures which oppose the Gospel usually involves suffering; throughout the book of Acts, confrontation with demons, idols and the occult was usually accompanied by confrontation also with human institutions, as for example at Philippi and Ephesus. These incidents always brought suffering to the church. Power encounter with demons or humans is effectuated through the suffering and triumph of the cross.

Ministries of healing are not necessarily related to demons or evil. We believe that prayer for the sick should be a normal ministry of the church, not only among Christians, but also a ministry by Christians for their Muslim neighbors. In many communities Muslims are being drawn to faith in Jesus the Messiah through the prayer ministry of the church.

The Nature of Conversion

What forms of social and theological change take place in conversion? Is the world view touched in the conversion process, or does the change of orientation take place at the value level of culture and psyche? In many so-called

Christianized societies, the church has achieved a fairly comfortable rapprochement with the mainstream culture. Is it right to expect Muslims to undergo a much more radical break with their culture than is true of Christians in so-called Christianized cultures, even though in many respects the Islamic culture may be more attuned to Biblical themes than is true of secular-Christianized cultures?

While these questions are urgent and significant, we perceive that the center point of conversion is a reorientation of life to a focused commitment to Jesus Christ as Lord and Savior and the amazing discovery that God is our loving heavenly Father. Sometimes conversion is an event. More often conversion for Muslims seems to be a process. Many in our own group had suffered much persecution after conversion. Yet the precious prize of knowing Jesus as Lord and Savior, God as Father, was a gift worth suffering for. The outworkings of that commitment are varied and fascinating and operate at many different levels of the psychic and the culture. Yet in every culture and within every person the center point of conversion is the confession that Jesus Christ is Lord and Savior and that God is our loving Father.

We are sobered, however, to learn that in some situations individual Muslims who confess faith in Christ do not become fully part of a believing community, and some therefore return to the Muslim community. Oftentimes believers also face pressure from family and the *ummah*. They may be ostracized from the economic structures of the Islamic community and become impoverished. The church must therefore become not only an evangelizing and nurturing community, but also a new and supporting family for the new believer. Conversion is not only to Christ, but also to the church, which must be ready to receive and encourage the new disciple.

We also believe that the church has a mission within Islam in addition to inviting individuals to faith in the Messiah. This is a witness to Islam itself, calling for a conversion within the spirit of Islam. This call is to consider the Spirit of Jesus in matters such as attitudes towards women and family, human rights, or ecology. It is a call to recognize the legitimacy of the witnessing church in their midst. The presence of the church should be an invitation to the *ummah* as a whole to a fuller quality of life. Prayer for the peace of the community is also a most significant ministry.

Exploratory Theological Considerations

We also commenced discussion on three theological concerns which merit much more thought than was possible in this brief conference. In essence the issues are: God in Islam and the Bible, Interpreting Jesus the Messiah and The Kingdom of God.

Muslim and Christian Perceptions of God

To what extent is the Biblical revelation of God as the one who reveals himself in loving covenant encounter with humankind, the one who is our father, our Abba, compatible with the Islamic perception of God, before whom Muslims bow in worship? How do we give witness to God as the one who chooses to reveal himself through his acts in history amidst the Islamic perception of God as the one who reveals only his will to humankind? How do we faithfully express the personal I-thou encounter of Biblical theology amidst an Islamic mystical (*sufi*) milieu which yearns for mystical absorption into divinity?

While we believe that in the Quran there is a greater openness to the revelation of Immanuel, God with us, than Islamic orthodoxy suggests, we nevertheless admit that we must ultimately let that judgment rest with the Muslims. Our primary task is not Quranic hermeneutics, important as that may be. Rather we are called to share the surprise of Biblical revelation with our Muslim friends.

Neither dialogue nor propositional polemics can adequately resolve these ultimate questions concerning the nature of God. Rather, let the accounts of God's acts of loving self-disclosure and encounter in Biblical salvation history speak to these issues. The accounts are witness enough! Let us tell of God's mighty acts, and invite Muslims to explore with us the Reality revealed in these accounts: Adam and Eve, Noah, Abraham, Ishmael and Isaac, Jeremiah, the Acts of the Apostles, but especially the accounts concerning Jesus who has revealed God to us as our Abba.

Interpreting Jesus Among Muslims

The Christian witness is that Jesus the Messiah is the definitive revelation of God and His will; in our conversations with Muslims, the cross therefore becomes the major stumbling block. Muslims ask, "Does not the crucifixion reveal God as weak and vulnerable? If indeed the cross is the revelation of God's love, then that love seems both cruel and weak, for if God is love, how could He permit the beloved Messiah to suffer so, and if God is all-powerful why did He not intervene and rescue the Messiah?"

We must seek for communication bridges which might be helpful. Some Christians search the Quran for paradigms of suffering for righteousness. Those themes are present in Islam; yet we wistfully admit that Islamic theology has mostly developed in directions which deny the efficacy of suffering love.

Perhaps we need other paradigms. Such starting points could involve the theological expression of prophethood, blessing, holiness, justice, honor, or kingdom. Consideration was given to the development of the theme of honor and shame in expressing the loyalty of Christ to God at Gethsemane and the blessing, generosity and blamelessness of God in raising Jesus from the dead.

The names of Jesus are helpful for interpreting his person, for in Semitic societies, the name is exceedingly significant. "What are the meanings of the names of Jesus?" is a question which is both theologically and culturally appropriate. During the early period of the Muslim era, that question seems to have been much on the mind of Muslims and particularly Muhammad. Too often in subsequent centuries that question has been mute for Muslims. It needs to be revived again, and that invitation to consider the meaning of the names of Jesus is the explicit call and mission of the church.

We recognize that Jesus is a figure in the Quran, with wonderful qualities and names attributed to him. We also believe that the Quran itself seems open and committed to the Scriptures which have been revealed formerly, Scriptures which are in the possession of the Christian church. The wonderful Quranic names for Jesus, and the Muslim respect for the previous scriptures can provide a helpful starting point for Christians to invite Muslims to explore the Biblical meaning of the wonderful names given to Jesus.

The Kingdom of God

Both Muslims and Christians are committed to the establishment of the Kingdom of God on earth and eternally. Muslims pray that God will reveal His guidance to them and prevent them from going astray. Christians also pray, "Thy will be done on earth as it is in heaven."

Communication with our Muslim friends concerning our commitment to the Kingdom of God is a basis for fruitful dialogue. However, in that witness we experience pain, for we quickly recognize that both the nature of the Kingdom and its implementation are vastly different from a Quranic or a Biblical perspective. The *hijra* and the cross are opposite to one another as the means through which the Kingdom is established. Islam and the Christian faith therefore move in opposite directions in their understanding of how God acts in history and how he brings about his will on earth.

The nature of these respective communities of faith, these regions of "peace," these expressions of the "Kingdom," are also irreconcilable. For Christians the center of the community of the redeemed is the Lamb slain and risen. Through his covenant blood the new community is created. Through his resurrected life it is sustained. This community has no locus except this one reality: the Spirit of Jesus is present wherever two or three or more gather in his name, and it looks forward to the fulfillment of the Kingdom at the second coming of Christ. The church is the sign of the presence of the Kingdom and a witness pointing to the eventual fulfillment of the Kingdom. The church is a community of hope, of pilgrimage towards the future and the ultimate fulfillment of the Kingdom at the *parousia*.

For Muslims the center of the Islamic *ummah* is the Quran, the book for guidance to the community of faith, a guidance which constantly invites that community to a geographical and cultural locus symbolized and ritualized in the Kaaba of Mecca. The *ummah* is a community which resists change as it seeks to preserve the original Islam of Adam. The faithful *ummah* is the expression of the Kingdom of God; therefore self-criticism by the *ummah* is hardly appropriate.

In our reflection on the Kingdom we discover, as we do at every turn, that within every area of convergence between Muslims and Christians we also experience the pain of divergence. It is the convergence and divergence between Messiah and Quran, between cross and *hijra*, between Pentecost and Medina, between Holy Spirit and Kaaba, between *parousia* and Adam, between pilgrimage towards the *eschaton* and the *hajj* to Mecca, between grace and *sharia*, between redemption and guidance.

Authentic Approaches

All of our theological reflection concerning mission and evangelism needs to be informed on one hand by the Scriptures and the Holy Spirit, and on the other hand by Christian experience in witness among Muslims, and by the questions which Muslims address to the church. The Bible needs to inform the manner in which we express mission in Muslim context. Thus the whole conference involved an interplay between theological reflection and experience. These twin realities informed our vision and plan for being faithful and fruitful witnesses among Muslims.

We explored four dimensions of modern mission among Muslims: National and international mission; Urbanization; Poverty and justice; Call, training and research.

National and International Mission

In many Muslim communities there are Christian churches which have preceded the advent of Islam; some of these were planted in the Apostolic period. Most have experienced centuries of pressure and even overt persecution. Like a rock, they have stood with a ministry of presence, prayer and witness. Their contribution to witness among Muslims is significant. Consultations on Christian witness among Muslims is impoverished when there is no representation from these ancient apostolic communities. Some participants who are working in areas where these churches are present felt that it would be wise to work with some of these leaders in regional consultations.

A witness springing from the indigenous roots of a culture is usually the most effective and authentic, whether those national roots be persons recently brought to faith in Christ or persons whose heritage has always been Christian. The danger of international involvement is that alien expressions of the Gospel may actually obscure the message or overwhelm the gentle, delicate life of a tiny congregation. Too often the expatriate missionary is insensitive to the indigenous church.

We need to rejoice whenever the church is present, whether they be churches with nearly two millenia of history and tradition, or a church only recently formed. Even when faith may seem weak, Jesus does not trammel the tender shoot of life. Let the church in cross-cultural missions also proceed with a spirit of learning, gentleness, humility and servanthood. Faithful mission is not always best expressed in activism. It is always essential to show sensitivity and respect to the church which is often already present in some form in the community to which the missionary goes.

Occasionally partnership with international missionaries is helpful as an encouragement, as a witness to the universality of the Gospel, as a sign of the nature of the church and to provide resources, skills, or ministries which are not present in the congregation which is present in a Muslim community. Expatriate presence may be especially necessary where there is no Christian witness, where the local church is a struggling minority or where the traditional church has become an ethnic enclave. In that case a multi-ethnic and multi-national expatriate involvement may be best.

However, in a number of Islamic societies the question of international missionary presence is mute, for visas are not available. In some circumstances where it is deemed advisable for internationals to be present, we need to attempt to enter the society through "tentmaking" or other approaches. This is especially true in situations where there is no Christian witness.

Nevertheless, tentmaking also poses special problems. What about integrity when the real intent of the "tentmakers" is evangelism rather than the job they have contracted? How does a tentmaker isolated from other Christians receive adequate spiritual support? How do they help an emerging fellowship develop links with a worldwide community of Christian faith? In spite of these problems, we believe that in certain circumstances tentmaking ministry performed with integrity and accountability is advisable.

Both the international missionary and the tentmaker need to be accountable to the church in the local community if one is present there. When the internationals function in an independent manner, it sometimes happens that they conduct themselves in a manner which jeopardizes or embarrasses the local church. The wisdom of the local church must be heard!

Urbanization

The city is a gift to the church as a special asset in Muslim evangelism. It is frequently in the city that persons begin to experience adequate freedom of choice to enable them to make decisions for the new community which may have been quite impossible in the traditional rural hinterland. At the same time, the kinship links between the city and the hinter-land mean that urban congregations do begin to touch the rural communities and in this way people groups which otherwise might never be reached by the Gospel may hear of Messiah through their urban kinspeople.

We were tremendously impressed by the phenomenon of world urbanization and recognized that some of the greatest cities on earth are now Muslim cities, as for example, Jakarta, Indonesia and Cairo, Egypt, both of which are super-cities. The growth of mega cities provides the modern church with unprecedented opportunity.

Poverty and Justice

In the city there are also the poor; urban centers in the Muslim world are often marked by intense poverty. Many of the world's 800 million desperately poor people live in cities which are predominantly Muslim.

The church is called to ministries of compassion to the poor. Throughout the centuries the faithful church has always expressed a holistic witness to the Gospel which includes medical, developmental, educational and justice commitments. A holistic ministry strikes a resonating chord with Muslims, for Muhammad himself was impressed with the fact that God cared for him as an orphan. In the care of orphans and the dispossessed, Christians are not only fulfilling the commission of Jesus to love the least of these, but are also speaking in ways which may be heard more effectively than many words spoken.

A holistic commitment to ministry is an appropriate response to the Muslim concern for *tauhid*. Holistic ministry is a sign that Christians also are committed to bringing all aspects of human life under the Lordship of Jesus Christ. One expression of that commitment is holistic ministry which authentically expresses the compassion of Jesus.

We must, however, never perceive of compassion for the poor as an evangelistic hook. We minister with compassion because of Jesus, not to gain converts. Holistic ministry is right, even if there is no evident response to the Gospel.

Leadership, Training and Research

Congregations worldwide need to call forth persons from various cultures for a commitment to Muslim evangelism.

Prayer and fasting for laborers needs to be combined with encouraging people to commit themselves to ministry among Muslims. Persons from multicultural backgrounds will be more effective than monocultural efforts in training and evangelism.

For the modern church in mission among Muslims, priority needs to be given to the training of evangelists and church planters. Jesus invested three years training twelve church planters.

Where are the authentic models of Christian missions and evangelism among Muslim peoples? We favor identifying several such models to share with the wider Christian community, for we recognize that models of ministry are one of the most effective training instruments.

Research is a central dimension of effective training. A network of research centers and resource pools needs to be developed. We recognize with appreciation that in all strategic regions, there are presently at least embryonic research and resource pool centers. Networking needs to be strengthened so there can be an increased flow of information between these various centers.

Most crucial of all is helping the information become connected with the trainee, with the person committed to frontier mission. In various locations around the world today there are regular seminars training Christians for Islamic witness and ministry. Cross-fertilization between these training centers would help to strengthen their overall effectiveness.

New Life

The conference concluded with communion. In communion we confess with joy and tears that Jesus the Messiah suffered and gave his life for us, that in him we have experienced the forgiveness of sin and the new life in the Kingdom of God.

Breaking bread and sharing the cup together shows that the Kingdom of God is established through the suffering of the cross, and that wherever Christians are involved in faithful witness, suffering is to be anticipated. Communion reminds us of the suffering, persecution, pressure and isolation which many believers in Jesus the Messiah experience in some Muslim societies. In the breaking of bread we demonstrate our participation in his body, the church, and our mutual participation in witness, in suffering, in ministry, in order that the eternal Kingdom of God may come in fullness.

Jesus the Messiah taught us to pray: "Thy Kingdom come on earth as it is in heaven!" May the church everywhere pray and fast in our day that the Kingdom may indeed become visibly present among all Muslim peoples to the glory of God the Father.

VARIETIES OF PEOPLE

"While they were talking and discussing together, Jesus himself drew near and went with them... And he said to them, 'What is this conversation which you are holding with each other as you walk?'"
— Luke 24: 15, 17

CHAPTER TWO

CONTEMPORARY TRENDS IN ISLAM

Kenneth Cragg

'When I see the world from the moon on television, I want to reach out and grab it for you, O Christ,' said Dr. Billy Graham, at the International Congress on World Evangelization at Lausanne. Perhaps many of us in world evangelism feel the way Graham does when viewing the globe. But does our desire to "reach out and grab" fit the pattern of our Incarnate Lord himself?

"Behold," said Jesus Christ in the Revelation to John (3:20), "I stand at the door and knock." He knocks, as a poet phrased it, to "pass the low lintel of the human heart."

In mission, the manner is the message. The Cross embraces the world but only at the price of its own hurt.

Above all else, mission must be pursued within the constraints of the gospel. For "as my Father has sent me, even so send I you" (Jn. 20:21). In mission the manner is the message. The Cross embraces the world but only at the price of its own hurt. The wounds of Jesus wait to win, they do not grab to take. Can it be otherwise with the faith, the church, the mission, that bear his name and "desire all nations"?

Much of Islam feels painfully misrepresented and denigrated by Christians.

It may seem harsh to open this chapter in this way. For what is initially quoted is well-intentioned. But it is always wise to interrogate our own enthusiasms, if only to avoid occasion whereby "our good may be evil spoken of." And there is another reason. It is that broadly the world of Islam is laboring—we might say smarting—under a long, often angry, sometimes distorting, sense of Christian misrepresentation and denigration, within the larger context of what it sees as Western exploitation, calumny and superiority complex.

It is not enough to deplore this state of mind, nor simply to query the grounds it alleges. For there is a sense in which things *are*, for relational purposes, what attitudes say they are. For moods are rooted in the psyche, and immune to any logic that might counter them.

The first implication for Christian witness from this situation is the *image* that witness bears, by and large, in the eyes of contemporary Islam. "Let not those that seek Thee be confounded through me," was the psalmist's plea (Ps. 69:6)—a prayer that is even more urgent in respect of those who believe they need not seek because they have already found.

Islam's sense of self-sufficiency prevents many of its adherents from seeking the relevance of anything else to its own positions.

We will have to take painfully to heart the degree to which, for so many in Islam, there is an instinctive and deeply rooted "rejectionism" towards the relationships which Christians would bring. Islamic identity, for a manifold of reasons, possesses a strong sense of self-sufficiency not readily open to finding or seeking the relevance of anything else to its own convictions.

Our first duty, then, is to take the measure of this posture of disavowal, resentment and "independence." Secondly, there follows a need to take stock of what is often (not always perceptively) dubbed Islamic "fundamentalism," which is so evident a factor in contemporary affairs. This must take us, thirdly, into some review of those trends in Islam which take active cognizance of modern tensions, responding to those areas of current experience, such as secularity, technology, the physical and social sciences, which cannot be ignored and with which, whether defensively or positively, Muslims must come to terms.

Clearly, such a threefold study of contemporary trends has to labor to comprehend a very wide panorama of evidence, only the main features of which can be reviewed, leaving a rich variety of local and esoteric aspects aside. We must not mistake a map for the territory. Further, it must be a study of articulate, intellectual and educational Islam, where the "trends" discernibly belong.

The presence of "Folk Islam" must also be remembered in assessing the active mind of the faith. But in this chapter we will not be involved with societal issues taken up by those who study contextuality within the several strata of economic, tribal or other denominators in society. What we shall explore is of course within these factors but should be distinguished from them. He is hardly a Christian Islamist who sees all religious faith reducible to some "sociology of religion," relevant as sociological criteria may be.

Reckoning with Antipathies

When in *Alice in Wonderland* Australasians are called "the people of the antipathies," (the tongue "slipping" around "the antipodes"), the phrase is one we could well borrow. The antipathies between Islam and Christianity are familiar enough, stemming from historical confrontation and doctrinal disparity. But leaving aside conquest, displacement, reversal, the Moors in Spain and their dislodgement, the Ottoman Turks in the Balkans and their tyranny, the Crusades both medieval and modern as Muslims see them, any Christian witness carries the burden of an interpretation of God and man which runs against the grain of the Islamic mind.

To the Islamic mind, the thought of divine incarnation offends both the unity and the majesty of God.

To the Muslim, "God in Christ" is an unnecessary elaboration of a divine mercy in forgiveness. The thought of divine incarnation offends both the unity and the majesty of God. The cross of Jesus could never be read as index to "the power and the wisdom of God." These are more properly vindicated in its prevention as ever happening to Jesus. For these and other reasons, the Gospels are not acknowledged as authentic Scripture; still less the Epistles. "Letters" from here to there on earth warrant no recognition as "sent down" from heaven.The church is based on a deep misconstruing of the ways and word of God. And Jesus must be freed from the calumny that ascribes to him some standing beyond prophethood which he himself never claimed or allowed.

All these areas of antipathy are familiar enough and they have often been disserved, even intensified, by the controversies which, since Abu Qurrah in the 9th century, have been used to handle them.

Today, as for the last 1000 years, East-West political and cultural alienations severely hamper communication between Christians and Muslims.

Our immediate concern is with contemporary alienations of political and cultural making. The over-all political situation in the Middle East has proved a witches' brew of them. The aftermath of the First World War is seen as defrauding Arab claims. The establishment of the State of Israel and its entail of displacement and exile means an experience of injustice, resentment and tragedy attributable to the West. There have been Western political machinations, not always so blatant as those which in the fifties reinstated the Shah in Iran, generating profound antipathy. The chronic polarization of communities in Lebanon sharpens Muslim/Christian strains everywhere else and seems itself incorrigible. Superpowers may not have created discords which have darkly local origins, but they certainly bedevil them further by their vested interests.

In Elijah's vision, "the still, small voice" could be heard after the fire and the earthquake. The still, small voice of evangelism today in the Middle East struggles for audibility in the midst of them.

Yet, ironically, technology and modern amenities make for a sort of "love-hate" relationship between Muslims and the West.

But if politically it is mainly a "hate" relationship (which we do well to appreciate and not dismiss as some externalization of guilt on others' part), it is a love-hate relationship over technology and modern amenities. These are irresistible, penetrating everywhere through airports, media, radio and TV, "pepsicolonization," and every kind of development, which some economies have been fabulously able to acquire and relish.

That tide may be turning now in the Gulf. But there, and everywhere, it leaves a deposit of changed values, of intrusive ideas and consumer indulgence—or privation by contrast. And the modern ethos of the technician, the surgeon, the engineer, the entrepreneur, the advertiser is highly liable to filch from people their former sense of the relevance, not to say the supremacy of God.

"Where does prayer come in where techniques obtain?", the lazy or the skeptic may ask. It tends to be the processes which we actually trust. The interventions of science in human behavior, in information-media, in sexuality, in production, and in social structure, have a way—by no means authentic— of displacing attitudes religious, reverent and dependent on providence. (We will think later of how such implications may be seen to be fallacious: the immediate issue is their growing prevalence).

To combat these dangers of the recession of the sense of God and his sovereignty, or of his absenteeism, Muslim custodians of faith and worship feel an ambiguous resentment with the West as the fountain and source of these disruptive influences. It is not that Islam is essentially anti-science. Quite the contrary. One of the complexities is that it was Islam in the middle centuries which tutored Europe in the physical, mathematical and chemical sciences, and the pupil has now bettered the tutor.

That reflection, however, is marginal compared with the burning theme, namely whether, and how, the Islamic world, can or will absorb the external techniques (for which it is avid) and somehow immunize those techniques (and themselves) from the interior consequences in the mind and spirit— consequences which, they would say, the West deplorably demonstrates in its secularity, religious indifferentism and moral decline.

Where materialism has replaced Islamic religiosity, Western goods are in effect the packaging; the real import is the mentality.

Some are blithely confident that Muslims can enjoy and digest all the facilities and keep at bay the irreligion. One writer sees the latter as something extraneous that got inside the crates that bring the cars, the computers, the TV sets.[1] A greater realism might well reverse the metaphor and see the goods as the packaging and the mentality as the real import. Secular habits and assumptions are more perceptively seen, it would appear, in the different imagery that runs:

> Secular inroads are like the *badu* in the proverb who, on a cold night, let his camel put his neck in the tent. The result was that after a while the camel had the tent to himself and the poor *badu* spent the night out under the open sky.[2]

It is just that awareness of the danger of being dislodged from one's own identity and heritage which makes "conservative" Islam adamant against the inroads of western habits of mind. The invasion may come, in part, in the off-loading of military hardware, with the technicians to man it, as in the Shah's Iran, bringing with them a swamping presence of attendant influences, Hollywood films, pop music and permissiveness. These, in turn, recruit and infect local "mediators" who are the more threatening because they are enemies in the camp. Sayyid Qutb and the Ikhwan al-Muslimun (Brethren) had little love for the likes of Umm Kulthum.

Television has a way of enthroning undesirable personalities on a popular adulation altogether denied to the "real" leaders of a sound society—that is, the Brethren themselves. Yet there are times when the invasive things seem irresistible, inasmuch as the concomitant apparatus of modernity cannot be halted or debarred. That realization, however, only makes the resentment the more complex and dogged. To the purist and the rigorist it almost seems like a forlorn situation in which they are quite literally "alienated" on their own ground. It is little wonder if reactions are stubborn and frightened.

One crucial area in this encounter is, of course, education. More particularly, higher education. The vital role of the Muslim nurture of Muslim children has been operative for centuries in Quranic recitation and the *kuttabs* of the mosques. Calligraphy of the Quran is the essence of art and *hifz* or *verbatim* recital of the sacred text, the gist of learning.

The skills and assumptions of technology are forward-looking, inductive, empirical, open-ended.

But such traditional education perpetuates a past, is authoritarian and retrospective. It sees truth as a precious hand-down from God and from his community. In contrast, the skills and assumptions of scientific education are forward-looking, inductive, empirical and open-ended. Technology requires the personnel that proceeds in that mentality. Development makes such education urgent, commerce and society being eager for its works and benefits. Thus there has long been a sharp dichotomy within Muslim education between the Azhar or Deoband-style and that of "polytechnics" and state colleges producing the technocrats.

Traditionalists fear not only for the vested interests of religious authority but for the very identity of Islam.

Traditionalists fear that the postures of the latter wean the young adults away from religion and piety. Higher education, therefore, needs to be taken under surveillance to prevent a drift away from faith in a significant sphere of communal life and to obviate a sort of "laicization" of leadership and decision away from *shaikhs* and *mullahs* and allowing *ijtihad* (the right to pioneer Islamic change) to non-"religious" minds. But it is not only the vested interests of religious authority which are at stake but, as those authorities see it, the very identity of Islam.

Higher education, of course, is not all in the physical and engineering sciences. In some ways the social sciences, psychology and sociology, may be even more lethal. For they tend to relativize all conviction to states of mind or factors of circumstance. Western sociology pretends to be "value-free." It serves the techniques of social analysis and contributes to competitive advertising but it dismisses any ultimate verdicts on truth and meaning. So there have been calls, in some Muslim quarters, for a complete "Islamization" of all knowledge.[3]

There have been, for example, a number of conferences in Saudi Arabia concerning education, the dangers it may hold for doctrinal adherence, and the ways in which the menace can be met.[4] It is feared that contemporary Arabic is losing its Islamic character through the influence of TV, advertisement and secular usages. The language of hedonistic life-styles supplants the vocabulary of true faith.

According to Muslim nationalism, Arabism and Islam should be synonymous. Christian Arabs are an embarrassment.

In another way the Christian minorities—Copts, Latins, Greek Orthodox and others, frail as they are—are perceived as a threat. They have behind them, of course, a 19th and early 20th century tradition of being protegés—and bridgeheads—of Western interests. In this century they have made strenuous efforts to identify wholeheartedly with majority Muslim nationalism.[5] But within those nationalisms this was never free of suspicion. Even where sincere still, it has an annoying quality in that Arab nationalism is expected to be thoroughly Islamic. Indeed Arabism and Islam should be synonymous.

Christian Arabs are a dubious embarrassment. Where Pan-Islamic feeling disputes and contests these nationalisms, the Christian elements, which should be aligned within them, are even more at issue. The handling of history in education, as well as the sciences, is also a concern here, lest the Islamic heritage should be diluted. In Malaysia there have been government decrees forbidding the use by Christians of terms like *Allah, Injil, iman* and *Rasul*, which—though they have a long and legitimate presence in Christian Arabic deriving from before Islam—many would like to arrogate to Muslims only.[6]

In all these unhappy ways, here only cursorily reviewed, we learn to measure the degree of antipathy the situation holds to what we seek and to whom we are. Perhaps, finally, the umbrage against "orientalism" must be noted. The West primarily, and Christians there secondarily, are seen as responsible for "image-making" about Islam and "the East" which has been condescending, superior, willful and—in a word—a travesty.

The charge, perhaps oddly, often comes from within the security of Western academic life. Its most influential exposition is Edward Said's *Orientalism*. Scholars, he alleges, have drawn an Islam and an East which is romantic, lethargic, odd and hidebound, the Islam these "reporters" envisage it to be. They never allow it to state its own case and exist in its own authenticity.[7] Scholarship has connived with denigration.[8]

When we move from academica to journalism the situation is even worse. *Covering Islam*—(a deliberately ambiguous title—i.e., journalistically reporting and concealing) documents the distorted image of Muslims in the American media.[9] These smartings of the soul need to be heeded and not merely scouted, even though in some senses what *Orientalism* complains of is sometimes identical with what Islamic fundamentalists denounce, namely an Islam assumed to be "immutable," "obscurantist," "supine" and "inauthentic."[10]

If we are sufficiently sobered, alerted and humbled by these perspectives of the situation for which our faith has to care, we are ready to move from the antipathies to some review of the responsive assertions of Islam of which the most evident, and strident, is "fundamentalism."

Taking the Measure of 'Fundamentalism'

The "measure" we have to "take" must include perception and not only regret. The term "fundamentalism" is, in one sense, a misnomer, if designating only *some* in Islam. Indeed, it is often difficult for Muslims to grasp just what outsiders mean when they use it.

Islam is essentially fundamentalist in a way that biblical Christian faith could never properly be.

Islam is essentially fundamentalist in a way that biblical Christian faith could never properly be. For the Quran is understood as the *ipsissima verba* of God himself, given in *Tanzil*, to Muhammad, in Arabic, as a transcribing of the divine Book in heaven. What Muslims have in revelation *per se* is a Book, a Scripture, not derived (as the Bible and New Testament are) from that which is more ultimate than itself, the "event" of Exodus, or the "event" of the Christ, from whence the "literature" derives to "house" the revelatory reality which is essentially in the history. For Christians "the Word was made flesh," and from him came the Scriptures *via* those who "beheld his glory, full of grace and the truth." "The Word" was not "made book."

The Quranic situation is thus in radical contrast. There is history within it but it is no more than incidental to the text, the *asbab al-nuzul*, or "occasions of (oracular) revelation." Muhammad's personality is garnered into Tradition (*Hadith*) and it is to this that Muslims often, and rightly, liken the Gospels we have. But the Gospels are Scripture to us because they reliably portray and enshrine the Jesus who, in word and deed and person, discloses the divine Nature.

This distinction is basic. To be determined by a text, understood as the Quran is, makes all Muslims "fundamentalist." But, given this fact, it is possible to denote by that term (at least for clarity among non-Muslims) those within Islam who intensify that sense of things, place themselves rigorously within the entire *Shari'ah* as revealed, and refuse in its interpretation any purely "spiritual," "liberal," or otherwise less than literalist, approach. The most notable exemplars in Sunni Islam today are the Wahhabis, the Ikhwan and the followers (in Indo-Pakistan) of Abu-l-Ala al-Maududi in Jama'at-i-Islami.

Among the most rigorously fundamentalist of the Muslims, the most notable are the Wahhabis, the Ikhwan and the followers of Abu-l-Ala al-Maududi.

Shi'ah fundamentalism diverges widely from Sunni rigor by virtue of its esoteric notions of authority and its doctrine of "the Hidden Imam." The latter is now represented by the Ayatollahs, among whom Ruhallah Khomeini in Iran is the most celebrated. But many of the impulses are the same in Sunni and in Shi`ah, as outlined above.

The Ayatollah Ruhallah Khomeini denounced *taqiyya*, the warrant by which the Shi'ah might act with docility under an unworthy ruler.

One main factor in Khomeini's ascendancy was his repudiation of the doctrine of *taqiyya* as totally inadmissible in the enormity of the Shah's règime. *Taqiyya* is that warrant by which the Shi`ah might act with docility under an unworthy ruler, concealing, yet also cherishing, their disavowal against a better time or a reasonable occasion of revolt. But this "quietism" Khomeini averred, could in no way longer obtain, given what the Shah's compromises of a true Islam were doing to Iran.

The Ayatollah was able, by renouncing *taqiyya*, to galvanize the masses and also to disqualify other Ayatollahs who advised its maintenance. The result became a vigorous, sometimes virulent, anti-Westernism and a rigorous Islamic authoritarianism even more extreme than its Sunni counterparts. There is, of course, more *charisma*, *mystique* and irrational fervor around Shi`ah leadership than is the case among the Sunnis where collective communal factors have more purchase on mind and temper.

Recruiting and riding all those emotions of antipathy, fundamentalism in the Ikhwan form sets itself strenuously against all that it sees within Islam as connivance with Western conspiracy. False "nationalisms" are an obvious culprit because they divide Islam.[11] Their "socialism" or their "open-door policy" anyway has not delivered the goods of social betterment nor the relief of poverty. It has only enmeshed Muslims in the multi-nationals' web of exploitation.

But, ideologically, these règimes have misled Islam and betrayed the past. The charge from "fundamentalists" often indicts the traditional `ulama' as mere mouthpieces of government policy, preachers become civil-servants controlled by authority and meekly submitting where they should be "contending for the faith."[12]

One of the striking features of this "fundamentalist" rejection of "Erastian" or, indeed, any other "Islam," is its insistence on describing all such as *Jahiliyyah*. The term abounds in their writing and speaking. The *Jahiliyyah* was the time of ignorance before the rise of Islam, the pagan obduracy of the unenlightened Arabs.

It might seem monstrous to apply this description to Muslims of their 15th century, as if the whole long history had been futile and "the last state as worse as the first." How can it be that revelation is not efficacious or that humanity can be so obdurate still? But to the Ikhwan al-Muslimun *Jahiliyyah* is not only a period in time; it is a state of heart and will, a condition of affairs at any time. It means man, as Sayyid Qutb phrased it, under "the domination of man, not that of God."

"Everything around," he wrote, "is *Jahiliyyah*: perceptions and beliefs, manners and morals, culture, art and literature, laws and regulations, including a good part of what we call Islamic culture."[13] His rejection of nominal Islam proceeds on the belief that *via* the whole *Shari`ah* a *Hakimiyyah*, or rule of God, is feasible. All rule must be in God's hands, and it can be there by due and rigorous conformity to the letter of the revelation. The fact that *Jahiliyyah* can be so perennial when the revelation is in hand does not seem to dismay this confidence. The cause lies in levity, laxity and *istighna`*—that arrogance of self-sufficiency against which the Quran warns and which modernity so far stimulates and abets.[14]

It should not be thought that such "fundamentalism" is obscurantist or irrational. In exponents like Sayyid Qutb it represents an intellectual persuasion deliberately chosen. He was, at the outset, a literary critic with a scholarship to the United States in that field. His "fundamentalism" was espoused without rejection of some of the principles of academic rationality.

Sayyid Qutb and his movement maintain a doctrinaire position "open" only within the exigencies of its closedness.

In Qutb's view, thought is not vetoed: it is exercised in submission to what is infallible and then consecrated to its defense. He rejects facile and puerile arguments, for example, about alleged scientific data in the Quran.[15] He and his movement represent that formidable religious phenomenon —a highly doctrinaire position adopted by a mind that is "open" only within the exigencies of its closedness, and all in the name of the security of a heritage and a commitment in faith.

"This Christian idolatry of the Trinity," writes Qutb, "and its notions of sin and redemption... make no sense at all."

All this means that it is not temperamentally ready to undertake the real onus of pluralism or to address properly the issue of minorities. Nor, obviously, is it disposed to listen to an alien witness. "This Christian idolatry of the Trinity," Qutb writes, "and its notions of sin and redemption...make no sense at all."[16] The mind of "fundamentalism" does not readily suggest a hospitality to anything outside the "sufficiency" of Islam to which it is committed.

This dimension of Islam has had some relative success, not least in Pakistan, in approximating règimes to its own point of view, via a tightening of the *Shari`ah* system. But more often it has registered frustration in the postures of the nation-state in general. At times that frustration has led to political conspiracy which has taken its toll, not least in the assassination of Anwar al-Sadat. Such will to insurrection has been based on an interpretation of Sura 5: 44-46, about "those who do not judge (rule) according to what God has sent down," (following their medieval mentor, Ibn Taimiy-yah), and sustained by their feeling that such "Muslim" unworthy règimes are the main obstacle to their cause.

Alternatively, the Ikhwan have favored a gradual approach, deploring unworthy rule and rulers but striving to encompass a truly Islamic power by biding their time and educating a virile, "puritan," resilient quality of Islamic practice in the population at large in hope of generating a ground-swell of change.

It seems clear that these efforts have been partially effective in quickening deep Islamic commitment, habituating it to exacting standards of devotion and fulfillment of the Five Pillars, and thus intensifying its authority, its vigilance and militancy against all that might undermine its loyalties.

Female roles are becoming even narrower in Egypt and Pakistan. And in Iran, women themselves have sought that backward trend.

Not least of these areas is that of the female role in society. There has been, for example, in Egypt and Pakistan, a marked impetus towards more traditional views of veiling and male control of female "living-space" and against female emanci-pation viewed as permissiveness or as a threat to the security of the Muslim family. What is noteworthy also in Iran is the degree to which women themselves have sought, more than merely acquiesced in, the version of themselves which those traditional views require and enjoin.[17]

But what of contrasted trends within Islam, opposed to "fundamentalism"? What of their rationale, their present standing and their discernible prospects and the factors both prompting and impeding them?

Other Islamic Measures of Islam

It may be invidious to think of contemporary trends in Islam under just two heads: "Fundamentalist" and "Other." The second may well be ultimately more significant. But the "fundamentalists" hold the headlines and would seem to be in some present ascendancy, though often seeing their counsels thwarted.

No single term fits Islam's "others." Whatever the varieties—liberal, radical, modern, progressive— a lively ferment of reflective thinking is going on.

We must give ear to what these say, even though they do not make the headlines fundamentalists do.

"Others" it is hard to denominate by any single term, such as "liberal," "radical," "modernist" or "progressive." But let there be no doubt that there is a lively ferment of reflective thinking. And there is a perception that there are vital tasks of mind and spirit to which Islam is summoned by the contemporary world for which it is authentically equipped. "Islam being what Muslims say it is,"[18] we must have a ready ear for what these "other" Muslims are saying, though the headlines may not be theirs.

It would be easy to cite the two celebrated "Muhammads" of Cairo and Lahore, Muhammad `Abduh (d.1905) and Muhammad Iqbal (d.1938), as pioneers respectively of rationalism and vitalism in Islam. But the former, though an influential reformer, lacked adequate successors, while the latter, as a poet-philosopher, was too elusive for average minds.

Both invoked *ijtihad*, or "enterprise" leading to loyal change, as open and legitimately to be exercised by "lay" Muslims as well as the `ulama'. They were ready for adaptation of the *Shari`ah* to changed conditions and saw Islam as essentially self-reforming in temper and in time.

One follower of `Abduh, `Abd al-Raziq, responded to the demise of the Ottoman Caliphate in 1924 by affirming that Islam had never been essentially committed to any political order, since Muhammad's mission had been a spiritual one and his own access to power had no necessary perpetuation within the faith. We find aspects of this theme recurring today. Much water, however, has gone under the mill since that far off first quarter of the century, and the "depoliticization" of Islam seems today, except in India and in the U.S. and European "diaspora" of Muslims, a very remote goal.

But it may be sound to begin a cursory review of what we have now to assess by taking up three related themes, rather than listing personalities within them. They are: (a) Thought about Islam and the State, (b) Religion and Contemporary Society, and (c) the Inward Crisis of Faith. That all these have deep implications for Christian witness will be obvious, involved as they all are in relevance of Christian faith.

1. Islam and the State

The division of the Quran and of Muhammad's *Sirah*, or prophetic career, into Meccan and Medinan parts is, of course, basic to Islamic faith, even though the Quran does not have the chronological sequence the Meccan/Medinan identification of the Suras might lead readers to expect.

What that division teaches and how it should be interpreted has become a fascinating issue in recent Muslim response to the impact of secularity. It had been broadly assumed for centuries that Muhammad as preacher and Muhammad as ruler were mutually authentic and that though he was final and unrepeatable *qua* prophet, he was rightly and duly "succeeded" as leader. That succession was the historic Caliphate through all its vicissitudes from Abu Bakr in 632 to the last Ottoman in 1924.

National statehoods, for the most part, took over from the Caliphate—fragmented to be sure, but in some sense functioning to supply the political dimension of what we must now call the *Dars* (pl.) of Islam.[19] Pakistan, of course, was deliberately created to ensure statehood for the majority of Muslim areas of the subcontinent as the only proper shape of "independence," though at appalling cost in life and suffering. But that very statehood consigned some (then) forty million Muslims to the permanent lack of it in the "secular" state of India. They, with others elsewhere inside non-Islamic règimes, have had to exist and survive (as the West might phrase it) just as a religion, that is, as a system of belief, piety, cult and code freely pursued but not dominating the body politic.

Contrary though it is to Islamic theory, the concept of Islam as "only a religion" is gaining some popularity among modern Muslims.

This necessary concept of "just as a religion," quite uncongenial as it is to Islamic theory and long practice, has come, in some quarters to be espoused even where it is not a factual necessity. It has its advocates, where Islam continues in political control, who plead it as the only way whereby Islam can truly address itself to its own non-Muslim minorities and—more importantly—fulfill its own inner meaning. The Caliphate, and any other politicization of Islam, should be seen as non-essential, as pragmatic solutions in given circumstances having no abiding logic or perpetuity.

Muhammad the ruler, the case runs, was just as unrepeatable as Muhammad the prophet. If so, the argument goes on, the really enduring message of the Quran must be sought and found in the Meccan period. For it is there that the primarily "religious" quality of Islam, the "essence" which was prior to the political/military order at Medina, is enshrined. This is not necessarily to disqualify Medina in Medinan time and place. It is to insist that contemporary time and place are not "Medinan."

The case is made strongly, for example, by the Republican Brothers in the Sudan, who write of "the Second Message of

Islam." By this they mean the original "first" message at Mecca, which becomes the "second" because it is now detached from the Mecca/Medina complex which, in its "unity" has been the historic, general, pervading, "first" message of traditional Islam through the centuries. The contemporary world needs to have Islam liberated from the integral role of the state.[20] For these thinkers the surest way to do so is to locate Islamic self-definition nowadays squarely within the spiritual message of the Meccan period when Islam was without benefit of power.

One writer in a UNESCO publication goes even further:

> If Islam is essentially consistent with human nature, the individual, whether Muslim or non-Muslim, should proceed in his own way to seek the fulfillment of his own nature with the aid of whatever help or guidance he himself may choose. Thus the constraint, the authoritarianism, of constituted institutions, fades away.[21]

More sober but still innovative, a well known Egyptian jurist describes how Medinan Surahs belonged not with a state but only with a community and yielded a *Shari`ah* relevant to that time and place. He finds the Quran giving no political injunctions about caliphate or necessary statehood. It is addressed, not to "citizens" as such, but to the "faithful." It is concerned with people as religious and relates exclusively to the soul and salvation. Its ethic is dynamic and even those specifics there are, are addressed to conscience nurtured by worship. The age-long pattern of religious law, under the control of rulers and teachers, he regards as a usurpation of God's authority. Theocracy on those terms is a tragic misnomer.[22]

India is clearly a realm where we would expect Muslims to emphasize the Meccan Quran. Though Indian Islam has its quota of "fundamentalists" it generates an impressive leadership in behalf of a "spiritual" version of Islam. The leading name is that of Maulana Abu-l-Kalam Azad of Delhi, who wrote a perceptive commentary on the Quran and played an important role in the first decade of independent India, repudiating the Pakistan solution as inappropriate to the genius of Islam.[23] Hasan Askari, sociologist and Muslim ecumenist, avers that Islam never intended a state-form. He wrote:

Muslim ecumenist Hasan Askari believes Islam can survive without political power.

> My profound conviction is that the Prophet of Islam did not create a state...The principles of the Caliphate and the Imamate are not Quranic. My belief is that Islam can survive without political power, without statehood.[24]

Muslims are better able to transform the social order and actualize a veritable *islam* by purely "religious" means and concepts. Comparably, Syed Vahiuddin argues that while the state has a curbing role within society it can "never judge what passes within the consciousness of man," and develops a dominance which can become tyrannical. At best it can only be a partial executant of a divine purpose for mankind.[25]

These views about the Meccan dimension as significantly separated from the Medinan do not commend themselves to the generality of Muslims anywhere. They call in radical question the whole import of the *Hijrah*, that Rubicon of original Islam.

While it is true that the Meccan Suras enjoin strictly on Muhammad the task of *balagh*, or "message-bringing," as his only vocation, the *Hijrah* nevertheless is seen as the authentic logic of the Meccan mission and in no way unwarranted. The Quran is not divisible in this radical way. Nor can it be made to support a case for a purely spiritual concept of Islam, an Islam happily shedding its political form and instinct.

For Islam to depoliticize would require a quantum leap of reform, unthinkable to the vast majority of Muslims.

But the fact that some can think such venturesome thoughts holds large implications for the Christian relationship.

Nor is this type of thinking—except where Muslims are minorities—anything more than marginal, with little chance of practical expression in the given temper of today. For Islam to depoliticize would require a quantum leap of reform.[26] Even so, that some can think such venturesome thoughts holds large implications for the Christian relationship. For they do focus attention on the nature and authority of religion itself, the how and the whence of human salvation. And they acknowledge that the problems of secularity are more than some Western disease or aberration from which Muslims can hold themselves scornfully immune.

2. Religion and Contemporary Society.

"Secularity" in the sense of statehoods that "hold the ring" impartially for a diversity of faiths in the citizenry is one thing. "Secularization" as indifference to, or abandonment of, religious faith altogether is another. The former need not necessarily lack a strong tradition, a faith-identity; the latter means a recession and forfeiture of the transcendent and of religious belief and practice.

As we have seen, contemporary technology, its assumptions and consequences, have worked, at least in the West, towards relinquishment of habits of worship. What place, people ask, does prayer have, amid the controlling techniques of the operating theater and the oil terminal? Islam, as we have noted, may believe itself proof against such surmises. Yet it does have intellectual problems which are distinctively its own in the vindication of its doctrine of God, of revelation and hu-man nature. Let us study its response here in respect only of the outward aspects of contemporary secularization, leaving to (3) below the inward aspects.

Many Islamic writers now warn about human arrogance and neglect of worship in a technological culture, in ways similar to those of Christian biblical writers.

Many writers in Islam today expound the answer their Quran directs and inspires them to give to the threat of human arrogance or human pretension and neglect of worship to which technological culture is liable. The elements of the answer are very close to dimensions of biblical and Christian faith and should be gratefully saluted as such. They hinge on the truth of humanity as being in trust with the world, having the *amanah* (33.72) taken in the primeval pledge, or consent made to the divine enquiry: "Am I not your Lord?" (7.172).

Thus all people's *imperium* is a gift, not for squandering or superbia (*istighna`*), but for gratitude, awe, and true *taqwa*, or God-fearingness. Man is no more, no less, than God's *khalifah* (2.30), the undermaster, deputizing for God in the immediate custody of the natural order which the divine mercy sustains and upholds. This is the sufficient answer to all secular "declarations of independence" of God, aggressively asserted or casually assumed.

This Islamic interpretation of man is underlined by the fact of natural phenomena as "signs" (*ayat*) or divine mercy. This, as Christians might phrase it, is the sacramental principle. The same "signs" which arrest and so enable the scientist in interpreting and controlling nature, are designed to arouse and sustain a deep, religious wonder, thanksgiving and consecration.

"Every one has somewhat to offer"—their sexuality first of all. For our procreative powers are the first sphere of our "sign" experience. The peasant, the farmer, the engineer, the surgeon, the merchant, the seaman, the craftsman, are all handling the *materia* of divine generosity. In dealing with things they are "having to do with God" as their source, sustainer, bestower and sovereign.

To deny this *shukr*, or gratitude, is *kufr*, or "atheism;" to think our competence our independence is *shirk*. It is *shirk* also to idolize our powers, to claim for our structures of trade, or nation, or power, or skill, any absolute quality. To give them a loyalty which acknowledges no referability beyond the market, or the profit, or the pride, or the right, is to repudiate *islam* and become *mushrikun*.

All history, then, is the arena of a crisis concerning our humanity, with the Satanic principle[27] set to defy God in the disputing of the dignity of man. This "accuser" (*Iblis*) of the divine design in the creaturehood of man has to be himself repudiated. We have "to give the lie to the liar." Thus the vindication of God in the enterprise of creation and of our creaturehood turns upon the fulfillment of man.

It is a precious fact that Muslim, Christian and Jew stand together in opposition to the secular presumption.

These are vital truths and the only sure response to the temptations of the secular presumption. It is of course, urgent to go further and ask *how* this human vocation, to be truly under God, is to be brought to pass. But that *how?* only arises when we are seen to be together on the prior issue *whether* it is this way with our humanity. That we are indeed together, Muslim and Christian (and Jew), thus far is a precious fact and crucial to any distinctive Christian witness about the *how* of our salvation in the grace of "God in Christ reconciling in the world" (2 Cor. 5:19).

It is this understanding which gives the lie to those enervating notions about the human condition which come from Freud and Marx and Durkheim and other challengers who interpret people as "religious" *via* neuroses, or by dint of an "opiate," or as symbolizing socialization. Galileo need not be seen, nor Darwin, as undermining this truth. For it does not hinge on a geocentric universe or Archbishop Ussher's Calendar. Creaturehood becomes all the more marvelous for its very capacity to comprehend the long patience and the vast perspectives of its own genesis and arena.[28] We have no reason, in God, to be either daunted or deceived by technology.

As the Islamic Council for Europe has it:

> Islam stands for a commitment to surrender one's will to the will of God and as such be at peace with the Creator and all that has been created by Him...As God is One and indivisible, so is life and man's personality...Everything originates from the one God and everyone is ultimately responsible to Him. Thus the unity of God has as its corollary the oneness of His creation. Distinctions of race, color, caste, wealth and power disappear: man's relation with fellow man assumes total equality by virtue of the common Creator.[29]

That conviction must be the context of any witness which asks about sin and perversity, about obduracy and evil, and what these may demand for their correction beyond the teachings of prophethood and the exhortations of goodwill. But those issues which took our Lord, and still take Christian faith, into Gethsemane only become crucial when the creaturely reality is firmly confessed and reverently received.

3. The Inward Crisis of Faith.

The assurance with which Islamic doctrine can interpret and potentially discipline current technology is not, however, free from issues at a deeper level. To affirm the human vocation as tenant-trustee of the good earth and viceregent in God's creation, is authentic and precious. Taken sincerely, it has grasped the technological temptation and can counter it. Nevertheless it is vulnerable to a more radical despair. It may well be undermined by an agnosticism of the kind preva-lent in the West, a hesitancy about commitment and convic-tion, generated by a variety of factors, some of which lie at the door of religion itself.

There is a cast of contemporary mind for which all dogma is suspect. To that mind, the more doctrinaire systems or faiths become, the less they are to be trusted or credited. How far, it is fair to ask, do trends in Islam register this mood today and what is the response?

If we look in contemporary Islamic literature rather than its scholarship, we can find suspicions of human absurdity, of nihilism, comparable to that in Western literature.

The Quran describes itself as "a Book in which there is nothing dubious" (2.2). Yet it is deeply aware of the chronic human capacity for "unfaith." Such "unfaith" is always reprehensi-ble. But what of the modern skeptics who are such on grounds—as they see it—of integrity and honest "unpersuad-edness"? Is there evidence in contemporary Islam of those suspicions of human absurdity, of pointlessness, or nihilism, frequent in Western literature? Have today's Muslims any kinship with the George Orwells, the Becketts, the Brechts, the Sartres, the Kafkas, of Europe whose skepticisms stem from theorists like Marx, or philosophers like Bertrand Russell and the logical positivists?

The answer is certainly yes, if we look at literature rather than scholarship. For it is in imaginative writing everywhere that such sentiments are most likely to find voice. Outright skepticism in theoretical form is rare enough among explicit writers, whether of intellectual or communist vintage.[30] But novelists and playwrights in the languages of Islam are cer-tainly portraying radical doubt and calling into subtle but un-ambiguous question the assured theism of Islam. In some ways Islam's very assurance invites the incredulity of those whose métier it is to depict and ponder the incongruities, the futilities, the pains and distresses of the human condition, the seeming absurdities of the mortal predicament.

Much the most celebrated of such writers is the Cairene, Najib Mahfuz (b.1911). The doyen of Arab authors, his short stories and major novels plumb the depths of wistful doubt and distrust of belief in God. *Awlad Haratina*, translated as *Children of Gabalawi*, depicts a forlorn human history dominated by "the big House" where, reputedly, lives Gabalawi, the divine author of all things, the enigmatic "God" whose creatures all people are. But he is the supreme "absentee." He never emerges from his supposed mansion. He only sends "messengers."

In the novel three of the messengers, recognizably (under their assumed names) Moses, Jesus and Muhammad, do indeed "improve" things for a while. But after their demise their followers quarrel and soon chaos and misery come again. The novel traces a vast panorama of history from Adam, Cain and Abel, to a nuclear scientist against a backdrop of Cairo "quarters." The last, in the manner Bertolt Brecht dramatized, becomes the pawn of political power greedy to wield the ultimate weapon he invents. The whole is a telling portrayal of modern fears and traumas, of the futility of religion and the inscrutable puzzle of "divinity." Is "the death of God" a hint, a calumny, a surmise, or a fact? And who is to know? and how? [31]

It may be surprising to find such "modernity" in a significant Muslim literary figure who was once an official in the Ministry of Religious Affairs. The writer, like many of his counterparts elsewhere, is elusive, preferring the gnawing open question to the brusque denial, whether for prudence, or for dubiety's sake. Yet what he intends to communicate is clear enough—all the more so for not being dogmatic.

Space does not admit of the elaboration of this dimension in the recent literature of Muslim countries. What certainly ministers to this vivid feature is what might be pointedly called the "irreligious hope." To ruminate over Lebanon is enough to encounter despair about religion, whichever religion it be.

At the core of the fissured antagonism is some *confessio*—a *confessio fidei*, belief encased in allegiance. These in their confrontation, develop into confessionalism which, in Lebanon (as in pre-partition Cyprus and elsewhere) becomes the political chessboard. When it sinks, and stinks, into chaos, "deconfessionalism" becomes the one, remote, impossible dream, a secular "salvation" from the desperate treachery of religion. This is the kind of world in which we propose to witness to a *confessio fidei*, the gospel of Christ. How can we do so where confessionalism is so tragically guilty?

Nor is Lebanon alone—except in intensity—in this issue. It would be tragic again if politics, say in Nigeria or Uganda, were to become "confessionalized," with parties and governments aligned with religions. In this sense peaceable coexistence is mandatory and a wise evangelism must live in those terms, respecting creed and cult and community while offering another faith and fellowship. But in Lebanon has not the voice of faith been almost silenced by the travesties of the faithless "faithful"? Has the outsider any warrant to be inattentive or sanguine when the weary secularists cry out: "A plague on all your houses"? [32]

God and faith and institutional religion under urgent interrogation is not, then, a situation unknown to, or negligible for, contemporary Muslims. Some at least of their number experience the unease and disquiet from which current agnosticism is born and any would-be evangelist must learn, with Ezekiel, to "sit where they sit." Such radical questioning may even paradoxically open a door of hope, insofar as it sobers religious confidence and quickens humble enquiry.

Certainly the Quran itself is no stranger to the errancies of which humankind is capable. Indeed it is full of somber reminders of the waywardness eloquent in the ruins of past generations. The readiness to read a *Jahiliyyah* in secular Muslims may perhaps admit, in other minds, of a contrasted readiness to find a spiritual *Jahiliyyah* in the orthodox and the militants. If so, the reproach will not be unique to Islam.

Christian witness plainly needs a long patience, a sense of the formidable "unwantedness" which stands in its way.

Our survey of trends, leaving much unexplored, has nevertheless yielded implications at every turn. Perhaps it is wise to leave them in the realism of the actual context we have reviewed. Christian witness plainly needs a long patience, a sense of the formidable "unwantedness" which stands in its way.

It is urgent for Christianity to diminish the occasions of the enmity that are within its own power. It must surely interpret *into*, rather than *against*, the themes in Islam and the Quran which have positive bearing on its witness to God in creation. Will not these be the surest route into the distinctive notes of the gospel about grace and redemption, sin and forgiveness? And will not these, in turn, be more fully heard in their true resonance if we can come into close sympathy with the pains and reactions of Muslims—of whatever "camp" or following—in the stresses of the world as they read them?

It is well to remember, if we return where we began, that there are "diversities of gifts" and so of ministries in the use of them.   The arts of personal evangelism were not here our concern, rather the tasks of discernment and perception that belong with the Christian theologian, determined to be neither daunted by obstacles nor deterred by tensions, but hopeful, resourceful and patient, in Christ, a steady listener with "the word in season" on "the tongue that has learned" (Isaiah 50:4).

NOTES

1. Dr. Izzedin Ibrahim, Chancellor of al-Ain University, Abu Dhabi wrote: "Various evils accompanying modernization have crept into the crates in which technology has been packaged"in *American/Arab Affairs* 4 (1983): 133.

2. Mushir al-Haqq, *Islam in Secular India* (Simla, 1962), 21.

3. E.g., Ziaddin Sardar, *Islamic Futures* (London, 1985) and Ismail al-Faruqi, *Islamization of Knowledge, General Principles and Work-Plan* (Washington, 1982).

4. S.S. Husain and S.A. Ashraf, *Crisis in Muslim Education* (Jiddah, 1979); G.N. Saqib, *Modernization of Islamic Education* (London, 1977); Rahat Nabi Khan, *Islam, Philosophy and Science* (Four UNESCO Lectures, Paris, 1981); and Ziaddin Sardar, *The Future of Muslim Civilization* (London, 1979).

5. Cf. the 1952 Egyptian slogan: "We are all Egyptians now."

6. A Draft Law (1984) in some Malaysian States, and enacted into Law in the States of Kelentan and Trengganu.

7. Edward Said, 1979.

8. The charge made of a number of Christian and other writers on Islam (including the present one) in: A.Hussain, R.Olsen and Jamil Qureshi, eds., *Orientalism, Islam and Islamists* (Vermont, 1984).

9. Edward Said, *Covering Islam* (New York, 1981); cf. Edmund Ghareeb, ed., *Split Image, the Portrayal of Arabs in the American Media* (Washington, 1983).

10. There is an intriguing parallel in the way in which political Zionism castigated diaspora Jewry in terms akin to those of the Anti-Semitic portrayal—i.e., that ghettoized Jews were hidebound, lazy, ingrown and futile. The difference, of course, was that political Zionism aimed to galvanize to action, the Anti-Semitic propagandists meant calumny and denigration.

11. At his trial on a charge of treason in Cairo in 1965, Sayyid Qutb insisted, with great courage, that loyalty to the *Ummah* of Islam should override the claim

of the *Watan* of the Egyptian State. The very jurisdiction of the court he regarded as a betrayal of true Islam since the state did not conform to the whole *Shari`ah* and violated Islamic community.

12. Even the *Azhar Journal* is taken to task for being effete, retailing innocuous subjects and failing to stand up to governmental power. The Brethren also complain that the share and quality of Quran reading and exposition on State TV leave much to be desired.

13. Sayyid Qutb, *Màalim` ala-l-Tariq* (Signposts on the Road) (Cairo, 1981).

14. *Istighna* is that attitude of men boasting of self-sufficiency: it is the vaunted illusion of resources that allow one to dispense with worship and think oneself "independent" of divine mercy. It occurs in the inaugural Sura, 96: "Man becomes insolent, thinking himself self-sufficient."

15. It has been frequently claimed by some Muslim exegetes of the Quran that modern inventions and scientific data, even nuclear fission, have been anticipated there and can now be detected in passages not hitherto appreciated for their prescience. Meanings earlier unsuspected disclose themselves as science proceeds. This stance, however, is strongly repudiated by others as the kind of corroboration the Quran, as a "spiritual" Scripture, neither needs nor approves. It is not confirmed by being supposedly "scientific," nor diminished as "guidance" for mankind by ante-dating so much that now needs that guidance. Muhammad Kamil Husain called all such exegesis "pseudo" *Mutanawwi`at* (Miscellanies) (Cairo, 1957) Vol.2: 29-37. Fazlur Rahman, *Islam and Modernity* (Chicago, 1982) also deplored it. But it continues to fascinate believers. Cf. the phenomenal success of the Arabic popular works of Mustafa Mahmud in Egypt in the seventies.

16. Qutb, 24.

17. One of the most explicit, even chilling, statements in this field is that of an English Muslim, R.W.J.Austin, "Islam and the Feminine," in *Islam in the Modern World*, eds. D.MacEoin and A. al-Shahi (London, 1983), 46: "The future of Islam as Islam must lie in its determination, whatever outside pressures be brought to bear, to maintain the patriarchal structures and values which alone can sustain the doctrinal principles on which monotheism claims to be founded." He adds: "Islam has . . . an inevitably secondary and satellite role for woman and what is feminine within the structure of its theology and society"(37). "Woman, despite her human and spiritual equality with man, is thought of only in terms of her relationship to some man"(43). Other Muslims would profoundly disagree with these dicta.

18. A remark of the Canadian Islamicist, Wilfred Cantwell Smith, in line with his emphasis on personal faith, as against the "-ism" (e.g. Hindu*ism*) of the comparativists. See also his comment that "the meaning of the Quran as Scripture lies, not in the text, but in the minds and hearts of Muslims." In "The True Meaning of Scripture," *International Journal of Middle East Studies* II (1980): 505.

19. The term *Dar al-Islam*, "the household of Islam," was of course always meant to be singular. The nation-states break up that unity but also claim to supply the political dimension of Islam and as such to be still "*Dars*." Yet to turn the phrase into the plural is to arrive at a contradiction in terms.

20. The Republican Brothers had their martyrs during the Numeiri règime in Khartoum. Their several publications include: *An Introduction to the Second Message of Islam,* 4th ed., 1980; *The Religion of Man: A New Conception of Islam,* 1979. Their leader was Mahmud Muhammad Taha.

21. Khan, *Islam, Philosophy and Science,* 127.

22. Muhammad Said al-ʾAshmawy, *Usul al-Shariʾah,* (Sources of the Sacred Law) (Cairo, 1979). His ideas were sharply attacked, e.g., in *Al-Daʾwah* Cairo (Oct. 1979).

23. See Himayun Kabir, ed. *Maulana Abu-l-Kalam Azad, A Memorial Volume* (New Delhi, 1959) and my *The Pen and the Faith* (London: George Allen and Unwin, 1985), 14-31. His *Tarjuman al-Qur'an* 2 vols. was translated into English by Syed Abdul Latif, (London: Asia Publishing, 1962-67).

24. Quoted by Y. Moubarac, *Verse et Controverse, Les Musulmans* (Paris, 1971), 132.

25. C.W. Troll, ed., "The Islamic Experience in Contemporary Thought—Syed Vahiuddin," in *Islam in India: Studies and Commentaries,* vol. 3 (Delhi, 1986), 71.

26. One forceful expression of the essentially political structure of Islam is in Ismail al-Faruqi, *Islam* (Illinois, 1979), where he interprets any Muslim "conversion" as a repudiation of the Islamic state and, as such, punishable by banishment, life imprisonment or death, being an act of political treason. "That is why Islamic law has treated people who have converted out of Islam as political traitors" (68).

27. Cf. Sura 2.30ff.

28. Our wiser sense of incredible dimensions of the universe in space and time in no way diminishes us. We are not vulgarized by sheer immensities: *they* are within our comprehension however much *we* seem marginalized by them.

29. Islamic Council of Europe, Statement.

30. One exception would be Sadiq al-ʾAzm, *Naqd al-Fikr al-Dini* (Criticism of Religious Thought) (Beirut, 1969).

31. *Children of Gabalawi,* Eng. trans. by Philip Stewart, (London, 1981). Mahfuz has also a short story, *al-Zallam,* about a malevolent deity against whom there is a revolt in the name of humane ideas which institutional religion has quite failed to understand or serve, and instead connives with injustice. See also *The Pen and the Faith,* 145-164.

32. Nasif Nassar, *Nawa Mujtamaʾ Jadid* (Towards a New Society) (Beirut, 1970), pleads Samman, *Nightmares of Beirut* (1980), is a collection of stories which depict an alienation close to nihilism, a disenchantment with religion conferring legitimacy on what is morally iniquitous.

CHAPTER THREE

POWER ENCOUNTER AND FOLK ISLAM

Paul Hiebert

Muslims' resistance to the gospel is due not only to their creedal simplicity and to historical confrontations, but to Christians' failure to deal with the common people's felt needs.

In the church today there is a growing interest in Muslim evangelism. Yet no other religion has shown so great a resistance to the gospel despite centuries of Christian missionary efforts.

In part, this resistance is due to the creedal simplicity of Islam, and to the historical confrontations that have taken place between Islam and Christianity. In part also, it is due to the fact that Christians too often have not dealt with the felt needs of the common people addressed by folk Islam. While responding to questions raised by orthodox Islam, we have overlooked the fact that most Muslims turn to a mixture of Muslim and animistic practices for answers to everyday problems.

The Phenomenology of Folk Islam

To understand power encounter in the Muslim context, we need to understand the role of power in folk Islam. We can then move beyond phenomenology to a Christian critique and a missiological response.

Folk and Formal Islam

A useful analogy: Think of folk Islam as inner city; think of formal Islam as suburbia.

Clifford Geertz compares culture to a city.[1] In the old inner part of the city, with its narrow, winding streets, dark corners and little shops there is often little apparent order; yet much is going on, and people of many kinds crowd the lanes and fill the cafes with raucous laughs and animated gossip. The suburbs surrounding the inner city are neatly-laid-out, with wide streets and spacious, well-designed houses arranged in

long orderly rows. Here, too, there is life, but not the bois-
terous crowds and disarray.

The analogy holds well for folk and formal Islam. Folk Islam
is inner city—a confusion of beliefs and practices with no
logical consistency, a bewildering array of small vendors, all
selling their wares. In folk Islam there is little effort to
develop a single, coherent system of beliefs. There are many
small markets, and many lanes to follow. Truth is not ratio-
nally proved—it is taken to be self evident. If we question it,
we only show ourselves to be fools.

Formal Islam is a suburb, the home of the orthodox and
specialists. Here truth is carefully laid out in formal propositions, and debated by experts. Large institutions dot the
area: schools training the next generation of believers,
mosques where the faithful gather at predictable times and
governments that maintain order. Broad roads enable the
residents to travel and maintain contacts with others in dis-
tant places.

While life in the suburbs is ordered and peaceful, the inner city
offers fun and action, so residents of the suburbs often go
there. For many of the common folk, however, the inner city
is their home, and they venture out to the suburbs only for
specific purposes.

Organization. Formal Islam is organized. On the 'little
tradition' level there are local mosques, schools and governments; local festivals and birth, initiation, marriage and
death rites; and local theologies.[2] On the 'great tradition'
level there are major centers such as Mecca and Cairo,
advanced seminaries, monastic orders and missionary
agencies. Many of the leaders are priests and prophets
formally trained in orthodox beliefs.

Folk Islam is more *ad hoc*. Traditions are handed down orally
from father to son, mother to daughter, master to apprentice.
There are few formal institutions, but many shrines, sacred
places, amulets, medicines and rites. The leaders are often
shamans—masters of ecstasy who deal with the spirit world,
heal and discern the future.[3]

Central Concerns. Formal and folk Islam each deal with
different areas of human concern. The former focuses on
ultimate questions: on the most comprehensive and lasting
nature of things, and on the origins, meaning and destiny of
the universe, of Muslims and of the Muslim. Consequently, it

examines cosmic, other-worldly realities: Allah, angels, *Shaitan* and *qismet* (see Figure 1).

Folk Islam concerns itself more with everyday human problems that cannot be solved by folk science with its herbs, medicines, proverbs, local lore and common sense knowledge. The domain of folk Islam includes such things as *jinn*, saints, sacred animals and shrines, evil eye, omens, divination, amulets and magic.

One of the questions folk Islam seeks to answer is the meaning of everyday life and of death. What is going on, not in some ultimate sense, but here and now? Does the story of my life, and of my family have a plot and purpose? Here life cycle rites such as birth and initiation rites, marriages and funerals make sense out of life by ordering it into stages and marking the transitions. Beliefs in heaven, saints and spirits help solve the problem of death.

Folk Islam focuses more on here-and-now concerns than on ultimate ones.

A second question has to do with the well-being of a person or group, and the threat of misfortune. Life is precarious at best. It is beset with illnesses, plagues, barrenness, accidents, drownings, fires, droughts, earthquakes and disasters of all sorts. To explain them, people talk of evil eye, curses, spirits and supernatural forces. To prevent them, people use amulets, talismans, divination, magic, astrology, spirit traps and repellents, rituals and many other practices. To deal with them, people turn to *walis*, shamans, medicine men, magicians, spirit healers, witch doctors and others.

A third question addressed by folk Islam has to do with success and failure. How does one find a suitable spouse for a child, succeed in business, win in gambling or pass a school examination? How does a tribe insure its prosperity, and guarantee victory in battle? Divination, omens, astrology, magic, ancestors, tribal gods and surrounding spirits can bring success. Similarly, curses, medicines, black magic, sorcery and witchcraft can secure the failure of rivals and enemies.

Another question has to do with the need to plan one's life, and the need to know the unknown—whether past, present or future. Who stole the money? Who is telling the truth? Will this business venture succeed? To answer these questions, folk Islam provides guidance by means of divination, dreams, oracles, omens or prophecies.

Other questions have to do with human relationships, and with relationships to ancestors, spirits, gods, demons, ani-

FIGURE 1

THE COSMOLOGY OF POPULAR ISLAM[4]

	CONCEPTS OF BEING	CONCEPTS OF POWER
OTHER-WORLDLY	Allah	$qadr$[a]
	archangels: Isrâfîl Jibrâ'îl angels: of no sex, good, created of light	books: especially Qur'an

THIS WORLDLY, EXTRAORDINARY	devils: Iblîs
	      others
	jinn:[b] sexed; many kinds,
	      usually bad
		magic & sorcery
		
		astrology

	prophets: apostles prophets	divination
NORMALLY UNSEEN		$baraka$[c]
	dead saints: good	$dhikr$[d]
	zâr[e] spirits	evil eye
	ᶜA'îsha Qandîsha[f], etc.	omens, prophylaxis
	quarîna[g]	vows, curses, blessings
	ancestors, souls of recently dead	
SEEN	living holy men (wali, pir)	sacred objects & numbers
	sacred animals & plants	/ dreams \
		< visions >
	pious Muslims	\ sleep /
THIS WORLDLY, ORDINARY	ordinary Muslims	herbs, drugs
	unbelievers	other natural forces
	animals, plants, insects	

a) *qadr*: 'fate' as expressed in *hadîth* literature.   *Taqdîr* is used in theological works.   Turkish: *kismet*.
b) *Jinn* are spirit beings below angels and above humans.
c) *Baraka* is the power of God's blessing or grace.
d) *Dhikr*: practice of a Sufi-type rite aimed at inducing ecstasy or trance.
e) *Zar* are spirits that possess people causing illness or abnormal behavior.
f) ᶜ*A'îsha Qandîsha*: a spirit found in Morocco.
g) *Quarîna* are a person's (evil) double or shadow spirit.

mals and plants (see Figure 2). Here one finds 'love magic,' fertility rites, medicines to test the faithfulness of a spouse, sorcery, witchcraft, curses and the like.

Truth and Pragmatism

One crucial difference between formal and folk Islam has to do with their central concerns. Orthodox Islam seeks truth—truth about the ultimate nature of reality; truth about the way to heaven. Consequently it is founded on revelation, insight and reason. Folk religion, on the other hand, focuses on problem-solving in everyday life. It is, therefore, basically pragmatic. Any method can be used so long as it works. Moreover, several methods may be used simultaneously without apparent contradiction, for one of them may work. A father with a sick son will ask the *mullah* to pray to God for him, tie an amulet to his arm to drive off evil spirits and give him modern medicine to kill the germs, all at the same time.

Given these differences, it should not surprise us that leaders of formal Islam are often in conflict with folk leaders who offer people immediate, pragmatic solutions to their every-day problems, and who often show little concern about truth or ultimate destiny.

FIGURE 2

CENTRAL QUESTIONS IN DIFFERENT EXPLANATION SYSTEMS

EXTRAORDINARY EXPLANATIONS:

FORMAL ISLAM	The nature of ultimate realities. The ultimate origins, purpose and destiny of: the universe, our people, myself.
FOLK ISLAM	The meaning of life and the challenge of death. Human well-being and the threat of misfortune. Success and the danger of failure. Human planning and control, the uncertainty of the unknown and the future and the need for guidance. Meaningful relationships and the fear of rejection, hostility and abandonment.

ORDINARY EXPLANATIONS:

FOLK SCIENCE	The nature and operation of everyday realities. The immediate stories of the universe, our people and myself.

Power and Power Confrontations

Power can be divided into two basic types: power that is exercised by living beings, and power that exists by itself. In formal Islam the former is found in Allah, angels and *Shaitan* who control human destiny. The latter is *qismet*, the cosmic force like 'fate' that also plays a part in human fortunes.

In folk Islam, beings such as *qarina, jinn, dews, als, pari* and spirits of various sorts have power to influence human lives. So, too, do saints, holy men, rulers and family heads. And so, too, do some animals and plants. Impersonal powers include *baraka*, the *evil eye*, astrological forces and magic.

Power Confrontation

Fundamental to many religions is the belief that reality is characterized by a conflict between good and evil. In orthodox Islam Allah is at war with *Shaitan*, and this battle involves the followers of both in *jihad*. Jacques Ellul notes,

> The word *jihad* has two complementary senses. It may denote a spiritual war that is moral and inward. Muslims have to wage this war within themselves in the fight against demons and evil forces, in the effort to achieve better obedience to God's will, in the struggle for perfect submission. But at the same time and in a wholly consistent way the *jihad* is also the war against external demons. To spread the faith, it is necessary to destroy false religions. This war, then, is *always* a religious war, a holy war.[5]

Rewards in this warfare are ultimate: paradise and the triumph of Islam. On this level we can examine the wars between Muslims and Christians during the rapid expansion of Islam and the reaction of the Crusades, as well as the present revival of Islamic fundamentalism.

In folk Islam, however, power conflicts take on another meaning. People in everyday life are believed to be at the mercy of evil powers: spirits, ghosts, demons, evil eyes, curses and sorcery. Their only protection is to seek the aid of Allah, angels, saints, charms, good magic and other powers. Here the consequences of this warfare are immediate: disease, drought and disaster on the one hand; health, wealth and prosperity on the other.

ERRATA NOTICE

Muslims and Christians on the Emmaus Road

MARC
World Vision International
919 West Huntington Drive
Monrovia, California 91016
(818) 303-8811

1. INDEX

This printing of *Muslims and Christians on the Emmaus Road* contains several errors in the index. The corrections   are as follows:

Eliminate:
- al ikraha
- Shari'ah a Hakimiyyah

Insert:
- la ikraha (*"let there be no compulsion"*), 120
- Hakimiyyah (*"rule" of God*), 30

Change:
- ayat (*lit. "signs", used of verses in the Quran*), 36
- Fatihah (*first sura of Quran, commonly used in Muslim public prayer*), 138, 306, 308, 309, 310, 311, 312
- haqiqa (*the divine "truth"*), 215
- Iblis (*the "Accuser", the Devil*), 37, 151
- jihad (*a spiritual "exertion" or war that may be inward/external*), 50, 319
- jinn (*spirit beings*), 47, 50, 53, 207
- shamans (*practitioners who deal with the spirit world, heal and discern the future*), 46, 47
- sifat (*God's attributes*), 188
- tariqah (*the divine "way", used of mystical brotherhoods*), 215

The index also contains errors in page references which will be corrected in the next printing.

2. PAGE 265

Page 263 is reprinted on page 265, which should be replaced with the facing page.

Manikganj, Bangladesh. I entered that small village as lacking in knowledge of Islam as the town was of electricity, running water, and paved roads. Sixty-two months later I emerged of somewhat sane mind and body but basically as ignorant of Islam as I had been when I initially set foot in our tin "honeymoon shack." I had not seen one Muslim come to Christ.

How typical this testimony is of so many missionaries. We have gone forth with the Word of God and faith but with a woefully inadequate understanding of Islam. Missionaries are now a new breed of probers and innovators. But are they in it for the long haul? One of my great disappointments in life has been to see sharp, well-educated missionaries with great potential call it quits after only one or two terms. Effective Muslim evangelism simply cannot be accomplished within minimal time commitments.

All the hassles and heartaches...have been eminently wothwhile in light of the end result: seeing the spiritual lineage of the firstborn of Abraham grafted into the body of Christ.

These are just a few reflections on lessons "being learned." My final summary statement is that all the hassles and heartaches of these many years have been eminently worthwhile in light of the end result: seeing the spiritual lineage of the firstborn of Abraham grafted into the body of Christ. These special believers are, to me, much more precious than fine gold or precious jewels!

The range of power confrontations is seen in Figure 3, and illustrations of the various types can readily be drawn from both formal and folk Islam.

Power Encounters

We are concerned here with certain types of power confrontations, namely those that take place between two religions, specifically between Christianity and Islam as Christians seek to win Muslims to Christ. These include *jihads* and crusades in which believers try to convert unbelievers by military force; opposition such as government officials prohibiting missionaries from preaching and persecution of those who convert to Christianity.

There are, however, two types of confrontations which are frequently referred to as 'power encounters.' One of these has

FIGURE 3

POWER CONFRONTATIONS IN HIGH AND LOW RELIGIONS

	GOOD	EVIL
OTHER-WORLDLY:	Allah Angels	Shaitan Demons
	Qismet	Bad fate
THIS-WORLDLY EXTRAORDINARY	Spirits Ancestors Walis, Pirs	Jinn, Zar Ancestors, Ghosts
	Baraka Dhikr, Blessing Good magic Amulets Sacred objects	Evil eye Curses, Sorcery Evil magic Evil objects
THIS-WORLDLY ORDINARY	Islam Person	Pagan religions Qarina (double)
	Natural forces	Natural forces

to do with public demonstrations of supernatural power, the other with the battle that takes place in the hearts of those wanting to become Christians.

Elijah's challenge to the prophets of Baal exemplifies one kind of power encounter.

Elijah's challenge to the prophets of Baal is one example of the first type of power encounter. Another is Rev. Lowder's violation of the religious taboos of the Budu in southeast Africa. Lowder knew that the people believed in a powerful royal spirit said to reside in leopard skins which were reserved for use by tribal chiefs. He obtained a leopard skin and went from village to village, trampling on it to show that he was immune to its power. This created much commotion among the people, and drew large audiences. C. T. Studd ate plantains cooked in a fire fueled by the medicines used in witchcraft. The fact that he did not die instantly convinced the people that he had superior powers.

In some instances such demonstrations of power have persuaded people of the superiority of the gospel and led to mass conversions. In most cases, however, they lead to increased opposition by the religious establishment, to persecution and sometimes even to death. This is clear in the case of Elijah. After he demonstrated God's power and killed the prophets of Baal, he fled for his life to the desert where he experienced severe depression. And there was no revival in Israel. Jezebel appointed new prophets of Baal and continued her persecution of God's people.

Conversion to Christ in a complex communal society may be an even more spectacular power encounter

The second type of power encounter takes place when new converts destroy their old gods. The confrontation is not between the missionary and the people, but between those who want to convert and those who do not; and, within individuals, between faith in Christ and fear of the old fetishes and medicines.

In these situations the pagan fetishes must be destroyed if Christ is to take their place. Allan Tippett writes,

> At the level of actual conversion from paganism...no matter how many elements may be woven into the conversion complex in communal society, the group action (which is not mass, but multi-individual) must fix itself in encounter at some material locus of power at some specific point in time. There must be a psychological moment or experience when the persons involved actually turn from the old god(s) to the new. There ought to be some ocular demonstration of this encounter, some specific act of faith. Both Christian and pagan alike frequently demand some such act to indicate the bona fide nature of conversion.[6]

Such power encounters cannot be precipitated by the missionary. If he or she destroys the fetishes, the people will remake them. In fact, if the people simply say that the gods have gone away, they may return. Only destroying them will do. Tippett notes,

> None but the tribe can destroy the tribal fetish (the chief as representative, acting in the presence of the group), none but the family (with the family head as representative) can destroy a family god, and a personal fetish can only be destroyed by the individual himself.[7]

To destroy one's fetishes and amulets is a fearful experience. There is always doubt, is Christ really more powerful than the *jinn* or *zar*? Can he protect new believers from the evil spirits, provide for their needs and heal them? In some instances a few members of the community destroy their charms and medicines as a test case, risking their lives for the rest. Illnesses and deaths during this early period of conversion are frequently taken to be signs that the old god and spirits are angry, and that the Christian God is not more powerful than they.

Theological Critique

Much has been written on a Christian response to orthodox Islam, but little on a Christian answer to the beliefs and practices of folk Islam. This is due, in part, to the growing influence of a neo-Platonic dualism in western thought following the Renaissance. The effect of this is to divide the world into two domains: spiritual and natural. The former has to do with other worlds, eternity and ultimate matters, and is the province of religion. The latter covers this world which is seen as an autonomous system operating by natural law.

The effect of this dualism on Christians is far-reaching. It has led to a division between evangelism (dealing with the spiritual side of humans) and social concerns (dealing with the natural side of humans). It has also led to a denial of the supernatural in everyday human life. Magic, which was a serious system of explanation in the Middle Ages, became sleight of hand, and spirits on this earth were relegated to myth. Even God's acts in the natural sphere were seen as exceptions to the natural order—as miracles. Consequently, western missionaries often had no ready theological answers for questions related to human crises, spirit oppression and witchcraft. Too often these were given to science for solution.

For most ordinary Muslims, folk Islam is a vital part of their lives, and if we want to work with them, we must develop a biblical response to the questions they face. To ignore these questions is to close the door to effective witness.

What theological affirmations can we make regarding God's involvement in everyday human life? And what are the pitfalls in developing such a theology?

Theological Affirmations

Beginning with the nature of God and his relationship to creation, we must include a theology of everyday existence.

A Christian theology of everyday existence must be subsumed within a broader theology of God, creation, sin, redemption and the Kingdom. To divorce it from these is to make Christianity a new 'social gospel' or a new magic. We must, therefore, begin with the nature of God and his relationship to creation.

FIGURE 4

GOD IN THE WHOLE OF HISTORY

GOD IN:	A THEOLOGY OF:
COSMIC HISTORY	creation, redemption, purpose, eschatology
HUMAN HISTORY	guidance, provision, healing, comforting
NATURAL HISTORY	creation, sustaining, disasters

God and Creation

In view of the influence Greek dualism has had on Western thought and theology, it is important that we affirm and experience ourselves that God is continually involved in all of his creation. He did not create the universe and leave it to run according to impersonal laws. He is at work not only in cosmic history, but also in the affairs of the nations, and in the life of every individual (see Figure 4). Furthermore, that work is characterized not only by righteousness and justice, but also by love and forgiveness. Consequently, we can go to him with our cares, knowing that he cares for us (I Pe. 5:7). It is important to emphasize this among Muslims, for they have a high view of the sovereignty of God, but know little of his concern for their everyday needs, and so must turn to folk Islam for answers.

concern for their everyday needs, and so must turn to folk Islam for answers.

A theology of God's involvement in human and natural history must be rooted in our understanding of him as trinity (see Figure 5). As Father, God is the sovereign ruler of history. In his providence, he works in everything for good for those who love him (Rom. 8:28). This is the large frame within which the other works of God must be understood.

As Son, God is present among us (Mt. 28:20; Jn. 17:23; Eph. 1:11-14). He encourages us in our victories, sustains us in our sufferings and is with us in our hour of death and resurrection. He is our exemplar.

As Holy Spirit, God works in us in power, enabling us to live victorious lives and to manifest the works of God on earth.

FIGURE 5

A TRINITARIAN VIEW OF GOD'S PRESENCE IN THE DAILY LIVES OF HIS PEOPLE

FATHER Providence	-maintains creation -superintends history
SON Presence	-is our exemplar in his incarnation. -leads us by the way of the cross and servanthood to hope and resurrection.
HOLY SPIRIT Power	-enables us to have spiritual victory. -manifests through us the power of God as a testimony of the Kingdom of God on earth.

In order to understand God's involvement in human and natural history, we need to develop biblical theologies; of human identity, guidance, healing, provision and hope, as well as theologies of death, suffering, disaster, loneliness and failure. We also need to develop theologies regarding ecology, and the church's responsibilities in a sinful, suffering world.

Power and Encounter

Because folk Islam focuses its attention on power, we must affirm that God is a God of power. We must affirm the mighty works of God in the lives of his people. But we must make clear that in a sinful world the way God uses his power is the way of the cross, not the sword; the way of suffering,

Power-conscious people need to see that God is a God of power— *and* that his way of using his power in people's lives is the way of the cross, not the way of the sword.

and not of ease (I Co. 1:18-25). God's war is with Satan and his followers, God's victory took place at Calvary.

The implications of this for power confrontations is profound. First, as Christians we are freed from the power of spirits and witchcraft. They no longer have hold of us (Gal. 4:3-7). This is indeed good news to most Muslims.

Second, we are called to challenge the structures and beliefs of existing religious systems, even as we invite their followers to turn to Christ. There are important truths in other religions that need not be destroyed, but other religions exist as systems in rebellion against God. They, therefore, oppose those from their ranks who turn to Christ.

Our invitations to Muslims to follow Christ should include demonstrations of God's power. These may include the passing signs of healing of those who are sick, and provision for those who are destitute. And they should surely include the more permanent signs of righteousness and transformed lives.

Demonstrations of God's power lead some to faith and others only to hostility. This was true even of miracles performed by Jesus.

We must remember, however, that such power encounters bring no easy victory. Some see them and believe. Others, particularly those representing the religious establishment, respond with greater hostility. This was clearly the case in the life of Jesus. John reports the miracles Jesus performed, and shows how these brought him into confrontation with the Jewish religious establishment. In chapter 2 Jesus overthrows the tables of the money changers in the Court of the Gentiles in the temple;[8] in chapter 3 he talks to a leader of the establishment; in chapter 4 he challenges the religious segregation taught by the Scribes and Pharisees; in chapter 5 he heals on the sabbath against institutional rules; in chapter 5 he challenges the leaders by showing up at the feast in Jerusalem; in chapter 8 he confronts their unforgiving legalism; and in chapter 9 he shows their powerlessness. In turn, the religious establishment baits him, attacks him and finally crucifies him. As Ched Myers points out, the cross in Jesus' day was neither a religious icon nor a metaphor for personal anguish and humility.

> It had only one meaning: that terrible form of capital punishment reserved by imperial Rome for political dissenters. Thus discipleship is revealed as a vocation of nonviolent resistance to the powers.[9]

The early church experienced the same response. Most signs and wonders led to imprisonment and death (see Table 1).

When we are involved in power encounters, we must be ready to pay the price, for the cross is the paradigm of how God works in human history (I Co. 1:18-25).

Finally, we must be deeply sensitive to the inner conflicts of those wanting to become Christians, and provide much pastoral care to those who have burned their old religious paraphernalia. It is easy for them to see every illness and misfortune as a sign that their old ways were right.

Discernment

Discernment is essential. All religions produce some kinds of signs and wonders.

Finally, in dealing with folk Islam we need a theology of discernment. Signs and wonders are not confined to Christianity. They are found in all religions. Reports of *glossolalia*, healings, miracles and resurrections are common in folk Islam. Scripture itself warns us to guard ourselves from being led astray, for Satan counterfeits God's work (Mt. 7:15-16; I Ti. 4:1,7; II Ti. 3:-4:5; II Th. 2:9-10). How should we respond to all this?

First, we need to test between what is real and what is not real. Not all reports are true, not all explanations valid. Christianity is deeply rooted in realism: it affirms a real God, and a real world created by God. It rejects the belief that reality ultimately exists only in the mind. Consequently, as Christians we affirm the need for reality testing.[10]

Second, we must test what is of God and what is not. It is too simple to say that what God's people do is of God (cf. Mt. 7:21-23), and that what non-Christians do is of Satan (cf. Num. 22-24), or to equate signs and wonders with miracles.[11] We need other tests.[12] Signs are not ends in themselves—they show us God's presence and point us his way.

Theological Cautions

In developing a theology of God's work in this world, there is a danger of buying into the explanation systems of this world—as the church did during the Middle Ages when it gave its approval to amulets, indulgences, saints and magic. Some of these dangers are:

The danger of confusing phenomenology and ontology. Experience is not the final arbiter of truth. It must be interpreted in the light of our theology.

TABLE 1

POWER ENCOUNTERS IN THE BOOK OF ACTS

Chapter	Encounter	Initial Response	End of the Story
2	Pentecost	Ridicule	Some believe
3-4	Heal the cripple	Amazement	Jail
5:1-11	Lying by Ananias and Sapphira		Death
5:12-42	Signs & wonders	Institutional reaction	Jail
6-8:3	Signs & wonders	Institutional reaction	Death
8:4	Sign	Imitation	Rebuke
9	Paul's opposition	Confrontation	Conversion
10	Reluctant witness	Vision	Obedience
11-12:19	Prophecy	Institutional reaction	Death
12:20-23	Herod's deification	God's judgment	Death
13:4-12	Encounter w/Elymas	Elymas becomes blind	Some believe
13:13-52	Preach	Many believe	Driven from city
14:1-7	Preach	Some believe	Driven from city
14:8-20	Heal crippled	Paul and Barnabas worshipped	Stoned and left for dead
16:16-40	Cast out demon	Attacked by crowd	Prison
17:1-9	Preach	Some believe	Attacked and had to flee
18:1-21	Preach	Jews oppose Paul	Persecution
19:8-20	Confront Jewish exorcists	Demon-possessed overpowers them	Burning of books
21-28	Confrontation with establishment	Prison	Death in Rome

The danger of self-centered narcissism. Folk religion is preoccupied with the self: with earthly health, success and power. God is indeed interested in us, but not in our self-centeredness. He calls us to a sacrificial ministry to a lost and broken world.

The danger of a new Christian magic. Given their self-centeredness, it is not surprising that in times of crisis humans seek control, even of God. They try to coerce him to do their will, rather than submit to his. The result is that Christianity has often become a new magic, stronger than the old.

The danger of introducing a new secularism. We must affirm God's wondrous works, but if we see God's hand only in miracles, we reinforce the dualism that gave rise to secularism. We need to affirm God's work in ordinary processes like medicine and counseling, as much as in extraordinary interventions.

The danger of making signs and wonders normative and ends in themselves. God's extraordinary works are signs—they point beyond themselves to lessons God is teaching us. Too often we focus our attention on the signs, not the messages, and see miracles as evidence of spirituality.

The danger of generating a false sense of guilt and failure among those who are not delivered. It is easy to rejoice with those who are delivered *from* illness, poverty or death, but what about those whom God chooses to sustain in their difficulties? By making miracles normative, we implicitly accuse those who do not experience deliverance of lacking faith or harboring sin. Yet it is they who need to see God's hand most in their suffering.

The danger of exalting a human leader. Folk religion centers around the 'big man': the *pir, fakir,* saint, shaman or miracle worker. The Scriptures speak of the church as a body in which Christ is the head, and in which no member has greater honor than the other.

The danger of pragmatism. Because folk Islam is concerned more with power than with truth, it is basically pragmatic in nature. Any means may be used so long as it solves the problem. In the end, however, pragmatism denies truth and leads to relativism.

Missiological Applications

What implications does all this have for evangelism among ordinary Muslims? How do we preach the good news of Christ's deliverance to ordinary Muslims, and how do we help converts move from their traditional beliefs to a biblical understanding of reality?

In critiquing folk Islam's beliefs and practices, ask: Which of them can the church reinterpret as Christian truth? Which are cultural understandings insignificant to Christian faith? Which must be rejected as antithetical to the gospel?

To answer these questions, we need a biblical critique of the beliefs and practices of folk Islam. Which of them can the church keep and reinterpret as bearers of Christian truth, which of them are cultural understandings having little to do with Christian faith, and which must be rejected as false or antithetical to the gospel? Here we must deal with such things as *jinns, qismet, baraka, dhikr,* evil eye, saints and ancestors, amulets, sacred sites and magic. The decisions must be made by the mature Christian leaders (missionary and national), and the people themselves.[13]

We need also a clear understanding of conversion. What changes must take place when a person becomes a follower of

Christ, and what changes are better left to spiritual growth and maturation? Clearly, concepts deeply embedded in the people's world view, such as *dhikr*, *jinns* and evil eye cannot be changed overnight. We can proclaim the power of God over them, but new converts' secret fear of them can persist for a long time. And what about amulets, medicines and other magical paraphernalia? Can these be eliminated over time by teaching, or are these among the items new converts must destroy in power encounters? What are the gods they must burn to break with their old ways? And how should we minister to new converts to bring them to spiritual maturity?

Closely tied to this are questions relating to the birth and growth of the church as a community of faith. When should it be formed, what should be its polity and how can we help the community mature? It is important to differentiate the spiritual progress of individuals from that of the church. The former are being led, the latter must do the leading. The former are in many stages of immaturity, the latter must define maturity. The church is a body that must provide the interpretation and application of Scripture. It is the guardian of Christian faith in a particular historical and cultural setting.

Christians' faithfulness in suffering, as well as God's demonstrations of power, bear witness that leads some to respond to Christ.

Finally, what part do power encounters of the first sort play in conversions and church planting? Prayers for the sick, poor, needy and dying are part of normal church life. But what about public demonstrations of power that seek to show the superiority of God over other gods and powers? Here we need to be careful not to go ahead of God's leading, for such demonstrations fail and discredit God if he is not in them. Moreover, we must realize that power encounters provide no easy victory. We must be ready to pay the price of persecution and suffering as opposition rises to this public proclamation of the gospel. But both demonstrations of God's power and the faithful suffering of his saints have borne and continue to bear testimony that lead some to hear and believe.

NOTES

1. Clifford Geertz, *Local Knowledge: Further Essays in Interpretive Anthropology* (New York: Basic Books, 1985). In this, Geertz extends the analogy which was originally used by Wittgenstein with regard to language domains.

2. The concepts of 'little tradition' and 'great tradition' developed by Robert Redfield have found wide acceptance in anthropology in the analysis of

institutional organization in complex societies. An example of this is McKim Marriott's analysis of the Indian scene. McKim Marriott, *Village India: Studies in the Little Community* (Chicago: University of Chicago Press, 1955).

3. Mircea Eliade, *Shamanism: Archaic Techniques of Ecstasy*, rev. ed., trans. W. T. Trask (New York: Pantheon, 1964).

4. Adapted from Bill Musk, "Popular Islam: An Investigation into the Phenomenology and Ethnotheological Bases of Popular Islamic Belief and Practice" (Doctoral diss., Pretoria: University of South Africa, 1984).

5. Jacques Ellul, *The Subversion of Christianity* (Grand Rapids, MI: Eerdmans, 1986), 101.

6. Allan Tippett, *People Movements in Southern Polynesia* (Chicago: Moody Press, 1971), 169.

7. Ibid., 203.

8. There is irony here, for the money changers had set up their tables in the Court of the Gentiles, which was intended to be the place for evangelism, where Gentiles could see the Jews in their worship of God. Those who converted were allowed into the Court of the Jews. Evangelism had been converted into business.

9. Ched Myers, "Embracing the Way of Jesus," *Sojourners* 16:8 (1987): 27-30.

10. E. S. Jones points out the fundamental difference between eastern and western religions. Judeo-Christianity and its heresies of Islam, Marxism, Secular Humanism and Capitalism are *realist* in nature. They affirm the existence of a real world independent of the human mind, and a real history distinct from fiction or imagination. It is not surprising that Christianity gave birth to science as the study of this real world and its history.

    Hinduism and its heresies of Buddhism and Jainism, on the other hand, are *idealist*. Reality ultimately lies not in an objective world without, but in a subjective world within. Here reality testing has no place.

    Today the West is being challenged by Eastern religions and the New Age movements, which have their roots in Hinduism and Buddhism, which challenge the realist foundations of Christianity.

11. In Scripture the terms "signs" and "wonders" are used of both ordinary and extraordinary phenomena. Their importance is not that they are 'miraculous' but that they are signs that God is present. For example, in the Old Testament the rainbow, the sabbath and circumcision are signs of God's covenants with his people. Similarly, the death of the first born son at the rebuilding of Jericho, and a second son at its completion were signs of God's judgment. Signs and wonders point beyond themselves to God and his world for a specific situation. They came at special times and did not replace the normal worship rites as the center of religion.

12. Cf. Paul G. Hiebert, "Discerning the Work of God," in *Charismatic Experiences in History*, ed. Cecil M. Robeck, Jr. (Peabody, MA: Hendrickson Publishers, 1985).

13. Ibid., 171-192.

CHAPTER FOUR

URBANIZATION AND ITS IMPLICATIONS

Harvie M. Conn

What are the connections between Islam and the cities of North Africa and the Middle East? What effect have the massive urbanization trends of the last three decades had on these features? What generalizations and stereotypes about the city can be corrected for their effect on strategy planning? Are there suggestions for strategy that might come from a better understanding of urbanization? These are the questions to be dealt with in this preliminary study—a tentative "work-in-progress."

The History of the Muslim Pre-Industrial City

Islamic civilization has always been predominantly urban. Islam has been wedded to the city. The urban lifestyle is not new to Islam historically or ontologically. Ira Lapidus, in his book *Middle Eastern Cities*, reminds us that Islamic civilization has always been predominantly an urban civilization.[1] He notes:

> For Muslims, cities often possess a special sanctity and are regarded as the sole places in which a full and truly Muslim life may be lived.[2]

V.F. Costello repeats the thesis:

> It has been argued that Islam has a preference of urban over rural societies, a preference rooted in doctrinal and historical conditions.[3]

This is not to say that Islam created the city. By the time of the advent of Islam, the whole of the Middle Eastern region from the Nile to the Jaxartes had been urbanized.[4] But Islam sanctified the city by building it as a presupposition into its religious system. The creation of a town was lauded as a highly praiseworthy act; pious legends about their foundation were innumerable.

> Blessings have always been associated with a stay at Medina. Special permission was needed to leave it. Contrariwise, the meritorious act *par excellence* was the *hijra*, the departure for Medina, the flight to the town.[5]

The rhythm of Muslim practices is designed for town dwellers. The gathering of the whole community for Friday prayer demands a fixed and permanent mosque, a requirement to be met by a fixed and permanent site.

> The mosque with its pool for ablutions and the complex installations this demands; the five daily prayers in response to the call of the muezzin; the ramadan feast with its active nights; these are all urban in character. Secondly, town life is not only essential to collective prayer, it is necessary to the dignified life which Islam demands. The *imam* needs to live the life of a townsman. Women should be veiled, which conflicts with the requirements of nomadic, or even rural, existence. This rigorous prudish ideal is that of the austere merchants of the Hijaz. There, still, Islam resorts to the decorum of the cities rather than the disorder of the fields or the desert. Its social constraints, just as much as its spiritual demands, make Islam an urban religion.[6]

The spread of Islam in the centuries following its birth followed an urban path. When European urbanism was undergoing the so-called Dark Ages, the Arabs were busy founding new towns and regenerating the old Roman towns of Egypt and the Levant and the Sassanian towns of Persia. Cities took on military and administrative significance as radiating centers of Islamization.

In later phases of the Islamic development, ruling Muslim groups did try to remain aloof from urbanism. And there were those countries like Syria which were as urbanized before Islam as afterwards, still others remaining with relatively little urbanization. But it is still true that

> in the Muslim world as in the ancient world, but unlike medieval Western Europe, the whole of civilization was found in the town; it was only there that administration, law, religion and culture existed.[7]

Urban artisans, merchants and tradesmen used the city's commercial webs to spread Islam along the caravan and sea routes. It moved throughout the interior of the vanquished countries along these same urban commercial routes. And, through the pioneering colonies of merchants and traders, it expanded beyond the borders of Islam's continuous territory into areas untouched by the nomadic conquests.

In the late 15th and early 16th centuries, urban decline began in the Middle East. By the end of the 19th century, the pre-industrial urban world of Islam had lost its vitality in the face of European expansionism.

Contact with the West in the 19th and early 20th centuries brought changes to the Muslim city, changes whose effects we still feel. An alien European invasion, initially through trade but later, in places like Egypt, through direct military action, began to force the transformation of the Muslim city from pre-industrial to one of trade and business. Seaport cities began to slowly grow, but at the expense of smaller towns.

In all this, one feature of Muslim urban demographics remained unique. While the West had exhibited a long history of social and ideological conflict between city and country, rural and urban,[8] Islamic social struggles were not formed along urban-rural polarizations.[9] Rather, "village-city differences resembled those between city quarters, between neighboring villages, and between city dwellers and villagers united against other parties."[10] In fact, if Egypt and Syria's histories are typical, they would indicate that in periods of a strong and centralized government the ties became stronger. And a weakening of government tended to separate them.[11]

Contemporary Urbanization Trends

Since the 1920s, and especially during the last three decades, urbanization has accelerated in the Middle East and in the larger Muslim world. The discovery and exploitation of oil in the Middle East has received much publicity. But that is only one reason for urban growth in that region. Other factors also take on significance, outside the area as well as in it.

The promotion of industrialization and other forms of economic development by state power; population growth and increasing migration to the city; foreign aid with the cities serving as points of contact with the aid-granting countries; internal political strife that has unsettled large groups of people; changes in foreign trade patterns and foreign relations; political centralization—all these have played a part in creating an urban Islamic world estimated by some to be 30% of the world's Muslims.[12]

The Middle East exemplifies the trend. By 1950, with a little over 3% of the world's population, it contained four of the world's 49 million-plus cities. If Europe, North America and the USSR are excluded, the number of such cities is reduced to 29. And the Middle East must then be seen as containing 14% of the large cities of the underdeveloped world.[13]   Costello says,

> Most of the countries [of the Middle East] now have more than one-third of the population living in towns, making the Middle East more physically urbanized than most of Tropical Africa, or of East, Southeast and South Asia.[14]

There is little sign of let-up in this dramatic picture. A 1987 report comments that

> the rate of growth in urban areas, especially in the main Arab cities, is about 6% per year...As a case in point, Cairo's population in 1920 was 875,000; by 1950 it exceeded two million, and by 1970 it exceeded 5 million. It may reach 20 million by the year 2000. Yet the city can only accommodate 1 million people.[15]

The urbanization rate of most Middle East cities exceeds that of most cities in other regions of the world.

The projected growth of other Arab cities looks very much the same. The so-called city states like Kuwait and Qatar are becoming urbanized at phenomenal rates of 10 and 15 percent annually. The cities of Doha and Kuwait will double their populations in less than ten years. Damascus, with a population of 850,000 in 1970, will likely reach 3 million by 2000. Baghdad will grow from a 1970 city of 2.2 million to 12 million by 2000.[16]

In the period between 1950 and 1970, urban growth in Northern Africa surpassed that of North America and all of Europe. The percentage increase of urban population growth in North Africa reached 51.6% (19.1% rural). In North America it was only 17.6%; in western Europe 18.7%; northern Europe was 9.8%.[17] By 1970, 42.9% of Algeria's population was living in urban areas with over 5,000 inhabitants. In Tunisia, the figure was 43.5%, Morocco 32.5%.[18] And the future? Algiers is projected to hit 4.8 million in 2000 (1.2 million in 1970), Tunis will go from 755,000 in 1970 to 2.3 million by 2000. Casablanca is expected to grow from its 1970 population of 1.4 million to 5 million by the end of the century.

In the process of urbanization, certain characteristics emerge that are significant for evangelistic strategy-planning. Here are a few of them.

1. There is the sudden eruption of what David Barrett has called non-Christian or anti-Christian urban supergiants, cities with over ten million inhabitants each. In 1958, Tokyo was the first to reach that status. By AD 2000, seven Islamic cities will have joined that category—Jakarta in 1989, Cairo in 1991, Baghdad, Istanbul, Teheran and Karachi in 1996, and Dacca in 2000. In addition, there will be three Hindu/Buddhist/Muslim supergiants: Madras in 1994, Delhi in 1996, and Bangkok in 2000.[19]

2. As is common in so many countries of Africa, Asia and Latin America, urban Muslim population is often crowded into one large city (designated "the primate city"). Far outstripping in size the second major city of the country, it is frequently the capital; its magnetic pull centralizes government administration, income and industry within its field.

So, by 1956, Teheran, with a population of 1,512,000, towered over Tabriz, with 390,000, and Isfahan, with 255,000. Baghdad, with about 700,000, compared to Mosul, with under 200,000. North Africa shows the same pattern. Casablanca, Algiers, Tunis and Tripoli each outclass all the other towns in their respective countries.

Massive human problems, including unemployment, under-employment and severe housing shortages, often outweigh the advantages of centralized infrastructures.

With this urban population concentration come massive human problems: unemployment and under-employment; the accumulation of wealth and professional resources in only one area; social and cultural changes, including severe housing shortages that take on runaway proportions.

3. Though the Middle East and the larger Muslim world have their great cities, "on the whole they are small by Western standards."[20] Where industrialization has invaded the city, this generalization must be modified. But the lack of large and heavy industry still remains a general feature of Middle Eastern cities in general. And that means less complex bureaucracies and small cities.

4. Migration from country to country has always played a key role in the expansion of the Muslim faith throughout its history.[21] Now it is intra-country migration that is deeply affecting the acceleration of urban growth (in tandem, of course, with natural increase). And, as in Egypt, this migra-

tion tends to favor the largest cities, bypassing those of moderate and small size. In fact,

> for the last three decades, cities of highest rank size have sustained average rates of growth which are more than twice the rate of natural increase, while smaller towns, of between 20,000 to 30,000, have failed to keep pace with rates of natural increase, i.e., have actually experienced net losses of population.[22]

The cities are not melting pots. Migrants' ethnic and sociocultural groupings remain strong within the urban setting.

5. As in other cities, there is little indication of a "melting pot" phenomenon. That is, the migrants do not lose their ethnic or sociocultural connections with the areas they come from originally. There are, of course, variations to this pattern. But, more often than not, migrants tend to concentrate in the city according to their home regions. A survey of Tripoli in 1917 showed that families from the Misurata area and from other regions were living in groups.

> In the shanty towns which began to mushroom outside the high walls built by the Italians, there was no pronounced differentiation by region of origin. More recently there has been some degree of concentration according to place of birth: migrants from the desert zone have tended to concentrate in the old city of Tripoli and in a group of shanty towns outside a southern gate.[23]

In cities like Cairo and Isfahan, migrants tend to live on the side of the city nearest their place of origin. Migrants may also cluster not only by residence but also by occupation.

6. Unlike other city centers, many urban dwellers

> exhibit characteristics and behavior patterns that reflect their rural or village background...Migrants do not simply pick up urban ways; they also, in effect, ruralize the cities. Many city dwellers are still tied to rural customs and culture, and migrants shape the city as much as the city shapes them.[24]

Janet Abu-Lughod, in her study of rural migrant adjustments to urban life in Egypt, speaks of the constant "ruralization" of cities like Cairo. In the incorporation of pre-existing village communities and their occupants, the migrants tend to reproduce for themselves a semblance of the way of life they left behind. They develop a variety of informal institutions, such as the village benevolent society, to make their transition to urban life more gradual and thus reduce cultural shock.[25] The pattern is typical of other cultural areas besides those of Islam.[26] So, despite its size, the city may be very rural in character.

Correcting Some Generalizations

In a way, rapidly growing cities such as Cairo are being "ruralized". At the same time, villages are being urbanized.

In creating an urban strategy for Islam, some stereotypes and generalizations need criticism. They crop up frequently in older missiological literature.

1. The alleged polarization between town or city and country continues to be a major one. Assuredly there are sociological and cultural differences.   Country areas, in matters of change, tend to be more conservative, slower to make shifts, more resistant to radical innovations, than towns and (even more so) the large cities. "Folk Islam," a synthesis of Animism and Islam with Animism dominating, may be more prominent in the villages than in those "orthogenetic" cities which see themselves as guardians of the Great Tradition, the purer Islam.

The Middle East certainly illustrates this. In fact, with increasing urbanization, traditional values are increasingly maintained in the villages.[27] Idealized in films, most of which are made in Cairo, city audiences see the village as the place where one can find peace, piety, understanding and unquestioning acceptance.[28]

At the same time, this generalization can be misleading. As we have said before, the polarization is less sharp than in the West. Islam, as a worldview, still binds city and village together. Networking, political, social and cultural, "ruralizes" the city and "urbanizes" the village.

Traditional Islam then continues to be extremely important, in both city and country. Even the changes we have noted towards religious understanding only serve to bring them together. Religion in the country takes on more the shape of religion in the city. Gulick's older judgment then may still serve us:

> Nothing…leads us to believe that Middle Eastern villagers and city dwellers differ essentially in the religious aspect of life, with the exception of the institutional features of Islam which are urban rather than rural.[29]

In countries where Islam is considerably less than dominant, the contrast between country and city attitudes towards the faith may be sharper. Where the city's role as change agent ("heterogenetic," to use the technical term) is stronger than its role as preserver and protector of the Great Tradition, the contrast will be greater. In such cases, good evangelistic strategy may deliberately choose the city as one with more potential for responsiveness to the gospel. But a simplistic appeal to differences between city and country is too general.

2. It has sometimes been argued that the cultural shock the migrant feels in moving into the city creates a setting of personal and social upheaval conducive to church growth. Behind the thesis is the presupposition, reinforced by past studies in urban sociology and anthropology, that the journey from peasant society to village to city always ends in social disintegration. Does the urban end of the continuum always represent social disintegration? Or merely progressive change?[30]

Applying it to the Muslim city, for example, reinforces these questions. Dacca, to cite one example, is a city of around three million people. But, in function and structure, it is a pre-industrial city, "a kind of urban village."[31] How strong will be the sense of dislocation for the migrant in such a city?

And what of Cairo? Abu-Lughod seems skeptical that there is adequate enough information to place too sharp a barrier along the continuum between an ideal folk society and urbanism. For one thing, the Egyptian village is hardly that isolated from the city. And, for another, "it is possible within Cairo to lead a fairly circumscribed existence outside the main stream of urban life".[32]

At this point, we are not trying to deny there is a gap. We are only questioning those who make it too large and pin too many evangelistic hopes on the dislocation it might create.

3. Another generalization is frequently linked to that of culture shock. The urban population is said to suffer from alienation and depersonalization, loneliness and loss of identity.[33] These needs, for the evangelical, are calls for the gospel. "Urban migrants," writes one such observer,

> become culturally displaced persons. Coming mostly from close-knit, face-to-face societies, the impersonal atmosphere of the big city produces a terrible loneliness. There is a breakdown of the social ties that formerly gave life its meaning, for families break up and friendships that have endured for generations are severed.[34]

Do urban migrants really break that severely their ties to their roots? One commentator observes that in the Middle East there is

> the tendency for individuals of the same family, sect, language, and dialect to live in the same geographical area, not only in the villages and small towns, but also in the large cities.[35]

There is a clinging to their rural locality roots by most urban Arabs. It is the place of origin and their family status there that give them a sense of identity and worth in the more anonymous society of the cities. Writes Costello, "There is little sign of the anonymity and alienation which were supposed" by earlier theories.[36]

Migration patterns themselves may also ease the transition. Movement to the city is not always and simply a move from the village to the large city. Chain or step migration may occur, the villager moving to a larger town, then a larger still, and finally the city. In the mid-1970s, for example, about 60% of the migrants to Teheran came from other urban places. And most had visited the big city before moving.[37] Costello affirms this as a general pattern throughout the Middle East. He indicates a number of migrants to the largest cities of the Middle East come from the smaller, traditional towns, hence the relatively high rates of growth in large cities and the slower growth of the small and medium-sized towns.[38]

To summarize, not everyone experiences entrance into the city as a shocking plunge; it is often more gradual, like getting your feet wet first.

In common with world patterns of migration, kin-based migration to the city is also common. The migrant tends to go to cities where he or she will find kin to cushion the effect of the transition and help locate work. Among kin will be found those comforting cultural similarities to ease the shift.[39] And, sometimes, as in Lebanon among the "old" families, kinsfolk will be richer and more influential. And the roles of poorer migrant and richer kin will be seen as that of a patron-client relationship.[40] So, in Teheran, over half the migrants in the mid-1970s had relatives in the city to which they went. And nearly 40% moved with their families.[41]

Given these patterns, it is difficult to speak of family disintegration, urban loneliness and loss of identity caused by the city or migration into the city. There are problems and felt needs in the city to which the gospel can and should respond. Family disintegration, depersonalization, *anomie* may be some of them. We are only saying now that they are not uniquely urban problems.

4. Frequently evangelical literature cites secularization as a uniquely urban problem and, often as not, an open door for the gospel. Secularization is said to be eating at the heart of the Islamic faith and leaving an empty room which Christianity can now occupy.

One cannot deny the impact of secularization on the Muslim city as on all the cities of the world. As Costello says,

> changes in religious habits frequently accompany a move to the city. A man may cease to pray five times a day as he is enjoined, perhaps praying only twice because of the constraints imposed on his time in the city.[42]

Even, however, as we acknowledge the reality of secularization in the Muslim cities, a number of qualifications are necessary. No commonly agreed on definitions of secularization, for example, exist in the evangelical community on the basis of which we may make careful judgments. We still possess only largely sermonic ones. We still therefore do not understand fully how the process of secularization works and what is its relationship to the evangelization of a Muslim people group.[43] And so we make too many generalizations.

"If urban Muslims are more free to change religious faith, they are also more free to forsake religious commitment of any kind."

For example, is secularization not a two-edged sword, cutting away not only at Islam but at any faith commitment, including Christianity? One personal correspondent, well acquainted with the Middle East, noted in a letter to me,"If urban Muslims are more free to change religious faith, they are also more free to forsake religious commitment of any kind."

Recent studies, for example, were done of the Arab-American community in North America. The research compared assimilation and adaptation by Arab Christians and Arab Muslims in this highly secularized continent. Syrian churches had been founded some 20 years before the existence of any mosque in the United States. But

> The number of the Arab churches today is not increasing in spite of the rapid increase in the number of the Arab Christians in America. It is estimated that no more than fifty Arab churches remain in America. On the other hand, the number of mosques has been increasing.[44]

Who is being more rapidly secularized than whom?

Shifts in marriage and family patterns occur more often than shifts in religious commitment.

As a matter of fact, a considerable body of scholarship exists showing that migration patterns from the Muslim world to North America have not deeply affected stability and commitment to the traditional faith.[45] In fact, as in the Middle East, Islam has acted as a basis for the unity of these migrant communities. Shifts in marriage and family patterns show clear signs of acculturation. But religious adjustments to a basic commitment are few.[46] The meager number of converts from Islam in North America is a testimony, not only to the neglect of them by the Christian church, but also to their resiliency of faith.

The picture would seem to be similar in the Peoples Republic of China and the USSR. In these two areas, where city and country are radically secularized, and where Muslims function as a beleaguered minority under severe pressure to conform,

> the experience of Muslim minorities...suggests that it may be useful to rethink older assumptions about Muslim minorities. The simple fact is that these large Muslim minority communities have survived. They have, even more, done more than survived. They appear to have grown and have not simply been withering away.[47]

Part of the difficulty in overestimating secularization among Muslims may be our tendency to define Islam solely in terms of its institutionalized aspects. Since those institutions are strongly urban in character, when we see them disused we assume a turning from Islam in the city; we see a process of secularization at work. We hear that only between one and five percent of immigrant Muslims attend mosque in North America.[48] And this sounds to us like a renunciation of Islam.

We must not forget the close identification of Islam as a religion with Islam as a culture. A Jew may be an atheist, never go to synagogue and have no commitment to Judaism as a religious system, and yet still consider his or her identity as Jewish, however secularized that person may be. So too, "a person who is only half Islamized still feels himself a Muslim and sociologically is firmly attached to a religion which he follows badly."[49]

Will the secularization process now affecting Islam, as it affects also Christianity, make the Muslim "more open" to the gospel? It may be too optimistic to use words like "more open." Can the situation also be described by saying they are "less closed"? After all, judgments as to the "winnableness" of a people to the gospel are made not solely on the basis of how close they have come to Christ, but how far away they have moved. And secularization, in its basic thrust, is a movement away.[50]

Strategy Suggestions and Urban Advantages

Even discounting all the false leads and faulty generalizations about the Muslim city and cities in general, there are functions and a style to the city that may offer us strategy advantages for evangelism. And, if "advantages" is too strong a word, we can call them urban "suggestions."

1. Where is the best place that offers the most potential (humanly speaking) for bringing Muslims to Christ? As one of my correspondents wisely commented, "I don't think it's a question of place so much as it is a question of their situation." Where will we go to find people in transition? Where are old patterns breaking up? Where will we find a greater degree of freedom for serious decision making? Where will we find an atmosphere more open to change?

Cities offer those possibilities in abundance. They are centers of change, and not only for themselves. They are the vehicles through which change is introduced into all Middle Eastern cultures.[51] There is a real degree of freedom in the city by comparison with the village or country. Close-knit social ties in the village or country, built out of kin relationships, tend to discourage change, experimentation; traditional patterns of behavior and values are more secure in the country.

By contrast, in the city the ties, though still there, are more loose. And there is a world of new ideas to bombard us through television or the university. Our move to the city has underlined our need to get into a learning mode—learning new trades, new skills, maybe a new language.

This does not always work to the advantage of the gospel. People far from their native community in an alien environment, notes one missionary observer, can become more tenaciously committed to traditional morals and belief systems than was true in the community from which they came. It is a sociological and psychological phenomenon which has to do with the attempt to preserve oneself, in the face of bewildering pressures, from change. In Nairobi, Kenya, it has been noted, the Somali Muslims living there were far more conservative and faithful in their attendance in the mosque than they had been in the villages of Islamic Somalia.

On the other hand, the experience of the Mennonite Church in Somalia illustrates the positive value of urban freedom. That church was enjoying a people group movement to the gospel among the riverine communities in the south. On occasions, hundreds of people would come together to hear the gospel. Then the government moved in and forced a cessation of all such activities. It was only in the cities that the church became established.

Cities multiply opportunities for reaching unreached people groups.

2. Cities also multiply opportunities for reaching unreached people groups. We have noted already the tendency of migrants from similar geographical areas and ethnic groupings to stick together in the city, occupying the same districts, even finding similar occupations. Every people group in the country will have its representation in the city. And, remembering the greater degree of tolerance to some extent characteristic of the city, they may be more amenable to new perceptions, even gospel perceptions, than they were in the country.

One such group uniquely shaped by the urban setting is designated the Transitionals.[52] They form one of three typological units of Middle Eastern society. People in motion, they lie midway between the Traditionals and the Moderns. The 1950 study that created the typology describes the majority of the Transitionals as born in the villages but now living in urban centers. They tend to be young unmarried males, relatively well-off and the most receptive to innovation. They are found scattered largely through the middle and lower classes, with the highest concentration among merchants and professional educators, students and industrial workers.[53]

Research carried on in 1973 used this typology to categorize converts to Christ in Lebanon, Jordan and Egypt. The study demonstrated that the Transitionals were the most receptive to Christianity. Of the converts surveyed, 75% were Transitionals, 17% Moderns and 8% Traditionals.[54]

Matheny's study, though suggestive rather than descriptive, also reminds us that the designation of "unreached peoples" is not to be limited strictly to ethnic groupings. In the cities, age and work groupings can also be highly significant in forming the core for an "unreached people."

Matheny's Transitionals, for example, are described as young. The young people from ages around 18 to 23, moving from rural to city areas, are said to be responding best to the gospel. One correspondent observed to me, "Bible correspondence schools in different parts of the Muslim world testify to the same thing."

In Turkey, it would appear that younger people especially prefer to pursue a secular path, rather than follow the old men to the mosque for religious discussions.[55] One observer in North Africa notes that alienation is a real problem among the youth: "My experience is...that frustration and dissatisfaction with traditional Muslim forms and restrictions causes a high degree of alienation in many of the younger generation North Africans." Whether frustration will turn to faith we will have to see.

It is interesting to note, in this connection, the effect that the generation gap plays on attitudes to Islam among Muslim migrants to the United States. In a three-generational study of over 400 Muslims in Toledo, Ohio, and Detroit, Michigan, it was found that "the further a generation is from the first, the weaker it is in the traditional religious beliefs."[56]

The research disclosed that

> the three items highest on the belief order of the Toledo third generation are general religious items shared by the prevailing religions in America: Protestantism, Catholicism, and Judaism.[57]

So, 100% of the third generation affirmed that there is a God, with 82% also believing that there is only one God and a lesser 78% confessing there is a Judgment Day. But only 64% could affirm that Muhammad is their Prophet and a smaller 61% that the Quran is God's Book.

And what about women in the city as an unreached people? Does the city open wider the door to reach women as an unreached people? What of the impact of alleged urban freedom on them?

The answer to this may vary more radically from country to country, and from city to city. A correspondent observes that young women in the southern towns of Tunisia never went out. But, further north in Tunis, besides going to school, they were allowed to go to town, to libraries and to shops, though not alone.

Jennings sees no single attitude to women in Middle Eastern cities. In Tripoli, women may go unaccompanied to the cinema in pairs, if lightly veiled. And once inside, they may smoke. In Kuwait City, by contrast, the cinemas are divided completely, half for families and half for single men. "Attitudes are usually more conservative in the provincial towns then in capital cities, and they vary from one urban district to another."[58]

It is while they are in transition that migrants seem most vulnerable and open to new ways.

3. Migration patterns need to be examined for their urban strategy potential. We have underlined the relative lack of polarity in Islam between the city and the country. But that does not mean there are no tensions in the transition. What about that immediate period of time between the migrant's discarding of rural ways and the initial exposure to the city, particularly the large city? If ever there was a time of uncertainty, concern and even fear, it would be then. It is a time of special vulnerability and openness to new ways.

At this point of transition, the fledgling urbanite can be truly uprooted. Surely in these circumstances, before new roots are laid, while plans are still tenuous and prospects are vague, evangelism may be the most fruitful.

Are we safe in saying then that, for this reason, a newer part of the city with expanding migrant population may be more receptive than an older, more settled part of the city? Or that a growing city may usually be more receptive than a static or declining one? Or that a shanty town, springing to life with a growing flood of migrants, has more potential than a settled residential area? Which areas might be wiser ones in which to initiate Bible studies when that is possible? How should this affect decisions by Christians as to where to live to bear testimony to Christ?

Further, given the links between Muslim country and city life, cannot those very links with the hinterland make it possible for the gospel to be communicated eventually to the countryside as well? We mentioned earlier the small Somali Christian fellowship that developed in Nairobi.

That fellowship, writes one correspondent, had considerable influence on the 300,000 Somalis living in northeastern Kenya. A number of believers had relationships in the hinterland. The word passed throughout the region that some of the Somalis in the city had become Christian. People would come from the country to investigate. And, in turn, occasionally visits would take place from Nairobi to the country, also attempting to interpret what was happening. These visits were being con-ducted by the new Christians.

4. Closely related to the growth of the Muslim city is the growth of the urban poor. The "have-nots" enter the grow-

ing cities from the villages and smaller towns, expecting to become the "haves." But the contrasts remain and the shanty towns grow. In the Middle East, it is this lower income group that constitutes the majority in all cities outside Israel.[59] And this pattern is not out of keeping with general world trends.

Since another chapter focuses on that lower income paper group, I shall only mention at this point the significance of these people in our thinking about the city. Surely, if anywhere in the city we will sense alienation, frustration and a lack of satisfaction, it will be among the poor.

Will the Christians of the Middle East, apparently enjoying the social advantages of relative affluence,[60] meet this challenge? I was intrigued to think of the possibilities in this when I read a Muslim study report entitled *Christian Missions in Pakistan*.

The single Christian experiment in evangelism detailed by the 16 page report was that of the Franciscan friars in Karachi. Seven new novices moved into a flat in a densely populated part of the city. The complex contained 140 families, of which only four were Christian. Their major task, the report continues, was to give witness to the Muslim families. Neighbors accepted the novices as simple, honest and God-fearing people.

The Muslim report concludes,

> This Roman Catholic approach to evangelism should be taken seriously and is very radical and bold. It deviates in its new form from the old methods because it penetrates into small urban housing societies and after entrenching itself there it spreads out its network for evangelizing the people. Not much effort is needed to draw the people into it. For it subtly preys on the neighborhood relationships which already exist among the people.[61]

Can a Muslim warning about an urban evangelistic method encourage us to wrestle again with our commitment to the poor and to the simple lifestyle?

Modern cities shape cultural and intellectual networks that reach far beyond their metropolitan borders.

5. Modern cities are preeminently culture shapers. They are the centers of cultural and intellectual networks that reach far beyond their metropolitan borders. The ideas, the value systems, the worldviews they spawn shape village as well as city. And when they are part of a country where all of life is directed by a Muslim ideology, that influence is even deeper.

When they are part of a country where all of life is directed by a Muslim ideology, that influence is even deeper.

What effect might there be for church planting in such settings if we found evangelical Christians whose gifts and cultural interests, in God's providence, could be placed at the center of that Muslim network?

There have been people who have come close to something like this. In 19th century Syria, the Uniate Melkite, Nasif al-Yaziji (1800-1871), has been called that century's "outstanding practitioner of classical Arabic." His friend and colleague, Butrus al-Bustani, through his dictionary, encyclopedia and experiments in periodical literature, was

> to influence much of subsequent Arabic prose and journalism. Before the last quarter of the nineteenth century, even Muslims were obliged to acknowledge the accomplishment and inventiveness of certain Christians in the language of the Koran.[62]

Among these men, and the societies for the renaissance of Arab learning and culture which flowed out of their emphases, were "the first stirrings of Arab Nationalism."[63]

More recently, in the struggles of Algeria for independence, a small group of French priests threw strong support behind the Front de la Liberation Nationale (FLN). Many found themselves honored by the Muslim country to which they had committed themselves.[64]

North African and Middle East Muslims generally see Christians as aloof from their countries' social struggles.

By and large, however, it would appear that in contemporary North Africa and the Middle East the perception of Christians by Muslims is quite different. Christians are seen as non-participants; they are judged as observers, not contributors.

To be sure, in a Muslim state where Christians must function in a uniquely second-class minority slot (the state of *dhimma*), it may be hard to expect more. And politico-cultural participation of a distinctly Christian sort will not be easy even with the freedom to do it.

Yet the major problem in this area may not lie with the Muslim side. Is it rather that for the Christian there is no sense of identity with the Muslim culture?

> A Maronite might well refuse to be called an Arab, identifying this term with Muslim. An Egyptian Jesuit, Samir Khalil, a Copt, has felt the need to plead with his fellow Christians not to deny their Arabness. Both Christians and Muslims have contributed to the growth of

Arabic culture, he argues, and their respective contributions are still needed.[65]

Fr. Samir calls this a "contemporary role," in which the two communities are made to complement each other. I am not sure I like this language. Any Christian contribution to nation building or to cultural "rebuilding in Christ," to be Christian, must do more than merely augment or add to. It must renovate, rejuvenate.

As an "outsider" to things Muslim, I may be far too naive in these matters. I shall appreciate the corrections of my brothers and sisters. At the same time, I recall the impact of a Francis Schaeffer in another non-Christian culture as he challenged that culture at its roots and, at the same time, encouraged fellow Christians to be positive culture builders in the cities of the world. What he called "pre-evangelism" I have no hesitation in calling "evangelism." His appreciation for art, music and philosophy established his cultural credentials to speak as he did. His convictions and his love, even though Christian, demanded a hearing.

Schaeffer's greatest impact came in the 1960s at a time of deepest disillusionment and frustration in Western culture. Will Islam enter soon a similar disillusionment as the urban movement for a "return to pure Islam" does not yield the hoped-for fruit of prosperity and well being? Then may come our greatest opportunity in the ideological and cultural arena. Where will our Schaeffers be to seize that opportunity?

While a substantial percentage of Muslims live in large cities, an even higher percentage of Christians do.

6. All these questions drive us to yet another urban asset—the church. It is estimated that worldwide 46% of all urban dwellers are Christians.[66] How large that figure is in Muslim or predominantly Muslim cities is not known to me. It would appear that in the Middle East their numerical strength is greatest in the urban centers.

In many a city the church is a sleeping giant.

In Egypt, for example, a 1978 study suggests that

> unlike the Muslim population, Egypt's Copts were prone to urban living. In 1960 nearly half (47%) were living in towns and cities with populations exceeding 35,000, as opposed to less than one-third of the Muslims (31%), and the general trend of rural migration to the cities has become even more pronounced among Christians in the last decade.[67]

In Syria, the 1960 census placed 62% of the Christian population in cities, as compared to a Muslim community of only
33% urbanized.[68] By 1957 over half (55%) of the Christian
population of Iraq was concentrated in the country's four
principal cities. And this compared with less than 20% of the
Muslim population. Significant also is the fact that Christians were found in virtually every quarter. Any segregation
that did exist was largely economic.

None of us needs to be reminded that this sleeping giant in the
city will remain asleep until it can be awakened. What can be
done to encourage reformation in the body of Christ? A massive concert of world prayer focusing on these churches? A
commitment to work within them for renewal? It goes without saying, I would assume, that all our strategy proposals
and suggestions "may have little content until and unless the
indigenous Christians of these countries...are drawn into the
discussion."[69]

Repeatedly charges are made that churches existing in Muslim majorities remain self-contained. Linguistic and social
barriers remain high between them and the majority community.

How many are like the small Iranian church and "its own in-
ability to adequately communicate to an influx of Muslim
converts"?[70]

One correspondent, well acquainted with the Middle Eastern
churches, remarks on the need to prepare the Christians in
urban congregations to welcome converts out of Islam "more
heartily and integrate them more fully in fellowship. These
converts, with some exceptions, are rather pathetic figures—
more of a curiosity than brothers in the faith—and not very
welcome in the social life of the congregation."

**Urban Christian
churches must learn
to welcome converts
from Islam more
heartily and
integrate them more
fully into the
fellowship of the
congregation.**

How can such a church, fearful of even the new convert, make
use of friendship evangelism? Studies in Iran point to it as
"one of the most effective methods" of bringing inquirers to
Christ.[71] Think of how its effectiveness might be compounded
in dealing with an urban newcomer, struggling with an
unknown and therefore frightening setting.

Conclusion

**Ultimately,
all God's cities will
come to him.**

As with all suggestions and strategies, we dream the plans
and God devises the realities. "The horse is made ready for
the day of battle, but victory rests with the Lord" (Prov. 21:31).

But one thing we know already about God's final disposition. His plan of salvation for the nations enfolds the cities by his grace. Even the inhabitants of Babylon will be given citizenship papers stating, "This one was born in Zion" (Ps. 87:4,6). The urban empires of Egypt and Assyria will hear the words of the Lord. "Blessed be Egypt my people, Assyria my handiwork, and Israel my inheritance" (Isa. 19:25). Damascus will be restored to its place within the boundaries of the people of God (Eze. 47:16-18).

These words of prophecy are not the careless words of over-done optimism. The New Testament stamps them as sure affirmations of hopes already begun to be fulfilled. Jesus has come to "preach the good news of the gospel to the other cities also" (Lk. 4:43). "A city of Samaria" rejoices in the gospel message of Philip, and the Word of the Lord begins to break out (Ac. 8:5,8). Damascus, a traditional enemy of the Lord's people, welcomes another enemy, Paul (Ac. 9:2), and sends him forth as an apostle to the cities. All God's cities will come.

NOTES

1. Ira N. Lapidus, ed., *Middle Eastern Cities* (Berkeley: University of California Press, 1969), v.

2. Ibid., 47.

3. V. F. Costello, *Urbanization in the Middle East* (Cambridge: Cambridge University Press, 1977), 6-7.

4. A. L. Oppenheim, "Mesopotamia—Land of Many Cities," in *Middle Eastern Cities*, ed. Ira N. Lapidus (Berkeley: University of California Press, 1969), 3-18.

5. X. de Planhol, "The Geographical Setting," in *The Cambridge History of Islam*, eds. P.M. Holt, Ann Lambton and Bernard Lewis (London: Cambridge University Press, 1970), 2:446.

6. Ibid., 446-447.

7. Claude Cahen, "Economy, Society, Institutions," in *The Cambridge History of Islam*, eds. P.M. Holt, Ann Lambton and Bernard Lewis (London: Cambridge University Press, 1970), 2:521.

8. Harvie M. Conn, *A Clarified Vision of Urban Mission* (Grand Rapids, MI: Zondervan Publishing House, 1987), 18-20.

9. Ibid.

10. Gabriel Baer, "Village and City in Egypt and Syria: 1500-1914," in *The Islamic Middle East, 700-1900: Studies in Economic and Social History* ed. A. L. Udovitch (Princeton, NJ: Darwin Press, Inc., 1981), 596.

11. Ibid., 641.

12. Richard V. Weekes, ed., *Muslim Peoples. A World Ethnographic Survey*, rev. ed., vol. I (Westport, CN: Greenwood Press, 1984), xxi.

13. Charles Issawi, *The Arab World's Legacy* (Princeton, NJ: Darwin Press, Inc., 1981), 298.

14. Costello, 33.

15. A. R. Omran, "The Arab World in the Year 2000: A Demographic Nightmare," in *Lebanon Monitor* II (1987): 5.

16. Ibid.

17. Kingsley Davis, *World Urbanization: 1950-1979*, 2 vols. (Berkeley: University of California Press, 1972), 2:200.

18. David B. Barrett, ed., *World Christian Encyclopedia* (New York: Oxford University Press, 1982), 136, 497, 677.

19. David B. Barrett, ed., *World-Class Cities and World Evangelization* (Birmingham, AL: New Hope, 1986), 10-11.

20. John Gulick, "Village and City: Cultural Continuities in Twentieth Century Middle Eastern Cultures," in *Middle Eastern Cities*, ed. Ira N. Lapidus (Berkeley: University of California Press, 1969), 123.

21. A. Ferre', "The Role of Migration in the Expansion of the Muslim Faith," in *Encounter 111* (1985): 2-16.

22. Janet Abu-Lughod, "Migrant Adjustment to City Life: the Egyptian Case," in *Urban Life: Readings in Urban Anthropology*, eds. George Gmelch and Walter Zenner (New York: St. Martin's Press, 1980): 77.

23. Costello, 48.

24. J. John Palen, *The Urban World* (New York: McGraw-Hill Book Company, 1981), 397.

25. Abu-Lughod, 77-89.

26. Douglas Butterworth and John K. Chance, Latin American Urbanization (Cambridge: Cambridge University Press, 1981), 139; and Richard Hostetter, "Voluntary Associations and Urban African Churches," in *Missiology IV* (1976): 427-429.

27. George Jennings, *Welcome into the Middle East!* (LeMars, Iowa: 1986), 52.

28. Ibid., 62.

29. Gulick, 140.

30. David Filbeck, *Social Context and Proclamation* (Pasadena, CA: William Carey Library, 1985), 40.

31. Ray Bakke, "Evangelizing the World-Class Cities," in *Together* (1984) 2:33.

32. Abu-Lughod, 8.

33. Filbeck, 146-147.

34. Edward Murphy, "Guidelines for Urban Church-Planting," in *Crucial Issues in Missions Tomorrow* ed. Donald McGavran (Chicago: Moody Press, 1972), 246.

35. Tim Matheny, *Reaching the Arabs. A Felt Need Approach* (Pasadena, CA: William Carey Library, 1981), 51.

36. Costello, 104.

37. M. Ray Brown, "The Adjustments of Migrants to Tehran, Iran," in *Urban Migrants in Developing Nations*, ed. Calvin Goldscheider (Boulder, CO: Westview Press, 1983), 236.

38. Costello, 47.

39. Brian M. DuToit, "Introduction: Migration and Population Mobility," in *Migration and Urbanization*, eds. Brian M. DuToit and Helen I. Safa (The Hague: Mouton Publishers, 1975), 8.

40. Jennings, 109.

41. Brown, 236.

42. Costello, 105.

43. Conn, 101-105.

44. A. A. Elkholy, "The Arab-Americans: Nationalism and Traditional Preservations," in *The Arab- Americans* (1969), 9-10.

45. Abdul Jalil Al-Tahir, "The Arab Community in the Chicago Area, A Comparative Study of the Christian-Syrians and the Muslim-Palestinians" (Ph.D. diss., University of Chicago, 1952); A. A. Elkholy, "Religion and Assimilation in Two Muslim Communities in America" (Ph.D. diss., Princeton University, 1960); and Atif Amin Wasfi, "Dearborn Arab-Moslem Community: A Study of Acculturation" (Ph.D. diss., Michigan State University, 1964).

46. Wasfi, (see note 45): 128-141.

47. John O. Voll, "Muslim Minority Alternatives: Implications of Muslim Experiences in China and the Soviet Union," in *Journal: Institute of Muslim Minority Affairs*, vol. VI (1985), 2:350.

48. Earle H. Waugh, "Muslim Leadership and the Shaping of the Ummah: Classical Tradition and Religious Tension in the North American Setting," in *The Muslim Community in North America* eds. E. H. Waugh, B. Abu-Laban and R. B. Quireshi (Edmonton, Canada: University of Alberta Press, 1983), 31.

49. Willy N. Heggoy, "Fifty Years of Evangelical Missionary Movement in North Africa, 1881-1931" (Ph.D. diss., Hartford Seminary Foundation, 1960), 64.

50. Conn, 112.

51. Jennings, 81.

52. Matheny, 5.

53. Ibid., 56.

54. Ibid., 6.

55. Trent Rowland and Frank Jameson, "Istanbul: Loosed from its Muslim Moorings," in *World Christian*, V. (1986) 6:24.

56. Elkholy, *Religion and Assimilation*, 176.

57. Ibid., 177.

58. Jennings, 118.

59. Costello, 81.

60. Robert B. Betts, *Christians in the Arab East* (Atlanta: John Knox Press, 1978), 131-136.

61. Abdul Karim Khan, "Christian Missions in Pakistan." *Situation Report* No. 9 (Leicester: The Islamic Foundation, 1981), 13.

62. Robert M. Haddad, *Syrian Christians in Muslim Society* (Princeton: Princeton University Press, 1970), 71.

63. Betts, 162.

64. John K. Cooley, *Baal, Christ and Mohammed: Religion and Revolution in North Africa* (London: John Murray, 1967), 310-319.

65. M. L. Fitzgerald, "Muslims and Christians in the Arab World," in *Encounter* (1985), 113:8.

66. Barrett, World-Class Cities, 15.

67. Betts, 64.

68. Ibid., 100.

69. C. C., "Response," in Seedbed I (1986), 2:26.

70. Don McCurry, ed., *World Christianity*. Middle East (Monrovia, CA: MARC, 1979), 32.

71. Ibid., 35.

CHAPTER FIVE

HOLISTIC MINISTRY AMONG THE POOR

Muhammadou Mensah

The contextualization of holistic ministry to the poor in Islamic countries deserves the attention of the Christian church at large.

When applied by practitioners, principles firmly held by conceptualizers often take on a variety of forms. Contextualization therefore must be emphasized in the midst of a biblical understanding of holistic ministry to the poor.

The vast majority of the world's more than 970 million Muslims live in poor countries. Because of this, the contextualization of holistic ministry to the poor in Islamic countries is not only relevant but deserving of the focused attention of the Christian church at large.

Government leaders in many poor Islamic countries are supervisors of Christian groups attempting to "help the poor." Such attempts are frequently seen as hidden agendas for converting Muslims into Christians. "Regardless of the truth or falsity of such a charge," Parshall suggests, "the main consideration is how orthodox Muslims perceive Christian social activities."[1]

Yet at the same time, there is also a growing openness in certain Islamic countries to allow Christian groups to become involved in development work. The opportunities present new challenges for Christians who want to share the gospel message in the midst of suspicious and even hostile Islamic communities.

All dehumanizing influences are antithetical to the liberating good new of the gospel.

Says Parshall:

All dehumanizing influences are antithetical to the liberating good news of the gospel of Jesus Christ. The Christian must involve himself in structures that allow a ray of hope to pierce the deep gloom of hurt and despair that often engulfs the Muslim peasant.[2]

The purpose of these pages is to foster dialogue concerning issues of working holistically with the poor in Islamic societies. Consider two short case examples which describe a Christian development agency attempting to apply some holistic development principles among the poor in two separate Islamic settings. The case studies are real although the names have been changed. Following each case example, a brief overview of some biblical foundations of holistic ministry is described. A suggested framework for applying holistic ministry and a starting list of principles is also included, plus a list of questions which can be used in discussion to enhance our common understanding of working with the poor in Muslim communities.

Case Example: Busafi

The population of the small country of Busafi is 6.5 million, of which 95% are Muslims. The Busafi people suffer from extreme poverty brought on partly by years of severe drought and partly through the effects of European colonial rule. Because Busafi's natural resources are few, some observers have become pessimistic about the opportunities for future economic growth. Nevertheless, international development agencies have been invited to focus their attention not only on the massive relief situation, but also on efforts to enhance long-term economic development.

One Christian development agency chose a particular simple strategy for assisting the people of Busafi. The agency's desire was to apply a holistic development strategy as much as possible in the midst of a very traditional Muslim society. The strategy focused first on providing sources of water for rural villages. The drilling of deep wells became the point of entry into the lives of the poor rural villages. From this point of entry, the ministry focus expanded to a child-centered and later a family-centered program emphasizing health, sanitation, nutrition and short-term crops. The program further broadened to encompass long-term issues including tree planting and general village agriculture.

Encouraged by an international development team, Islamic community leaders helped describe what a better future for their community would look like.

Throughout the process of broadening the scope of activities, special attention was given to allowing Islamic community leaders to help describe what a better future would look like. The image of a better future became the hope and encouragement of the Busafi people. The international development team, comprised of technicians and managers from four continents, has played a catalytic role in encouraging local discussion about the better future.

Outsiders were viewed with both suspicion and curiosity.

In most rural villages throughout the world, outsiders would be viewed with both suspicion and curiosity. This was especially true in Busafi where strong Islamic traditions dominate normal community life. The development team discovered, after some frustrating encounters, that holistic development in Busafi must be limited to existing Islamic beliefs about the nature of God. Thus, a better future can be seen as Allah's intentions in Busafi society. Persistent biblical reflection on linking the Christian world view with the Busafi world view became the challenge of the team leader and development project staff.

The well drilling crews, trained to strive for professional excellence and maximum efficiency, sank 40 wells in six months with an outstanding success rate of striking water in 35 of them. The team has reached such proficiency that wells can now be completed in less than one week at a cost of under $10,000. The Prime Minister marveled at how this could be done when the norm had been $120,000 per well in one month's time each. He has visited some project sites himself and has sent cabinet ministers and department heads to witness this wonder and study its secrets.

The Provincial Governor has also been curious about something else he observes. Once he invited the team for a midnight dinner, at which he said,

"Even though you are a multi-racial, multi-national group," marveled the provincial governor, "you live in harmony. How can such a thing be?"

Friends, you are a multi-racial, multi-national group. Around this table we resemble the United Nations. And yet you start each day with worship and joyful singing and then go out to live in harmony. How can such a thing be?

Perhaps the most puzzling question of all, which is asked by many, is why the team has left the capital city and located the agency office in a small provincial town where they, their wives and children suffer heat and dust during the day, cold at night, and the fatiguing sight of constant suffering. "Just to be with you," is all the team members have to say, but their presence has won them such credibility that they receive overwhelming outpouring of welcome wherever they go.

The team's choosing to live among the needy has won them credibility and welcome.

The project director both personifies the message of the project and tries to articulate it. Although not speaking Arabic or tribal dialects, he is able to communicate in French. Highly person-oriented, he easily relates to people of all levels. Being non-white and from a colonized country himself, the project director has an advantage in gaining identification with the people.

He has won admiration, not only for western management skills and organization, but also as a man of piety and dedication to God. When asked what is the secret of success in striking water, he answers "prayer and fasting," and goes on to invite the people to join him and his team in petitioning the Lord to send the water and abundant blessing on the land.

The project staff consistently identify themselves—whether in public gatherings, with mullahs, or with the elite and officials—with one simple message which speaks to the questions people frequently ask. This is an example of the message they share:

"We are Christians sent by God...to serve you. That's why Muslims and Christians can serve together."

We are Christians sent by God who is the God of love and of hope. He is the creator who never forgets or leaves you. He is compassionate toward your every cry for help. God makes people love one another. That is why he sent us to serve you. That is why Muslims and Christians can work together in harmony to restore well-being to the people and bring renewal to the land.

Although Jesus Christ is not mentioned in the "cooperative agriculture" document, the attitude and desires of Jesus are reflected.

Special project events are used as occasions to express deeper meanings which underlie needs in the project. A significant event is the signing of the agreement of cooperation between the agency and the village. The agreement, written upon parchment in Arabic, French and the tribal dialect, makes fundamental propositions about a Christian view of life contextualized in a Busafi community.

For example, special reference is made to Allah's desire that all people should enjoy abundant life including adequate water, housing, health, livelihood and so forth. The document also states that Allah is concerned about the daily needs and desires of his people, the common people of Busafi. It speaks of God's love and attentiveness to people's prayers. Although the name of Jesus Christ is not mentioned in the document, the attitude and desires of Jesus are reflected.

The sign of the cross on the public markers has led to discussion of Christian issues.

After much discussion with the people under the trees of the public square, the covenant is signed in a solemn ceremony by the elders and the project director. At this point a public marker is unveiled which indicates that the people of (the village is named) and (the agency is named) covenant to work together in making this place to become more and more like God wants it to be.

The sign of the cross is displayed prominently on a marker in the center of the village. The presence of the sign of the cross has raised issues. Conversations have become occasions for the men in the village to talk with the director and staff members about what Muslims and Christians believe. Jesus, as Messiah, is of *great interest*. Especially controversial issues are his divinity and whether he actually died on the cross. Other topics include the Books of God, the prophets, worship, salvation and the *shari'a* of Islam, as compared to the Christian law of love.

Much interest focuses on Jesus as Messiah. Points of controversy include his divinity and whether he actually died on the cross.

The need to understand this strange new world of thought has driven the team to further study and reflection upon their experience during weekly scheduled reflection/sharing sessions. Each session starts with prayer and Bible study. Following this, time is given to discussion of a basic study paper which gives guidelines for holistic ministry. The paper is an in-process biblical study which the agency views as its own philosophical understanding of ministry and its particular calling.

Certain key study books that have been assigned for reading are also discussed. One text, *Islam and Christianity* (1980), has been an especially valuable guide to non-polemical conversation with Muslims on issues about which there could be a breakdown of relationships. The book is a written dialogue between Badru Kateregga and David Shenk, formerly university faculty colleagues in Africa, one a Muslim, the other a Christian. Their conversations give very readable, factual knowledge about major issues debated between Muslims and Christians. Moreover, an attitude is conveyed. In these exchanges both sides listen deeply and sympathize with the perspectives of the other. Yet both sincerely believe in the truth of their faith and do not hesitate to witness to it as effectively and persuasively as they possibly can.

Every week, team members share with each other highlights of their experience.

Finally each team member shares with the group highlights of experiences encountered during the past week. Such sharing may concern problems and issues of a technical nature or tough questions raised in conversation with Muslims, or it may include something of a personal nature. The purpose of the exercise is to try to distill and write down principles learned from experience which can help one live a more deeply disciplined life during the week ahead.

All try to contextualize visions of a better future, as desired by Allah, into practical measures.

Thus, while the well drilling was used as an entry point into the Busafi community, the effects of the total development process are much broader. Attempts are continually being made to contextualize the visions of a better future, as desired by Allah, into practical measures in daily life. The key to the process is not only in the relative success of the contextualization but, more importantly, in the ability of the Christian project staff to remain tolerant, flexible and yet consistent in building relationships.

A principle stressed by the team director: the Christians' mission must be accomplished through genuine fellowship with God and with one another.

The director says that the main principle they have discovered so far is that their mission has to be accomplished through genuine fellowship with God and with one another, for in fellowship, the life and love flowing in and through the Godhead flows through them. As a result, they have something to share with the Busafi Muslims among whom God has sent them.

Case Example: Komanu

Komanu's Christians (less than 1 percent) are mostly converts from animist or Hindu background. Their worship and beliefs bear little resemblance to the dominant Muslim culture.

The nation of Komanu, with more than 80 million inhabitants, is one of the poorest countries in the world. Approximately 87% of its population are Muslims, with 12% Hindu and less than 1% Christians. The Christians of Komanu, most of them converts from animist or Hindu background, have been strongly influenced by Western Christianity. The form of worship and resulting belief systems bear little resemblance to the dominant Muslim culture.

Because of political and religious sensitivities, the Komanu Christian church has largely avoided expansion into Muslim areas. In recent years, however, a small group of believers have begun to focus on evangelism in predominantly Muslim communities. The results of these efforts are being viewed with fear and suspicion by the traditional Christian church at large.

The central government of Komanu has been fairly open to Christian missionaries and Christian development organizations to operate in the country. However, warning is given to all Christian groups concerning proselytizing or "conversion of Muslims into the Christian religion."

Aware of these complexities, one Christian development agency is attempting to explore new approaches for ministry among the Muslims. Having operated in the country for approximately 12 years, the agency has focused on working with the mainline denominations in providing child and family assistance. However, most of these efforts have been in non-Muslim areas or communities.

The new strategy: place selected Christian couples in Muslim communities.

In an attempt to apply holistic ministry in Muslim communities, a new strategy was initiated. The strategy essentially encouraged the selection, training, placement and follow-up of groups of Christian couples (husband and wife) in predominantly Muslim communities. Some of the key characteristics of the strategy:

- Committed Christian couples are selected and paid a small salary by the agency.

- The couples are trained by the agency and assigned to some village for a designated period of time.

- The couples are responsible for finding suitable housing in the village. In most cases the village leaders were encouraged to help provide this.

- The couples' major activities are to focus on organizing the community and motivating the villagers. This includes organizing savings groups, cooperatives, development committees, women's clubs and vocational training groups.

The Christian couples' witness here must be primarily through example. But they are prepared to answer questions when asked.

- A small amount of money is made available for "seed projects," such as purchasing tools, seeds and other supplies.

- Christian witness is focused through the lifestyle of the individual couples. In other words, the focus is on modeling and exemplifying a Christian witness while also being prepared to talk about Christianity when asked.

One couples agreed to stay in a barn when no better lodging was offered. Their humility gained them greater acceptance and trust.

As one might imagine, a multitude of problems have been encountered by the approximately 20 Christian couples sent into the Muslim villages. Many of the couples reported having serious problems gaining acceptance even to work or reside in their villages.

For example, in one village the only place offered as accommodations was with the animals in a barn. After a number of days the couple agreed to stay with the animals. As a result of this servant-like humility, the Muslim owner of the house invited the couple to stay with them in his own home. Such action over a period of time helped the Christians to gain the acceptance and trust of the community people.

In another village, two couples gained acceptance because of their focus on assisting the widows and divorced women. Because of the generosity and friendliness given to these outcasts, the village people began joining in the co-op activities.

Since none of the Christian couples were originally from a Muslim background, the program began with an intense period of training. Follow-up training events were then scheduled every few months. A focus of the training was to help the couples contextualize their Christianity in a way that may not be totally foreign to the Muslim community residents. Worship and the observance of special religious ceremonies began to take on a distinctly different look from those of the traditional Christian churches.

For mutual strengthening, the couples meet as often as possible, at least once a week with one or two other couples and once a month with the larger group. The time is used primarily for sharing, reflection and Bible study.

The couples describe their primary goal as one of living the Christian life by example, with Matthew 25 as their guide—caring for the hungry, the stranger, the naked and the prisoner as expressions of Christ. They are quick to suggest that following the example of Jesus is difficult, but nevertheless, they strive to be humble and sympathetic.

In spite of risk, some Muslims have requested baptism. In at least one village a result of open baptism has been rejection of the couples and the development of a near-riot situation.

In months just prior to this writing, the couples faced dilemmas, including questions about responding to a growing number of Muslims desiring to become baptized. Recognizing the political and religious implications this will have throughout the country, the agency has attempted to discourage such activity. However, some of the couples have gone ahead and openly baptized villagers. A result in at least one village was rejection of the couples and the development of a near-riot situation.

By using unconventional means for worship and the expression of their Christian faith, they have come under attack from both Muslim and Christian circles. In addition, some Christian development workers have criticized them for focusing too much on a new form of worship to the exclusion of the needs of the poor.

To this charge, the couples' response is that in order to experience long-lasting results with the poor, relationships must be built first. In order to build these relationships, the couples are focusing on a contextualized form of Christianity that, in their minds, will help to break down traditional barriers between Muslims and Christians.

Although the couples have lived in the villages of Komanu for more than two years, the signs of economic development are difficult to see. Attitude change, however, has become apparent in some villages. Recognizing the problem of even communicating with Muslims in most of the villages, the couples have spent much of their time in building relationships. As attitudes become more open, it is hoped, deeper values will also be changed, resulting in different lifestyles and behavior.

The Need For Understanding World View

Although the two cases described above differ in approach and geographic setting, they do emphasize the need for understanding the Islamic world view which may differ from location to location. As an understanding occurs, a new appreciation can be made of the biblical foundations upon which holistic ministry is built. Parshall compared elements of Muslim world views, which he also equated with the Old Testament Hebrew tradition, to those of Western Christians.[3] The accompanying chart lists eleven concepts with a short description of Hebrew/Muslim and Western Christian views.

The Need for Understanding Holistic Ministry

Muslims may see wholeness as part of Allah's intention for humanity, and yet feel that Christians doing holistic ministry are trying to use physical, medical and social inducements to convert them.

As we begin to better understand the Muslim world view, it becomes increasingly apparent that to the Muslim, there is a natural unity in all of life. Wholeness or completeness is part of Allah's intention for humanity. However, at the same time, many criticisms are made by Muslims who feel that Christians try to use physical, medical and social inducements to convince Muslims to become Christians.

Several of the following pages suggest some of the biblical foundations for holistic ministry. Attempts must continue to be made to bridge the gap of misunderstanding between Muslim and Christian concerning holistic approaches to serving the poor.

The designation "holistic ministry" seems to have become popularized to correct a theological imbalance of both Liberalism and Evangelicalism since the middle of the 19th century.

The former under-emphasized ministry to human spiritual need (especially humankind's lost condition), while the latter under-emphasized the need for ministry to the physical and social side of human life.

Comparison of World Views

Concept	O.T. Hebrew and Muslim	Western Christian
1. **Unity**	Emphasis on unity in all of life	Emphasis on unity only if it has pragmatic value
2. **Time**	High respect for the the past and tradition	Orientation toward the future
3. **Family**	Solidarity	Emphasis on individual
4. **Peace**	Harmony, integration Total way of life Internal and external characteristic	Contentment A segment of life Internal characteristic
5. **Honor**	All-important consideration	High priority
6. **Status**	A matter associated with family name, age	A result of wealth, accomplishment
7. **Individualism**	Subordination to emphasis on group	High regard for independence
8. **Secularism**	A totally unacceptable trend	A largely acceptable trend
9. **Change**	An undesirable phenomenon	A highly desirable phenomenon
10. **Equality**	A theoretical ideal which is not practiced	A theoretical ideal which is not practiced
11. **Efficiency**	A matter of little or no concern	An imperative

Holistic ministry is attempting a genuine, balanced approach to the redemption and growth of persons, whole persons. The approach focuses on what God—who is both Creator and Redeemer—has revealed as his intentions for human life. Like Jesus, who "grew in wisdom and stature and in favor with God and men," holistic ministry strives for an integration between the growth of persons spiritually, physically, mentally and socially, founded upon a response to the good news of the Kingdom of God.

Tracing   Biblical   Themes :
'Covenant of Peace' and 'The Kingdom of God'

The kingdom of God is also the reign of right relationships.

The biblical basis for holistic ministry can be examined by reflection upon two interlocking concepts: "the Kingdom of God" and the "Covenant of Peace." The Kingdom is God's sovereign rule in nature and in history. The Covenant of Peace is not mere absence of conflict; it is the condition of well-being, peace and harmony wherever God reigns. It characterizes the state of appropriate relationships under God's kingship. Therefore, in simple terms, the Kingdom of God is also "the reign of right relationships."

Some Biblical Teachings about Wholeness in God's Kingdom

There will be wholeness in the Messianic Kingdom. The biblical revelation of this Kingdom provides guidelines as to God's intentions for the believers' personal and community life. It provides goals as well as standards of ministry. Consider the following major tenets of God's revelation:

In Eden—Where Harmony Reigned

The setting in which God placed humankind was a garden full of beauty and freshness. Here our first parents were intended to dwell in perfect harmony with God, with self, with others and with creation. God's reign was complete and all was peaceful.

The Fall—Where Covenant and Wholeness was Shattered

God's peace in Eden did not last long. By a tragic choice, Adam and Eve and the rest of humanity became separated from God. Harmony with God was shattered. A flaming sword kept the rebels away from the tree of life (Gen. 3:24). Harmony with self was replaced with fear and shame (Gen. 3:10). Harmony with others, for which we were created, was now broken (Gen. 3:12). Harmony with nature and within nature, was disrupted, for "creation was subjected to futility" and "bondage to decay" (Rom. 8:20, 21).

In Abraham—Pronouncement of a Destiny

The treasures of God's shalom were to be broken open and lavished upon Abraham and his descendants. Yet all of God's investment in Abraham had to be turned over into Abraham's investment in others—never selfishly hoarded. The wonderful destiny of the chosen people was that they were to model in the earth the highest values of God's Kingdom: Loving God with all their hearts and loving their neighbors as themselves. The Covenant initiated by God between himself and Abraham would surely succeed in recreation of the whole world because of the prophetic word in the Covenant at Ur: "All people on earth will be blessed through you" (Gen. 12:3).

In Laws Providing for Cleansing and Forgiveness from Sin

During the long period of wandering, God continued to desire right relationships in his creation. God made provision for people to be redeemed from sin and rebellion against him. The tent in the midst of the camp was a beautiful, restful tabernacle where God dwelt, a special place where he would meet with his people. In order for them to be fit to stand in God's presence, they had to be cleansed of their sins. The laws instructing them in God's provision for their forgiveness climaxed in the day of atonement when a solemn offering was made for all the people and the blood was put on a goat which was then taken out into the desert (Lev.16).In the weekly Sabbaths (Ex. 20:24), and in the various feasts (Lev. 27), Israel was to meet with God, rejoice and celebrate God's bounty and his kind purposes for their lives.

In Laws Preventing Social and Economic Injustice
God also gave laws to insure that all people would receive justice. Justice due to the poor was not to be perverted. False charges were forbidden, and bribery was not to be practiced. Foreigners were not to be oppressed. Every 50th year the land would return to the original family, emphasizing that God is the real owner of the land and preventing huge land accumulations. All debts were canceled (Lev. 25:10-24). Lending laws protected the poor from unjust loans (Deut. 24:10-13). Just wages for workers were mandated (Deut. 24:14-15). Tithes were given to provide for the landless, the aliens, the orphans and the widows (Deut. 14:22-29). In addition, the Sabbath year provided for rest for the land while providing food for the poor (Ex. 23:10-11).

In Long Exile

However, the people failed to obey. They perverted justice, oppressed the poor and even prostituted themselves before foreign gods and goddesses. Instead of sharing God's blessings they became selfish hoarders. Isaiah called the people to "cease to do evil, learn to do good, seek justice, correct oppression, defend the fatherless, and plead for the widows" (Isa. 1:17). But despite the repeated warnings of the prophets, the people continued on their evil paths. God's anger was ignited. The land suffered because of their wickedness. Finally, the Lord delivered them to their enemies and sent them into long, lonely exile.

But God still did not give up on His creation. Even in exile the covenant of peace was not forgotten. Through the prophet Jeremiah, God spoke:

> I will fulfill to you my promise and bring you back...For I know the plans I have for you, plans for peace and not for evil, to give you a future and a hope (Jer. 29:10-11).

In Jesus Bringing the Long-Awaited New Creation, the Kingdom

Jesus began his ministry announcing that "the Kingdom of God is near." Later he said, "It has already come upon you." Kirk suggests that Jesus showed by his actions that God's Kingdom was at work through him:

> Jesus reversed every aspect of life which was hostile to God's new world: disease; demon-possessed; guilt; a ritualistic empty religion; a cast system of purity and impurity; the shortage of food (he fed the hungry crowds); hostile nature (he calmed a storm); economic exploitation (he drove the money-changers from the temple); even death. The Kingdom marks the end of all that disfigures creation or destroys what God created "very good."[4]

Jesus brought the long awaited liberty of God's creation. In this creation, people are wholly reconciled to God, to one another and to nature; fear, aggression, selfishness, falsehood and suffering are banished.

In the Reconciliation of the Cross

Adam's sin destroyed the covenant of peace between humankind and God, between people and people, as well as peace within nature. There can be no peace with God until sin's reward is given. The first move to restore broken relationships was made by God himself. God's holy wrath was diverted from us to Christ who suffered in our place in order that we might be reconciled to God.

As Christ's disciples and as citizens of the new order yet to come, we attempt to live out our lives in light of the future. The work of peace becomes an integral part of our existence. In this respect, Nicholas Wolterstorff asks,

Shalom is both God's cause in the world and our human calling.

Can the conclusion be avoided that not only is shalom (peace) God's cause in the world, but that all who believe in Jesus will, along with him, engage in the works of shalom? Shalom is both God's cause in the world and our human calling. Even though the full incursion of shalom into history will be a divine gift and not human achievement, even though its episodic incursion into our lives now also has a dimension of divine gift, nonetheless it is shalom that we are to work and struggle for. We are not to stand around, hands folded, waiting for shalom to arrive. We are workers in God's cause, his peace-workers. The "missio Dei" is our mission.[5]

Suggested Framework for Examining Holistic Ministry

In light of the need for understanding the Muslim world view and understanding holistic ministry, the following is a suggested framework for examining holistic ministry. The categories include: 1) development by the people, 2) Christ-like groups of believers, 3) family life, 4) food, 5) shelter, 6) health, 7) learning opportunities and 8) economic viability.

These categories can be used to assess the general situation as well as the impact of a particular development process within a community. In each category are a series of standards. Some are listed as generic; others would need to be contextualized within a particular Muslim setting. Emerging from these questions or standards would be a list of possible indicators of values to be used to show evidence of holistic development. Such values might include awareness of God's presence, hope for the future, increasing self worth, care for the weak and attitudes toward women.

I. Development by People

1. All members of the community have opportunity to participate actively in the development process according to ability.
2. All members of the community share fairly in the benefits of development.
3. The community provides adequate support for those who are vulnerable and unable to care for themselves.

II. Christ-like Groups of Believers

1. The community is able to recognize Christ's portrait in its midst, through a growing body of believers who:

a) confess Christ's Lordship,
b) increasingly demonstrate Christ's character in their actions, values and attitudes,
c) commit themselves to God's ongoing purpose,
d) call the whole community to be reconciled with God, with one another and with the environment.

III. Family Life

1. The family life and the relationships in the community are consistent with biblical views, specifically:

   a) stable families based on love, faithfulness, responsibility, care and the ideal of monogamy;
   b) parental responsibility for nurture, discipline and spiritual welfare of children;
   c) respect for and care of the aged;
   d) wider community responsibility in caring for members of bereaved or broken families;
   e) respect for women.

IV. Food

1. All families in the community can obtain sufficient food for adequate nutrition and regular diet.

V. Shelter

1. All community members have adequate access to shelter or protection from outside dangers and the weather.

VI. Health

1. All members of the community have reasonable access to sufficient and safe water.
2. The community has awareness and understanding of principles and practices related to nutrition, mother and child welfare, family planning, and preventive and promotional health care.
3. The community has reasonable access to adequate health care facilities.
4. The community is motivated to utilize the available resources for promoting good health.

VII. Learning Opportunities

1. All community members have access to formal and non-formal education in cultural context that will help release their God-given potential and prepare them to

function adequately and with dignity as contributing members of society.

VIII. Economic Viability

1. The community generates sufficient resources to provide for the basic needs of all families.
2. The community resources are shared in a way that insures no member is deprived of the basic needs.
3. The development of responsible behavior toward the environment will be integrated in all economic activities.

Realization of the indicators above illustrates a community's change of values: from a sense of helplessness to optimism and participation in a change process; from carelessness about family responsibilities to caring and stability; from primitive views of health to a better understanding of appropriate health practices; from inadequate education and skills training to the development of their potential so they may contribute more to society and possess self-dignity; from disrespect for the environment to responsible behavior.

Permeating everything is a desire for justice for all so that no one is deprived of basic resources or rights or opportunities to grow.

"...to encourage a community of people...to move toward recognizing the presence of Allah's covenant of peace, the presence of God's kingdom."

A large concern is to encourage a community of people, within their particular context, to move toward recognizing the presence of Allah's covenant of peace, the presence of God's Kingdom. It involves trying to enter into the people's world view and influence their life orientation and thus their behavior. In this process, the Holy Spirit is active as a "go-between" in relationships, helping people to be sensitive to the need for change.[6]

The Holy Spirit is... a "go-between" in relationships, helping people to be sensitive to the need for change.

Although the values of the entire community cannot be affected at once, usually the influence of a few committed leaders spreads and keeps the community atmosphere more and more open. One author has suggested that we aim at a series of "mini transformations" in the lives of people if we want to see communities changed.[7] A small percentage will be closed to change; more will be neutral or have a wait-and-see attitude. Only a small group or "core group" of community members are typically the instrument used by God to keep the momentum moving.

The realization of the Kingdom of God comes in such areas as sharing, compassion, reconciliation, trust, forgiveness, justice

LINCOLN CHRISTIAN COLLEGE AND SEMINARY

for others, equality, honesty, listening, sympathizing, cooperation and peace making. The assumption is that all good values have their source in Jesus Christ. For this reason, holistic ministry is just as concerned, or more so, to address values as it is to improve material benefits. And this process may start with true values that are already among the people, affirming them, and building upon them. Though the non-believer may never have heard of the "Kingdom of God," yet, as John Bright concludes:

> ...for the Kingdom he yearns. Even thousands who have never in their lives darkened a church door grope blindly after it unwittingly. For the hope of it is engraved in the very necessity of man's nature and he can no more escape it than he can escape himself.

Holistic ministry, then, involves cooperating with the Spirit.

Holistic ministry, then, involves cooperating with the Spirit to assist individuals and groups of people in moving toward the return of the covenant of peace—and the full realization and enjoyment of the Kingdom of God with all of its inherent values. This movement towards the Kingdom is part of our conversion process. Its evidence is continued openness and value change so that we become more and more the kind of people God wants us to be, the kind of community God wants us to experience.

Principles for Action

Holistic ministry in Islamic settings needs, of course, to be contextualized. The application of development activities follows from an appropriate understanding of the Muslim world view, the biblical foundations for holistic ministry and the freedom of God's wisdom to work through his people. As we learn more about particular applications of holistic ministry in Muslim settings, it is helpful to have a list of guiding principles. The following is a list of some general statements. Specific statements related to Islamic settings need to be elaborated.

- Right relationships in the entire realm of creation is a function of a right relationship with God.

- The intentions of God are summed up in the concept of wholeness or God's covenant of peace.

- Holistic ministry assumes a process of mending or restoring poor relationships.

- Holistic ministry assumes there is a new meaning and purpose (destiny) for a better future.

- All manifestations of God's covenant of peace are essential personality traits of the one Isaiah calls Prince of Peace.

- God's desire is to remove any barriers hindering right relationships, through a process of conviction, forgiveness and cleansing.

- God's desire is for people to live in right relationships with a sense of justice. God's view places high emphasis on justice in social relationships as well as on individual redemption from sin.

- Because people have a tendency to fall out of harmony, God warns his people of judgment and holds out promises of reconciliation when they return.

- God has provided a model for peace by incarnating himself in Jesus. He also calls for us to follow the model.

- The messianic age (Kingdom) has already come and is here, but at the same time is not yet fully consummated.

- The eschatological vision (the restored creation) stimulates and guides Christian social action and evangelism.

- The vision of God's Kingdom allows for the transformation of minds, attitudes and belief systems in individuals and communities.

- Holistic ministry requires the contextualization of the gospel of Jesus Christ to different cultural groups.

- Contextualization of holistic ministry can only occur as we understand and enter into the particular world view of individuals.

Conclusion

Although the case studies are related to the work of large, well-funded agencies, the biblical foundations with their implications for today and the general principles stated apply to any holistic Christian ministry among Muslims no matter how limited the financial, material and human resources might be.

NOTES

1. Phil Parshall, *New Paths in Muslim Evangelism: Evangelical Approaches to Contextualization* (Grand Rapids, MI: Baker Book House, 1980), 183.

2. Ibid.

3. Ibid., 66.

4. Andrew Kirk, "The Kingdom of God," in *The Lion Handbook of Christian Belief* (New York: Lion Publishing, 1982), 318.

5. Nicholas Wolterstorff, *Until Justice and Peace Embrace* (Grand Rapids, MI: Eerdmans, 1983), 72.

6. John V. Taylor, *The Go-Between God: The Holy Spirit and Christian Mission* (New York: Oxford University Press, 1972).

7. S. Kindervatter, *Non-formal Education as an Empowering Process* (Center for International Education, Amherst, MA: University of Mass., 1979).

SCRIPTURAL PERSPECTIVES

*"And beginning with Moses
and all the prophets,
he interpreted to them
in all the scriptures
the things concerning himself"*
— Luke 24: 27

CHAPTER SIX

RETHINKING THE GOSPEL FOR MUSLIMS

Colin Chapman

Part of their resistance to the gospel is our fault.

Having thought and prayed about what we are doing in engaging with the House of Islam, we now go on to consider what is involved in the communication of the gospel. Wherever there is resistance to the gospel, it is easy to find reasons *on their side* for such rejection. But what if some of the responsibility is *on our side*? If the Christian Church has contributed to the misunderstanding and rejection, we need to recognize that we have an obligation to look again more carefully at the way we articulate the message.

This challenge that faces us is described in the Report of the 1981 Pattaya Consultation, *Christian Witness to Muslims*:

> As soon as we begin to listen to Muslims and try to share the gospel, we begin to realize how difficult it is to express ourselves in a way that Muslims understand. The painfulness of this experience ought to drive us back to the Bible, in order to learn new ways of understanding our faith and relating it to the Muslim mind.[1]

After giving several examples of areas in which we need to rethink and restate our faith it goes on to say:

Believers who come from an Islamic background need the freedom to think through these issues. The Holy Spirit can and will lead them in their search for effective ways of communicating to the Muslim mind.

> If the gospel was first given to us in an Eastern context, it ought to be possible for us to get behind the Graeco-Roman patterns of thought through which we have interpreted it, and express it once again in ways that make more sense to the Eastern mind. We also need to encourage believers who have come out of an Islamic background to have the freedom to think through these issues; and trust that the Holy Spirit can and will lead them in their search for effective ways of communicating to the Muslim mind.[2]

If we can see how this rethinking and restating works out in a completely different context, we may be in a better position to appreciate what is involved in the Islamic world. One of the best and most moving examples in recent years is Vincent Donovan's account of his work among the Masai in Tanzania. In his book *Rediscovering Christianity*, he describes how he, as a Catholic missionary, abandons the mission station approach and goes out to live with the tribes people where they are, to listen to them and understand their world view. This leads him to find radically new ways of sharing the good news about Jesus. On the last page of the book he gives what he calls "An African Creed":

> We believe in the one High God, who out of love created the beautiful world and everything good in it. He created man and wanted man to be happy in the world. God loves the world and every nation and tribe on the earth. We have known this High God in the darkness, and now we know him in the light. God promised in the book of his word, the Bible, that he would save the world and all the nations and tribes.
>
> We believe that God made good his promise by sending his son, Jesus Christ, a man in the flesh, a Jew by tribe, born poor in a little village, who left his home and was always on safari doing good, curing people by the power of God, teaching about God and man, showing that the meaning of religion is love. He was rejected by his people, tortured and nailed hands and feet to a cross, and died. He lay buried in the grave, but the hyenas did not touch him, and on the third day, he rose from the grave. He ascended to the skies. He is the Lord.
>
> We believe that all our sins are forgiven through him. All who have faith in him must be sorry for their sins, be baptized in the Holy Spirit of God, live the rules of love and share the bread together in love, to announce the good news to others until Jesus comes again. We are waiting for him. He is alive. He lives. This we believe. Amen.[3]

Despite wide differences between Muslims around the world, enough is distinctive about the Muslim mind-set so that we can find more intelligible and relevant ways of expressing the Gospel.

It is all so beautifully African, and gives us the feeling that the gospel has truly taken root in African soil! If this, then, can be a model of what the contextualization of the gospel is all about, can we not find similar models which are appropriate for Islamic contexts? Although there are considerable differences of language and culture between Muslims of different countries, enough is distinctive about the Muslim mind-set throughout the world for us to hope that, if we persevere, we may find ways of expressing the good news that are more in telligible and more relevant to Muslims than the traditional ways we have inherited.

Like Paul dialoguing with Areopagites, we can dialogue with Muslims about God and his prophets, God and his Word, God and his mercy.

We look first, therefore, at the way Paul faces the challenge of a new and different kind of audience at the Areopagus in Athens. Then, after seeing some of the basic principles of his approach, we try to apply the same approach in exploring three themes which arise out of our dialogue with Islam: God and his prophets, God and his Word, and God and his mercy.

Paul at the Areopagus

No doubt we have all studied Acts 17 in the context of various disciplines of theological study. In studying doctrine, for example, we have asked: What does the passage teach about the difference between general and special revelation? What does it say about eschatology and the fate of those who have never heard the gospel? And in the context of philosophy, the question often is: What is the rationale for Paul's apologetic here, and to what extent does he succeed?

But what happens if we leave such familiar territory, and look at Paul's address in the context of our thinking about Islam? The question then becomes: In what ways can Paul's approach to this particular audience be a model for our proclamation to Muslims today? In order to do this we need to explain briefly what Paul seems to be doing at each stage of the argument and then suggest, with the help of examples, how this approach can work in the context of our relations with Muslims.

Meeting Face to Face

All that happens in Athens grows out of Paul's meeting with people on the streets, and the distress he feels over religion that has gone sadly wrong: "...he was greatly distressed [exasperated, NEB] to see that the city was full of idols. So he reasoned in the synagogue...as well as in the market place with those who happened to be there" (vss. 16-17). The address at the Areopagus was not written in a study!

Too often, sophisticated organization and technology seem to prevent personal contact with the people we are supposed to reach.

It seems such an obvious point that it hardly needs to be made. But in an age of missionary societies, conferences, reports, computers and statistics, it sometimes feels as if everything conspires together to prevent the missionaries from having any personal contact with the people they say they want to reach.

As I sit teaching in the ivory tower of a theological college, I realize that I cannot go on forever telling stories beginning,

"When I was in Cairo..." or "When I was in Beirut..." A thriving Muslim community sprawls near my doorstep in the inner city areas of Bristol. And some of the most significant events during my course on Islam are the visits we make to the mosque in the center of the city.

On the last visit, only a few days ago, our host invited us to visit him in his home to watch a video "which proves mathematically that the Quran must be the Word of God." I have been waiting two years for an opportunity of this kind, and look forward to taking up the invitation!

For some of my friends, however, living in a totally Muslim community is a very different matter. This came home to me with special force this summer when a Lebanese Christian friend wrote to me, describing the distress he experienced in his contact with Muslims during Ramadan in another country in the Middle East:

> The month of Ramadan has just finished. Particularly on this occasion I am having first class contact with Islam and its practices. The legalism, the Judaism, salvation by works and hypocrisy is just killing. Being invited to so many dinners I eat so much during this month, but also suffer so much spiritually. I find myself completely helpless being evangelized rather than evangelizing. It is a faith so much rooted in the hearts of people. Anything else contradicting their Book is false because God has actually and verbally spoken. What is contrary should have been manipulated. Whoever believes that evangelism, mission and good Christian life will bring about conversion and change in this part of the world is dreaming. 1500 years testify to this...

If the problem for the writer is that he is so close to Muslims and so much on his own, the problem for many of us is that we are nowhere near to this kind of "eyeball to eyeball" encounter.

Understanding Their World View

We can take it for granted that Paul has had enough first-hand contact with the religions of the Mediterranean world to understand what he sees in Athens. He observes the folk religion that is being practised all around him; but at the same time he knows what the poets have said (v. 28), and is not taken by surprise when faced by the philosophers (vss. 18-21).

One might similarly assume that Christian missionaries among Muslims would have the same kind of understanding of Muslims, their culture, their world view and their religion. Unfortunately, however, this has not always been the case. D. B. MacDonald, the founder of the Islamic Center at Hartford Seminary, spent almost a year in Cairo in 1907-1908, studying Islam and meeting Christian missionaries. In a letter written later to Constance Padwick about his time in Egypt, he made this sad comment about the missionaries he had met:

"(The missionaries) did not understand the Muslims because they were not properly trained for the work...."

> I was profoundly conscious that they [the missionaries] did not understand the Muslims because they were not properly trained for the work—were in fact, as far as Islam was concerned, horribly ignorant...The result for me was that I made up my mind if ever I could do anything to train missionaries to Muslims to know Islam, I would put my back into it.[4]

"....were in fact, as far as Islam was concerned, horribly ignorant."
—D. B. MacDonald, founder of the Islamic Center at Hartford Seminary, c. 1909.

Temple Gairdner was one such missionary who wanted to learn from MacDonald, and in 1911 spent six months of a sabbatical studying under him in the USA. It seems, however, that it took some time for Gairdner to appreciate what his teacher was trying to do. Several years later MacDonald recalled in a letter how Gairdner once expressed his acute frustration and disappointment to him: "I came here thinking that I would get from you knock-down arguments to use with Muslims, and you are teaching me only to understand them!" The record of Gairdner's later ministry suggests that MacDonald's method was entirely appropriate!

With all the renewed interest in Islam in recent years, one hopes that the same cannot be said about today's missionaries. I venture to suggest, however, that we still have some way to go, not only in understanding the world view of Islam but also in allowing this understanding to shape the way we articulate our faith to Muslims. My example to illustrate this point is one which I put forward with some trepidation, since it comes from the journal called *Seedbed*, which is concerned with these very same issues. The following is entitled "The Prophethood of Christ" and begins as follows:

> Christians have generally neglected the Biblical doctrine of the prophethood of Christ. Some traditions do assert Christ's fulfillment of the three Old Testament themes of Prophet, Priest and King. However, while his priestly and kingly roles have been treated extensively, relatively little attention seems to have been given to his prophetic role, leaving us theologically ill-equipped to deal with Muslim teaching on prophets. Faced with Muhammad's claim to

prophethood, Christians have tended to overlook the relevance of biblical teaching on the prophethood of Christ and have stressed instead his Deity. This article attempts to redress the balance...[5]

After helpful sections "The New Testament Evidence," "The Character and Qualifications of a True Prophet," "The Prophet like Moses" and "Is Christ the Final Prophet?", the article concludes:

Christ is a prophet! He fulfilled the role of prophet, and His prophetic work will only be consummated at His second Coming. Fundamentally, Christ as prophet must be interpreted in terms of the Mosaic model of covenant mediator. The root problem with Muslims is that they do not really believe in the God of Moses. Hence the sense of God's holiness and man's sinfulness is lacking, and the radical solution of Scripture is replaced by a legalistic code. As a consequence, the general revelation man has of his sinfulness is suppressed and avoided. [This article has not examined the Muslim doctrine of prophets directly, but is written as a stimulus, to help us to rethink prophethood in Biblical terms. If Muslims at least understand the Biblical view of prophethood, they will be a step closer to acknowledging Christ as Savior—and Lord.][6]

What seems to happen in the article is that, faced with the Muslim challenge concerning the prophethood of Muhammad, the writer responds by simply restating a traditional Christian understanding of prophethood. He certainly gets to the heart of the matter when he points out that the difference between Muslim and Christian ideas of prophethood can be traced back to fundamentally different diagnoses of the human condition. But if he had first tried to examine more fully "the Muslim doctrine of prophets," he might have had to come back to the Scriptures with a different set of questions. And his restatement of a Christian understanding of prophethood would then be more closely related to the Muslim mind.

To communicate effectively with the Muslim mind, a Christian theologian must know Muslim thought about prophethood.

If, therefore, our rethinking about prophethood is done in isolation, without careful study of the Muslim mind, the danger is that what we offer the Muslim may be little more than a reworking of traditional Christian theology;. And if this theology was worked out by theologians who knew little or nothing about Islam and never had to face any challenge from that direction, it is not likely to communicate very effectively with the Muslim mind, however loudly it is proclaimed.

Entering into Debate

It is not long before Paul finds himself being drawn into discussion and debate. The philosophers "...began to dispute with him...'What is this babbler trying to say?'" Perhaps it sounds as if he is talking about a new god and his consort (Jesus and "Resurrection," *anastasis*). And so the challenge goes out: "May we know what this new teaching is that you are presenting? You are bringing some strange ideas to our ears, and we want to know what they mean" (vss. 18-19).

Some Muslims simply have no interest in open dialogue with anyone who has a non-Islamic viewpoint.

In some situations our problem with Muslims is that they are not interested in open discussion. They are happy to present Islam as the Final Religion and answer our questions. But our very Western idea of dialogue does not make much sense to them.

Thus, for example, at the end of a very helpful time of questions during our recent visit to the mosque, I asked a final question: "We appreciate your hospitality and would like to return it in some way. Would you and any of your community be interested in visiting a church or coming to our college to hear how we understand our faith?" The answer was polite but clear: "There are too few of us looking after our own community, and we do not really have the time to meet with people of other faiths. Also, it might be confusing for any Muslims who are not sure of their faith. But for those of us who are sure about our faith, there is nothing we can learn from Christians, because it is all there in the Quran. We have got it all in Islam." With this kind of mentality it is not so easy to win a hearing!

In some situations, on the other hand, it is *our* prejudices which make it impossible to have any discussion. A Ugandan Christian tells me that for him, Muslims are people to keep away from, not to get close to. And a leading lay person in England is known to have expressed the wish in private that his government would turn all the mosques in Britain into public conveniences. If this is how any of us feel in our heart of hearts about Islam, it is not surprising if we simply reinforce the fears and prejudices which have been built up in European Christians over the centuries, and never have the opportunity to enter into a genuine discussion with Muslims.

Thankfully, however, there are many situations where Christians find they can enter into the same kind of discussion as Paul did. Here, for example, is a letter from an American who spent some time in England in preparation for working in a Muslim country overseas:

An interesting thing happened last Tuesday evening—I was invited to a Qur'an study in…There were six women and five men at the meeting, mainly from South Asia but a few from Jamaica, all now living in England. It was most rewarding for me to have gone. The Muslims were studying the Qur'an like I used to study with other college students during my IVCF days. They were asking questions about the text, seeking to interpret it.

We studied Sura 55 (The Beneficent), which deals in the latter verses with heaven or Paradise. It was interesting to hear how they dealt with the verses about the physical delights of Paradise. I felt some of their explanations were quite understandable. I have often heard Christians criticize Islam because of these verses.

After the study they proceeded to ask me questions about the Bible for two hours or so. I tried to be honest with them during the meeting and to explain that I had a real desire to learn something about Islam, not to debate about different religions. I avoided the questions about the deity of Christ, and the crucifixion because I felt trying to answer in a few sentences would not be helpful to the Muslims. I told them to read the Injil for themselves and then we will talk about the message it speaks.

The meeting opened my eyes to the great value of talking openly and honestly and personally with Muslims. More was accomplished in that meeting than in my entire time passing out tracts in London.

At the end of the meeting I again stressed my desire to know more about Islam and to better understand what it was like to be a Muslim in the so-called Christian West. They then apologized to me for not allowing me to think about the questions before I came. They then encouraged me to ask them questions. At the end of the meeting the leader told me I was talking about Islam except for my understanding of Jesus. One of the women then asked me how I deal with sin in my life as a Christian, because she has struggled with sin herself. They invited me back every Wednesday and said if there was a topic I would like discussed, to let them know.

I made no apology to them for being a follower of Messiah Jesus, but through listening and seeking to understand them, I feel I have gained their respect and the beginnings of a friendship...I am excited about what God has done.

Perhaps he need not have been so pessimistic about the value of his tract distribution. But it is clear that this Christian's experience marked a genuine breakthrough for him in his relations with Muslims.

Establishing Common Ground

Is it just that Paul starts where his listeners are in order to find a way in? This view does not sound very convincing in someone who is so concerned about integrity (2 Cor. 1:12; 2:17). It makes more sense to think that Paul genuinely believes that the Athenians already have some ideas about God. Although he is fully aware of all the excesses of idolatry (v. 16), he is still prepared to use the word for "God" which they use: "...I even found an altar with this inscription: TO AN UNKNOWN GOD (*agnosto theo*). Now what you worship as something unknown I am going to proclaim to you. The God (*ho theos*) who made the world..." (vv. 23-24).

In an article entitled "Paul in Athens: Pseudo-philosophy or Proclamation? A Missiological Study of Acts 17:16-34," Myrtle Langley recognizes that there can be different ways of explaining Paul's approach:

> Did he mean, "The God whom I proclaim is in fact the one whom you already worship without knowing it," or "What therefore you worship as unknown, this I proclaim to you," or "What you worship but do not know—this is what I now proclaim"? The Greek can sustain all. I think the Jerusalem Bible translation makes more sense in the context.
> Whichever, Paul is declaring the existence of one God, and all worship, however misguided and distorted, insofar as it is directed to deity, is worship of the Creator, whose existence biblical religion does not attempt either to argue for or to prove, but rather assumes. A case can be made out for placing the main emphasis of Paul's remarks on ignorance, rather than idolatry.[7]

Muslims can agree with almost everything in Paul's address to the Areopagites. The significant thing to notice, however, when we look at the address in an Islamic context is that there is nothing in the whole address with which a Muslim would disagree, except perhaps the reference to people as God's "offspring" in verse 28, and certainly the reference to the resurrection of Jesus in verse 31. At every point there are extraordinarily close parallels between Paul's words and the teaching of the Quran. Some of these can be seen by putting verses from the Quran alongside sentences and phrases in Paul's address:

> "The God who made the world and everything in it is the Lord of heaven and earth and does not live in temples made by hands..." (17:24).

> Knowest thou not that it is Allah unto Whom belongeth the sovereignty of the heavens and earth; and ye have not, beside Allah, any friend or helper? (Q 2:107).

"He gives life and breath and everything else..."(17:25).

> Look, therefore, at the prints of Allah's mercy [in creation]: how He quickeneth the earth after her death. Lo! He verily is the Quickener of the Dead, and He is able to do all things (Q 30:50).

"From one man he made every nation of men ..." (17:26).

> O mankind! Be careful of your duty to your Lord Who created you from a single soul and from it created its mate and from them twain hath spread abroad a multitude of men and women

"...so that men would seek after him and reach out for him and find him" (17:27).

> Allah it is who raised up the heavens without visible supports, then mounted the Throne, and compelled the sun and the moon to be of service, each runneth unto an appointed term; He ordereth the course; He detaileth the revelations, that haply ye may be certain of the meeting with your Lord (Q 13:2).

> So give to the kinsman his due, and to the needy, and to the wayfarer. That is best for those who seek Allah's countenance. And such are they who are successful (Q 30:38).

"...though he is not far from each one of us" (17:27).

> We verily created a man and We know what his soul whispereth to him, and We are nearer to him than his jugular vein (Q 50:16).

"...we should not think that the divine being is like gold or silver..." (17:29).

> Lo! Allah pardoneth not that partners should be ascribed unto him. He pardoneth all save that to whom He will.

Whoso ascribeth partners unto Allah hath wandered far astray (Q 4:116).

"...in the past God overlooked such ignorance" (17:30).

Is it a judgment of the time of (pagan) ignorance that they are seeking? (Q 5:50).

Bedizen not yourselves with the bedizenment of the Time of Ignorance. Be regular in prayer, and pay the poor-due, and obey Allah and His messenger. Allah's wish is but to remove uncleanness far from you, O Folk of the household, and cleanse you with a thorough cleansing (Q 33:33).

"...but now commands all men to repent for he has set a day when he will judge the world..." (17:30).

Lo! that wherewith ye are threatened is indeed true, And lo! the judgment will indeed befall (Q 51:5-6).

They ask thee of the Hour: when will it come to port? Why (ask they)? What hast thou to tell thereof? Unto thy Lord belongeth (knowledge of) the term thereof. Thou are but a warner unto him who feareth it (Q 79:42-45).

Muhammad must have heard of these ideas either from the Jews or from Christians, or through the general religion of Arabia.

If we go on to attempt to explain all these common elements, the most obvious suggestion (which of course is totally unacceptable to Muslims) is that Muhammad must have heard of these ideas either from Jews or from Christians, or else that these ideas had already been absorbed into the general religion of Arabia. Tor Andrae is even more specific in suggesting that at an early stage Muhammad must have heard a missionary sermon. He begins by asking how we can account for the fact that while Muhammad clearly had some contact with Christians and knew something about their faith, his knowledge of Christian beliefs and practices remained so incomplete and sketchy. "This riddle," he suggests, "can be solved only in one way":

At some time Mohammed must have heard a Christian missionary sermon. As I have tried to prove in an earlier work on the origin of Islam, one often notices in Mohammed's revelations a fixed rhetorical scheme with approximately the following outline: (1) A description of the blessings of God as revealed in His providence, especially in the wonderful creation of man, and the life-giving rain which brings about productive growth for the nourishment of man. (2) The duty of man, therefore, to serve God alone in faith and good works. (3) The judgment and retribution which shall come upon all who do not fulfil this duty.

Ever since,the days of the Christian apostles this has been the prevailing style of Christian missionary preaching. We know that none of the Oriental churches carried on so active a missionary programme as did the Nestorians, who established important Christian churches in Central Asia, India, and China. It is not overbold to assume that Nestorian monks from the Arabian churches in Mesopotamia, or from Nejran in Yemen after the Persians had conquered this country in 597, in the course of their preaching tours among their pagan countrymen, visited Hejaz, with whose capital city the Christian Arabs maintained a lively contact. As a matter of fact, tradition tells of a Christian preacher named Quss ibn Sa'ida, who is said to have been Bishop of Nejran, but who belonged to a tribe living at Hira in Mesopotamia, whom Mohammed is supposed to have heard preaching in the market at Ukaz.

The word falls by the wayside and upon stony ground. But when it finds a receptive spirit its power is often greater than we are able to comprehend. The message which Mohammed heard concerning the one God, His goodness, and His judgment, took root in his soul. Many years passed; the outward conditions and the associations in which the message reached him faded from his memory; but the word lived.

Unrealized by him, [the word's] innermost meaning, the creative energy of its ideas, became Mohammed's personal spiritual possession. It was intensified by what he heard from time to time concerning the Christian hermits and itinerant preachers, who also occasionally passed through Hejaz. And it is part of the mystery of the inspiration of the Prophet and of the poet, that the power which these ideas wielded over his soul was never fully clear to him until, like a revelation from above, they emerged in a new form of unsurmised and incomprehensible clarity and consistency. No more than other inspired men could Mohammed recognize his own reminiscences and ideas in this new form.[8]

Even if this is no more than speculation, the important point for us at this stage is that we need to recognize the considerable amount of common ground between Christianity and

Islam. We probably have far more in common with Muslims than Paul had with his audience in Athens!

Challenging their World View

Verses 24-28 appear to be a very straightforward statement of Christian beliefs about creation. Myrtle Langley suggests, however, that it is not quite as simple a statement as it seems, and that Paul's approach at this point is influenced by the distinctive beliefs of the two main groups of philosophers who are in his audience.

The Epicureans advocate a "philosophy of materialism and despair," which amounts to a kind of practical atheism. The Stoics teach pantheism and materialism, combined with a strong moralism. At several points in the address, therefore, Paul sides with the Epicureans against the Stoics, and at others with the Stoics against the Epicureans. It looks as if Paul is deliberately trying to divide his audience, as he does with the Sanhedrin in Acts 23:6.

To establish some common ground with his listeners of two different philosophies, Paul was willing to recognize any expression of truth, wherever it was found.

What Paul is trying to do is to establish *some* common ground with *both* these schools of philosophy, and he is prepared to quote from Greek poets (Epimenides—6th century; Aratus—4th century; and perhaps also Cleanthes—3rd century) in order to strengthen his case. It is not until verse 29 that he reaches a climax in his argument and openly challenges idolatry as something totally inconsistent with the idea of God as Creator. And in order to do so, he is willing to recognize *any* expression of truth, wherever it is found. In the words of Myrtle Langley, "Paul has need to enlist the help of Greek philosophy if he is to clinch his argument...All wisdom, biblical and Hellenistic, is welcome if it can be shown how ridiculous it is to maintain that the creator of living men can be contained in dead matter."[9]

But what would it mean to challenge the world view of Islam in the same way? At the very least, the example of Paul ought to convince us that there is still a place for apologetics in our dialogue with Muslims. There has been such a strong emphasis in recent years on cultural issues and contextualization in Muslim evangelism, that we have sometimes been given the impression that "if only we can get 'the cultural thing' right, we will be able to turn back the tide." I doubt that Paul the apologist would agree!

This should not be seen, however, as an excuse for returning to the polemics in which so many Christians have engaged in the past. Nor should it mean that we go on reprinting for worldwide circulation in the 1990's Pfander's great work which was produced in India in 1835. For many of us today his *Balance of Truth* sounds uncomfortably culture-bound. It is somewhat rationalistic in its argument, and the way in which Pfander decides what are the criteria for deciding whether the Quran or the Bible is the Word of God looks a little too much like the football player who not only decides where the game is to be played, but also moves the goal posts to suit himself.

Are there, therefore, other ways of challenging the Islamic world view today which do not mean fighting the old battles all over again? The following three examples show how Temple Gairdner and Kenneth Cragg attempt to press home their challenge. The first deals with the question of whether or not God can be known; the second is concerned with our diagnosis of what is wrong with humans; and the third has to do with the question of power in religion.

(1) The God of Orthodox Islam becomes an 'Unknown God.'

Temple Gairdner spent much of his time during his sabbatical under D. B. MacDonald working on a translation of one of Al-Ghazali's treatises, *Mishkat al-Anwar*. In his introduction to the text he puts Al-Ghazali's mysticism in context, and points out where his mysticism led him, or in some cases where it *would* have led him if he had been more consistent:

> In Ghazali the most extreme Agnosticism and the most extreme Gnosticism meet...What saved God for him from his obliterating agnosticism was the experience of the mystic leap, his own personal *mi'rai* ...The man who had thought his way out of both atheism and pantheism... would have been left at the end of the quest, by his thinking alone, with an Unknown and Unknowable Absolute.

> God's unity and perfection are only preserved by relieving Allah of all describable part or lot in this function, and ceasing to predicate anything whatever of Him or attribute anything whatever to Him. So agnostic is the thought-basis of his Gnosticism. The divine unity becomes not so much the Light of Lights as Hegel's "night wherein all cows are black."

> Every Sufi—every merger of the All in the One—who goes as far as Ghazali evidently had gone in his mystic experiments, must be perpetually trembling on the edge of the pantheistic abyss. He does not pretend to know

intellectually. His experimental gnosis is an intellectual agnosis, and an agnosis which must seem to him continually oscillating between an extreme pantheism and an extreme deism.[10]

Although we must recognize that Al-Ghazali is not fully representative of Islam at this point, Michael Nazir-Ali sums up the attitude of Orthodox Islam very fairly when he writes:

> Islam not only believes in the hiddenness of God, but, more seriously, in the impossibility of ever knowing Him. The most that can be said is that believers know His will which He has revealed to them.[11]

(2) Islam's diagnosis of the human condition is too optimistic.

In the following extracts from the account of the *Chambèsy Consultation*, Kenneth Cragg challenges the traditional Islamic understanding of man's sinfulness, as already expressed by Al-Faruqi, and points out how this ultimately affects the Muslim's response to the Christian understanding of salvation:

> Going back to your exegesis of the verse in *Surat al-Ahzab*, we take the point that there is a kind of natural Islam of nature—that is, *islam* with a small "i," as it were—and there is a volitional Islam, on the part of man. But in the conclusion of that verse, after man has accepted the trust, the Qur'an says: "Indeed he is a wrongdoer and rebellious" —which is what the Psalms describe when they speak of the "froward," i.e., both ill-advised and obstinate. It is this area that I am so deeply concerned about in your paper because, if I may put it this way, there is a certain naiveté about principles of reason, and about your alternative of the world being either full of fools or of people who are prepared to be persuaded.
>
> Is there not a third possibility that there is a kind of quality of...perverseness?—for which law, exhortation, argument, do not suffice. Indeed they may provoke the very disobedience they condemn. Could it not be that it is this perversity of man which is implied in that particular verse of the Qur'an? There seems to be a real emphasis upon man as being in trust and at the same time distorting the trust he was given; the trust, if you like, is simply the context of the distortion.
>
> Your paper, in its very real concern which we all share for a right and true humanism, neglects this dimension which,

perhaps in some emphases exaggeratedly, nevertheless essentially has been at the core of the Christian tradition about man, and the sense of the divine responsibility which Christians understand in terms of that saving intervention which you say is psychotropic folly...or whatever.[12]

(3) The Islamic attitude to power is based on the example of Muhammad, which was totally different from that of Jesus.

In his book *Muhammad and the Christian*, Cragg attempts to answer the Muslim complaint that Christians not only refuse to recognize Muhammad as a prophet, but also shrink from any Christian evaluation of the man and his message. In one chapter he focuses on the question of power, and points out the glaring contrast between Jesus and Muhammad at this point:

> Could it be that Islam stands among religions as the most forthright witness to the reality of power as a "friend" that cannot be dismissed, but that the Christian must never forsake the contrasted witness of Gethsemane and the New Testament that it [power] is an "enemy" who must always be distrusted?

> ...if the friend/enemy of power has to be conceded, it will always need most urgently the disqualifying disavowal, the *al ikraha* ("let there be no compulsion") of the Qur'an (2.256), the "put up thy sword" of Gethsemane. To the Christian mind, nurtured by Jesus and the Gospels, it will always be a burden and a tragedy that force has been so uncomplicatedly enshrined in the very canons of Islam via the pattern of the *Sirah*. For that sufficient reason, any appreciation of Muhammad *in situ* must resolutely retain the contrasted meaning of the love that suffers as the Christ. Christianity in history has so far and so readily besmirched its own originating nature as to make that resolve paramount in all its external relationships, lest its own temptations should be mistaken by others for its—or their—proper terms.

> So, in their origins in Jesus and Muhammad an abiding, and irreducible, disparity persists. It must be allowed to stand without compromise and without concealment.

Realism, which is Muhammad's own plea, "may perhaps invite both Islam and Christianity .to a closer perception of the due limits of the political order vis-a-vis the things of faith."

For the rest, the realism which is the Prophet of Islam's most obvious plea, as we have generously seen, may perhaps invite the two faiths to a closer perception of the due limits of the political order *vis-a-vis* the things of faith. At best the state can only achieve a modicum of justice, holding the ring for spiritual forces which it cannot itself embody or absorb into its order. Such possible achievement will always be dogged, and perhaps destroyed, by the perennial temptations, the compulsiveness, besetting statehood in the actual world. To be sanguine here is to be deceived. To be an easy "realist" is to be unrealistic.[13]

If Cragg's critics feel that he goes too far in his attempt to understand Islam from within, they cannot fail to notice the sharpness of the challenge which he addresses to Islam at this point.

Interpreting what God has done in Jesus

Paul's approach to the Athenians may provide a valuable corrective to an unbalanced kind of thinking.

Paul's address is thoroughly *God*-centered: God has created; God wants people to seek him and find him; God will judge; and God has appointed a man by whom he will judge. The address is suddenly brought to an end when Paul speaks about the resurrection; but even this is expressed in the context of what *God* is doing; he is going to judge his world *through Jesus*, and he has put the matter beyond all doubt by *raising him from the dead*. The man Jesus therefore plays a crucial role in the outworking of God's plans for the world. It is through knowing Jesus that we know more clearly what God is like and what is the standard by which we shall be judged.

Paul's approach here may provide a valuable corrective to an unbalanced kind of "Jesus-centered" thinking common among evangelical Christians. An article about Islam and the uniqueness of Christ in a popular Christian magazine for teenagers made the following statements:

> In Islamic faith there is no place for a personal, compassionate God. Heaven is the place you go to if you have done more good deeds than bad. Christianity is about a relationship with a person—Jesus, the Son of God—who in a loving and caring relationship chooses to involve himself with people even to allow his death on the cross.

The devout Muslims I know would have good reason to protest against this caricature of their faith. But in addition to this, the writer's emphasis on our relationship with *Jesus* sounds different from the language of the New Testament: "Now this is eternal life; that they may know you, the only true God, and Jesus Christ, whom you have sent" (Jn. 17:3). "Through him [Jesus] we both have access to the Father by one Spirit" (Eph. 2:18). "And our fellowship is with the Father and with his Son, Jesus Christ" (1 Jn. 1:3).

If we accept the need to be more God-centered in our statement of the gospel, one way of explaining our faith to Muslims is to start from one or more of these simple propositions:

God creates.
God is one.
God rules.
God reveals.
God loves.
God judges.
God forgives.

Both Christians and Muslims can assent to these seven basic statements without hesitation. The question about each statement, then, is not whether but how.

Both Christians and Muslims can assent to these statements without any hesitation. But as Kenneth Cragg would say, "The question is not *whether*, but *how*." The issue between us is not *whether* God forgives, but *how* he forgives; not *whether* he reveals, but *what* he reveals and *how*. Let us then take each of these propositions and indicate briefly how they can be explored in the context of this kind of dialogue.

(1) God creates.

Islam has such a clear doctrine of creation, that there is no chance of confusing the Creator with his creation. After talking to a Hindu or a Buddhist, we become aware of how much we share with Muslims. If we are looking for areas to explore differences, we may want to find out to what extent the Muslim thinks of humans as being created "in the image of God." But unless we really know what we are doing, perhaps it is better simply to rejoice in the fact that we have so much in common in our doctrine of creation.

(2) God is one.

We can agree with the Muslim that "There is no god but God," because we believe that "The Lord our God, the Lord is one" (Deut. 6:4). We, like Muslims, believe in the oneness of God. But the question at issue is: what kind of oneness are we talking about? Are we talking about a strictly mathematical kind of unity? Or can we think of the more complex unity of the atom, or the unity that creates "one flesh" in marriage?

(3) God rules.

He rules as king in complete control of the world he has made. But how does he exercise his kingly rule? And how, in particular, does he react when people reject his lordship over their lives? The Christian sees God's response coming to a climax in the life of Jesus, whose message is: "The time has come...The kingdom is near. Repent and believe the good news!" (Mk. 1:15). Jesus enters into his glory as the Messianic king only through suffering: "Did not the Christ have to suffer these things and then enter his glory?" (Lk. 24:25). Those who enter the kingdom of God, therefore, are those who live under the authority of Jesus as members of the new community he called into being. Muslims, on the other hand, associate the kingdom of God with the House of Islam, so that entering the kingdom of God means living according to the law revealed through the Prophet.

(4) God reveals.

But what does he reveal? We believe that God has revealed *himself*: "No one has ever seen God, but God the only (Son), who is at the Father's side, has made him known (*exegesato*, has given us an exegesis of God!)" (Jn. 1:18). In his high priestly prayer Jesus prays: "I have revealed you (or your name) to those whom you gave me out of this world" (Jn. 17:6). The Muslim, however, can never make such a claim. Although the Sufis come close to Christian language in speaking about knowing God, the position of Orthodox Islam is fairly summed up in these words of al-Faruqi:

> He [God] does not reveal Himself to anyone in any way. God reveals only His will. Remember one of the prophets asked God to reveal Himself and God told him, "No, it is not possible for Me to reveal Myself to anyone. "...This is God's will and that is all we have, and we have it in perfection in the Qur'an. But Islam does not equate the Qur'an with the nature or essence of God. It is the Word of God, the Commandment of God, the Will of God. But God does not reveal Himself to anyone. Christians talk about the revelation of God Himself—by God of God—but that is the great difference between Christianity and Islam. God is transcendent, and once you talk about self-revelation you have hierophancy and immanence, and then the transcendence of God is compromised. You may not have complete transcendence and self-revelation at the same time.[14]

(5) God loves.

John sums up the meaning of the incarnation with the words: "God so loved *the world...*" (Jn. 3:16). Paul similarly understands it all in terms of love: "God demonstrates his own love for us in this: While we were still sinners, Christ died for us" (Rom. 5:8). Christians have sometimes refused to recognize that the Quran *does* speak about the love of God. But while there are many verses which speak about God loving, the crucial question is: who does he love? We shall see later that the Quran states clearly which kinds of people God loves, and which he does *not* love.

(6) God judges.

We both believe in the Day of Judgment, and look forward either with confidence or with dread to the end of the universe as we know it. But on what basis does God judge? Paul sees that it is the function of the revealed law in Scripture to expose "the exceeding sinfulness of sin" (Rom. 7:13 AV), while those who have not known the law will be judged by the law that is within their hearts (Rom. 2:14-15). Either way, all people stand condemned before God (Rom. 3:19, 23). While the Muslim would see the function of the written law in similar terms, he does not share the Christian conviction that sin is *sinfulness* and is more like a fatal disease than simply weakness or a series of mistakes.

(7) God forgives.

But *who* does he forgive, and *how* does he forgive? In Islam, when people repent, God forgives, as it were, by a word. But if the sacrificial system of the Old Testament taught the Jews anything, it was that forgiveness involves suffering. Divine forgiveness can never be a simple amnesty or a reassuring "*ma'lesh*"—that wonderful word in colloquial Arabic which means everything from "never mind" to "it doesn't matter"! As we shall see in the parable of the two lost sons, the father *himself suffers* as he forgives his son and welcomes him back home.

What then have we been doing? We have started from common ground—from propositions which we can affirm without hesitation along with Muslims. We have then tried to recognize frankly the differences between us in answering questions which arise out of these basic convictions. And instead of trying to dictate the criteria by which we decide whether a particular belief is true or false, we are simply asking: which of these answers makes the most sense of all that we know about the universe and about ourselves? And are we prepared to live with all the consequences of what we believe about God?

God not only invites but commands all people to repent. At the end of the day, however, if we are to let God be God, we as human beings do not have the luxury of deciding what we are going to believe. For if God is God, and if the resurrection of Jesus means what Paul says it means, God not only invites, but *commands* all people to repent and change their minds (Ac. 17:30).

NOTES

1. Report of the 1981 Pattaya Consultation, *Christian Witness to Muslims* (Lausanne Occasional Paper No. 13), 13-16.

2. Ibid.

3. Vincent Donovan, *Rediscovering Christianity* (London: Student Christian Movement, 1982), 200.

4. D. B. MacDonald, quoted by Mike Shelley in "Temple Gairdner" (doctoral diss., University of Birmingham, to be presented 1988).

5. "The Prophethood of Christ" in *Seedbed*.

6. Ibid.

7. Myrtle Langley, "Paul in Athens: Pseudophilosophy or Proclamation? A Missiological Study of Acts 17:16-34," *Bulletin of the Evangelical Fellowship of Missionary Studies* 10 (September 1980): 59-74.

8. Tor Andrae, *Mohammed: The Man and His Faith*, trans. T. Menzel (London: George Allen and Unwin, 1936), 90-92.

9. Langley.

10. Temple Gairdner, trans., "Al-Ghazali's Mishkat al-Anwar and the Ghazali Problem," *Zeitschrift für Geschichte und Kultur des Islamischen Orients*, 1914.

11. Michael Nazir-Ali, "The Christian Doctrine of God in an Islamic Context" (prepared for the Zeist Conference, 1987).

12. Kenneth Cragg, *Christian Mission and Islamic Da'wah: Proceedings of the Chambèsy Dialogue Consultation* (Leicester: The Islamic Foundation, 1982), 45-46.

13. Kenneth Cragg, *Muhammad and the Christian* (London: Darton, Longman and Todd, 1984).

14. al-Faruqi, *Chambèsy Consultation* (see note 12), 47-48.

CHAPTER SEVEN

THE GOD WHO REVEALS

Colin Chapman

In this chapter we shall take Paul's method in his Areopagus address (noted in the previous study), and see how it can be worked out in greater detail with three themes familiar to Muslims: God and his prophets, God and his word, God and his mercy.

God and His Prophets

Let us see how far we can walk along the same road with the Muslim before we come to the fork where our paths diverge.

Here is a theme fundamental to Islam: God responds to human ignorance by sending prophets and messengers /apostles. Our first task, therefore, is to understand how Muslims think about these prophets. In doing so we want to recognize all the common ground we can find between the two faiths, working within that area where the two circles overlap. Or, to change the metaphor, we want to see how far we can walk along the same road with the Muslim before we come to the fork where our paths diverge.

When we then turn to the Scriptures, we are trying to look in a fresh way at how they describe the relationship between God and his prophets. We want to see if we can correct any Muslim misunderstandings of Christian beliefs, and we want to find new ways of restating the gospel that really engage the Muslim mentality.

Jeremiah reveals much about himself as a prophet, and about the inner agonies of his ministry

We shall choose Jeremiah as our example of a biblical prophet. Why Jeremiah? One reason is that we know more about the life and personality of Jeremiah than about almost any other prophet in the Old Testament. Just as 2 Corinthians lays bare the heart of Paul and reveals much of his thinking and feeling, so the book of Jeremiah reveals much about him as a man and as a prophet, and in particular about the inner agonies of his ministry. Another reason is that since Jeremiah stands halfway between Moses and Jesus, he may have something to say to those who cannot make such a huge leap at one go from Mount Sinai to the Garden of Gethsemane.

Islamic Teaching about God and His Prophets

The following summary of Islamic teaching is based largely on the summary given by B. D. Kateregga in *Islam and Christianity, A Muslim and a Christian in Dialogue*:

1. A messenger/apostle (*rasul*) is sent with a divine Scripture to guide and reform humans. The four most important are those through whom Scriptures were revealed: Moses, David, Jesus and Muhammad.

A prophet (*nabi*) carries information or proclaims God's message, but is not given Books like the messengers. Thus all messengers are prophets, but not all prophets are messengers.

2. Both prophets and messengers were given a message by God through revelation (*wahy*) for the guidance of a group or nation. They all brought essentially the same message—the message of Islam. Almost every nation has had its messenger or prophet. Twenty-five are mentioned in the Quran (e.g., 16:36 and 2:136) and 124,000 in *Tradition*.

3. All God's prophets were trustworthy, knowledgeable, and obedient to God. They were the best examples of moral trust. They were all human beings, but protected by God from serious sin and bad diseases. They set very good examples with their own lives, although (according to strictly Orthodox teaching) they were not sinless.

4. We must accept *all* God's prophets and messengers, and denying any one of them constitutes unbelief (Q 4:150-151). Some prophets were more highly endowed than others (especially Moses and Jesus, Q 2:253), but it is sinful to elevate any one prophet and put him on a higher level than the others.

5. Many prophets were mocked and rejected (Q 15:11; 17:94). Some prophets were delivered by God—for example, Noah (21:76; 26:118; 29:15,24; 37:76), Lot (21:71,74; 26:170), and Moses (28:20-22; 26:65). It is worth noting that in several of these passages the word used is *najjainahu* ("we delivered him"), where the verb is the same as that used in the Arabic Lord's Prayer for "deliver us." It seems to be understood that God is in some way *obliged* to rescue his prophets; he *must*

intervene to save them from the hands of people—for example:

> Then shall we save Our Messenger and the believers, in like manner (as of old). It is incumbent upon Us to save believers (10:103). Allah delivereth those who ward off [evil], because of their deserts. Evil toucheth them not, nor do they grieve (39:61). In Allah we trust...of Thy mercy save us from the folk that disbelieve (10:85).

6. Some of the prophets, however, were killed "wrongfully"(e.g., Abel, Zecharias and Yahya. 2:61, 87, 91; 3:21, 112; 4:155, 183; 5:70). Those who were responsible for killing the prophets were later punished by God (2:61; 3:21).

7. Muhammad is "the seal of the prophets" (33:40). In receiving what was revealed to him, he was to recite the stories of the previous prophets, partly as a warning to unbelievers (46:30-34), and partly as an encouragement to himself to persevere with patience in the face of opposition (46:35).[1]

A Study in the Life of Jeremiah

Jeremiah's account speaks of a clear-cut call from God. Some accounts of Muhammad's call speak of a nocturnal vision; others of a vision in clear daylight.

Below, we note briefly 13 of the main characteristics of the ministry of Jeremiah. In some cases we notice where there is anything similar or significantly different in the ministry of Muhammad.

1. The prophet has a clear call from God at the beginning of his ministry (1:1-19), in which he feels that God has laid his hand on him (v. 5), promises to give him the words to speak (v. 7), and to rescue him from enemies (v. 8). Later in his ministry, when experiencing hostility from the people, he questions several elements in the original call he has received (15:11-18). It is interesting to compare this language with that of the Quran and the early accounts of the call of Muhammad in the early *suras*, some of which speak of a nocturnal vision in a dark cave, while another speaks of a vision received in clear daylight.[2]

Both Jeremiah and Muhammad warned of judgment to come.

2. Jeremiah declares the judgment of God which will fall on a stiff-necked, stubborn and disobedient people (e.g., 11:9-17; 19:15). Similarly Muhammad speaks of the judgment of God which is imminent, and tells many stories of God's judgment on sinful people in the past.

3. Jeremiah calls for repentance (e.g., 1:1-8). Muhammad has a similar message of judgment to proclaim. But whereas Jeremiah is recalling his people to obedience to a law revealed centuries before through Moses, Muhammad claims to bring a new revelation for the Arabs which is basically the same as that revealed through previous prophets.

Jeremiah identifies himself both with his people and with God.

4. Jeremiah is identified with his people and, because of his identification with them, confesses their sins and prays for them (8:18-9:1; 14:7-9; cf. Lam. 3:1-51, especially 40-47).

5. At the same time, Jeremiah is identified with God, sharing the anguish of God over his sinful people (6:9-12; 14:17-18—though it is not always clear whether the "I" refers to God or the prophet). The Quran never uses language of this kind to describe God's response to evil—it is far too human an emotion to be ascribed to God. It is therefore inconceivable that Muhammad as prophet should be identified with God in this way.

God-given tests enable Jeremiah to distinguish between true and false prophets.

6. The prophet has to wrestle with the distinction between true and false prophets, and is given several tests to determine the difference (23:9-40).

7. He receives God's message in different ways, and there is considerable variety in the kind of language used to describe the process of revelation. Sometimes he is said to recite the words that are given to him by God (1:7). Elsewhere the reception of the message is compared to drinking (23:9). In another place he listens to the words he is to convey (23:18). In one case he receives the message during a dream (31:23-26; but contrast 23:29).

In the Muslim mind, revelation came from God through Muhammad almost as if he were only a typewriter.

This language is of special interest when we appreciate how Muslims think of the process of revelation and inspiration: Muhammad is simply the human vehicle through which an eternal message is delivered to humans. He is almost like a typewriter used by God to deliver his word, or a pipe through which words are conveyed like liquid.

8. His message is rejected, and he is rejected (11:18-23; 12:6). Gerhard Von Rad makes the significant comment that in Jeremiah we see "a shift in the centre of interest from the *message* to the *messenger*."

9. He suffers great indignities and is treated cruelly. For example he is put in the stocks (20:2); he is imprisoned (32:2); left in a muddy cistern (38:1-13); humiliated by the king (chap. 36); finally he is bound and taken to Babylon but later freed (chap. 40).

10. In his agony he pours out his complaint to God (especially 15:10-18 and 20:7-18), asking for judgment and vengeance on his enemies (20:12; cf. Lam. 3:58).

Muhammad learned from the examples of earlier prophets who had suffered persecution.

When Muhammad is persecuted, he is given in the Quran examples of prophets who have suffered before him, and have been patient in their sufferings. Bell believes that the example of Moses leading his people out of bondage and suffering in Egypt may have made a strong impression on Muhammad. For if God brought his people out of Egypt, surely he can also deliver the Muslim community, and the pattern of the Exodus is therefore repeated in the *Hijrah*.[3]

11. Jeremiah has a message of hope—but only after judgment (30-33, especially 30:3, 18; 31:2, 16-17). He is even told to buy a field to demonstrate the certainty that there will be a future for the people in the land (chap. 32).

12. His life ends in misery and shame as he is taken down to Egypt (43:1-13, esp. 4-7). At the end of the book we are left asking the question: Did God keep his original promise to deliver Jeremiah?

Greater than Jeremiah's suffering was the suffering of Jesus. Difficult as this is for Muslims to contemplate, it is an essential part of the story of prophethood.

13. Jeremiah and Jesus. Whereas Jeremiah is called to take the cup of the wrath of God and make all the nations drink it (25:15-31), Jesus in the Garden of Gethsemane finds that *he himself* is being called to drink the cup of wrath. What makes the prospect of his coming death so much more intolerable, therefore, is that he knows that those who should drink the cup are "all the wicked of the earth" (Psalm 75:8).

The story of how God dealt with a prophet in the Old Testament and how the people treated him, affords some clues about what we can say to the Muslim about prophethood:

Does not people's treatment of prophets such as Jeremiah reveal a deeper problem in human nature than mere "weakness" and "forgetfulness"?

• Do you as a Muslim take seriously enough the perversity of humans in their rejection of the Word of God? You say that people are created "weak," and suggest that all people need is law and admonition, combined with the example of the prophet. But look at the way the people of Judah treated the prophet Jeremiah! Is there not something more seriously wrong with human nature than mere "weakness" and "forgetfulness"?

• What do you understand about the inner experience of the prophet or of any prophet? In the light of the experience of Jeremiah, do you accept that suffering may be a necessary part of the prophetic experience? And how do you explain the fact that God does not always seem to deliver his prophets?

Jeremiah's suffering mirrors God's suffering as he bears with his people and forgives them.

• What does it mean if the prophet is willing to suffer? Does it not say something about how God deals with evil? Does it not suggest that judgment is not the only response God can make to evil? If this can be so, the prophet's suffering can become a kind of mirror of the suffering of God himself. The prophet's suffering can then be an indication of the way that God himself suffers as he bears with his people and forgives them.

• How do you understand God's involvement in this prophet? Is there not a sense in which the honor of God is tied up with his prophet, so that what the people do to *him*, they are doing to *God*? If so, is God bound to deliver his prophet? If he is bound, why the exceptions? Why did he allow some to be humiliated and killed? What does it say about God that when the preaching of his Word draws out the worst in people, he does not rescue his servant, but allows him to suffer?

These questions can only be answered by Christians when they have been with Jesus in Gethsemane, and begun to understand that "God was in Christ..." (2 Cor. 5:19). But if Jeremiah is halfway between Moses and Jesus, perhaps he can help the followers of the prophet not only to appreciate the questions, but also to catch a glimpse of what the fuller answers can be in Jesus.

God and His Word

Like the New Testament, the Quran gives Jesus the title "Word"— but with a different meaning.

The choice of this theme arises out of the fact that both the New Testament and the Quran give Jesus the title "Word":

> In the beginning was the Word, and the Word was with God, and the Word was God . . . (Jn. 1:1).

> The Messiah, Jesus son of Mary, was only a messenger of Allah, and His Word which He conveyed unto Mary, and a Spirit from Him...(Q 4:171).

Although we have here some obvious common ground, the problem is that the same title is interpreted differently in the two communities. So do we simply have to accept that we are poles apart, or is there any possibility of building bridges?

Jesus as "Word" in the Quran

The following verses describe the annunciation of the birth of Jesus to Mary:

(And remember) when the angels said: O Mary! Lo! Allah
giveth thee glad tidings of a word from him, whose name
is Messiah, Jesus, son of Mary...(Q 3:45-48).

Another important verse in which Jesus is spoken of as God's
Word comes in the context of an appeal to Christians not to
exalt Jesus too highly:

O People of the Scripture! Do not exaggerate in your
religion nor utter aught concerning Allah save the truth.
The Messiah, Jesus son of Mary, was only a messenger of
Allah, and His Word which he conveyed unto Mary, and
a spirit from Him. So believe in Allah and His messengers, and say not "Three"—Cease! [It is] better for you!
Allah is only One God...(Q 4:171).

If we go on to ask how the title "Word" is interpreted in the
Quran, a later verse in Sura 3 gives the answer:

Lo! The likeness of Jesus with Allah is as the likeness of
Adam. He created him of dust, then He said unto him:
Be! and he is. (Q 3:59)

The traditional Muslim interpretation of the title has
therefore been that Jesus is the Word of God in the sense that
he was *created by the Word of God*.   Thus the commentator
Bidawi says: "Jesus, is called 'a word,' because he came into
existence by God's command without a father, so that he
resembled the new creations, who are the world of
command." Razi gives a different explanation: that Jesus
was called a word because he was the fulfillment of the word
spoken by the prophets.[4] Yusuf Ali's comment on Q 3:5 is:

Notice: '*a* Word from God', not '*the* Word of God', the
epithet that mystical Christianity uses for Jesus...Jesus
was created by a miracle, by God's word 'Be', and he
was.[5]

**Some sources of
Muhammad's ideas
about Jesus need to
be seriously
questioned.**
What then do we do when faced with these Islamic
interpretations? One natural response on our part is to
investigate sources and ask where Muhammad might have
heard these ideas. Although the title is found only in five
verses in the New Testament (Jn. 1:1, 14; 1 Jn. 1:1, 10; and Rev.
19:13), the idea of Jesus as the eternal word of God was developed by certain theologians between the 2nd and 4th centuries, notably by Clement of Alexandria.

It is significant, however, that the title was used much less
after this time, and was not used in any of the major creeds.
Geoffrey Parrinder suggests this may have been because the

Logos idea had also been used by various Gnostic sects. The example he gives is the apocryphal Acts of John, written about the 2nd century A.D., which describes the disciples taking part in a dance, "going round in a ring," saying to Jesus: "Glory be to thee, Lord: Glory be to thee, Grace: Glory be to thee, Spirit."[6] The fact that this same document says that Jesus was only crucified in appearance (cf. "They slew him not nor crucified, but it appeared so unto them..." Q 4:157), suggests that Muhammad may well have found the title "Word," as well as the Quranic idea of the crucifixion, in heretical Christian sources like these.

This kind of enquiry about sources makes a great deal of sense to us, because it helps us to understand how Muhammad may have come in contact with these ideas either in Arabia or Syria. Unfortunately, however, it is anathema to Muslims, because they believe that the words of the Quran were revealed directly from God. Their concept of divine revelation rules out the possibility that what is recorded in the Quran could have come to Muhammad from any human source.

Another possible response is to use the kind of argument first developed by St. John of Damascus in the 7th century. In his treatise *De Haeresibus* he speaks of Islam as "the Heresy of the Ishmaelites," and gives a clear idea of how he must have engaged in discussion with Muslims in Damascus less than 100 years after the Prophet's death. He suggests that when Muslims accuse Christians of *shirk* (i.e., of associating a created being with God the Creator), we should reply that in our eyes Muslims are guilty of *mutilating* God by refusing to believe that the Word of God is fully divine:

> Since you say that Christ is Word of God and Spirit, how is it that you revile us as *Hetairiastai* (Associators)? For the Word and the Spirit are not separated from the one in whom they are by nature. If therefore His Word is in God, it is evident that the Word is also God. But if the Word is outside of God, then according to you God is without reason and without life. And so, fearing to provide an Associator for God, you have mutilated Him. It were better for you to say that He has an Associate than to mutilate Him, and to treat Him as stone, or wood, or some insensible thing. Wherefore you speak falsely of us when you call us "*Hetairiastai*", but we call you "*Koptai*" (Mutilators) of God.[7]

We want to say to the Muslim: "We understand what *you* mean when you say Jesus is the Word of God or a Word of God. Will you allow us to explain what *we* understand by that title?

Whether or not these two approaches bring us any nearer together, our main desire should be to come back to the Gospels to see what light they shed on the title "Word." We want to say to the Muslim: "We understand what *you* mean when you say Jesus is the Word of God or a Word of God. Will you allow us to explain what *we* understand by the title?"

We will need to begin with the prologue to John's Gospel, and say something about the background of ideas which must have influenced John. Greek philosophers centuries before had thought of the logos (word or reason) as the rational principle by which the universe is sustained. And the Jews, probably under the influence of Greek philosophy, had reflected on the role of the creative word of God in Genesis 1, and of the Wisdom of God described in Proverbs 8:22-31.

Thus when John spoke of Jesus as "the Word," most of his readers would have connected the title with one or both of these ideas which were common in the 1st century. But they would not fail also to take note of John's incredibly bold claim that the eternal *logos* of God "*was God*" (Jn. 1:1), and that he "*became flesh and lived for a while among us*" (1:14).

Words of command can get things done and achieve certain ends. Thus when John speaks of Jesus as the Word of God, he means that it was *through Jesus that the universe was created*: "Through him all things were made; without him nothing was made that has been made" (1:3). Whereas the Quran speaks of Jesus as *created by the Word of God*, John believes that God *created the universe through Jesus the eternal Word*. But words also reveal a person's mind and character. So when John thinks of Jesus as the Word of God in this sense, what he means is that Jesus *reveals God* in the fullest way that is possible: "No one has ever seen God, but God the only (Son), who is at the Father's side, has made him known" (1:18).

Although only one New Testament writer refers to Jesus by the title "The Word," much can be gained by noting how the Synoptics bear out the meaning of that title in their respective accounts of Jesus' words and works.

If then the title is used by only one writer in the New Testament, and this is what he seems to understand by it, where else do we need to look? We might say that we do not need to go any further than this. Much can be gained, however, from looking at the Synoptic Gospels, which give us a different kind of account of the life and teaching of Jesus. We may then see how the Apostle John, writing in the 90's of the 1st century and reflecting on all that he and the other apostles had seen and heard of Jesus of Nazareth, could have come to think of him as the eternal Word of God.

We notice first of all examples of how the words of Jesus affect the created order (the so-called "Nature Miracles"). We then look at healing miracles, in which the words of Jesus bring about a cure. Finally we see examples of Jesus pronouncing words of forgiveness. All the examples are taken from the Gospel according to Mark. In each case we note in the column on the right the recorded words of Jesus, and in several cases we also note significant parallels in the Quran.

1. The word of Jesus working in creation:

He calms the storm: "Quiet! Be still!" (Mk. 4:35-41)
He feeds the 5,000 after giving thanks (Mk. 6:30-44).

This miracle is of special significance for us, since it is referred to indirectly in the Quran. In the Sura entitled "The Table Spread", the disciples are reported as praying, "Send down for us a table spread with food from heaven" (Q 5:114).

It is also helpful to notice the verse in the Quran in which Jesus speaks of his miracles: "I fashion (akhluqu, create) for you out of clay the likeness of a bird and breathe into it and it is alive, by Allah's leave" (Q 3:49). I know of one Muslim whose pilgrimage to faith in Jesus began when he thought about the implications of the word "fashion" or "create": surely only God can create—so how can Jesus here speak of himself creating something?

2. The word of Jesus in healing :

Like the Gospels, the Quran relates accounts of Jesus' healing people by his word.	
man possessed by evil spirits	"Be quiet! Come out of him!" (1:21-25).
the leper	"Be clean!" (1:40-45).(cf. in the Quran: "I heal...the leper." (Q 3:49).
the paralytic	"Your sins are forgiven" (2:1-12).
Legion	"Come out of this man, you evil spirit!" (5:1-12).
sick woman	"Go in peace and be freed from your suffering" (5:21-43).
raising the dead girl	"Talitha koum! Little girl, get up!" (5:21-43). (cf. in the

	Quran: "I raise the dead, by Allah's leave" Q 3:49).
healing the deaf and dumb	"Ephphatha! Be opened!" (7:31-37).
healing the boy with a spirit	"You deaf and dumb spirit, I command you, come out of him and never enter him again" (9:14-32).
healing of blind Bartimaeus	"Your faith has healed you" (10:46-52). (cf. in the Quran: "I heal...him who was born blind" Q 3:49).

3. The word of Jesus in forgiving:

the paralytic	"Son, your sins are forgiven" (2:5).

The reaction of the Pharisees to these words ("He's blaspheming! Who can forgive sins but God alone?" 2:7) is exactly the same as that of the orthodox Muslim who knows that the Quran says: "Who forgiveth sins save Allah only?" (Q 3:135).

In the power of his words to do what only God can do, (especially the forgiving of sins) the absolute uniqueness of Jesus is shown.

With the memory of these events and these words indelibly printed on his mind, the Apostle John recognizes that the words of Jesus have power to still the storm—which is something that only God can do ("He stilled the storm to a whisper." Ps. 107:29). He remembers also how his words brought healing and forgiveness—which once again is the prerogative of God himself ("He forgives all my sins and heals all my diseases." Ps. 103:3). If, therefore, the words of Jesus have the power to do things that only God can do, Jesus must be the one through whom God has spoken and acted in a special way.

The title "Word" which John gives to Jesus is therefore firmly grounded in all that John remembers of Jesus. For if the words of Jesus were in effect the words of God, is it not natural to think that Jesus is in himself the Word of God? And if the historical Jesus spoke and acted in this way, speaking and creating, healing and forgiving word of God, then the risen and ascended Jesus can still speak these words to us today. The Word of God cannot be less than or other than God himself.

God and His Mercy

"In the name of God, the Merciful, the Compassionate..." says the Muslim in the *Fatihah*. "How can I find a merciful God?" cries Luther in his despair. It is one thing to proclaim the mercy of God, but another to be sure of experiencing that mercy.

Thinking about the mercy of God brings us nearer the heart of the matter. For how do we benefit from God's prophets and his Word, unless they communicate God's mercy to us in our need?

God and His Mercy in the Quran

We can summarize the Quran's teaching about mercy in the following way:

1. God is merciful and forgiving (*rahman, rahim, ghafur*).

Your Lord is a Lord of All-embracing Mercy, and His wrath will never be withdrawn from guilty folk (Q 6:147). Despair not of the Mercy of Allah, who forgiveth all sins! Lo! He is the Forgiving, the Merciful (Q 39:53, cf. 23:118).

2. God loves certain kinds of people: those who do right (2:145; 3:134; 3:148; 5:13, 93), those who turn to him (2:222), the pure (2:222), the God-fearing (3:76; 9:4, 7), the patient (3:146), the trusting (3:159), the upright (5:42), the equitable (49:9; 60:8) and those who do battle for his cause (61:4).

> **Quranic teaching about God's love is notably narrower than that of the New Testament.**

God does *not* love certain other kinds of people: aggressors (2:190), the corrupt (5:64; 28:77), the evil unbelievers (2:276), the ungrateful (22:38), the braggart boasters (31:18; 57:33), the prodigals (6:141; 7:31), the proud and boastful (4:36), the unbelievers (30:145), the wrongdoers (3:57, 140; 42:40), the treacherous (4:107; 8:58; 22:38), those of harsh speech, (4:148), the transgressors (5:87).

3. Forgiveness is associated with obedience to God and his Prophet.

If you love Allah, follow me. Allah will love you and forgive you your sins. Allah is forgiving, Merciful (Q 3:31; cf. 8:29; 19:95; 20:73; 46:31; 57:28; 61:11-12; 71:3-4; 19:95).

4. God's forgiveness is inscrutable—he forgives whom he wills.

He [Allah] will forgive whom He will and He will punish whom He will (Q 2:284; cf. 3:129; 5:18; 5:40). Knowest thou not that unto Allah belongeth the Sovereignty of the heavens and the earth? He punisheth whom He will, and forgiveth whom He will. Allah is able to do all things   (Q 5:40; cf. 48:14).

5. We cannot be sure of forgiveness: God will show mercy on the Day of Judgment.

We ardently hope that our Lord will forgive us our sins because we are the first of the believers (Q 26:51)...and who, I ardently hope, will forgive me my sins on the Day of Judgment (Q 26:81; cf. 13:41; 66:8).

6. There is *no* forgiveness for certain sins, like *shirk* (association).

Allah pardoneth not that partners should be ascribed unto Him. He pardoneth all save that to whom He will...(4:116; cf. 4:48, 137, 168; 9:80; 47:340).

God and His Mercy in the Teaching of Jesus

Many Christians have believed that in the preaching of the gospel, *law must precede grace*. We have seen the Letter to the Romans as *the* definitive presentation of the gospel, and have therefore generally thought that we must *first* proclaim the law in order to bring people to an awareness of their guilt, and *only then* preach grace. The Bible Selections publication entitled *The Message of the Tawrat, the Zabur and the Injil,* which was prepared for Muslim readers and published first by the Bible Society in Lebanon, is based on this model of the gospel. Thus the first four studies have the following titles:

1. God is one and has created man to serve and love him.
   God gives man his laws.
3. God warns man of the consequences of failure to keep his laws.
4. God is merciful and loving and wants to forgive.

The remaining studies go on to present Jesus as God's answer to people's need. However, three fundamental questions need to be raised concerning this approach:

1. Is this the *only* model of the gospel?
2. Is this model of the gospel true to the teaching of Jesus?
3. Is this model of the gospel appropriate for the Muslim?

These are questions which have been raised by Kenneth E. Bailey, and arise out of his life-long study of the parables, concentrating especially on their literary form and on their context in Middle Eastern peasant culture.   Three of the parables are of special importance for us:

1.   **The Prodigal Son** (Lk. 15:11-32. See *The Cross and the Prodigal* and *Poet and Peasant* and *Through Peasant Eyes: A Literary-Cultural Approach to the Parables in Luke*);
2.   **The Two Debtors** (Lk. 7:36-50. See *Through Peasant Eyes*);
3.   **The Good Samaritan** (Lk. 10:25-57. See *Through Peasant Eyes*).[8]

Bailey's study of the parables leads him to sum up the gospel proclaimed by Jesus in the words: "The Costly Demonstration of Unexpected Love." The basic message here is that God loves. His love is totally *unexpected*, since we would not expect him to love his rebellious creatures. Not only does he proclaim his love, he *demonstrates* it in action. And this demonstration of his unexpected love is *costly* to him, for he really suffers in the process of forgiving people their sins.

In the parable of the father and the two lost sons, the gospel is conveyed not through a series of propositions but through the story of broken relationship restored by humble confession and acceptance of the father's mercy and grace.

We shall concentrate here on the parable of the Father and the Two Lost Sons (as it should be called, rather than "the parable of the Prodigal Son"). We shall see what it teaches about the mercy of God. Bailey summarizes the significance of the prodigal's homecoming as follows:

> On his return, the prodigal is overwhelmed by an unexpected visible demonstration of love in humiliation. He is shattered by the offer of grace, he confesses his unworthiness, and he accepts restoration to sonship in genuine humility. Sin is now seen as a broken relationship which he cannot restore. Repentance is now understood as acceptance of grace and confession of unworthiness. The community rejoices together. The visible demonstration of love in humiliation is seen to have clear overtones of the atoning work of Christ.[9]

If this is the thrust of the parable, what would happen if, instead of presenting the gospel in a series of propositions (like "All men are sinners" and "Jesus died to atone for our sins") we attempted to recover the lost art of *telling stories*? And how could this interpretation of the parable be presented in a popular form?

The Father and His Two Lost Sons – A Parable

Interpretation	Scripture	Application
Incredibly, in spite of all that the father has already suffered, he rushes out to welcome his son home. Perhaps the people of the village think *he* is now bringing disgrace on himself by welcoming his son who is in disgrace! But instead of punishing him, he forgives him, and receives him back as a full member of the family. He is so happy that he wants everyone to join in a party to celebrate his son's homecoming.	He was still a long way from home when his father saw him; his heart was filled with pity; and he ran, threw his arms around his son, and kissed him. "Father," the son said, "I have sinned against God and against you. I am no longer fit to be called your son." But the father called to his servants. "Hurry!" he said. "Bring the best robe and put it on him. Put a ring on his finger and shoes on his feet. Then go and get the prize calf and kill it, and let us celebrate with a feast! For this son of mine was dead, but now he is alive. He was lost, but now he has been found." And so the feasting began.	Here we see a picture of God as a loving Father who loves *all* people and wants them to come back to him. He comes to each of us offering his forgiveness. And forgiveness is not an easy thing for God—it costs him something to forgive. But he accepts us just as we are and welcomes us with joy.
It is sad that the older brother is *not* happy to see his younger brother welcomed home. Perhaps he has always been a dutiful son at home, but never very close to his father. Now he is so angry that he insults his father in front of all the guests.	In the meantime the older son was out in the field. On his way back, when he came close to the house, he heard the music and dancing. So he called one of the servants and asked him, "What's going on?" "Your brother has come back home," the servant answered, "and your father has killed the prize calf, because he got him back safe and sound." The older brother was so angry that he would not go into the house.	If we are religious people, it is all too easy for us to practice our religion outwardly, while our hearts are far from God. And it is a special temptation for us if we are religious to think that we are better than other people.
How is the father going to respond to this new disgrace? The older son deserves to be punished for behaving like this. But again the father does not want to punish him, and instead he goes out to plead with his son to come in and join the party.	So his father came out and begged him to come in. But he spoke back to his father, "Look, all these years I have worked for you like a slave, and I have never disobeyed your orders. What have you given me? Not even a goat for me to have a feast with my friends! But this son of yours wasted all your property on prostitutes, and when he comes back home, you kill the prize calf for him!" "My son," the father answered, "you are always here with me, and everything I have is yours. But we had to celebrate and be happy, because your brother was dead, but now he is alive; he was lost, but now he has been found."	God has a right to punish us for all the wrong things we have done, and we expect that he will punish people in this life and on the Day of Judgment. But God surprises us and does something that we might not expect: he comes to us where we are to show how much he cares for us and loves us.

Jesus' parable of the prodigal's return is especially informative to Muslims about the Father's love and eager forgiving.

The following paragraphs are from a tract which is intended to present the parable itself and this interpretation of it for Muslim readers. The front page has the title: "A Story Told by Jesus ('Isa), Son of Mary", and the parable is printed in full on the cover.

On the inside pages the parable is divided into smaller paragraphs, and printed in the center of the page. In a column on the left is a brief explanation of what is happening in the story, while on the right are some comments to draw out the meaning of the story. On the facing page is a representation of the section which tells of the prodigal's homecoming and the reception he receives from his father:

The surprising thing about the parable is that we are left with a real "cliff-hanger" ending: how does the younger son respond to his father's unexpected demonstration of love? The final paragraphs explain the significance of this ending and present the challenge to the reader.

Interpretation	Application
And what is the end of the story? Did the older son apologize to his father and join in the party to welcome his brother? Or was he so angry that he wanted to do something violent to his father?	Perhaps there was no ending to the story Jesus told because all of us who hear the story today have to make the same kind of decision that the older son had to make: will we thank God and worship him because of the way he loves us and the way he demonstrates and proves his love for us? Will we think of ourselves not just as servants, but as sons and daughters who can approach God as a loving and forgiving Father?[10]

Here is New Testament scholarship at its very best! Bailey's interpretation makes such perfect sense of the parable and enables us to see it in a new light. But it also seems tailor-made, as it were, for the Muslim mind. The prodigal's face-saving plan of serving his father as a servant/slave is so close to the thinking of Muslims. To them, therefore, the message is that God wants us to be closer to him than servants—he wants us to be sons and daughters. If forgiveness were simply a matter of words, the father could have sent a message through a servant. But in forgiving and in demonstrating his mercy, he himself suffers, because he takes upon himself all the wrongdoing of his son.

The process of repentance in the son certainly began in the far country; but it comes to a climax when he sees how his father has proved his love.

We can now look back at our earlier summary of the teaching about God's mercy in the Quran and, without trying to overdraw the contrasts or to see differences where there are none, notice how the message of this parable addresses that world view point by point:

1.   Here we have no differences, for the whole message of this parable is that God is merciful and forgiving.

2.   God does *not* only love those who love him. The father in the parable loves *both* sons and shows the same kind of forgiving love to both of them.

3.   God's forgiveness is associated with the one who proclaims and declares that forgiveness to people. The father himself welcomes his son and reinstates him in the family. When Jesus declares, "Your sins are forgiven," it is because he speaks with the authority of God himself. So what Jesus does, God does; and what God does, Jesus does.

4.   God does indeed show mercy on whom he wills (Rom. 9:18); but we *can* know where we stand before him. The way the father shows his love for both his sons shows how God's love is extended to us all, and how he takes the initiative and comes to meet us and welcome us home.

5.   We *can* be sure of God's mercy and forgiveness. We do not have to wait until the Day of Judgment before we know how we stand before him. The prodigal knows that he is forgiven because of the way his father goes out of his way to show that the wrongs of the past are forgiven and forgotten.

6.   The only unforgivable sin in the teaching of Jesus is what he calls "the sin against the Holy Spirit" (Mk. 3:23-30—i.e., attributing the work of God to Satan and calling what is good evil). If the older son in the parable refuses in the end to accept the mercy shown to him by his father, he is spurning his father's love, and the breach in their relationship looks as if it must be final. But this is only *after* the father has demonstrated his love for his son in a way that is beyond all doubt.

If we have prayed for *parresia* (boldness and freedom of speech) with the Jerusalem Church (Ac. 4:29) and with Paul (Eph. 6:19-20), could this way of understanding and articulating the gospel be part of the answer to our prayer?

NOTES

1. B. D. Kateregga and D. W. Shenk, *Islam and Christianity, A Muslim and a Christian in Dialogue* (Paternoster, 1980).

2. Cf. Tor Andrae, *Mohammed, The Man and His Faith* (Harper & Row, 1955), 43-52.

3. Richard Bell, *The Origin of Islam in its Christian Environment* (London: Macmillan, 1926), 122 ff.

4. Geoffry Parrinder, *Jesus in the Qur'an* (Faber, 1965), 45-46.

5. Yusuf Ali, *The Holy Quran, Text, Translation and Commentary* (Leicester: The Islamic Foundation, 1975), 133.

6. Parrinder, 45-48.

7. John W. Voorhis, trans., "The Apology of John of Damascus," *The Muslim World* (1934), 394-395.

8. Kenneth E. Bailey, *The Cross and the Prodigal* (St. Louis: Concordia, 1973); *Poet and Peasant*, and *Through Peasant Eyes. A Literary-Cultural Approach to the Parables in Luke* (Grand Rapids: Eerdmans, Combined Edition, 1976), 158-206.

9. Bailey, *Cross and Prodigal*, 206.

10. "A Story Told by Jesus ('Isa), Son of Mary," a tract.

CHAPTER EIGHT

DIFFERENT DIAGNOSES OF THE HUMAN CONDITION

J. Dudley Woodberry

When Christians share the "good news of salvation from sin" with Muslim friends, it is often not heard as "good news." This is largely because Muslims have traditionally not diagnosed the human condition as pessimistically as the Bible does; so they have not seen the need for as radical a solution.

Islamic theologians generally see no need for human nature to be *transformed*; only to be *guided*.

Two contemporary Muslim writers illustrate this common perspective. Badru Kateregga says, "Muslims believe that man is fundamentally a good and a dignified creature. He is not a fallen being."[1] From a similar premise Isma'il al-Faruqi continues, "Islam denies, therefore, that God had to ransom humanity by means of oblation and sacrifice."[2]

In this study we shall first look at the Islamic materials supporting this optimistic analysis of human nature to see why so many Muslims are only looking for right guidance, not the transformation of their natures. Secondly, we shall look at other Islamic sources that suggest that the problem is graver. Thus it is hoped that Muslims, on the basis of their own writings, will search for a more drastic solution, and that we all, joined in our common sinfulness, may receive the redemption God offers.

An Optimistic Muslim Diagnosis of Human Nature

Muslims find support for their optimistic analysis of the human condition in Sura 30:30 (Egyptian ed.)/29 (Fluegel ed.):

So set your face to the religion as one of the pristine faith (*hanif*)—the state of natural purity (*fitra*) in which He created people. There is no changing of the creation of God. That is the eternal religion.

The traditionist al-Bukhari (194-256 A.H./810-870 A.D.) relates that Muhammad said on this subject: "No child is born except in the state of natural purity (*fitra*) and then his parents make him Jewish, Christian, or Magian."[3]

Additional support for this perspective is found in the quranic account of Adam and Eve—at least in certain features of the story. Sura 20:115/114 says, "We [God] made a covenant with Adam before, but he forgot, and We found in him no determination." Muslims have tended to focus on Adam's forgetfulness here rather than on his rebellion or the disobedience reported in verse 121/119: "Adam rebelled against (or disobeyed—'asa) his Lord." One reason for their selectivity may be that in Muslim thought Adam is a prophet, and traditionally they have not viewed prophets "warts and all."

In any event, the consequence of Adam's act, according to the Quran, is a descent from the Garden to the earth "for a time," after which God turned toward him [in mercy] (2:36/34-37/35)—all without the need for an atonement.

The passage goes on to repeat the command to descend [from the Garden] "all together" and adds, "yet there shall come to you guidance from Me, and whosoever follows My guidance, no fear shall be on them, neither shall they sorrow. As for the unbelievers...those shall be the inhabitants of the fire" (23:38/36-39/37).

Here those who have "fallen" (if we may use the word) seem capable of following the guidance of God without transformation or new life; they do not echo the words of Paul: "I can will what is right, but I cannot do it. For I do not do the good I want, but the evil I do not want is what I do" (Rom. 7:18-19). Since they do not utter the same cry of despair, they do not see the need for a new infusion of the Spirit of God to transform and give new life (Romans 8)—although they share the record of the breathing of God's spirit into our first ancestor (15:29; 32:9/8; 38:72; Gen. 2:7).

Adam and Eve Revisited

The Prophet Adam, in the traditional Islamic view, did not fall; he *forgot*.

At times the Quran indicates a more critical human predicament. When we reexamine the quranic accounts of Adam and Eve, we see a number of elements that are often passed over. First, there is an awareness that, if humans are created, then they will be corrupt. With reference to the creation of Adam we read:

> And when the Lord said to the angels, "I am setting in the earth a viceroy," they said, "What, will You set therein one who will do corruption there, and shed blood, while we proclaim Your praise and call You holy?" He said, "Assuredly I know what you know not" (2:30/28).

The subsequent quranic account confirms that corruption and sin against other humans is what resulted when they were given power and freedom. God's response indicates a knowledge of this and, it would appear, a solution.

Secondly, the Devil (*Iblis*) foretells that he will master and pervert most people. After he disobeyed God by refusing to bow down to Adam, he says, "I shall assuredly subjugate his seed, save a few" (17:62/64). In another account of the story, Satan tells God, "As You have perverted me, I will sit in ambush for them...You will not find most of them grateful" (7:16/15-17/16). In still another rendering of the story Iblis says, "As You have perverted me...I shall pervert them, all together, except those of Your servants among them that are devoted" (15:39-40). Subsequent history in the Quran and human experience have shown these not to be idle boasts; they have been difficult facts to explain if humans are basically good.

Thirdly, some verses reflect the biblical perspective that Adam knowingly disobeyed or rebelled against the will of God. The account of the fall of Adam in Sura 20 starts with the biblical concept of a covenant: "We [God] made a covenant ('*ahidna*) with Adam before" (vs. 115/114). As we have noted, Muslims have tended to focus on Adam's subsequent forgetfulness in the same verse, but this is hard to correlate with Satan's reminder to Adam and Eve of God's prohibition (7:20/19). In fact, the subsequent eating of the fruit is described in very strong words: "Adam *rebelled against* (or *disobeyed*— '*asa*) his Lord and *went astray* (or *erred*— *faghawa*)" (20:121/119). This latter description reiterates the biblical portrayal of that sin as disobedience and rebellion.

While differing in details, quranic and biblical passages on Eden are significantly parallel.

When we probe deeper to ascertain the nature of the rebellion, we note, fourthly, that in both the Bible and the Quran, Adam rejects the type of creaturehood God has assigned to him even though the details are different. In the Bible the temptation is to become "like God knowing good and evil," and they ate of the Tree of the Knowledge of Good and Evil (Gen. 2:17; 3:5-6). In the Quran the temptation is to "become angels or...immortals" (7:20/19) and they ate of the Tree of Immortality (20:120/118-121/119), which was barred to them by the cherubim in the Genesis account (3:24). In both renderings, however, Adam and Eve reject their form of creaturehood assigned by the Creator.

Fifthly, with respect to who was responsible for Adam and Eve's disobedience, they said, "Lord, we have wronged ourselves" (7:23/22), indicating they were at fault.[4]

When we look, sixthly, at the results of their action, we again note biblical parallels. They have a sense of shame (7:22/21; 20:121/119). While the Quran implies they consequently hide from God, the eminent historian and commentator al-Tabari (224-241 A.H./839-855 A.D.) quotes the Jewish convert Wahb ibn Munabbih as making this explicit: Adam hides in a tree because "I feel ashamed before You, O Lord."[5] They confess that unless God forgives them and has mercy on them they will be "among the lost" (7:23/22). They are expelled from Paradise and have enmity between them (2:36/34, 38/36; 7:24/23; 20:123/121).

How has the expulsion from Eden affected the subsequent generations of the human race?

Muslim answers vary but include some nearly biblical perspectives.

The question arises as to whether or not the Quran and Muslims see any implications of these events for the human race. As for the expulsion from Paradise, Sura 2:38/36 puts the command in the Arabic plural form, indicating more than two ("Get you down out of it, all together"), instead of the dual form ("Get you down, both of you together"—20:123/121). Muslim commentators have normally accounted for this plural by including Iblis in the expulsion with Adam and Eve[6]— not by including the human race even though humans remain on earth.

The authoritative traditionist Muslim (202-261 A.H./817-875 A.D.), however, makes a connection between the sin of Adam and the descent of the human race when he recounts a story by Muhammad in which Moses says to Adam: "because of your sin you caused mankind to come down to earth."[7]

The contemporary Egyptian Muhammad Kamil Husain, however, while noting a difference between Muslim and Christian views of the implications of the account, affirms that Muslims "believe in the sin of Adam and his involving us in expulsion from paradise."[8] Thus he recognizes some consequences for humans in general.

As the expulsion from Paradise is put in a plural as well as a dual form, the same verses declare enmity between those expelled. Of particular interest is a comment on the enmity by al-Tabari, on the authority of the convert from Judaism Wahb ibn Munabbih, in which God says to the serpent, "You shall be an enemy to the children of Adam and you shall bite his heel, but wherever he finds you he shall crush your head."[9] This not only relates the events to subsequent generations of people but is an obvious reference to Genesis 3:15, which Christians have traditionally understood to refer to the conflict culminating in the crucifixion where Jesus is wounded by Satan but where the former ultimately defeats the latter.

Does the story of "the fall" give any insight into our nature? Sura 7:26/25-27/26 makes it an illustration and warning about Satan's continued temptations to the "Children of Adam." The recognized traditionist Tirmidhi (d. ca. 270 A.H./883 A.D.) relates that Muhammad noted that Adam's descendants repeated the sin of their ancestor: "Adam forgot and ate of the tree and his offspring forgot; and Adam sinned and his offspring sinned."[10]

Muhammad associates a deficiency in humans to Adam and Eve, according to Ibn Sa'd (ca. 168 A.H./784 A.D.-230/845) in his biographical dictionary. Here the Arabian prophet says, "As regards Adam and Eve men are like a deficient grain measure which they will never succeed in filling."[11] Since the next sentence is about the Judgment Day, the human deficiency is apparently a moral one.

Kamil Husain does not go so far as to say that human nature has a bias to wrong, but he sees the story of Adam as symbolic of the human condition and as dealing with the fundamental nature of humans.[12] When the account is interpreted in this way, there can be much common ground for Muslims and Christians.

The contemporary Islamic scholar Uthman Yahya sees humans in two distinct states: the original prototype and the actual condition. But after asking rhetorically, "Where is salvation and by what means is it to be made real?"...

Another contemporary scholar from al-Azhar and Morocco, Uthman Yahya, goes further in recognizing a "fall" in the race. Unlike most Muslims, he distinguishes between humans in two distinct states:

the first is his original constitution, the prototype created in the image of God, the second man in his actual condition.

As contrasted with his prototype man in his actual state is feeble (Sura iv. 28), despairing (Sura xi.9), unjust (Sura xiv. 34), quarrelsome (Sura xvi.4), tyrannical (Sura xcvi.6),

lost (Sura cv.2), etc....we see clearly in the light of these
quotations that there are two distinct states of man: that
of his original nature and that of his fall.

But if with the sin of Adam man has lost the state of Eden,
it is by the crime of Cain that this sin has entered actively
into humanity.

...if...man, as he actually is, is incapable of living in
perfect blessedness, where is salvation and by what means
is it to be made real?[13]

Yahya gives the traditional Muslim answer: divine guidance.
We might ask, "Is this enough?"

The Subsequent Quranic Narrative

Quranic accounts of
humankind's
corruption abound.

Satan's prediction that he would master and pervert most
humans (7:16/15-17/16; 15:39-40; 17:62/64) is borne out in the
subsequent quranic narrative.[14]   After Adam and Eve disobeyed, the Children of Adam are warned, "Let not Satan
tempt you as he brought your parents out of the Garden"
(7:27/26). Next Cain murders Abel (5:27/30-30/33). Each
community is sent an Apostle (16:36/38), but one after another
they reject him—the people of Noah, the Pit, Thamud, Ad,
and Pharaoh, the brothers of Lot, the men of the Grove
(Midian), and the people of Tubba' (50:12-14/13). Others are
added—the people of Abraham and Moses and many cities
(22:42/93-45/44). Generation after generation were destroyed when they did evil (10:13/14; 17:17/18; 19:98, etc.).

There were exceptions such as those to whom Jonah preached
(10:98), but the majority seem to be evil:

We sent Noah and Abraham, and We appointed
the Prophecy and the Book to be among their seed; and
some of them go aright while many of them are perverse
(17:26).

If people are basically
good, how do we
account for the
quranic quotations of
most people
rejecting right
guidance?

If only there had been among the generations before
you men of perseverance restraining from corruption in
the earth—except a few of these whom We delivered
from amongst them (11:116/118).

The portrayal goes on: "Most men are not believers" (12:103);
"Most of them do not believe in God" (12:106); "Most men do
not believe" (13:1). The Quran recounts, "We sent Apostles
among the people of old, and not a single Apostle came with

out them mocking him" (15:10-11). Again the question haunts us: If people are basically good, how do we account for the quranic quotations of most people rejecting right guidance?

Human Nature in the Quran

We have noted Sura 30:30, the verse traditionally used to indicate the state of natural purity (*fitra*) in which people are created. There are, however, many other verses which indicate a more critical human predicament. Perhaps the clearest of these is Sura 12:53, where Joseph refers to his temptation with Potiphar's wife and says, "The soul is certainly an inciter to evil." This does not place the blame on Satan or Potiphar's wife, but indicates a problem at the core of human nature. This statement carries added force because it comes from Joseph, as the text indicates and most commentators concur, rather than from Potiphar's wife. This confession led Ahman Zaki, at the 1956/57 session of the Arabic Academy in Cairo, to affirm that the soul of humans can be inherently wrongdoing [15] —an affirmation Christians too would make.

"If God were to punish men for their wrongdoing," says the Quran, "he would not leave on earth a single creature."

Other passages refer to humankind as sinful (or unjust—*zulum*—14:34/37; 33:72), foolish (33:72), ungrateful (14:34/37), weak (4:28/32), despairing or boastful (11:9/12-10/13), quarrel-some (16:4), and rebellious (96:6). The Quran concludes, "If God were to punish men for their wrongdoing (or injustice—*zulm*), he would not leave on earth a single creature" (16:61/63). If this is the verdict, is there not a need for a radical solution?

Sin in the Quran

Since we have been looking at some of the negative characteristics of human nature, we need to relate these more broadly to the nature of sin in the Quran. The words for sin in the Quran share root meanings with similar words in other Middle-Eastern languages and cultures. Instead of focusing on the root meanings of words, which are often used interchangeably, it is more helpful to identify the relevant elements of a quranic world view.

In the Quran, as in the Bible, *God* is related to *humans* through a *covenant*.[16] This covenant is not like those between equal parties, but is in the form of the Mosaic covenant (Exodus 20). In it, on the basis of the care of the Lord (vs. 2), the subjects must abide by certain stipulations (the Decalogue).[17]

The idea of a covenant is more marginal in the Quran than in the Bible; nevertheless covenants are made at the time of Adam (20:115/114), Noah, Abraham, Moses, and Jesus (33:7). Unlike the Bible, all the covenants that are mentioned here seem to be in the Mosaic form—only indicating obligations by humans (e.g., 2:83/77-84/78; 5:7/10).

Three biblical aspects of the covenant appear in the Quran:
—the *personal* element,
—the covenant's *revealed*ness,
—its forming the basis of *the law.*

There are three aspects of the covenant that are significant for an understanding of sin in the Quran as in the Bible. First, there was a *personal* element behind the moral law. God himself gave the covenantal commands in the Quran (5:7/10) as in the Bible (Exodus 10:1-2). Thus sin was not mere aberration from cosmic harmony as in ancient Egyptian religion,[18] but was the breaking of a relationship and disobedience or rebellion against God (7:77/75; 10:15/16; 50:24/23; Isaiah 59:2, 13; Nehemiah 9:26).

The Quran does not have a highly personal confession like Psalm 51:4: "Against You, You only, have I sinned." Nor does it develop the personal human analogies found in Hosea (where sin against God is compared to marital unfaithfulness) or in the story of the Prodigal Son (Luke 15:11-32). But God is behind the covenant; so sin is *proud self-assertion* on the part of humans (e.g., 25:21/23; 38:74/75-75/76; 96:6-7; Psalm 10:2-6; 1 Timothy 3:16). When humans become anthropocentric as in the "tribal humanism"[19] of pre-Islamic Arabia, rather than theocentric, it is sin.

The second significant aspect of the covenant for an understanding of sin is that it is *revealed* (3:81/75-84/78; 5:47/51-48/52). Thus sin is *disbelief* (e.g., 3:86/80). In contrast to ancient Mesopotamian religion where this revelational element is not found, the Quran, like the Bible, adds this element of sin.[20]   Although Sura 7:28/27 indicates that the pagan Arabs claimed divine sanctions for their traditional practices, the religious ideas—especially in northern and central Arabia—were vague. The Quran gave a clear idea of revelation; so sin as disbelief took on a new clarity.

The third and most prominent characteristic of the covenant is that it forms the basis of *Law*. Sin, then, is *transgression* of that law (2:229; 66:6; Joshua 7:11; 1 Samuel 15:24; Nehemiah 9:26; 1 Timothy 1:9). This is in contrast to the paganism of Arabia where people's actions were based on common practice. Quranic law, like biblical law, was not based on the Ideal or an abstract idea of law as in ancient Greece. Rather it is God's revealed will expressed through his commands. Although the concept of the Scriptures being on a "Preserved Tablet" in heaven (85:22; cf. 43:4/3) might be interpreted as indicating a static concept of the revealed law, the progressive nature of the commands to meet new situations gives a more dynamic concept of law in the Quran. As in early Israel, the ideal community in the Quran was a theocracy. Hence the law applied to every area of life.

Although the Quran does not spiritualize the law to the extent the Bible does, it recognizes that the heart attitude is more important than the external act.

The Quran never spiritualizes the law to the extent of some of the biblical writers—especially in the New Testament. Jesus considered the Pharisees sinful because of their pride, even though they strictly observed the Jewish Law (Matthew 12:34; Luke 18:11-14). Nevertheless, the Quran recognizes that the heart attitude is more important than the external act (see, e.g., 2:173/168).

The greater contrast relates to the function of the law. In the New Testament the law is considered important (Matthew 5:17; John 14:15; Romans 7:7, 20) but insufficient (Matthew 5:20; Romans 3:20). It requires a righteousness it does not give the power to perform. Thus the New Testament spells out the human predicament of which we have seen evidences in the Quran and its interpreters.

Extra-Quranic Witness

Obviously space only permits an even more cursory glance at materials outside the Quran. All we shall seek to show is that there continues to be an awareness in the Muslim community that there is a basic problem in human nature.

Traditions

The most celebrated traditionist al-Bukhari attributed to Muhammad the words, "Satan touches every child when it is born, whereupon it starts crying loudly, except Mary and her son."[21] This idea of something that needs to be corrected from the earliest stage of development is found even in Muhammad according to his earliest biographer, who quotes him as saying:

> Two men in white raiment...opened up my belly,
> extracted my heart and split it; then they extracted a
> black drop from it and threw it away; then they washed
> my heart and my belly with snow until they had
> thoroughly cleaned them.[22]

What is wrong becomes more specific in a tradition of Ibn Hanbal (164-241 A.H./780-855 A.D.), who lent his name to one of the orthodox schools of law. He relates that the companions of Muhammad confessed to him that "we have no control over our hearts." He did not take issue with their awareness of their condition but directed them to the quranic statement "God charges no soul save to its capacity" (2:286).[23]

In the discussion "Adam and Eve Revisited" above, we have noted traditions of Muhammad from the canonical or semi-canonical collections which indicate that Adam and Eve's descendents not only repeat their sins but have a deficiency.

.i.Theology;

When we move on into the development of Muslim theology and philosophy, we see the theme of *al-nafs al-ammara* (the uncontrolled appetitive soul or carnal desire) running throughout its literature.[24] It is always there to lead astray.

The eleventh-century Islamic fundamentalist Ibn Hazm believed that the human soul, if left to itself, would spontaneously incline to dishonesty. The near-contemporary Muslim theologian al-Ghazali believed that the fall is repeated for each individual.

Ibn Hazm (384-456 A.H./994-1064 A.D.), a champion of fundamentalist doctrine, believed that the human soul, if left to itself, spontaneously inclines to dishonesty.[25] What could be closer to a Pauline view of human nature?

The most celebrated of all Muslim theologians al-Ghazali (450-505 A.H./1058-1111 A.D.) believed that the fall is repeated for each individual. He identified in humans four kinds of base inclinations: those of savage animals, those of the beast, those inspired by the devil, and those arising from pride and ambition.[26] The Christian would certainly agree that each individual repeats the sin of Adam and would see the act as arising from pride and ambition as we rebel against our creaturehood and the obedience due our Creator.

Shi'ite Thinkers

Turning to contemporary Shi'ite thinkers, we see a clear awareness of evil in human nature. The internationally recognized scholar Sayyed Hossein Nasr, while believing there is a way of escape, speaks of the "limited prison" of a person's "carnal soul."[27]

One of the clearest analyses of human nature was given by Imam Khomeini on the occasion of the Inauguration of President Khamene'i on September 4, 1985, when he said of humankind:

> If the whole world is gathered and given to him, he will not feel satisfied. You see that the mighty who have great power seek more power...Arrogance should be stopped and ego should be controlled in everything.

The downfall of man is that he wants absolute power, i.e., the power of God.[28]

Considering the human predicament, is not a person's appropriate response: "God make an atonement for me!"? If this is true, is not the answer the cry of the publican in the temple (Luke 18:13)? And should not the cry be more than just the common translation "God be *merciful* to me a sinner?" Should it not be the more specific one supported by the Greek: "God make an *atonement* for me"?

To underline his basic premise Khomeini urged:

> You should pay attention and all of us should pay attention [to the fact] that man's calamity is his carnal desires, and this exists in everybody, and it is rooted in the nature of man.[29]   Amen!

NOTES

1. Badru D. Kateregga and David W. Shenk, *Islam and Christianity* (Nairobi: Uzima Press Ltd., 1980), p. 109.

2. Isma'il R. al-Faruqi, *Islam* (Niles, IL: Argus Communications, 1979), p. 10.

3. *Sahih al-Bukhari: Arabic-English*, trans. Muhammad Muhsin Khan (Beirut: Dar Al Arabia, 1985), VI, 284 (Bk. 60, chap. 230, trad. 298).

4. For interpretations of the meaning of the common quranic reflexive verb "to wrong oneself," see Muhammad Kamil Husain, "The Meaning of *Zulm* in the Qur'an," trans. and ed. Kenneth Cragg, *Muslim World*, XLIX (1959), pp. 196-212.

5. Abu Ja'far al-Tabari, *The Commentary on the Qur'an (Jami al-Bayan 'an Ta'wil ay al-Qur'an)*, trans. and ed. J. Cooper (Oxford: Oxford University Press, 1987), p. 251.

6. Al-Tabari, *Jami al-Bayan* (Cairo: Dar al-Ma'arif, 1332/1954), I, 535-36 in Mahmoud Ayoub, *The Qur'an and Its Interpreters*, I (Albany: State University of New York Press, 1984), 84.

7. *Mishkat al-Masabih*, trans and ed. James Robson (Lahore: Sh. Muhammad Ashraf, 1963), I, 23 (Bk. 1, Chap. 4, Sec. 1).

8. "The Meaning of *Zulm*," p. 205.

9. *Jami al-Bayan* (Cairo, 1954 ed.), I, 524-26 in Ayoub, p. 83.

10. *Mishkat*, I, 31 (Bk. 1, chap. 4, sec. 3).

11. *Kitab al-Tabaqat al-Kabir*, I (Leiden, 1905), 11-16 in *A Reader on Islam*, ed. Arthur Jeffery ('s-Gravenhage: Mouton & Co., 1962), p. 190.

12. "The Story of Adam" (*Qissat Adam*), trans. and ed. Kenneth E. Nolin, *Muslim World*, LIV (1964), 7.

13. "Man and His Perfection in Muslim Theology,", XLIX (1959), 22-23.

14. Of help in preparing this section has been an unpublished paper by Ernest Hahan, "The Response of Nations to Their Prophets" (Toronto: Fellowship of Faith for Muslims, 1982).

15. Husain, "The Meaning of *Zulm*," p. 205.

16. On the relationship between biblical and quranic covenants, see Arthur Jeffery, *The Quran as Scripture* (New York: Russell F. Moore, 1952),   pp. 39-41.

17. For an analysis of the form and its antecedents, see George E. Mendenhall, *Law and Covenant in Israel and the Ancient Near East* (Reprinted from *The Biblical Archaeologist*, XVII (1954, pp. 26-46, 49-76) (Pittsburgh: the Biblical Colloquium, 1955), pp. 32-34.

18. See John A. Wilson, *The Burden of Egypt* (Chicago: Chicago University Press, 1951), p. 48; Henri Frankfort, *Ancient Egyptian Religion* (New York: Columbia University Press, 1948), pp. 73-74.

19. See W. Montgomery Watt, (Oxford: Carendon Press, 1960), pp. 24-25.

20. See George Ernest Wright, *The Biblical Doctrine of Man in Society* (London: SCM Press, 1954), p. 30n; Theophile J. Meek, trans. "The Code of Hammurabi," *Ancient Near Eastern texts*, ed. James B. Pritchard (Princeton: Princeton University Press, 1955), pp. 163-80.

21. *Sahih al-Bukhari*, VI, 54 (Bk. 60, chap. 54, trad. 71).

22. Ibn Hisham, ed., *The Life of Muhammad*: (Ibn) Ishaq's *Sirat Rasul Allah*, trans. A. Guillaume (London: Oxford University Press, 1955), p. 72.

23. Ibn Hanbal, no. 3071 in Kenneth Cragg and Marston Speight, *Islam from Within: Anthology of a Religion* (Belmont, CA: Wadsworth Publ. Co., 1980), pp. 90-91.

24. H. A. R. Gibb, "The Structure of Religious Thought in Islam,"   *Muslim World*, XXXVIII (1948), 28.

25. R. Arnaldez, "Ibn Hazm," *Encyclopedia of Islam*, 2nd. ed. (Leiden: E. J. Brill, 1960-), s.v.

26. A. J. Wensick, *La Pensée De Ghazali* (Paris: Adrien-Maisonneuve, 1940), pp. 47-49. For this reference I am indebted to an unpublished paper of Ernest Hahn, "The Unforgivable Sin" (Toronto: Fellowship of Faith for Muslims, 1982).

27. *Ideals and Realities of Islam* (London: George Allen & Unwin, 1966), p. 38.

28. "Islamic Government Does Not Spend for its Own Grandeur," *Kayhan International* (September 4, 1985), p. 3.

29. Ibid.

CHAPTER NINE

CULTURALLY RELEVANT THEMES ABOUT CHRIST

Evertt W. Huffard

Paul communicated the gospel in terms of the historical reality of the death and resurrection of Jesus Christ. It was an event that demanded a response of submission to Christ as Lord because, as Paul wrote, Christ "was put to death for our trespasses and raised for our justification" (Rom. 4:25).

Muslim objections to the event of the Cross spring more from cultural values than from historical criticism.

Muslims have consistently rejected the resurrection and the role of history in God's revelation. However, their opposition to the event of the Cross usually comes as an appeal to cultural values rather than to historical criticism.

This chapter will identify a cultural theme that significantly influences evangelical theology. It will also contrast that theme with the presuppositions reflected in the Muslim response to the Christian message.

While Muslims and Christians worship the same God, each group's criteria for the uniqueness of the divine nature reflects a different socio-cultural context.

While both faiths worship the same God, their criteria for the uniqueness of the divine nature reflects the socio-cultural context of each group. To communicate effectively, there is a need, as Kenneth Cragg has shown, for each to understand the other's world view.

The issue, then, between Islamic and Christian theology is not about acknowledging God rightly, which we both seek to do. It is about how, and by what criteria, he is rightly recognized. What we both need here is not recrimination about our theologies but patience about their frames of reference.[1]

The Cross and the Theme of Love

From the earliest efforts to communicate the gospel to Muslims, evangelists have usually begun with what they identified as the irreducible minimum of the Christian message. It was the message that had moved them to a life of service and sacrifice. A few examples from the past and present will illustrate this observation.

To the Muslim, love is not the essential theme it is to the Christian. Nor does the Muslim see the Cross as an expression of God's love.

Raymond Lull, the first missionary to Muslims, challenged Islam for its lack of love. When he sailed for Tunis in 1292, at the age of 60, two of the many books he had written were *The Book of Love and the Beloved* and *The Tree of Love*. Lull, a mystic and poet, identified love as the distinctive element of Christianity. Zwemer quotes him as saying:

> ...inasmuch as the Christians believe more than this,
> and affirm that God so loved man that He was willing to
> become man, to endure poverty, ignominy, torture, and
> death for his sake, which Jews and Saracens do not teach
> concerning Him; therefore is the religion of the
> Christians, which thus reveals a Love beyond all other
> love, superior to that of those which reveals it only in an
> inferior degree. Islam is a loveless religion.[2]

Rahbar, among others, would agree that traditional orthodox Islam is far less concerned with the theme of love. He observed that "unqualified Divine love for mankind is an idea completely alien to the Quran."[3]

In 1933 an editorial in a Cairo newspaper made the claim that the death and resurrection of Christ were not vital elements of the Christian faith. The Muslim writer assumed that Christianity was "a religion for the inculcation of monotheism, morality and ethics" like Islam and Judaism. Temple Gairdner wrote a response to explain the necessity of the Cross as a prerequisite to glory, based on the statement of Christ to the disciples on the road to Emmaus (Lk. 24:26). However, Gairdner did not develop that text. He shifted from this theme of glory and honor to the personal love of God:

> Yes, God was essentially in Him. Therefore in the crucified
> Messiah the perfect holiness and perfect love of God, uni-
> ted, were shown forth, demonstrated to the whole world
> on the stage of place and time...The message of this was
> carried everywhere by those who received it. And thus
> mankind perceived the extent of its sin and the extent of
> the love of God: the nations perceived it: individuals per-
> ceived it: "I" perceived it. It was "for the world," "for me."[4]

In more recent years, authors such as Kenneth Cragg and Phil Parshall have expressed a similar theology of love. Cragg will take Christian themes and find parallels or potential parallels within Islamic theology. In this process he has identified love as the irreducible minimum:

> It has often seemed to me that the Christian could "inset" the whole Christian drama of "God in Christ" within the *Bismillah*. He believes that in the love which in Christ undertakes our human tragedy the eternal mercy, or grace, of God becomes operative in an enterprise which suffices for our human salvation and authenticates to us, in the face of evil, the almightiness of God as love...At all events, it is the New Testament's theme of divine initiative through the love that suffers which anchors me to my Christian conviction.[5]

He has also suggested that Muslims who believe in Christ be called "lovers of Jesus."[6]

Parshall develops the theme of love as an important thematic bridge to folk Muslims because it is the force behind God's involvement in history:

> Love is a supra-cultural truth. This concept is part of every religion of the world...Man acknowledges the need to love and be loved, both on a human and a divine level. To the mystic, love is the very core of his being...So there is a necessity to point out that love is the motivation for God's divine plan for the redemption of sinful man.[7]

Abdol Massih, in the compendium on *The Gospel and Islam*, identified love as the "Key to incarnational witness."[8] But we must ask, the key for whom—the speaker or the hearer?

Are there not cultural reasons why to the Western ear, "God is love" rings better than "God is Spirit," "God is just" or "God is true"?

Lull, Zwemer, Gairdner, Cragg, and Parshall are just a few examples of the prevailing power of the theme of love as the "core" of the gospel of Christ. When we begin to study Scriptures with an Islamic set of questions in mind, we are challenged to raise the question of why our Christology places much greater emphasis on one specific theme within the Johannine corpus (specifically 3:16; I Jn. 3:1; 4:7-11) rather than another theme in Scripture. What influence does our cultural context, with its individualistic presuppositions, have on our theology? Why, for example, does "God is love" (Jn 4:16) have a better ring to Western ears than "God is Spirit" (Jn 4:24), "God is just" (2 Thess. 1:6), or "God is true" (Jn 3:33)?

These are serious questions in view of the fact that Muslims do not see the love of God in the cross nor do they feel compelled to limit their theology to such a theme.

The Muslim Response

In 781 A.D., Caliph Mahdi defended the Muslim rejection of the Cross by appealing to our assumed ethic: "It was not honorable to Jesus Christ that God should have allowed Him to be delivered to Jews in order that they might kill Him."[9] In the dialogue between Kateregga and Shenk, the Sunni Muslim made it clear that a suffering prophet would not be morally acceptable or honorable:

> Muslims believe that Allah saved the Messiah from the ignominy of crucifixion much as Allah saved the Seal of the Prophets from ignominy following *Hijra* ...the scheme of moral values on which Christian conduct is based is somewhat similar to that of Muslims, although *love is made to supersede every other moral value in Christianity* [emphasis mine]. This over-stressing of "love" in all aspects of the Christian life has at times, in Muslims eyes, rendered the Christian ideal of conduct more theoretical than practical.[10]

An Iranian student rejected the Cross for the same reason:

> We honor him (Jesus) more than you do...Do we not honor him more than you do when we refuse to believe that God would permit him to suffer death on the cross? Rather, we believe that God took him to heaven.[11]

Sayyed Hossein Nasr, a Shi'ite philosopher, hurls a similar challenge. He presents Muslim theology as more holistic than any other religion by bringing about an equilibrium in life through the Shari'ah:

> In this sense its [Islam's] method is in contrast to Christianity in which love plays the central role and sacrifice is the outstanding virtue. For this very reason Christians have often criticized Islamic virtues as being mediocre and contributing simply to a social equilibrium whereas the Christian love of sacrifice seems to a Muslim as a kind of individualism which breaks the universal relationship between what is natural in man and the Divine Being. Yet, both the Islamic virtues leading to equilibrium which prepares the ground for contemplation and the Christian stress on love and sacrifice are means whereby man can escape the limited prison of his carnal soul and come to realize the lofty end for which he was put on earth.[12]

The epistemological basis for the Muslim denial of the event of the cross rests on a single *ayat* in the Quran. While acceptance of the divine authority assumes that God only has to speak (once), and it is, there is evidence throughout the Quran that repetition and hyperbole are used according to rhetorical and literary styles of Arabic for stress and emphasis of important commands. This being the case, the opposition to the Cross is so strong among Muslims one would expect at least a whole Sura dedicated to the reasons why Allah would not allow such to happen to one of his great prophets. However, the Quran almost ignores the Cross. The only reference reads:

> ...and for their [the Jews'] saying: "We slew the Messiah, Jesus son of Mary, the Messenger of God"—yet they did not slay him, neither crucified him, only a likeness of that [shubiha lahum] was shown to them. Those regarding him; they have no knowledge of him, except the following of surmise; and they slew him not of a certainty—no indeed; God raised him up to Him; God is All-mighty, All-wise (4:157/156-157).

The vagueness of this text produced a wide range of interpretations in the history of Quranic study.[13] Therefore, with so little Quranic support, we must search elsewhere for the source of the Islamic rejection of the Cross. There are historical, cultural and political factors to consider. Cragg has observed that "there is the historical denial of its actuality, the moral refusal of its possibility and the doctrinal rejection of its necessity."[14]

All of these reasons are not of equal importance. Since historical evidence is of limited epistemological value in Islamic theology; and the Quran gives little doctrinal instruction for rejecting the Cross, the primary source of opposition is cultural, a difference in world view.

I am of the opinion that if this ayat did not exist in the Quran or if a Muslim were persuaded to exegete it within its immediate context, admitting that it may not be strong enough evidence to deny the crucifixion, he or she would still reject the gospel as it has been communicated. When the gospel message is confined to a theme the Muslims cannot accept, and when Muslims so contextualize Allah that His nature is limited by their own cultural value system, communication becomes impossible.

Conflicting Paradigms

Evangelical theology is heavily influenced by a Western individualistic world view that amplifies the values of freedom, equality and personal love. On the other hand, Islamic theology has a symbiotic relationship with a community deeply rooted in the group-oriented pre-Islamic Arab culture that champions the values of honor, authority and loyalty.

In very broad sweeping terms, the Western Christian [specifically the American middle class] lives within an individualistic society where relationships are expected to be horizontal. Fathers want to be buddies and friends to their sons; all people are to be treated equally. Social relationships are maintained by love and shared interests. Personal rights are valued to the extreme of lawlessness or relativism in society. The stress on a "personal Savior" in Evangelical circles disturbs the Muslim as an attempt to bring God down to the human level.

The Arab Muslim lives within a group-oriented context where vertical relationships have priority. The group/ vertical structure is maintained by loyalty to the family and respect for authority. Fathers want to be respected and honored by their sons; people are treated on the basis of their status and age. The cultural theme most valued is honor and the greatest fear is shame. This cultural value is often pushed to the limits of pride and aloofness in a secular context, and to deism in the religious sense.

The paradigms that emerge from the themes of love and honor find their fullest expression within the family. For the American family, mate selection is based on a personal free choice after which the couple lives independent of their parents. Love is assumed to be the starting point and sole criteria for the relationship. If a husband and wife in the American society become "incompatible," there are far fewer concerns about dishonoring their vows than about demanding personal rights. It is assumed that if love no longer exists, divorce is justifiable.

Within the Arab Muslim family structure, relationships begin with honor and grow in love. Love is not the only consideration in the selection of a mate. The mate must be one that honors the family. Thus, a man may not marry the woman he loves but he learns to love the woman he marries. The couple must then live in a good relationship with each other and the community because divorce would bring unforgivable shame on the whole extended family.

Muslims are convinced they honor Jesus more than Christians do.

The theological; implications of these social phenomena may be obvious. Muslims would see nothing but shame in the Cross and must do all they can to defend the honor of Jesus as a prophet of Allah. Thus, they are convinced that they honor Jesus more than Christians do. And the preoccupation with the need to bring all people to the love of Jesus seems to them unnecessary.

Christian evangelists, on the other hand, prefer stressing the humility of Christ, the equality of Christ with humans and the evidence of God's love for all humankind. The Cross is valued as the event that confirms the love of God for all humankind, due to his willingness to be like us, one of us, and with us. That is, in the incarnation and the Cross, God identified himself with humans (Phil. 2:6-8). What God did through Christ was for us. The evangelistic goal then is to help a new believer "fall in love" with God in response to the loving sacrifice of Jesus. However, to the Muslim, this Christology is too anthropocentric and does not honor God adequately.

Must all relationships with God begin with love? What other biblical values belong in our criteria for the worship of God?

The contrasts in paradigms raises new questions for both the Christian and Muslim. As a Christian, I can only address the new questions on my side of the dialogue (and would urge the Muslim to do likewise). For example, must all relationships with God begin with love? Are there other biblical values that should be included in our criteria for the worship of God? If so, could one initially respond to God at any other juncture and leave love to the work of the Spirit in the Christian maturation process? The quest for answers to such questions may constitute the initiation of a valid incarnational witness among Muslims.

Seeking Culturally Relevant Themes

The fact that the synoptic Gospels make very little reference to the love of God, and that Luke says nothing about *agape* in Acts, could suggest that the theme of love was not as fundamental to the *kerygma* of the early church as it has become today.

The assumption that agape is the copyright and "core" of the Christian faith precludes the possibility of any other starting point in a relationship with God. Although the importance of love in the Christian life (as per 1 Cor. 13) as a motive for discipleship and missions is unquestionable, there are other biblically valid themes to be considered, such as blessing and honor.

As in Muslim marriage, which is based initially on honor rather than on love, the biblical theme of blessing rates high in the Muslim concept of relationship to God.

The desire for blessing is prominent in the Quran and is a primary felt need in daily life throughout the Middle East and Africa. A blessing is conferred on a family when a son is born, when the ritual of circumcision is observed, and when the "right" marriage is made. In the community, the blessings of God are confirmed in prosperity and power. The Muslims attribute all these factors of daily life to God as the ultimate source of blessing.

Scripture passages on blessing can serve well as points of contact in Christian witness to Muslims.

Larry Lenning has developed the theme of blessing as a theological; bridge for Muslim evangelism in Africa. In *Blessing in Mosque and Mission* [15] he identifies eight New Testament passages in which God is the source of blessings in fulfillment of his promise to Abraham (Mt. 25:34; Ac. 3:25-26; Gal. 3:8-9, 14; Eph. 1:3; Heb. 6:7-8, 12-15; I Pe. 3:9).

The blessings of God were included in Paul's defense of the necessity of the Cross. To those who could not accept it, he wrote:

> Christ redeemed us from the curse of the law, having become a curse for us—for it is written, "Cursed be every one who hangs on a tree"—that in Christ Jesus the blessing of Abraham might come upon the Gentiles, that we might receive the promise of the Spirit through faith (Gal. 3:8-9).

The redeemed were reminded that blessing is not an end in itself but is a means to a holy and blameless life:

> Blessed be the God and Father of our Lord Jesus Christ, who has blessed us in Christ with every spiritual blessing in the heavenly places, even as he chose us in him before the foundation of the world, that we should be holy and blameless before him (Eph. 1:3-4).

Those who live in an extended family setting know the value of being blameless. For them, "blamelessness" is synonymous with honor. One maintains honor by living without shame or blame in the community.[16]

John saw in Jesus a quality of life that fully revealed the blameless nature of God. In the *doxa* of the Lord, God showed his grace and truth (Jn. 1:14). No one can blame God for breaking a covenant with Noah or Abraham. Jesus fulfilled the promises of God and proved his word was good.

To summarize, a legitimate response to the Cross could be a response to the love of God [implying a horizontal relationship vis-a-vis the incarnation and personal gift (Jn. 3:16)] or to the honor of God [suggesting a vertical relationship vis-a-vis Lordship and submission (Jn. 5:22-26; Phil. 2:9-11)]. The limitations of world view may prevent us from seeing more than one aspect of God's divine nature.

Does not a biblically-based Christology bridge both worlds and at the same time challenge both?

The Christian and the Muslim must be reminded that God cannot be limited by our cultural categories. A biblically-based Christology has the power to bridge both worlds and at the same time challenge both. Did not Jesus do this in his personal ministry? For instance, the Jews bound God to their Sabbath sanctions, prohibiting him from healing on the Sabbath. However, Jesus defended his Sabbath activity by saying, "My Father is always at work to this very day, and I, too, am working" (Jn. 5:17).

Islamic theology amplifies the transcendence of God while evangelical theology amplifies the immanence of God. Instead of exploring the doctrinal and historical reasons for this, our immediate missiological concern is bridging the cultural and theological gap. The post-resurrection appearance of Christ to Mary illustrates both natures of God in Christ. He called Mary by name, implying some degree of intimacy, but did not allow her to embrace him, maintaining some distance (Jn. 20:16-17). He was like humans from birth to death, but was transcendent in that he never dishonored God, as all humans do.

Christ's death and resurrection is a greater sign of power than his avoidance of death could have been.

When God makes his will known to humans, can we not expect it to be in a flawless form—be it written or personal? Would there not be justification within a monotheistic theology to claim that God's honor and power would be more obvious in a perfect, loyal and honorable human than just in a perfect written Word? If so, the death and resurrection of Christ would be a greater sign of power than the avoidance of death.

Humans fear and avoid death because they cannot create life but God transcends human limits. Is it the "*shubiha lahum*" (the likeness of a crucifixion of Jesus; 4:157) or the resurrection that reveals the true nature of the "*al-Asma' al-Husna*" (the Beautiful Names of God)?

Cragg raises a similar question when he asks: "Is it possible that you can be found forbidding things to God in the interest of what you think is his dignity?"[17] Cragg responds with a phrase that has become a worthy trademark in most of his publications, namely: "Let God be God."[18]

Paul encountered constant and violent opposition to the message of the Cross. For Muslims, as for Jews, it is a stumbling block to a faithful response to God (I Cor. 1:23). But are there not those who have greater difficulty with the paradigm employed to interpret the event?

To deny the centrality of the event to the gospel is syncretism. A contextualized Christology for Muslim evangelism must also begin with that event but could employ a paradigm to stress the vertical relationships between God, Christ and humans. If we were to use the paradigm of honor in expressing the meaning of the Cross to Muslims, our Christology would have much more to say about loyalty, generosity and blamelessness in understanding the glory of God as revealed through Christ.

1. The Loyalty of Christ

God's honor was established in Gethsemane and on the Cross by the loyalty of Christ to God and to his divine will. This testifies to the fact that Christ is not another god or a "partner" with God, which is *shirk* [cf. Cragg's informative discussion of "what Christology is not, what Shirk is, and what is not Shirk."][19]

As a mediator between God and humans, Christ is blameless. As any mediator in an Arab community knows, mediation involves vulnerability. The honor of the mediator is always put to the test and only a few people could qualify to settle a dispute between two families or villages. Christ had to be vulnerable but he served the purposes of God and humans unlike any prophet in history.

The cultural hermeneutic of Islam assumes God is limited by the same parameters of death as humans. Therefore, they try to "help" Christ avoid the cross. A theology of honor affirms that the glory, transcendence and authority of God is best realized by performing something beyond all human capabilities but in harmony with the nature of God—a "re-creation," or a resurrection.

In the Old Testament, false prophets were those who tried to circumvent the plans of God. The most vivid example comes from Jeremiah. He prophesied the exile would last for 70 years (29:10-11) but Hananiah claimed it would be two years (28:13) and Shemaiah a short time (28:27-28). Both prophets were punished for rebellion against the Lord. They tried to reason away the plans of God. "For I know the plans I have for you, says the Lord, plans for welfare and not for evil, to give you a future and a hope" (29:11). The parallel to the Cross seems appropriate.

By cultural norms, the exile was a shameful event in Hebrew history, for the temple of YHWH, representing his presence among people, was destroyed. The surrounding nations might assume YHWH was too weak to protect his own dwelling place. To cover the "shame," false prophets tried to defend God's honor, as they saw it, by assuming it would only be temporary. Although they may have feared the possibility that defeat represented the death of Israel and YHWH, they were unattentive to God's plan, one beyond their comprehension but for their good. To reason away the need for the Cross circumvents the loyalty of Jesus to God's will—to a divine plan beyond human reason, one to give us "a future and a hope."

2. The Generosity of God

In an Arab village the cultural code of reciprocity requires honorable responses. To deny the Cross, they need to see, is a refusal to accept God's generosity, thus dishonoring the giver.

Secondly, the Cross is more than a theological abstraction expressed in terms of propitiation and reconciliation. In a very real sense, it was the fullest expression of the generosity of God. As recipients of God's generosity (grace), the cultural code of reciprocity in an Arab village requires honorable responses. To deny the Cross is a refusal to accept the generosity of God; it is to dishonor the giver.

As Paul pleads, "you were bought with a price, so glorify God in your bodies" (I Co. 6:20). Paul assumed his audience knew how to honor God in their bodies as they would honor their family and community, by maintaining a blamelessness in the transitions of life and graciously accepting the gift of God— eternal life.

3. The Blamelessness of God

Muslims reject the Cross as morally unacceptable, as if the resurrection were an impossibility for God. That is, they assume Jesus would not be honored if allowed to die on the cross. Quite true, if he were left in the tomb. But, could God not exercise the same power displayed in the beginning to recreate life in Christ? If so, God could not be blamed for abandoning a prophet, forgetting his promise, or dishonoring Jesus.

In a Christology of the honor of God, Christ's resurrection day confirmed and revealed God's blamelessness.

A Christology of the honor of God in contrast to the love of God interprets the day of the resurrection of Christ as the day the blamelessness of God was historically confirmed and revealed to all people. His promises were fulfilled and his generosity revealed.

By far the most frequent use of *doxa* (glory) in the New Testament is in reference to the resurrected Lord (cf. Rom. 6:4; I Co. 2:7-8; Heb. 2:10). Twice John notes that certain statements regarding Jesus were made before he received *doxa* (7:39), and shows that his death would be an occasion to honor God (21:19). God confirmed his moral dignity and honor in faithfulness to a covenant. He was transformed from shame to glory.

The human response to God's glory is obedience and submission. Thus Paul relates the glory of the resurrection to baptism:

> We were buried therefore with him by baptism into death, so that as Christ was raised from the dead by the glory [honor] of the Father, we too might walk in newness of life (Rom. 6:4).

Baptism is not accompanied by some strange physical phenomena or bright lights (as some may limit the meaning of *doxa*). But, with each baptism, the credibility, the blamelessness, the trustworthiness, and the promises of God are confirmed. All people can live new lives because they are upheld by the blamelessness of God—a quality of the divine nature that responded with power to Jesus in death on the cross. It is a human response to the Cross because of a similar process of the "bringing of many sons to glory" (Heb. 2:10).

Peter believed many "honors" would follow the crucifixion. What were these honors (*doxa*: "glories" in KJV, RSV, NIV) that were to follow (I Pe. 1:11)? Were they a series of strange phenomena? Certainly the walking through walls, the Ascension and the Pentecost experience would qualify. But the submission to God, as seen in Thomas' exclamation of lordship (Jn. 20:28), and the renewed and dynamic fervor of the apostles, and the expression of repentance at Pentecost also confirm the continued glorification of God among people in grace and truth.

God's nature was revealed in Christ in a way it had never been. His glory was no longer trapped within the Holy of Holies of the temple, for Jesus became the full exegesis of God

(Jn. 1:18). Even Abraham would rejoice in seeing the fulfillment of God's promise to him (Jn. 8:49-56).

As churches in every generation fulfill the mission of Christ they share in the honor and glory of God among all nations. Peter knew his hope was based on God's blameless response to the Cross. "Through him you have confidence in God, who raised him from the dead and gave him glory, so that your faith and hope are in God" (I Pe. 1:21). That glory, as Paul would observe, is maintained in the community of faithful disciples:

> Now to him who by the power at work within us is able to do far more abundantly than all we ask or think, to him be glory in the church and in Christ Jesus to all generations for ever and ever (Eph. 3:20-21).

Could it be that the greatest struggle Paul had in his quiet time in Arabia was the shift from his rabbinic paradigm to "Let God be God"? He had to adjust his world view to the possibility of the Cross and the implications of a risen Lord.

NOTES

1. Kenneth Cragg, *Jesus and the Muslim: An Exploration* (London: George Allen and Unwin, 1985), 191.

2. Zwemer, 1902, cited in Francis M. Dubose, ed. *Classics of Christian Missions* (Nashville: Broadman, 1979), 127.

3. Daud Rahbar, *God of Justice* (Leiden: E.J. Brill, 1960), 172.

4. W.H. Temple Gairdner, "The Essentiality of the Cross," in *The Muslim World* 23 (1933): 250.

5. Kenneth Cragg, "Being Christian and Being Muslim: A Personal Debate," in *Religion* 10 (1980): 203.

6. Kenneth Cragg, *The Call of the Minaret* (Maryknoll, NY: Orbis, 1985), 319.

7. Phil Parshall, *Bridges to Islam* (Grand Rapids: Baker, 1983), 130.

8. Abdol Massih, "The Incarnational Witness to the Muslim Heart," in *The Gospel and Islam*, ed. Don McCurry (Monrovia, CA: MARC, 1979), 85.

9. Quoted by J. Windrow Sweetman, *Islam and Christian Theology* Part 1, Vol. 1 (London: Lutterworth, 1945), 31.

10. Badru D. Kateregga and David W. Shenk, *Islam and Christianity: A Muslim and a Christian in Dialogue* (Nairobi: Usima Press, 1980), 141-142, 163.

11. Livingston Bently, "Christ and the Cross," in *The Muslim World* 41 (1951): 5.

12. Sayyed Hossein Nasr, *Ideals and Realities of Islam* (London: George Allen and Unwin, 1966), 38.

13. Cf. Mahmoud M. Ayoub, "Towards an Islamic Christology (II): The Death of Jesus, Reality or Delusion?" in *The Muslim* World 70 (1980) 2: 101-102.

14. Kenneth Cragg, "Islamic Theology: Limits and Bridges," in *The Gospel and Islam*, ed. Don McCurry (Monrovia, CA: MARC, 1979), 202.

15. Larry G. Lenning, *Blessing in Mosque and Mission* (Pasadena: William Carey Library, 1980).

16. Cf. Evertt W. Huffard, *Thematic Dissonance in the Muslim-Christian Encounter: A Contextualized Theology of Honor* (Ph.D. diss., Fuller Theological Seminary, 1985), 227-275; Bruce J. Malina, *The New Testament World: Insights From Cultural Anthropology* (Atlanta: John Knox Press, 1981), 45ff.; and Eugene Nida, *Exploring Semantic Structures* (Munich: Fink, 1975), 131-132 for a synchronic study of these terms.

17. Kenneth Cragg, "Legacies and Hopes in Muslim/Christian Theology," in *Islamochristiana* 3 (1977): 9.

18. Ibid., 4 & 10; Cragg, "Islamic Theology,"275; Cragg, "Being Christian," 199; Cragg, "Greater is God," 29; *The Call of the Minaret*, 201.

19. Cragg, *Jesus and the Muslim*, 203ff.

CHAPTER TEN

THE NAMES OF CHRIST IN WORSHIP

Lyle Vander Werff

'The Messiah': Focus for Muslim-Christian Encounter

The basic question: Who is the Christ? Pivotal to Christian-Muslim dialogue and Christian witness to Muslims is the question of the Messiah's identity. Scholarly Muslims and Christians agree that the question that both divides them and holds the promise of their ultimate reconciliation is: "Who is the Christ?"

Dr. Mahmoud M. Ayoub of San Diego State University insists that the crucial issue for Christian-Muslim discussion is Christology. His thesis: "Muslims and Christians can, and must, learn much from the man Jesus of Islam and from Christ the Lord of Christianity."[1]

He argues that Muslim responses to the question, "What think ye of Christ?" (Mt. 22:42) must be taken seriously by Christians, not simply "judged and found wanting." Muslim formulations must be understood before they can be assessed or measured by God's revelations. While we may not be able to accommodate Ayoub's desire for an ecumenism which acknowledges these formulations as "authentic expression of the divine and immutable truth," we can respect this search for an answer concerning Christ's identity and his role in God's sovereign plan. To his credit, Ayoub urges Muslims to

> likewise rethink their own understanding of the true meaning of Islam as the living up to the primordial covenant between God and all human beings and the divine reaffirmation of this covenant in a variety of expressions to a religiously pluralistic world.[2]

Ayoub urges his readers to focus on Christology:

> This can only be achieved through honest and sincere efforts by us all to be existentially involved in the meaning and purpose of our existence in a world of sin and imperfection, but a world sanctified by the divine presence among and within us.[3]

The challenge: To interpret the New Testament for Muslims in a way that considers the Islamic context but does not betray the text.

Kenneth Cragg in *Jesus and the Muslim* agrees that Christology is at the heart of Christian-Muslim encounter. Not only does he bid Christians to study the Islamic portrayal of Jesus in the Quran and Traditions, but to learn how to interpret the New Testament for Muslims in a fashion mindful of the "Islamic situation." Such witness must consider the context but not betray the text. He writes:

> A sensitive Muslim introduction to the New Testament has long been a need, unmet in our relationships. There can be no more urgent desire, in this field, than to have the New Testament seriously read and studied in the Islamic world.

He goes on to say,

> The best way to face them [the issues] is to merge into one the study of the Islamic Jesus and the New Testament Christ, to have the Christian literature through Muslim eyes and the Quranic Jesus for Christian perception.[4]

In admirable fashion, Cragg does just this as he strives to reinterpret the Jesus of the Bible for the Islamic setting. Such an exploration must reach both ways as we live in the hope of what God is yet to do.

Few are as sensitive as Cragg to Islam's "long vista" (*qiblah*) towards Christ. He argues that Christians need to recover the Semitic background of Jesus and to realize how the Quran struggles to recover Jesus from the Jewish distortions and Christian controversies of the seventh century. We need to educate both Christians and Muslims about the milieu in which Islam was born, to generate a historical awareness of what prompted Jewish-Christian-Muslim differences, while at the same time we must witness to the eternal nature of the Christ and his reconciling work in history.

I propose that one way this witness can effectively be made is by a devoted recital of the biblical names of the Christ followed by careful exposition and discussion of the revealed New Testament meaning of these names wherever Muslims show interest. May all be pointed to the glory of God! *Bismillah!*

Respect For Muslims as 'Truth-Seekers/God-Fearers' Who Long For a Fuller Knowledge Of The One True God and His Messiah

Conversing with Muslims over the years, I have been struck by their fascination (and frustration) with Jesus. They are willing to confess so many of the biblical tenets, and yet are left suspended, not being able to pilgrimage farther in their walk with him. Christians are, I believe, to be companions and witnesses to such Muslim brethren so that together they might move beyond fascination and seminal faith into fuller obedience and fulfillment in their common human longing. Even as Jews turning to Jesus find fulfillment, so Muslims submitting to the Messiah can experience maturation to the glory of God. In him the Gentiles rejoice!

I agree with Samuel M. Zwemer's assertion (in 1912): "To help our Moslem brethren to answer this question ["What think ye of Christ?"], we must...lead them up to higher truth by admitting all of the truth which they possess."[5] Christian scholars and missionaries have not always been so considerate of the Muslim's posture concerning Christ. We rejoice, however, in the development of evangelical and ecumenical approaches that are empathetic without compromising the gospel, the hope of humanity.[6]

In my studies of Islam and contacts with Muslims, I have come to appreciate Muhammad's awareness of the One God and the earnest quest of those who bear the name Muslim. The Quran provides clues as to this unfinished search (even though at times Islam gives the impression of the finality of its answer). When one comes to love these "Muslim brethren," he longs that they might share the fullness of God's blessing in the Messiah. This should not curtail our affirmation of any truth declared in Islam that is consistent with the biblical record. Whatever is just and good in other religions will find deeper meaning and final formulation in Christ. All truth is God's truth and it shall finally stand under his advancing rule in his Messiah.[7]

We are...to move beyond the reviling rhetoric and combative apologetics of earlier centuries and...

Fairness and justice oblige Christians to respect such questing by Islam's prophet and peoples. The charity of Christ bids us to move beyond the reviling rhetoric and combative apologetics of earlier centuries and to recover the evangelical spirit and style of Jesus as we reach to our Muslim neighbors.

...to recover the evangelical spirit and style of Jesus as we reach to our Muslim neighbors.

Those who would witness must be in dialogue with Muslims, listening to their longing after God, their struggles and their statements of conviction. Witnesses to Christ must speak of the realities of God, his grace and redemptive rule in Jesus. This may take the form of more conversational exchange, best attained in everyday contact.[8]

Those who would witness of Christ to Muslims must develop an intimate walk with God, a deep spiritual dedication and devotion. Only from that reference point can one recognize a Muslim's hunger for God and address it. Deep speaks unto deep. Effective witnesses are, as Paul writes, "spiritually discerned." They must, as Fenelon said, "practice the presence of God." They must live lives centered in Christ, assured that ultimately "every knee shall bend" to him so that they are not devastated by each contrary wind and storm. Such proleptic celebration provides the patience vital to Christian witness amidst Muslims.

We must appreciate the Meccan background of Muhammad as he fought against its pagan idol worship. Like the Hebrew prophets, he challenged the polytheistic baalism which deified nature and fertility and confused them with God. (Something of his stern reform prevails in the reluctance to employ terms such as "begotten," "sonship" and "three.")[9]

Early in his career at Mecca and again at Medina, Muhammad probably received support from Jews and Christians, but as that waned, tension developed. He was surely frustrated when each group prided itself in what it possessed (Sura 23:53; 30:32) and that they only reported to him those portions of their Book (Sura 3:23; 4:44, 51) which backed their case. The fact that he had only partial access to these earlier successive revelations prompted a longing for the full word of God.[10]

The early Meccan Suras reflect that Muhammad's developing spiritual consciousness was empathetic to the biblical sources. In a sense, the Quran stops with Sura 5, where Jesus remains a "mystery." In the Quran, the title "Christ" (Messiah) is used but never defined. Undiscussed are those profound New Testament mysteries of Jesus' incarnation, trinitarian relations, resurrected Lordship and coming kingdom.[11] The Quranic portrait of Jesus is thus limited but embryonic.

Chronologically, the fifth Sura suggests that Islam still "waits" some fuller disclosure of the Christ who will come again as the Judge. Clearly Muhammad never knew the full gospel delivered by the Apostles, nor the church catholic, nor the fuller New Testament theology that shapes Christian life. He did contend with the distortions of Christianity found among Monophysites, Nestorians, and desert pilgrims but lacked opportunity to attain the larger picture. Massignon often drew attention to Muhammad's longing for genuine knowledge of Jesus Christ. This inner disposition may be found in what is often misinterpreted as a negation. "If the All-Merciful has a son, then I am the first to serve him" (Sura 43:81) is more faithful to the Arabic text than Pickthal's "The Beneficent One hath no son. I am first among the worshippers." The Arabic at this point does not indicate a "contrary to fact condition," but communicates a genuine openness to the truth!

Muhammad argued for a more inclusive view of covenant; he contended against Jewish and Christian exclusiveness. In this he was true to the biblical vision over against some of his ethnocentric critics. There is room for the descendants of Ishmael's line and all peoples in God's promises to Abraham. It is remarkable that "the Table Spread" (title of Sura 5) is a "table spread with food from heaven" (Sura 5:114) not unlike the bread from heaven in the fourth Gospel. Jesus petitions God as "the Best of Sustainers" and serves as host of that table.

The challenge Christians face is to show how the Messiah is truly the mediator of God's sovereign grace and rule (Sura 5:120). The transcendent God does extend his offer to all Muslims and will finally in the Last Judgment require all peoples to submit to his Messiah's authority.

How this mystery of the Messiah's rule will finally gain top priority in Muslim circles leaves all of us who claim to be disciples of Jesus humbled, expectant and hopefully engaged in witnessing.

The Need To Stimulate The Development of Christological Thought Among Muslims

Giulio Basetti-sani is probably correct in suggesting that Islamic Christological development was cut short:

"The Christian apostolate, over 13 centuries, have been unsuccessful because they never found out who the Muslims really are."
—*Giulio Basetti-sani*

This beginning of a progression in the direction of knowledge and acceptance of Christ as Son of God was arrested for centuries, and perhaps turned aside, in the development of Islam after the time of Mohammed. This happened because there was no one to help Islam continue on the right path to the house of the Father and fulfill its role as a catechumenate for the sons of Ishmael. More and more, I have been convinced that the Christian apostolate, over a period of 13 centuries, have always been unsuccessful because they never found out who the Muslims really are. It has never been able to help them retrace their steps to those first miles of the arrested march and lead them toward the complete encounter with Christ, the Son of God, sole Mediator, sole Savior.[12]

The cultural explosion and the military expansion of Islam in the one hundred years after Muhammad aroused the reactionary fears of Christians which in turn found its worst expression in the crusades and the centuries-long cold war of words. Only brave souls among Eastern Christians who were true neighbors to Muslims and exceptional Europeans like Francis of Assisi and Raymond Lull began to thaw the icy barriers prior to the Reformation. Protestants since then have joined Roman Catholic and Orthodox Christians in a search for the path which will lead them to their Muslim neighbors and together to God in Christ.

The King's pattern for proclamation and presence...can cure our dividedness and make of all peoples one household of faith.

We desperately need an evangelical spirit and style to be Christ's instruments of reconciliation and peace. We need to discover the King's pattern for proclamation and presence which is persuasive without compromising, which can cure our dividedness and make of all peoples one household of faith.

Call Muslims to Return to the Roots of Biblical Faith

We must bid Muslims to heed the Quran's injunction to consider and reconsider the former revelations, namely the Law, the Prophets and the Gospel. In a remarkable way, the New Testament is the most complete and normative statement about Jesus the Messiah, and all else is preliminary (O.T.) or commentary (Church Fathers, Talmud, the Creeds, the Quran).

There is merit in struggling to understand the Quranic commentary, for such is the essential history of the Muslim community of believers. The Christological comments of Quran, Hadith, pietistic Muslim literature and modern Muslim preconceptions of Christ warrant careful study.[13]

When it comes to the great issues of faith, the Quran bids its readers to turn to the earlier revelations given to Jews and Christians.

We can appeal to the Quranic injunction that Muslims should consult the other Scriptures (O.T. and N.T.) for the truth. When it comes to the great issues of faith, the Quran bids its readers to turn to the earlier revelations given to Jews and Christians. Sura 10:95 (Pickthall) declares,

> And if thou art in doubt concerning that which We reveal unto thee, then question those who read the Scripture (that was) before thee. Verily the Truth from thy Lord hath come unto thee. So be not thou of the waverers.

This key verse affirms the credibility and authority of the Law and Prophets, the Gospel and Epistles, available in Jewish and Christian circles.

This makes a powerful case for inviting Muslim friends to hear and heed the biblical witness to Jesus the Messiah. Our goal must be to assist Muslims in acquiring the fuller revelation of God's Messiah as fellow servants. Abdul-Haqq writes,

> Therefore, a strategic point of contact between Islam and Christianity is Jesus Christ. About Him we can speak from our Scripture (Injil) to their Scripture (the Koran) legitimately and fruitfully.[14]

Regrettably, Islam has sometimes had a Christian presence without a Christian witness of the Word to give meaning to that observed. Nor can the Word be effective without loving deeds. There were many words, many deeds; bitter words, bitter deeds; but not often the witness of the Word.

Muslims do respect the Word, the Scriptures. We need to learn how to let the Word speak more clearly on its own. We need to rediscover the kerygmatic, declarative approach. This is the hope lying behind a recital of the names of the Messiah. Such recitation may trigger dialogue and fresh reading of the New Testament. It may lead to a theological reconstruction like the Messianic mosque or a "Muslims for the Messiah" movement. Jesus Christ will gain pre-eminence wherever the Spirit works until all declare that "Jesus is Lord."[15]

Other passages commending the revelations of the Old and New Testaments include: Sura 4:163-165; 21:7; 32:23f. The fact that custody of these Scriptures was with Jews and Christians produced tensions and limited access (Sura 2:75-78,113; 3:93f., 98; 5:43f.; 10:95f.) The authority of the Law (Taurat) and Gospel (Injil) is acknowledged and all readers are commanded to believe in the Old Testament and New Testament Scriptures (Sura 2:1-5; 5:46-48, 68f.; 21:7; 62:5). Muslims are warned to receive the whole message and not to reject any part of it (Sura 2:89, 136; 4:136, 150-152; 40:70-72). The whole Bible must be placed in the hands of the whole Muslim world.

Only with the background of the Bible does much of the Quran make sense.

Exactly how should the relationship between the biblical materials and the Quran be defined? Some evangelicals are fearful lest they give the impression that the Quran is on a par with the Bible's authority. To avoid giving this impression, some completely avoid any reference to the Quran. Yet, one's interpretation of the Quran cannot long be hid. One can and should show respect for the prophet's book and yet not abandon loyalty to the authority of the Bible.

Allow the Muslim reader to discover for himself that the Bible is a more complete historical narrative and theological; reflection on God's redemptive, regal actions covering long stretches of time, while the Quran is a historic commentary, didactic in format. The Quran contains little narrated history, but is a book of lessons, warnings, instructions and exhortations. The Torah contains much expository prose, the prophets employ inspired oracles, while the Quran often uses elliptical, sophisticated poetry. The Bible is a composite featuring many authors, the Quran speaks with a solitary voice.

Only with the background of the Bible does much of the Quran make sense. Take for example the Joseph narrative in Genesis which is a necessary backdrop to Sura 12 and its understanding. Such an example should help spur Muslims into reading the biblical record. Radical differences between biblical and Quranic materials have been noted.[16]

Muhammad appears receptive to the counsel of Christians and the former revelations on several occasions.

> And argue not with the People of the Book unless it be in (a way) that is better (fairer), save with such of them as do wrong; and say: We believe in that which hath been revealed unto us and revealed unto you: our God and your God is One, and unto Him we surrender (Sura 29:46).

Muhammad expressed genuine affection for Christians.

This yielding to the authority of the Scriptures, including the *Injil*, is most significant. Muhammad was a man under the Word! If authority was granted by Muhammad to all revelations, then surely the New Testament would be the document par excellence concerning Jesus' death, resurrection and as cension. Muhammad expressed genuine affection for Christians, those who humbly confessed "our Lord" and bore witness to the truth of God's revelation in Christ (Sura 5:82-86).

Muhammad, as I view him, is a radical Arab Protestant Hanif, protesting the cantankerous arguments of his day and the misuses of Scripture while at the same time affirming the authority of these former revelations. It is a tragedy that the Hebrew Old Testament as well as the Greek New Testament were inaccessible to Muhammad, even though translations of Gospels and Pauline Letters in Syriac, Ethiopic and Arabic were beginning to circulate in the region. Equally tragic was Muhammad's lack of training, which compelled him to rely on oral transmitters or his Jewish rivals. Their proud claim to being the exclusive people of the Book surely alienated this prophet of Arabia (Sura 6:156-158).

It appears that Muhammad often appealed to the Scriptures in his deliberations with his contemporaries (Jews, Christians and tribal Arabs) in order to authenticate his own revelation (Sura 4:150-52; 13:36l 26:192-197; 46:10). He contends that the Quran is an attestation to the Bible (Sura 2:89; 3:48; 5:48; 6:93; 35:31; 46:11f.; 46:30).

Muhammad criticizes the Jews for concealing or mishandling the Scriptures (esp. Sura 2), but it is interesting that he never levels such charges against Christians! It must be noted that the Quran itself never develops the charge of the corruption of the Hebrew-Christian Scriptures found later in Islam.

The Quran argues that the words of the Lord cannot be changed (Sura 6:34; 115f.; 10:65). The Quran honors the direct disclosures of God through Jesus Christ, confirming that which came before (Sura 5:46f.; 57:27). The Quran sees Jews and Christians pitted against each other and Muhammad sides with the latter. The Quran defends Jesus Christ against his critics.

The Case For The Names of The Lord's Christ And Their Recitation

Muslims recite the exalted and exalt the recited.

Muslims recite the exalted and exalt the recited. They recite the beautiful names of God and they worship by means of recitation. They esteem the Quran as "the recited revelation," while the Hadiths are unrecited or read disclosures. The idea of recitation carries with it a sense of esteem and authority. The power of the spoken Word prevails.

Concerned Christians must recover the power of the "names of Christ" and their public recital in worship and witness. They need to develop a mode of witness which employs recital of the biblical names and claims of the Messiah.

Sweetman, Cragg, Abdul-Haqq and others have indicated that the great names or titles of Jesus occupy a strategic position in any effective witness to the Messiah's identity and role. Witnesses to Muslims must master an understanding of the biblical list of Messianic titles, probing deep into their biblical meaning and addressing these to the Muslim context/Islamic situation until the Truth is acknowledged by all (Muslim, Christian and other) in a fresh kingdom realization.[17]

The Power of "Name"

In the ancient world, a name generally conveyed meaning and power. It could spell out status, record an event, celebrate a transformation, or admonish in prophetic fashion. While the use of names for persons and phenomena might occasionally seem common, the names associated with God were profound and awesome.

The Quran centers on God and his name. His holy names are mentioned more than 10,000 times (the name *Allah* occurs over 2,500 times). He is all-present and all-powerful. Every part of creation is viewed as subordinate to his transcendent, majestic dominion.

After uttering a name for God or Jesus, Muslims often pause and "bless his name."

In the ancient world, a name for God often stands as "a double" for God himself and is to be treated with the same awe or honor that his very being deserves. Thus to speak "in the name of God" is a fearsome act, for as one deals with the name, so one deals with the divine entity. The personal name of God is always more than a label, it is the very clue to his being (nature) and doing, the handle by which humans address and gain access to his presence. In this tradition, Muslims often pause after the utterance of a name for God or Jesus and "bless his name."

While a name of God reveals, it also conceals much of his mystery.

Biblical revelation in a very real way is the revelation of divine names. God is known by the titles which he discloses (Gen. 14:22; 16:13; 17:1; Ex. 3:1-4:17; 5:22-6:8). The divine name Yahweh is either a simple indicative or a causative indicative of the verb "to be" meaning "he is" (alive, present, active) or "he brings into being." Yahweh is the God who is and acts in majesty.

While a name of God reveals, it also conceals much of his mystery. Language is limited. Like an orb, only one side faces the beholder. A name of God always anticipates a fuller expression, a progressive understanding.

While a name may not convey magical power, knowledge of the name of God is essential for an intimate relationship with this God of power (Ex. 33:12, 18-19; Jn. 17:6). Knowledge of God, of his name, results from divine initiative, not human discovery. God acts for his own name's sake (II Sam. 7:23; Ezek. 20:9, 14, 22, 44; Neh. 9:10). That is to say, God is equal to his name and more. While God is always greater than his names, what may be known of him is bonded to his names.

"Believing in his name" involves an experience of him and a commitment to him (Jn. 3:18; I Jn. 3:23), a knowledge of his very essence and action. His people are those called and kept "in his name." Such experience moves beyond revelation to redemption to glorification. The "name-theology" of the Bible leads into the unapproachable presence and glory of God, for his name signifies none other than himself. A name is never a mere label, but signifies the real personality of him to whom it belongs. All the attributes and actions of God are associated with a name.

> In the New Testament,...the names of Jesus become signs pointing to his identity, relationships, authority and actions.

Similarly in the New Testament, the name and names of Jesus become signs pointing to his identity, his relationships, his authority and his actions. It is on this backdrop that the names of the Messiah are to be understood.

The Messiah: His Names and Claims

> While the Quran acknowledges Jesus as the Messiah, it leaves the title and concept of Messiah/Christ quite undefined. Few tasks equal the challenge of bearing witness to the Messiah.

For the Muslim, the title and concept of Messiah/Christ remain quite open, fluid and undefined. We noted that in the Quran the title "Christ" is left undefined. Few tasks equal the challenge of bearing witness to Jesus as the Messiah. The Quran's acknowledgement of Jesus as the Messiah provides a natural opening for a mind-enlarging and life-enriching testimony. In the Muslim world, the concepts/names of the Messiah stand like large containers waiting to be filled or refilled by the Holy Scriptures and human experience in faith. The Quran offers clues to the Messiah's identity, yet remains an enigma to be illumined. The Quran offers homage and yet mirrors the unresolved controversies raging in the milieu in which Muhammad sought after God.

How should the names of the Messiah be introduced? Begin with the Old Testament names and promises of the Messiah.

Allow the Hebraic/Semitic testimony to the One Sovereign God and the promise of his Messiah to establish itself.

If Quranic references are to be considered, treat them like intertestamentary documents (e.g., the Apocrypha), valid where they are consistent with biblical revelation. Can we not acknowledge Muhammad as a prophet late-born, sent to the Arab peoples to arouse their hunger for the One God? Muslims are to be respected as seekers and submitters and are to be encouraged in their zeal to come to the Messiah. The challenge is to show them how the Messiah stands above every prophet and every book of revelation as Lord, the singular executive of God's name.

Allow the testimony of the New Testament to come as fulfillment. Interpret contextually those messianic titles at which Muslims are prone to take offense (e.g., Son of God) so the real issues of life are faced.

It is the Bible's very diversity in unity, transcending cultural contexts, that provides its strength of witness of Jesus.

Christian witnesses must acknowledge that the Bible is a library of 66 books and not one book as the Quran. It covers the disclosures of God and the experiences of the faithful over many centuries. There is a variety of vocabularies and many views rendered in "sundry times." There may be several "theologies" in the Bible, according to some scholars. Yet in the New Testament there emerges a united witness, a coherent theology, a worldview.[18] It is this diversity in unity, transcending cultural contexts, that provides the Bible's strength of witness to Jesus. For this reason, we must allow the multiple witnesses from Genesis to Revelation to speak for themselves, for the Holy Spirit is able to employ all in calling humans to faith and fullness.

Conclude by confessing that the Sovereign God is above all Scriptures, and that his Messiah (the eternal, living Word of God) is above all books!

All three monotheistic faiths affirm God's involvement in history and humanity, without equating Creator with creation.

Messiahship ultimately means that "Jesus is Lord." All three monotheistic faiths affirm God's involvement in history and humanity. They acknowledge contact but do not equate Creator with creation. All three agree there must not be confusion of Creator and creation (which Islam calls *shirk*). Christianity claims to avoid this confusion too in spite of its radical message of divine invasion (incarnation), sacrificial redemption (cross and resurrection), dynamic rule/kingdom of God, ongoing mediation (Christ as mediator, Trinity) and consummation (return of the Lord). "Jesus is Lord" (I Cor. 12:4) is the church's earliest confession.

Pronouncing the names of the Messiah is a form of honoring "the kingdom, the power and the glory" of God.

Pronouncement of the names of the Messiah is a form of honoring "the kingdom, the power and the glory" of God. Like the Lord's Prayer, such pronouncement voices prophetic awareness and proleptic hope, considering the future "as good as happened," celebrating the promise of God which will surely become fact in Christ.

Such pronouncement of the names of Christ will appeal to those who respect the recitation found in the *Shahadah*, which is likewise offered as both praise and profession. Such is not a matter for debate. By employing the biblical titles/categories with a minimum of systematized, rational commentary, one can avoid making it a matter for argument. Thus we should recite the biblical testimony to the One God who through his Messiah and Spirit extends himself toward us $(1 \times 1 \times 1 = 1)$.

A Model for Recital: The Beautiful Names of God

The devotional use of names is certainly apparent in Islam. At four points in the Quran, the "most beautiful names" of God are mentioned (Sura 20:8; 17:110; 7:179; 59:24). Students of Islam know that the beads of the Muslim rosary (*subha*) are often used by adherents of Islam in recitation of Allah's names. As one fingers the individual beads, he quietly and reverently repeats the 99 names of God that are familiar. The actual number of names of God may soar upwards to one thousand, but these select 99 are recited in worship. Next to the Quran, these names are held in highest respect. Professor Hitti once suggested that the treatment of these names as found in Al-Ghazali's *Al-Maqsad Al-Asma* comes closest to a Christian viewpoint.[19]

A study of the 99 names reveals that a number of these have their source in the Old Testament, and several of them are not even mentioned in the Quran. Sweetman writes:

> ...all the foregoing would appear to be names which have no sort of originality in Quranic usage, but rest on the foundation of a common stock of ideas. And in addition, even the anthropomorphisms of the Quran and the Old Testament are similar, both speaking of God's hand, His face and His being seated upon the Throne. So strong, indeed, is the Biblical influence (not, of course, by direct literary dependence) on the formulation of the canonical list of the Divine Names usually called *al Asma ul Husna* (the Ninety-nine Beautiful Names) that we find therein names which have little or no foundation in the Quran, but have in the Old Testament, e.g., *al Mani*, the Hinderer...[20]

The early Islamic use of the 99 names to describe God's attributes (*sifat*) shows the concern for unity and yet manifoldness, for transcendence and immanence. There is heavy emphasis on knowledge of God's existence as immutable creator who reaches down into the world (not rising up from the world) to act. Jews, Christians and Muslims agree on this theistic movement. These names employ anthropomorphic and metaphoric use of language as do the titles of the Messiah.

The ritual recitation of these names gives them a creedal or confessional nature. Although the selection of the 99 names may have been quite arbitrary, they are an effective means for worship and witness. Therefore I propose that in similar fashion, Christians living among Muslims be urged to employ a similar mode of witness to Jesus the Messiah. There could be merit in forging a unique litany or confession regarding God's Messiah in special consideration of the Muslim world.

Our goal should be to claim for Christ nothing beyond what he claimed and to deny nothing which he claimed. It must be a witness to the truth about him and to the new reality which accompanies his coming kingdom.

Of necessity we must wrestle with the tensions between divine transcendence and immanence, between divine unity and manifoldness, between kingdom come and kingdom coming, as revealed in the Messiah. We can assist our Muslim friends to see that the issues involved in New Testament Christology are unavoidable issues for every true "submitter" in faith.

Proposed List of Messianic Names

1. The Messiah as the Eternal Word and Spirit of God (stress his pre-existence and the role of Word and Spirit).

2. Jesus the Son of Mary (stress his humanity, personhood, virgin birth, incarnation, miracles/signs, sinlessness).

3. The Messiah as Prophet among the Prophets (stress his prophethood and yet show how the office of Messiah stands above that of prophet).

4. The Messiah as God's Suffering Servant (stress the importance of Jesus' death, resurrection and ascension).

5. The Messiah as Redeemer and Mediator (stress how this is the logical outworking of Jesus' cross, resurrection and ascension to rule, the truth about sin and salvation).

6. The Messiah and the Language of Sonship and Trinity (study the transcendence, immanence, the nature and action of God and the limits of human language). Emmanuel!

7. The Messiah Who Reigns as Lord and Who Will Return to Establish God's Kingdom and Before Whom Every Knee Shall Bend (study the king and kingdom in eschatological perspective).[21]

The Nature and Style of Our Worship/Witness

A worthy objective in recitation of Messiah's names: to allow the total impact of the Word and Spirit to evoke a response in hearts.

The goal must be to recite these names as Scripture recites them and to allow the total impact of the Word and Spirit (rather than our digressive interpretations and dialogues) to evoke a response in the hearts of our Muslim neighbors. We must invite a response to Jesus' claims: his call to discipleship, to fellowship in his body, and to obedience/submission to his rule. Dialogue and nurture will naturally follow such stirrings by the Spirit.

In this open recitation and public introduction to Jesus the Christ, there may be prayerful utterance, chant and song; standing, hand lifting, head bowing, kneeling and prostration. Such a recital would always be first and foremost worship (lifted up to God) and secondly witness (testimony to all those present). It would borrow from the best of Protestant piety and the liturgical riches of Eastern Orthodox and Roman Catholic communions, besides harnessing modes of expression familiar to Muslims. Its orientation (*qiblah*) may at times be upward in honor of the ascended Christ who shall return, and may at times take the form of a circle turned inward to acknowledge the community of Christ, and at times outward to express the church's mission and concern for the world.

I urge that our witness should take the form of a direct recital, an adoring witness, an undebatable praise of the Messiah. We need a confessional, creedal format drawn directly from the Scriptures, carrying the weight of Scripture which the Quran acknowledges in its own enigmatic fashion. We need to employ the names of the Messiah which will challenge the Muslim to study the Old and New Testaments. Is it not possible for the church to work on a biblical confession that can function in the Muslim context in the same way that the Apostles' and Nicene Creeds functioned in their original contexts? We need such a litany of praise, a confession, as a vehicle for honoring God in Christ among our Muslim friends and for urging their obedience to his call.

Evangelicals who have insisted "no creed but the Bible" and those from confessional communions of the Reformation (as well as Roman Catholic and Orthodox traditions) can be united on this employment of Jesus' biblical names. We need to be one in such a confession that the Muslim world might believe that God and his Messiah and his Spirit are One (Jn. 17:21). Such a liturgical confession finally will be doxological! *Bismillah!*

An Experimental Litany [22]

I Bear Witness to the Messiah's Names
in the Fourth Gospel

The Messiah is the Word of God eternal with God and of God as life, light, and love incarnated as a human being, dwelling among us, full of the grace and truth of God, revealing God as "Father" as only he could (Jn. 1:1-18).

The Messiah is "the Lamb of God who takes away the sin of the world" (Jn. 1:30), baptizing with the Holy Spirit (Jn. 1:33).

The Messiah alone is worthy of the title "Son of God," describing the spiritual bond of the Messiah to God (Jn. 1:34, 49). Some erred when they tried to kill Jesus because he called God "Father" and himself "Son" because they misunderstood the relationship and rejected his reign (Jn. 5:17-47).

The Messiah is known as: teacher or rabbi (Jn. 1:38; 41) bridegroom or groom (Jn. 2:1ff.; 3:22-36) able to grant rebirth and eternal life to all who believe in his name (Jn. 3:1ff.).

The Messiah is the Living Water, God's gift of salvation, teaching us how to worship God in spirit and in truth and viewing humanity as a field ready for harvest (Jn. 4:1-42). "If any one thirst let him come to me and drink" (Jn. 7:37-39).

The Messiah is the Bread from heaven, Bread of life, sent down from God to all who hunger for eternal life (Jn. 6).

The Messiah is the Light of the world, who liberates from sin (Jn. 8:1-30),whose person is the Truth that sets free (Jn. 8:31-36). In him the glory of God predates Abraham (Jn. 8:48-59) and enables the blind to see (Jn. 9:1-41).

The Messiah is the Door giving access to God's kingdom, the Good Shepherd who sustains the flock (Jn. 10:1-18). Some hated him because he claimed, "I and the Father are one" and "I am the son of God." The Messiah is one with God in purpose and spirit (Jn. 10:22-42).

The Messiah is the Resurrection and the Life who raises Lazarus and is raised by God in victory and vindication (Jn. 11). He is anointed for kingship and sacrificial death. He approaches the cross as "the hour of glory," the time in which God's glory shines and the ruler of the world is cast out and humanity given the choice of faith or unbelief (Jn. 12).

The Messiah is the Way, the Truth, and the Life. No one comes to the Father but by him (Jn. 14:6). This .i.Servant;- Master promises to send the Holy Spirit, Counselor, the Spirit of truth (Jn. 14:16-17).

The Messiah is the True Vine, binding true believers like branches to the Father and calling his disciples "friends" (Jn. 15).

"This is eternal life, that they know thee the only true God, and Jesus Christ whom thou has sent" (Jn. 17:3). Jesus prays that his disciples "may all be one; even as thou, Father, art in me, and I in thee, that they also may be in us, so that the world may believe that thou hast sent me" (Jn. 17:21f.).

The Messiah is king but his kingship transcends this world. By his cross and resurrection,the glory of God shines most clearly. Those who believe that "Jesus is the Christ, the Son of God" have "life in his name" (Jn. 20:30-31).

NOTES

1. Mahmoud M. Ayoub, "Towards an Islamic Christology: An Image of Jesus in Early Shi`i Muslim Literature,"*The Muslim World* LXVI (July 1976): 163-188.

2. Ibid., 165.

3. Ibid., 188.

4. Kenneth Cragg, *Jesus and the Muslim* (London: George Allen and Unwin, Ltd., 1985), xiv f.

5. Samuel M. Zwemer, *The Moslem Christ* (Edinburgh: Oliphant, Anderson and Ferrier, 1912), 8; Lyle Vander Werff, *Christian Mission to Muslims: The Record* (Pasadena, CA: William Carey Library, 1977), ch. 4 and app. K.

6. Several of these studies have fastened onto the Quran and its compatibility with the Bible's message [cf. R.C. Zaehner, *At Sundry Times* (London: Faber & Faber, 1958), 209, 216; Geoffry Parrinder, *Jesus in the Qur'an* (London: Faber & Faber, 1965), 173; Kenneth Cragg, *The Event of the Qur'an* and *The Mind of the Qur'an*; and William A. Bijlefeld, "Some Recent Contributions to Qur'anic Studies," *Muslim World*, 64 (1974): 79, no. 1]. It must be admitted, however, that the meaning of a Quranic passage is always subject to the varied Muslim interpretations. Wilfred Cantwell Smith insists that "no statement about a religion is valid unless it can be acknowledged by that religion's believers." Nevertheless, the Quran speaks for itself, standing in Islam as an authoritative word from God and not simply as the product of Muslim .i.theology ; [cf. W. Montgomery Watt, *Muhammad at Mecca* (London: Oxford University Press, 1953), x; Parrinder, *Jesus in the Qur'an*, 10). Thus it is legitimate to deliberate as to which interpretation of a text is closest to the truth.

7. Muslim piety surprises those who study it. See *Muslim Devotions—A Study of Prayer-Manuals in Common Use*, by Constance Padwick, which shows the Muslim's search for the living God. Modern Iranian poets focus not only on Jesus as the miracle worker, but on the persecuted Jesus with whom they can identify in their own social and political struggles. While it may be true that some classical Persian poets slandered Jesus and his crucifixion, there is positive identification with Jesus' person and suffering. Sometimes there is a link made between Jesus and the martyr Husayn bin 'Ali (Muhammad's grandson, the third Shiite Imam). Shiites view his death at Karbala (A.H.61/A.D.680) as a judgment of Ummayad corruption. [Sorour S. Soroudi, "On Jesus' Image in Modern Persian Poetry," *The Muslim World* LXIX (October 1979): 221-228].

8. For an excellent set of interviews, read "Conversations in Cairo: Some Contemporary Muslim Views of Other Religions," by William E. Shepard, professor of the University of Canterbury, Christchurch, New Zealand, *The Muslim World* LXX, 3-4 (July-October 1980): 171-195.

9. Fazlur Rahman, "Islam's Attitude Toward Judaism," *The Muslim World* LXXII, no. 1 (January 1982):1-13.

10. In Rahman (note 9) Muhammad felt the Jewish and Christian pressures to follow their way (Sura 2:12, 111). He was very much drawn to the Christian view, preferring them because "among them there are priests and monks and they are not conceited people" (Sura 5:82). He experienced the truth that "We [God] cast in the hearts of his [Jesus'] followers kindness and mercy" (Sura 57:27). Muhammad was clearly in awe of the biblical disclosure and the faith which gripped Jews and Christians. He longed for a similar redemptive experience and guidance for his people. He wanted for them the heritage of Abraham, Moses, David and Jesus. He earnestly believed that he stood in this lineage and was sent to call others back to the worship of the One God, the Creator Lord.

11. True, the Quran refutes some of the heterodox and heretical movements of the day (Trinity as God, Jesus, and Mary; or the monophysite view that Jesus is only God and not human). The fact that Muhammad countered such

tritheism should not be equated with a rejection of the Trinity. Later Muslim theologians may employ these verses and other Hadiths in anti-Jewish, anti-Christian polemics, but this is a far cry from the initial confessions of Muhammad which were closer to Christian orthodoxy than to many of the Jewish and Christian deviations of his time. Even at Medina where Muhammad was often embattled with his fellow Arabs and Jewish neighbors, he did not pit himself against the Hebrew prophets or Jesus the Christ.

12. Giulio Basetti-sani, *The Koran in the Light of Christ* (Chicago: Franciscan Herald Press, 1977), 32.

13. E.g., Muhammad Kamil Husain, *The City of Wrong* (Amsterdam: Djambatan N.V., 1959): 59.

14. Abdijah Akbar Abdul-Haqq, *Sharing Your Faith with a Muslim* (Minneapolis: Bethany Fellowship, 1980), 21.

15. The Quran's teaching about Jesus is very Christological and not simply about the life and ministry of Jesus. It reflects the great Christological discussions occurring in Christian circles in the 7th and 8th centuries. It reflects the debates between Cyril of Alexandria and Nestorius, the arguments about the nature of Christ, docetism, dualism, polytheism, exaltation of Mary, and the mediation of saints. It was a world in which a genuine witness to Jesus as Savior and Lord was often missing. We must assist Muslim scholars and leaders in recovery of this historical context. More than one Christian leader in the Middle East identifies with the experience of Anglican minister R.A. Lindley, writing in *Bible Lands*, Winter, 1985. He tells of an elderly Muslim Sheik who requested certain Bible aids with these words,

I love Jesus. I have great affection and loving respect for our Prophet Mohammed, he is after all the Founder of my Faith, but as a lawgiver he is hard to love. I do however love Issa and you have more to read about him in your Bible than we have in the Koran...

There are many such searching spirits who would meet the Messiah. We owe them our fullest cooperation in the quest!

16. Marilyn R. Waldman, "New Approaches to Biblical Materials in the Quran,"*The Muslim World* LXXV (January 1985): 1ff.

17. We are indebted to the careful comparative scholarship of James Windrow Sweetman, *Islam and Christian Theology; a Study of the Interpretation of Theological Ideas in the Two Religions*, Parts. I-II (London: Lutterworth Press, 1945-). Sweetman, who served both at the Henry Martyn School of Islamic Studies (India) and at Selly Oak Colleges (Birmingham, England), supported the view that we must urge Muslims to study the Old and New Testaments as basic foundations of the true faith in the One God. The Quran can be seen as a .i.theological; commentary representing the unique insights of the Arab cultural-historical context.

18. Lyle Vander Werff, "The Exalted Christ: An Exegetical Comparison of Several Christological Passages of the New Testament" (Thesis, Princeton Theological Seminary, 1961).

19. Robert C. Stade, trans., *Ninety-Nine Names of God in Islam* (Ibadan: Daystar Press, 1970).

20. Sweetman (note 17 *Islam and Christian Theology*), 1966: 201.

21. In a another paper I will discuss the Christological significance of these names within the Quran's comment and the Muslim context.

22. Similar unpublished litanies have been prepared by the author on the Names of the Messiah in the Law, the Prophets, the Writings, the Synoptic Gospels, the Acts of the Apostles, the Letters of the Early Church and the Revelation of John.

FORMS OF WITNESS

And their eyes were opened and they recognized him . . . Then they told what had happened on the road.
— Luke 24: 31, 35

CHAPTER ELEVEN

HERE IS HOW I SHARE

Muslims can express many perspectives and reveal diverse varieties of felt needs. The attempt here is to derive practical suggestions on witnessing from a number of effective practitioners—male and female, from several cultures. All base their sharing on genuine friendship and listening, and all relate their witness to practical problems in everyday life.

Missionaries are often perceived as relating to Muslims only on the spiritual level in, for example, Bible studies. But the first writer, from a Muslim culture, sees the coffee house as the most strategic place to influence people. It is like the central circle of a spider's web that leads into all segments of society, providing a natural network for communication.

Women in the Muslim world present a special problem because of their insulation from many areas of public life. The second writer tells how she relates to women in their national context, including their folk beliefs and practices, and she shows the relevance of Jesus' interaction with women.

When these women go into a Western context, they acquire new felt needs—especially the need for friendship. The third writer, who first ministered in the Muslim world and now works in the West, shows how she meets the need for friendship and how she uses the natural ways there are for sharing through the meanings of festivals and stories.

The fourth writer, a missionary who works with Muslims, shows how he illustrates these stories with flannelgraph. Then he describes the phenomenon so common in Muslim conversions, that of dreams or visions.

Finally, a national from the Muslim world who is primarily involved in outreach through radio and Bible correspondence courses, shows how he seeks to separate Christ from the cultural baggage of the West so that Muslims might meet him and experience the gospel in culturally relevant forms.

IN COFFEE HOUSES

Hasan al-Ghazali

Where but in the *magha* can one find an environment so conducive for developing cultural awareness, for becoming a true friend, for sharing Christ in an appreciated context?

I spend from 9 to 11 a.m. daily in my "office," the *magha* (the coffee shop). This is the hub of our ministry, the launching pad for evangelism. These are the most important hours of the day, neither a lazy way to pass the morning, nor a waste of time. Here is where I let out the net to fish.

Every level of the sociological scale is represented in the *magha* In one week I met the university dean, laborers, teachers, students, communist party members and Muslim brotherhood leaders.

In order to win these people, I need to be informed on a wide variety of subjects related to their daily lives. If religion is the only subject I can deeply discuss, most will become bored quickly. So I talk on secular topics and current affairs and inject Christian viewpoints and philosophy—usually new ideas. The Spirit of Truth will continue to shed light on what belongs to him. These "darts" open the way for further inquiry into my beliefs.

I see a common problem in Muslim countries, and many nationals tell me they have observed the same thing. The missionaries only relate to them on the spiritual sphere of their lives—Bible studies, meetings and so forth. Because they have few other social functions, the nationals feel that missionaries do not relate to their daily lives and cannot understand their struggles. The coffee shop is the hub of daily life; it has played an influential part in the making of Arab history. Coups and revolutions have begun there, and in one instance, the first radio release of a new government was written there.

Leaders in society train disciples; business transactions are conducted and students study there. It is the central circle of the spider's web where you build up contacts in a network into all segments of society. It is the most strategic place to influence people.

In the city where I live, each *magha* is patronized by a specialized clientele. There is a certain coffee shop for teachers, smugglers, police, students and so forth. "My" *magha* is patronized by university professors, high school teachers and, of course, some secret police. We meet daily and become united like a family. The relationships grow strong enough so problems are shared at a deeper personal level. Through this coffee shop I have influenced six people to write their B.A. theses on Christian-related topics. Several were converted and many are reading the Bible. Hardly a week passes without requests for Bibles.

Following initial discussions, we invite people to our home for deeper talks. But it is very important to speak the kernel of our message in the coffee shop. We must have the same language in private as in public. If you are vague in public and only open on the religious subject in private, you become an object of suspicion. "Why didn't he say that at the *magha*?" "What are his real motives?" We must teach our converts to be bold by setting the example at the first meeting with them before conversion.

The police have not been suspicious about our activities or motives. They know we are active Christians and will hear the same story in the street as in the house. They might not like it but they do not suspect us of having political or even professional religious aims. I have a clear identity as a business man, and my witnessing is just a natural expression of my personal faith. My business profession separates me from professional religious workers; therefore I need not be concerned about appearing too "religious." Muslims expect people of faith to share their faith, just as they do with us.

One morning in the *magha* I was discussing the Lebanese civil war with a teacher. When I mentioned that I follow Christ (I do not use "Christian"), the discussion was brought to an abrupt halt. "What! I have been wanting to learn about Christianity for a long time. I teach at a number of schools and the students ask me about Christian beliefs. We only know what we've been told about you Christians. I want to hear from a Christian what you believe." He came home with a friend, and they took notes until 2 a.m.

After finding interested people we visit their homes and involve the family in the friendship. We center on the family unit and try not to let inquirers isolate themselves from the family. Once friendship is established, we include the family in Bible studies and invite them to see the Jesus video (Campus Crusade version).

When the family are our friends, they are not suspicious of "Ahmed's" relationship with us, and cannot very well forbid him to fellowship with us.

Our first convert here, a young woman, is facing strong opposition from her husband and family. Yet, as they are also our friends, they do not forbid us to see her. We still have access to the house and continue witnessing and encouraging her. While they reject our religion, they appreciate our friendship and good influence on their daughter's life, which changed radically after conversion.

Her brother, a university graduate, wrote his thesis on al-Hallaj, a great Muslim Sufi, who denied Islam and requested to die the way Christ did. They crucified him on a pole. This brother defends the daughter's right to believe in Christ. He was the opening into the family. I met him at the *magha*. He is now a believer and teaching at a university.

If we can get support for the new believers within the family, they will have the security they need to stay firm. As there are no "churches" existing to strengthen young believers, we must recognize the importance of family evangelism.

In the Middle East the existing churches refused to become "family" to Muslim converts. Consequently, many single men have fallen back from following Christ.

To sum up the importance of a regular presence in the coffee shop, I believe it is the most strategic place for integration in all levels of society, for gaining an intimate knowledge of fellow patrons, receiving an education on culture and a natural bonding place—not to mention picking up all the current town news. To not be part of a *magha* group is to fail to be integrated into Arab society. It is therefore to forego the most strategic place for evangelism.

WITH WOMEN IN THE EAST

D. Smith

Singleness and marriedness each provide special points of contact for meaningful woman-to-woman sharing of social and spiritual concerns.

During my 18 years as a teacher in an Arab country, I became aware of cultural thought patterns and traditions through my students and their families. They, in turn, carefully watched me and inquired about my beliefs and practices. I soon realized that sharing the gospel with them involved my whole life—my words, my actions and my thoughts. Out of this background of observing and questioning has grown my approach to the evangelism of Muslim women.

Most women I meet in the Arab world are curious. Since I too like to find out about their lives, it takes only a minute before we are well involved in a series of questions and answers. They delight in the intricacies of family relationships; so I must pay close attention to names, numbers, kinship terms (an aunt may also be a sister's mother-in-law!). Then they want to know about my family.

My celibacy into middle age astounds them. I take this as an opening to talk about God. He provides security and protection. He directs and leads in the decisions of marriage and employment. I also believe that remaining celibate in a society that views women in terms of sexual fulfillment is a way to make a statement of her value as a person, created in the image of God. From a different perspective, married colleagues add to this picture of personal worth. Husband-wife relationships of mutual submission, respect and love express profound truths about man and woman and God.

One of their questions about my lifestyle concerns prayer. My answer to "Do you pray?" is to compare their outward physical washing with the inner cleansing provided by God through the blood of his sacrifice. Sometimes I draw upon their knowledge of the provision of a sheep for the son of Abraham. I usually talk about a holy God, a clean heart and free access to him at any time. I may even give examples of what I say in prayer—to praise him, to confess sin, to intercede for others. In all of this I wish to share the reality and nearness of my heavenly Father while guarding the respect due to his holy name.

Personal preparation for ministry to these women is essential. Praying, reading and meditating are a part of my daily life so that the thoughts I share with my Muslim friends come sincerely from my own interests, questions and convictions. First, I pray in a more general way for God to bind evil forces and free the hearts of women to hear his Word. I hold a certain woman in prayer before God and wait on him for a special truth to share in terms of her needs. Then I study relevant Scripture passages in Arabic and I think of their application in terms of that particular woman—examples from her daily life and personal interests. Before I meet my Muslim friend, I commit the visit to God and pray for her to be at home with free time to sit and discuss. Then I relax, enjoy my time with her and her family, trusting God to work.

Much of my time with my friends is spent listening. Even if I have heard the same religious views many times, I try to recognize their importance to this woman and look for openings to take her from her known world to spiritual truth. I want to sow seeds of truth and encourage every sign of hunger for righteousness she expresses.

When a woman shows interest, I use some type of inductive Bible study (oral or written, depending on literacy) with questions to help her interact directly with the Word. I want her to learn from the beginning not to be dependent on my presence for her relationship to God. Teaching through the use of questions also helps me determine the woman's real comprehension of the Scripture. Then I can explain further before I seek to lead her into personal application.

Once when I was trying to help a young woman find a way to read daily from the Word, we discovered that the best time for her was the evening news hour when everyone was watching television. Like many women who are at the beck and call of family all day long, she needed help to see the importance of study and meditation, and to find the application in her home situation. Some time later, this same friend, used to applying the Word from our inductive approach, voluntarily explained Christ's mediation from her own experience of looking for an intercessor in a complicated bureaucratic situation.

Several women have felt free to confide information about themselves and their families to me, a foreign teacher and friend, for I am a safe person without ulterior motives to betray them. These confidences (about bitterness, sorrow and heartbreak caused by divorce, illegitimate children, poor health, death) give opportunities to counsel and to share God's love, pardon and provision in Christ. There may be an opportunity to pray openly then, or to promise to do so at home.

As I listen to modern young women discussing their roles in present day society, I learn much of their conflicts, hopes and fears. Then I seek to present thoughts of God's purpose in creating women, and I mention our responsibilities, along with our failures as sinful persons. These young women often blame their society and express their hope to change it. Yet they rarely recognize the selfishness and sinfulness of the human race. After some years of involvement in the women's movement, one of my friends has said that she now sees what I meant by our Christian teaching of the need for change in the human heart.

When possible, I try to turn to a passage where Christ is talking with a woman. He never despises her or treats her as a sexual object, but rather offers her eternal life, pardon, healing and value. The miracles and parables of Christ are other passages of Scripture that also relate to the interests and circumstances of women. I like to use basic items from her daily life—bread, water, clothing—as a helpful way to illustrate Scriptural truth so that she will be able to remember a Bible verse and our discussion when she looks at that object.

One of my colleagues often uses Old Testament stories with the children of the family she is visiting. One day after drawing pictures of the story of Noah and teaching a song about the flood, she returned later to hear how an overflowing bucket of water had flooded their apartment. That Bible lesson will long be remembered. Usually her stories with the children lead into a time of talking with the women. My colleague encourages any sign of truth evident in those conversations. She asks thought-provoking questions in such an original way that the women (and I) spend hours wondering what she means—and we are stretched in our perception of God and his righteousness.

Sometimes I introduce a discussion on the attributes of God. If I have been reading or meditating on this subject, I find it is quite natural to ask a friend how she thinks of God. The subject of idolatry seems related to the Islamic view of not associating anyone or anything with God. I like to share those different ways that we allow something to become so central in our lives that it actually pushes God to one side—family, possessions or position.

Again and again I find that the barrier against the gospel of Christ is due to women's strong attachment to folk Islam and the animistic practices it encourages. From birth to death, some 'superstitious' practice binds them to the spirits. A woman goes to a saint's tomb and asks for a child: she returns to carry out her vow when the child is born. Children are protected against the 'evil eye' by many charms and amulets. Marriages are made and broken by sorcery. Sick people are healed by the intercession of dead 'saints.' Houses are built, fields are plowed, diplomas gained—all through the power of the saints' tombs (*marabouts*).

Victory through the powerful name of Jesus Christ must be proclaimed to break the bondage of these women who dearly guard the traditions of their ancestors. They confide in me about these practices: I long for their deliverance, but personally I have seen little breakthrough here. My present concern is to focus prayer and proclamation of the gospel for his victory over their bondage. I seek his wisdom and power in applying the message of deliverance to the lives of women in the Muslim world.

WITH WOMEN IN THE WEST

Alberta Standish

Genuine friendship and presentation of the *person* of Christ through story, imagery, poetry and suggestion is for most Muslim women more appropriate than intellectual, theological presentations of the gospel.

There are about 485 million Muslim women in the world, living in 50 different countries. They come from many different ethnic backgrounds and have a wide variety of needs. They are highly educated and uneducated, rich and poor, married and even single. They are traditional homemakers and modern career women. But many of their lives are characterized by insecurity and fear—fear of illness, death, rejection and the spirit world. Even though they fear the spirit world, they also look to it to give them power and control. They may use helpful or harmful magic to give them the power and control they feel they need.

Because they are *women* and their felt needs are more psychological than theological, more relational than informational, they need to be understood and they need to have the love and power of Christ related to them at the point of felt need. Intellectual, theological approaches of the gospel usually do not communicate. Neither do apologetics. In the following paragraphs, I will give what others and I have found helpful in sharing the love of Christ with Muslim women.

Practical Approaches

In sharing the gospel we must remember first of all that our message is a *Person* we have experienced, not a doctrine or a system or a religion or a book or a church. It is a *Person* we have a relationship with. Muslim women are interested in relationship but they do not know that they can have a relationship with almighty God who, they assume, is far away and to be feared.

We must also remember that Muslim women, for the most part, think in an Eastern way, not using Western linear logic. We must learn to communicate truth by imagery, poetry and suggestion.

Friendship

Relationship is so important in Eastern culture. And relationships with Muslim women cannot be hurried. They take time. Walls of suspicion and distrust must be broken down with patience and love.

Ways that this can be done include being a *learner* of their language, customs and food. So much of a woman's life centers around the preparation of food. In addition, it contributes to her worth as a wife and mother. Have her teach you to prepare local dishes. *Visiting* is the primary form of "entertainment" in Eastern cultures. Get into the habit of regularly visiting the Muslim women with which you want to develop friendship.

Serving her practical needs is another way of breaking down barriers. Show an interest in *her* rather than just her soul. The importance of relationship is seen in times of personal crisis. Crisis inevitably comes, and when it does, if you have a relationship of trust with your Muslim friend, God will open many doors of witness. Fuad Accad has said, "Build bridges of relationship that will bear the weight of truth."

Sharing Your Life in Christ

I have found that sharing stories about my life in Christ—that intimate, personal relationship I have with him—is an effective way of communicating God's character of love and care and the relationship he desires to have with us. This can be done by:

- telling her the "story" of how we came to know Christ; giving her the surrounding details, the emotions you felt, thoughts you had, what you prayed and so forth; using vocabulary and truth that she can identify with (e.g. "I believe that God is one and that there is no other god besides him").

- sharing what our feasts (Christmas and Easter) mean to us personally.
- sharing stories of God's answers to prayer.

- giving examples of God's personal provision and protection.

Relating to Muslim and Christian Holidays

Ramadan and Id-al-Adha (Feast of Sacrifice) are excellent times to relate to our Muslim friends with visits and in some cases, the giving of gifts. These feasts may also give the opportunity to discuss spiritual issues, and (at Id-al-Adha) the biblical story of Abraham sacrificing his son.

Story Telling

Jesus was an expert story teller, and we can learn so much from his example. Many of his parables can be retold in Islamic dress if we take the time to think and prepare ahead.

Bible stories of Jesus relating to women are also very effective—for example, Jesus raising the widow's son to life, healing the woman with the issue of blood (Mk. 5) and healing the woman on the Sabbath (Lk. 13). These stories are especially good because they deal with issues that are very important to Muslim women (i.e., the death of an only son, menstrual bleeding and evil spirits or *jinn*). Be in the habit of collecting other good stories that illustrate spiritual truth.

Poems and Songs

Often in Eastern cultures it is a "shame" to express deep feelings in conversation, but it is perfectly acceptable to express them in poems or songs. This also seems to be the case when expressing spiritual truth. This is an area that needs further development.

Prayer

Praying with our Muslim friends over their specific needs demonstrates love, reveals our intimate relationship with God and brings Christ's power to bear on their lives.

Signs and Wonders

Jesus said that the Kingdom of God would be accompanied by healing and the casting out of demons (Mt. 12:28). Because much of the world view of Muslim women contains the supernatural, we need to be praying that Christ would reveal himself—even through dreams, visions, miracles and power over demons, as he deems best.

Drama

This is another area that could be developed. For example, parables and Jesus' encounters with women could be acted out and then discussed.

For the most part, we are seeing very few Muslim women coming to Christ around the world. We need to be asking ourselves, "Why?" I believe that one of the reasons is that the church has overlooked them and taken for granted the fact that they can be reached in the same way as some of their husbands or fathers are—through a more intellectual presentation of the gospel.

It is going to take Spirit-filled, creative Christian women who will find the key to unlock the hearts of their Muslim sisters. Samuel Zwemer put it this way: "What the women of the Muslim world need supremely is the sacrificial service of their Christian sisters."

THROUGH RELATIVES

Ray Register

Hospital contacts sometimes lead to fruitful ongoing ministry to extended families.

The most practical means of evangelism for me in our area has been preaching in ward services at the local evangelical hospital, using the parables of Christ with a Child Evangelism flannelgraph presentation. I have done this regularly each month for the last 15 years. (This keeps the presentation simple and on my level of Arabic!) This has given me exposure to hundreds of Muslims from villages in Galilee and the West Bank.

In 1966 a Muslim villager who had visited the hospital came to me and invited me to come to his encampment near the Sea of Galilee, where his family was engaged in sheep raising. He had a dream as a boy of angels in heaven singing "Glory to God in the highest and on earth, peace, good will to men." Later, as a young man he purchased a Bible from the Christian engineer at the hospital and found the verse. Through a series of visits our friendship deepened.

His father died, leaving him responsible for his 12 children and his mother's 12 children. Several days after his death, the father appeared to him in a dream and told him, "Follow the *kasees* (the pastor); he will show you the right way."

He has taken me as a brother to visit his sisters and his wife's married sisters in four other villages on the Muslim feast days and on other occasions. I take along the flannelgraph or a Christian film and usually have a presentation for the family after the customary meal. In a recent visit to a village of one of his relatives I met a young Muslim lady who became a believer while a student in the United States. My wife and I have been discipling her through personal visits and prayer, and have a counseling ministry with her and her husband.

My friend has never taken a decisive step to leave Islam and become a "Christian." I am not sure he ever will. It would be a great cultural jump. He has made a profession of faith to me privately after studying the booklet "Seven Muslim Christian Principles," and is presently doing his own topical study of the Bible. He does not pray in the mosque, but I have visited the mosque and had several talks with the young sheikh in my friend's home.

He is so cautious that he will not arouse the opposition of other villagers to his associating with the "foreign Christian." He occasionally attends special evangelistic meetings and enjoys powerful preaching. He helps me in choosing young Christian Arabs who feel called to witness to Muslims. On the surface he appears to be a very simple, uneducated and unimposing "fellah." He has some of the typical prejudices of a villager toward the Bedouin and others. But lately he has been engaged in a study of his family tree which has opened unexpected new doors.

"Muhammad" found that he has relatives scattered across the West Bank into Jordan and into Saudi Arabia. In the last six months we have made numerous visits into West Bank villages to meet these relatives, some of whom are substantial men in their communities. In general they are much more influential than my friend and his family in the little Galilee village. They have unofficially "adopted" me into their tribe! They are open to my presentation of the gospel in ordinary conversation and generally have more contact with the West than Muhammad's Galilee relatives.

One cautionary note: I fear they have seen me as another source of foreign funds that are flooding the West Bank. I have checked on sources of various development projects and have responded to their inquiries that this is not my major area of concern. But I have been involved in head-start kindergarten programs in Galilee villages; this gives me some expertise in advising this kind of project. I would not hesitate to be involved if I found it was a way to open their villages for further gospel sharing.

THROUGH CONTEXTUALIZED FORMS

Sobhi Malek

An essential of any valid strategy: meet Muslims at their level.

First of all, I want to share three personal convictions:

1. Winning Muslims to Christ is a reality. It is not impossible, as the devil has wanted the church to believe over the centuries. We *can* win Muslims to the Lord. It has been done and it should continue to occupy our minds and hearts.

2. Evangelizing Muslims has been one of the greatest challenges confronting the church since Muhammad said he heard a voice ordering, "Recite in the name of thy Lord..."

3. One can foresee a great move of the Holy Spirit among Muslims such as has never happened before in all the history of that segment of the world population. I believe that we will see individuals and families, groups and multitudes of Muslims submit their life at the cross of Jesus and declare that he is Lord, to the glory of God the Father. A simple grasp of the future implications of present-day happenings leads one to foresee such a phenomenon. Hence, the church must prepare for such an ingathering.

Now to our subject: Practical Means of Evangelizing Muslims. For this I have neither an exotic recipe nor a step-by-step formula. However, I do wish to emphasize one essential of any valid strategy: meet Muslims at their level. If our goal is to minister to Muslims, we have to meet them exactly where they stand. So important is this factor that it will decide whether or not they understand and accept the message we offer. Certainly Paul had this in mind when, inspired by the Holy Spirit, he stated:

> I am a free man, nobody's slave; but I make myself everybody's slave in order to win as many people as possible.

While working with the Jews, I live like a Jew in order to win them; and even though I myself am not subject to the Law of Moses, I live as though I were when working with those who are, in order to win them. In the same way, when working with Gentiles, I live like a Gentile, outside the Jewish Law, in order to win Gentiles. This does not mean that I don't obey God's law; I am really under Christ's law. Among the weak in faith I become weak like one of them, in order to win them. So I become all things to all men, that I may save some of them by whatever means are possible (I Cor. 9:1922, TEV).

Theological Level

We need to meet Muslims at their level in two major areas: theology and culture,

The serious theological controversies between Christianity and Islam have often frustrated and rendered unproductive many an endeavor to lead Muslims to Christ. These issues touch some of the most basic tenets of the faith: the divine authority of the Bible, the Trinity, the deity of Christ, his Sonship and his crucifixion. In addition, these controversies bring into focus some Islamic beliefs Christians find totally unacceptable. For example: the Quran is God's final revelation to humans; Muhammad was the last, the greatest and consequently the seal of all the prophets; and God wants all people to convert to Islam.

As serious as these issues may be, I do not think they form a hurdle impossible to cross or that we should begin evangelizing a Muslim by confronting these controversies.

I do believe it is our duty to smooth out theological obstacles and explain things to our Muslim friends in a satisfactory way. However, I want to emphasize here, from personal conviction and practical experience, the importance of first presenting Christianity as a practical encounter with the Christ.

One of the first steps in ministering to a Muslim is to take him by the hand and introduce him to Jesus. I want my Muslim friend to walk with Jesus on the hills of Judea, sit with him by the Sea of Galilee, listen to him teach, watch him do miracles, hear him pray, talk with him, see him crucified and watch him come to the upper room alive on resurrection Sunday. I want my Muslim friend to experience Jesus first. Then we can talk about the theological controversies.

Biblical Christianity is not a dogma to be learned. It is first of all a personal relationship with Jesus. When ministering to a Muslim, one must always remember that we are not trying to win a theological debate. These are futile approaches. Rather, we are trying to help a precious eternal soul find peace with God through the living Savior and Lord. The Muslim, like any other person, has serious needs and my goal is to help him, not defeat him.

Cultural Level

Reconciliation with God at the cross of Calvary is a universal message. It is for every person from every culture, race, language and social setting. Acceptance or rejection of this message is influenced by its "package" —whether or not it is communicated in a way that is sensitive to the cultural traits of the receptors, appealing to their tastes and meaningful to them.

In many cases, Muslims do not want to accept the gospel or even hear it because they see it as a threat to their cultural traits, to the solidarity of their Islamic community. Often, the gospel strikes them as alien because of the way it is offered to them. They mistakenly conclude that in order to become a Christian, one must renounce his own culture, lose his identity and betray his own people.

I believe that when we present the gospel to Muslims in a "gift-wrap" that is authentically culturally Muslim, the possibility of a positive response is high indeed. Let me state this in other words. If we want Muslims to consider the gospel seriously, with the possibility of accepting Christ, we must present the good news in a form that appeals to them culturally and attracts their attention.

Western cultures are not necessarily biblically based. We must avoid offering our own cultural traits or achievements as the gospel. Rather, we need to seek molds and forms which look very Muslim as a "gift-wrap" for Christ's message when we offer it to our Muslim friends.

God desires to meet Muslims without having them convert to another culture. He wants to use their own cultural traits as a vehicle to communicate his truths more effectively. Muslims can accept the Lord, give their total allegiance to Jesus Christ, become authentically Christian and yet retain their Islamic culture. God is blessing these emphases today as increasing numbers are turning to Christ in faith.

IN THE INDONESIAN CONTEXT

Chris Marantika

How can the gospel be communicated in a meaningful way to the Muslims of Indonesia? To answer this we shall need to look at the problems of evangelism among Muslims and then at the type of Muslims found in Indonesia.

Argumentation, condemnation and confrontation have naturally failed to win a Muslim hearing for the gospel.

A tragic fact is that Christians often have looked upon Muslims as enemies. They have not loved them as Christ intended them to do. The church, consequently, has engaged in negative argumentation, condemnation and confrontation toward Muslims. Thus it has not been able to win a hearing among the people.

Biblical messages that will win a hearing need to be formulated. A bridge needs to be built; a "point of contact" needs to be created. In order to formulate messages that win a hearing, build bridges and create "points of contact," it is necessary to understand first what Muslims think about the Christian message. As Zwemer put it:

> Not our ignorance, but our accurate knowledge of the Muslim Christ will enable us to show forth the glory and the beauty of the Christ revealed in the New Testament to those who ignorantly honor Him as a mere prophet.[1]

The Composition of Islamic Adherents

Three varieties of Muslims make up the Islamic population of Indonesia —and of many other predominantly Muslim nations.

Muslims comprise approximately 77 percent of Indonesia's population. They may be classified into three major groups. The largest group consists of the fanatical Muslims, who make up 37 percent of the Muslim community and are scattered throughout the nation, occupying such main areas as West, East and North Central Java, Sumatra and surrounding islands, South Celebes and North Malucca provinces.

Gospel bearers should know which variety of Muslim they are addressing in a given setting.

Djayadiningrat, a student of the Hollander Snouck Hogronje, who was renowned for his knowledge of Indonesian Islam, called this group "the white people who live religiously."[2] They are concerned with the orthodox religious doctrines, faithfully observe the fundamental rituals of Islam, such as daily prayers, strive to relate Islamic doctrine to daily life and conscientiously embrace a worldwide Islamic fellowship.[3]

The second group consists of mystic Muslims who are dispersed mainly among millions of people in Java and Sumatra. This group is more tolerant of Christianity than are the fanatics, because of the moderating influence of Buddhism and Hinduism. More people from this group have come into the fold of Christianity than from the first group. The highest goal of their teaching is complete submission to the divine way *tariqah* and complete absorption of one's being into the divine truth *haqiqa*.[4] The object of all their efforts is the absorption of self into the Ultimate Being.

The third group consists of the statistical Muslims, the *abangan* or the "red people,"[5] who also are scattered throughout the nation of Indonesia. It is primarily from this group that people are turning toward Christ in great numbers. They comprise about 30 percent of the Muslim community, but do not live religiously. They observe the rituals of Islam, but are not personally committed to its teachings. Their beliefs overlap many of those of the previous group but draw more heavily from the earlier animistic Javanism of the peasants. They are nominal and syncretistic rather than orthodox.

This three-part classification of Islamic adherents seems to be true in many countries with different degrees of commitment. Evangelistic efforts should be prepared to appeal to each of these different mentalities.

Relevant Approaches

Ability to present the gospel in a way that wins a hearing in each context is an art in itself. Gospel bearers to the Muslims should take into consideration the acceptable attitudes, patterns of thought, patterns of social structure, the law of the country and relevant methods. New ways can be developed to evangelize positively, constructively and creatively and, at the same time, comply with the law and maintain peace among the people.[6]

The mentality of people is sometimes classified into three categories:

One is the rationalistic-logical pattern of thought, dominant in the Western world.

Another is the imaginative-mythological pattern of thought, dominant in Africa and Latin America.

The third is the intuitive-meditative-mystical pattern of thought, dominant in Asia.

Indonesia, with the largest Muslim group in the world, possesses the third pattern of thought, combined with a little of the second pattern. The message presented should appeal to the intuition and the imagination of the people. The Christian message of God's acts in history, because of his love and care for people, will appeal to this kind of mentality if it is presented with a story-telling approach.

Each culture has been shaped by at least four structures of society:

1. the individual structure
2. the family structure
3. the community structure
4. the tribal structure

Each people group in each Islamic country should be studied to determine what structure is the most important to the people. The evangelistic efforts and the formation of the church should be patterned accordingly.

The most important and practical structure among Indonesian Muslims is the second structure: the family. This is being promoted by the government as well. The third structure—the community—is also being observed to a higher degree than previously. The fourth—the tribal structure—even though it has been used extensively in the past by missionaries and is still being tightly held by the old established churches, is under attack by the new generation.

Relevant Methods

Almost all legal methods used in world evangelization today can be used in Indonesia, as long as they are practiced with much care, and with attention to the above principles. There are seven methods, however, which have become the most relevant methods in Indonesia.

One is *personal evangelism*. In this case, many of the materials produced by such organizations as Campus Crusade for

Christ and the Navigators are applicable with minor modification for Muslim countries.

The second important method is *household evangelism* (not house-church evangelization). This approach emphasizes the use of a divine institution (the family) for world evangelization. Besides having a strong biblical and a healthy .i.theological; basis, it also appeals to the oriental Islamic mind-set and social structure.

Making a family tree is a good practice. The church, then, can develop special yearly prayer programs and step-by-step evangelistic programs to approach Muslims who are relatives of church members, taking courage from the divine promises (Ac. 16:31-32; Lk. 19:9), as well as the example of our Lord (Jn. 4:44-54; Lk. 19:9) and the early church (Ac. 16:14; 18:8; I Cor. 1:16).

The third relevant method is the *church planting* one. This method calls for the formation of a local church after 30 baptized believers exist in a community. The believers should be taught for four to six months with lessons on basic Christian doctrines and then be challenged to follow through with the baptismal ceremony. A simple church building should be erected immediately if possible. Local authorities should be asked to inaugurate the building. It gives immediate legal identity and credibility to the local congregation.

A shortage of educational institutions for that nation's eager learners makes public education a particularly fruitful field for Christian ministry in Indonesia.

The fourth relevant method is *public education*. Besides the strong desire of the younger generation to be educated and the lack of educational institutions to provide for the great number of qualified children, a reason for this is that the law of Indonesia requires every school child to be steeped in one religion. Religious instruction is a compulsory course from elementary school through the university.

This measure taken by the government, intended to counteract Communism, has become a blessing in disguise for Christianity. Our evangelistic efforts among the young could be concentrated on establishing thousands of Christian schools. Even though some students would remain as Muslims, they might have a very favorable attitude toward Christianity. This approach has been very successful in the past and is still a wide-open door today.

The fifth method is *renewal conferences* for Christians in different walks of life, such as Christian farmers, Christian teachers, Christian doctors, Christian fishermen, Christian intellectuals and so forth. The conferences should focus upon training these people to bear witness for Christ wherever they are, by means of word and deed.

The sixth method is *social service projects* as pre-evangelistic means. They provide a way to be present in a community and to be sensitive to an open door for presenting the gospel.

The seventh relevant method is *theological;education*, with strong biblical emphasis and theological exercise, balanced with a strong evangelistic program. This has been practiced in Indonesia through the Evangelical Theological Seminary of Indonesia, which requires its students to plant a church with at least 30 baptized believers before graduation.

Christians can be found in every Islamic country in the world.

Through a new pattern faithful to the biblical teachings and relevant to the Islamic context, evangelization of the world's Muslims in this generation is not impossible.

One of the most exciting things in this generation is the fact that Christians can be found in every Islamic country in the world. Should a new pattern, faithful to the biblical teachings and relevant to the Islamic context be found, the evange lization of the Muslims of Indonesia and of all other nations in this generation would not be an impossible task. After all attempts have been made to present clear, relevant, challenging, biblical messages on Christ, one must sit back and wait by faith to observe the working of the Holy Spirit in convicting and redeeming those whom God "in love...has predestined to the adoption of sons...to the praise of the the glory of his grace" (Eph. 1:5-6). *Surely, Muslims are winnable.*

NOTES

1. Samuel Zwemer, *The Moslem Christ* (1912), 8.

2. Kenneth W. Morgan, *Islam, the Straight Path: Islam Interpreted by the Muslims* (New York: Ronald Press Co., 1956), 384.

3. Clifford Geertz, *The Religion of Java* (London: Free Press Glencou, Collier-MacMillan, 1960), 126.

4. Harun Hadiwijono, *Kebathinan Islam Abad XVI* (Jakarta: BPK Gunung Mulia, n.d.), 7-16.

5. Morgan, *Islam, the Straight Path*, 384.

CHAPTER TWELVE

SOCIAL AND THEOLOGICAL CHANGES IN CONVERSION

Tokumboh Adeyemo

This study is based on examination of three competing religions among the Yoruba people of southwestern Nigeria. The religions examined were African Traditional Religion (ATR), Islam and Christianity. The primary research objective was to investigate the ideas of salvation and conversion, paying particular attention to the problems of continuity and discontinuity in conversion experience from a socio-theological perspective.

Definition of Terms

In this study the following working definitions are adopted:

FAITH is simply defined as a spiritual apprehension of divine truth apart from proof, which is expressed through a system of religious beliefs and practices.

SALVATION has been variously described as deliverance from one's enemies, real or potential; submission to a supreme Being resulting in peace; or a reconciliation with God with attending forgiveness and peace. This concept is separately considered under each system.

CONVERSION is a change of adherence from one religion or faith to another, which can take place at any one of the following three levels (or a combination of levels):

EXTERNAL: changes at this level are nothing more than paraphernalia conformity. They are usually shallow, sometimes superficial and transient.

AUTHORITY: changes at this level are a bit deeper than the first level. They touch on why people do what they do and where or to whom they turn for support, such as a book, cultic rules and regulations, a tradition or a person. This level is also called mythical or a value level or ADAPTATION.

ONTOLOGICAL: changes at this level take place at the very tenor of one's being, right at the central core. It is not just a question of form but of essence, not of sound but of sense, not of action but of existence. At this level, change is described as TRANSFORMATION.

CONTINUITY and **DISCONTINUITY**. By continuity, we mean a set of beliefs or/and behaviors carried from one faith into another when conversion takes place. Discontinuity stands for the opposite—that is, beliefs and behaviors abandoned upon conversion.

African Tribal Religion among the Yoruba

ATR is the indigenous faith and practice of the Yoruba people of Nigeria. It is the heart of their culture and traditions. It is the product of their perception, encounter, reflection upon and experience of the universe in which they live. Speaking generally, the Yoruba world exists in two spheres: the visible, tangible and concrete world of people, animals, vegetation and other natural elements; and the invisible world of the spirits, ancestors, divinities and the supreme deity. Yet it is one world, indivisible, with one touching upon the other. One of their proverbs says: "Our world is like a drum; strike any part of it and the vibration is felt all over.

"Our world is like a drum; strike any part of it and the vibration is felt all over."

Basic elements of the African Tribal Religion

Basic elements of faith in ATR include:

1. Belief in the existence of lesser gods and a High God.
2. Belief in spirits, both good and evil.
3. Belief in the ancestors.
4. Belief in cultic prohibitions (called taboos) and moral violations which can cause disruption of human relationship.
5. Belief in sacrifices performed for various purposes such as warding off evil or securing ancestors' support.
6. Belief in the continuing existence of the dead in the visible world, a position where they could be of help and assistance to the living.
7. Belief in partial reincarnation.

8. Belief in judgment from the High God and/or the dead or the living community of elders.

The traditional religion is expressed and has expressed itself in the way the Yoruba have always regulated their relationship both with nature and with their fellow humans. Because of this, in some cases, some animals have been regarded as sacred to devotees of any particular divinity (such animals are called "totem animals"), some natural phenomena such as baobab trees, hills and rivers have been deified, and some ancestral heroes have been worshiped.

Basic functions of the African Tribal Religion

In a society with a strong sense of community cohesion where the traditional religion is at the heart of culture, one is not surprised to find that ATR has served the following functions among the Yoruba:

1. It has been used as a medium of education, for example, taboos have been used to teach dietary laws, and initiations and rituals have been used to teach sexual morality.
2. It has inculcated a life of communion, union and responsibility.
3. It has served as the repository of the people's history and cultural values in some cases.
4. It has been used as a control of social organizations.
5. It promotes respect for old age in the community.
6. It has preserved some of the traditional works of art and craft.
7. It has been generally tolerant of and hospitable to other religions.

Since the advent of Nigeria's political independence in the early 1960s, ATR has enjoyed some measure of resurgence. The reasons for this are diverse, including: a) the desire for a cultural and spiritual heritage uncontaminated by colonial or Western influence; b) the desire for a supposedly dignified historical and religious identity; c) a reaction against "imposed" systems; and d) in some cases, spiritual aspirations and needs of African people which have not been satisfactorily met by imported religions.

Basic values among the Yoruba

The Yoruba, like many other African peoples, are preoccupied with the following values:

1. The sacredness and sanctity of life. Life is believed to be the property of the Supreme Deity, which no man can bestow nor has the right to terminate.
2. People-centeredness. Things are made for the benefit of humans. Some even think that the gods exist for the benefit of humans.
3. A sense of community. A Yoruba is a being-in-community. He is a part of an organic whole.
4. Holistic approach to reality. No dichotomy exists between the sacred and the profane. This places religion right at the center. It is by it that meanings are determined.
5. Material blessing and community acceptance. To be materially rich is regarded as a blessing from the gods or ancestors. To be poor is like a curse. The community accepts and often reveres the rich but despises the poor.
6. Sense of shame rather than guilt. In matters of morality a sense of shame is more pronounced than a sense of guilt.
7. Possession of power. Acquisition of life force or power through divination, mastery of macrocosm or allying with ancestral powers is an obsession among the Yoruba. By this they believe they can manipulate elemental force and ward off all untoward spirits.

Ideas of Salvation

The basic motivation for societal existence is the preservation of life. This puts humans right at the center of their environmental stimuli.

Their world is not seen as mechanistic like that of the West but dynamic. It is a moving equilibrium that is constantly threatened and sometimes actually disturbed by natural and social calamities. The events which upset it include natural disasters (such as droughts and famine) and epidemics as well as sorcery and other antisocial forces.

Yoruba ATR focuses on *warding off* cosmic and social evils. Their witchdoctors, herbalists and ancestors are "saviors."

The Yoruba believe that these cosmic forces and social calamities are controllable and should be manipulated by them for their own purpose. Thus, the *warding off* of these cosmic and social evils (or, stated positively, maintaining ritual equilibrium) becomes the central focus of religious activities and their salvation. Those who can wield powers in the society, such as witchdoctors, herbalists and ancestors, are regarded as "saviors."

The Yoruba deal with sin as an act and not as human nature. In one of their proverbs they say: *Omo titun ko lese lorun,* meaning: "A newborn baby has no sin." Sins are graded as major and minor. Major sins include violation of religious taboos, adultery with a neighbor's wife, murder and witch-craft. Minor sins include acts like lying, petty stealing or cheating. People are reminded of the law of retributive justice to discourage sins. However, when a sin occurs, especially a major sin, forgiveness consists of community acceptance after a prescribed penalty has been fulfilled.

To them, forgiveness consists of community acceptance after a prescribed penalty has been fulfilled.

To the Yoruba, religion basically originates not with belief in God—this is assumed—but with an opposition to removable evils; and it terminates not with home in heaven, but with the maintenance of social and cosmological balance in the here and now, and community remembrance of people after their death.

Generally speaking, the Yoruba will not really worship anything they can manipulate. Neither are the divinities and ancestors worshipped for their own sakes. Worship in the form of sacrifices, libations and offerings is rendered with an expectation of commensurate return.

For purposes of discussion, it can be summarized that among the Yoruba religionists, salvation is:

a) preservation of life
b) warding off of evil
c) community acceptance and remembrance after death
d) material blessings.

Conversion in African Traditional Religion

ATR knows almost nothing of conversion as a total break from one faith to another. Rather, new gods are added to the old—except that in marriage a bride is expected to forsake her former religion to embrace that of her husband.

The idea of conversion as a total break from one faith in favor of of another is foreign to ATR. Among the Yoruba it never happened before the advent of Islam and Christianity. What did occur before the entrance of Islam and Christianity could be described as the accumulation of more gods to the existing ones.

This happened frequently in warfare. When a clan or tribe was invaded and captured by another, the captors would carry away the gods of the captives and simply place the captured images alongside their existing ones just as the Philistines did with the ark of the Lord of Israel (see 1 Samuel 5:1-12).

The captives or "converts" are made to observe the religious practices and festivals of their captors. More often, change in this manner is essentially external conformity. The converts abide by the rules and regulations of their new cult to the extent that they do not contradict their old beliefs. Where there is conflict, two lines of action are open: the captives may reject the new cultic demands at the risk of punishment, or they may syncretize. There is overwhelming evidence for the second option.

The closest to a total break from one divinity in favor of another within the Yoruba pantheon is in the case of marriage. The Yoruba believe that a woman has no religion or faith of her own as such. She is expected, upon marriage, to embrace that of her husband over against that of her parents (especially her father) which she has hitherto followed.

Cases of real conversion from Islam or Christianity to ATR are almost nonexistent. Among the few encountered in our research, the majority came from the elite or intellectual class. One such case is that of Professor Wande Abimbola, the current vice-chancellor of the University of Ife, Nigeria. During an interview with him, he professed to have been a Christian during his secondary school days in a mission school until he became disenchanted and started to search for his cultural roots and identity. This he claimed he found in *Ifa*, the Yoruba god of oracles. He later read African languages and linguistics and wrote his Ph.D. thesis on *Ifa*.

Professor Abimbola has published a number of excellent literary pieces on the subject. His conviction and argument is that the universal God has revealed himself to all peoples of the world in particular ways. In his view, people can only find meaning and fulfillment as they respond to God in their particular way. He concludes that it is not only wrong but sinful, therefore, for a Yoruba man to respond to God in, for example, an Arabic or Jewish way.

Often change of this type occurs at the authority level. Many a cultural revolutionary who once espoused Christianity or Islam as a student during the colonial days has turned to ATR. It is observed, however, that many of those interviewed are only theoretical adherents rather than practitioners. Where cases of re-conversion are found among the less educated, the common practice is that of syncretism.

Continuity and Discontinuity

Syncretists do not care about continuity or discontinuity. Theologically and sociologically, they simply accommodate.

In the case of syncretists, the question of continuity and discontinuity does not arise. Theologically and sociologically, syncretists simply accommodate. But in the few cases of re-conversion, especially of a cultural revolutionary or a nationalist, it is one of radical repudiation of the sacred books and the founders of Christianity and Islam as foreign ancestors.

Islam Among the Yoruba

Like all other non-Muslims, Yoruba's ATR adherents are regarded by Muslims as infidels and a mission field.

Islam entered the Yoruba land primarily through the north by the hands of Hausa and Fulani traders. Since Islam is a book religion and the Yoruba were largely illiterate, propagation was mainly by oral communication. Islam preaches peace through submission to Allah and the brotherhood of all Muslims. All non-Muslims are regarded as *kafirs* (infidels) and are considered as a mission field.

Ideas of Salvation

Salvation consists of believing in Allah and doing deeds of righteousness. "Those that believe and do deeds of righteousness, those are the inhabitants of Paradise, there they shall dwell forever" (Sura 2:75). Later in the same Quranic portion, the idea is expanded as follows:

> True piety is this: to believe in Allah, and the Last Day, the angels, the Book, and the Prophets, to give of one's substance however cherished to kinsmen and orphans, the needy, the traveler, beggars, and to ransom the slave, to perform the prayer, to pay the alms (2:172).

Yoruba Muslims teach that to escape hell and be a candidate for paradise, one must forsake all other gods and turn to only Allah.

Among the Yoruba Muslims, teaching about paradise and hell is very prominent. To escape hell and be a candidate for paradise one must forsake all other gods as Abraham did and turn to only Allah (2:257; 6:79). The areas of good deeds often advocated by Yoruba Muslims are: kindness, alms-giving, prayers, fasting, making pilgrimage to Mecca, and the necessity of a good character.

Sin, say the Muslims, is neither hereditary nor inevitable, but acquirable through choice and avoidable through knowledge and divine guidance.

Associating anyone or anything with Allah is an unpardonable sin in the teaching of Yoruba Muslims. They believe that sin is sinful nature. Rather, sin is acquirable through choice, but also avoidable through knowledge and true guidance from God. In Islamic teaching, a human is fundamentally a good and dignified creature, weak but not fallen. Furthermore, Islam does not identify with the Christian teaching that a person needs to be redeemed. Instead it teaches that Allah loves and forgives those who obey his will. A person experiences peace through total submission to Allah's guidance and mercy.

Instead of redemption, Islam teaches forgiveness for those who obey Allah's will.

Islam expresses itself in materialistic categories with a high degree of accommodation among the Yoruba. There is no certainty or assurance of paradise, since Allah reserves the prerogative to do whatever he chooses with his creatures.

Coupled with this is the disquieting Quranic teaching that a Muslim must face the punishment of the grave first (19:71).

On the other hand, every devout Yoruba Muslim holds the belief that paradise (or eternal life) could be earned by piety and good works. Sura 18:29, which reads: "Allah does not leave to waste the wage of him who does good works," is a common quotation. The analogy of a scale is often used. It is strongly believed that in the day of judgment Allah will balance on scales a Muslim's good deeds over against his evil deeds. Destiny depends on which way the scale tilts. In summary we can say that the idea of salvation among Yoruba Muslims consists of people's works and God's mercy.

Ideas of Conversion

In occasional waves of reformation, Muslims seek to become pure and to convert infidels. At such times, intolerance is greater towards ATR adherents than towards Christians.

With the Yoruba, tribal or family solidarity is given preference to religious allegiance. It is not uncommon to find adherents of the three religions living under the same roof. This encourages religious toleration. Frequently all members of an extended family participate in one another's religious festivals. From time to time, however, waves of reformation bring the call for compromising Muslims to become pure and convert the infidel. At such times, intolerance is greater towards the religionists than towards the Christians.

Conversion to Islam means admitting that there is no other God but Allah, and recognizing Muhammad as his apostle. A ritual bath usually follows, along with adoption of an Arabic name and repudiation of any other form of worship.

Conversion into Islam from either ATR or Christianity takes a simple form of admitting that there is no other god but Allah and recognizing that Muhammad is his Apostle as expressed in the Kalima. This is usually followed by a ritual bath, the adoption of an Arabic name, and a repudiation of any other form of worship than Islam. A new convert is taught to accept the articles of faith and to practice the five Pillars, especially the Ritual Prayer. Stress is placed on a new social identity. Among some sects new converts are made to wear white robes and to conform to the idiosyncrasies of the group. A strong sense of community solidarity is soon inculcated into the new convert.

It is fashionable among the Yoruba, especially among the illiterates, to become Muslims. In some quarters it is almost a group phenomenon. Reasons advanced by new converts interviewed (a few claimed to have been Christian before) include the following:

a. That Islam preaches peace
b. That Islam promotes one community
c. That Islam offers material prosperity
d. That Islam admits the traditional practice of polygamy.

At best, conversion into Islam takes place at the authority level, where one adopts a new name, new rules and regulations and a new religious system. Values change as one copies the traditions of the new community. However, in a majority of cases, mixing or accommodation is normal.

Continuity and Discontinuity

Syncretism , nevertheless, abounds among the Yoruba, sometimes mixing in elements of Christian practice as well as of ATR.

As in ATR, cases abound of syncretism in Islam among the Yoruba. A case in point is that of my aunt, a former Christian who married my uncle, a Muslim. Under pressure she was given an Islamic name and ritually bathed. She made a pilgrimage to Mecca. Asked about the practice of her faith, she admitted a degree of confusion. She said: "When I sit down to pray five times daily, I find myself reciting the Psalms or calling upon Jesus." Similar things can be said of many who profess conversion into Islam but still engage in traditional religious festivals.

Where genuine conversion takes place at the authority level, new converts faithfully adhere to the Quran and the Sunna. The concept of gods in the hierarchical pantheon is purged and the idea of a mediator between God and humans is eradicated. Worship undergoes a radical change, with new paraphernalia, and a change of place of meeting and language (Arabic), as well as mode of worship. This aspect, more than any other, gives a distinct socio-cultural expression to conversion in the Islamic faith. The Pilgrimage to Mecca is also a big event. More than performing it as a religious duty, many Yoruba Muslims desire to perform it because of the socio-economic status it confers.

Christianity among the Yoruba

Christianity came to Yoruba land through the south about the same time as the colonialists landed. Thus, commerce, civilization (or colonization) and Christianization came hand-in-hand. We leave the evolution of the alliance to the historians to determine its successes and set-backs. Also, since my audience is steeped in the Christian doctrine of salvation and conversion, it suffices to summarize the main tenets and then illustrate them by a personal testimony.

Ideas of Salvation

Four cardinal truths are often emphasized in connection with salvation. These are: (a) the doctrine of original sin—every person is a sinner by nature; this results in the acts of sin and causes unhappiness and misery; (b) reconciliation to God through Christ and forgiveness by his blood; this results in peace and joy; (c) power to live a victorious life by the Holy Spirit; and (d) the assurance of eternal life with Jesus. All of this is by grace.

Ideas of Conversion

Inner transformation, accomplishable only by the Holy Spirit but receivable by faith, is the essence of Christian conversion.

Becoming "new" is the preoccupation. Emphasis is on an inner transformation, a work wholly attributed to the Holy Spirit, but receivable by faith. As evidence of this happening, some churches demand manifestation of spiritual gifts; some ask for fruits worthy of repentance; some call for a walking worthy of the gospel; most require obedience to the Word of God. Almost invariably, demands for water baptism and participation in a local church follow.

In the church, along with genuine believers, can be found nominal Christians and pseudo-converts.

As there are nominal Christians in the church, there are also pseudo-converts. Our research even identified a few cases of people who claimed to have undergone double conversions—for example, a Muslim converted to Christianity and then back to Islam.

What happens where a genuine inner transformation takes place in the life of a Muslim who becomes a Christian? To this I shall speak from personal experience.

Continuity and Discontinuity

1. Understanding God in personal terms and in a personal way as my Father—this was a revolution. It changed my whole .i.theology; and practice. However, this did not happen all at once. It took time as I studied the Bible. In fact all I remember of my moment of conversion is deciding to follow Jesus, the giver of life (John 10:10) rather than Muhammad and the way to God he brought.

2. The corollary to understanding God as Father was my accepting Jesus Christ as my sole Mediator who offers me access to God. Theologically speaking, the *kalima* (confession of faith in God and Muhammad's apostleship) is where it began for me. Jesus became to me more than a prophet. At that initial stage I had problems with the doctrine of the Sonship of Jesus and, of course, the Trinity. But I was convinced as well that Jesus was not a man elevated above men as prophets were. Something was unique about him. At that time I settled for his Mediatorship. I have grown beyond that since.

3. A new attitude toward the Bible followed. From a critical, destructive and polemical attitude, I turned to loving, reading, believing, obeying and applying the Bible to my life. In this exercise I discovered many truths, supreme among them the assurance of life beyond the grave with Christ, who says: "Because I live, you too shall live" (John 14:19). I also realized that knowing him puts me under urgent obligation to share him and what he offers with others. So I began with my immediate family. Today five of them have been converted.

4. The next big change in me was my prayer life. It was quite a struggle and a time of confusion. For days following my conversion, I would go to the mosque to offer the *salat*. But an inner witness would say to me: "But these people are not following me correctly," or "But you are not following me here; this is not my house." On a couple of occasions, I left the mosque in the middle of prayer. I realized that I should identify with Christians, but I also knew that would mean persecution from my people.

Finally, through the encouragement of the man who was discipling me, I went away to the prayer mountain to fast and pray for three days. That did it! It was during that period that the Lord confronted me with the words of Psalm 27:10 that says: "When my father and mother forsake me, the Lord will receive me." I decided there and then to follow Jesus at whatever the cost. Indeed persecution followed, but the Lord has been faithful to his Word.

5. My next discovery was that the Holy Spirit is a person and that through his power I can live for Christ, tell others about him and be victorious. I started seeing results of prayer. Yet I had nothing—no talisman, no magic—just the name of Jesus Christ! When my people saw this, they started calling me by nicknames "prophet" or "son of Jesus." As a result of seeing Christ's power, they started moving from hostility to skepticism and later to neutrality and some to faith in Christ.

Soteriologically, Islam and Christianity cannot both be right. Islam does not agree with Christ's claim.

6. By this time my set of friends started changing. Some of my old Muslim friends called me a traitor or a rebel, worse than Satan. Some predicted that after a few months I would come back to my senses. Of the few who remained friends, some have been converted. Yes, the Lord is able. What the Muslims are looking for is not just a definition but a demonstration of the power of the gospel. And we must not be ashamed of it!

With love in our hearts, tears in our eyes, purity in our lives, justice in our hands and power on our heads, we must boldly take the gospel of peace and offer it to every Muslim.

7. Finally, I have come to the conclusion that they and we Christians cannot both be right. One of us must be wrong, because the two orders are soteriologically different. Unfortunately, Islam does not agree with Christ's claim. With love in our hearts, tears in our eyes, purity in our lives, justice in our hands and power on our heads, we must boldly take the gospel of peace and offer it to every Muslim. May the Lord help us!

OLD FORMS AND NEW MEANINGS

*He appeared to be going further, but they constrained him
saying, 'Stay with us for it is toward evening.'...
So he went in to stay with them.
When he was at table with them, he took the bread and
blessed, and broke it, and gave it to them.
And their eyes were opened
and they recognized him...
Then they told...how he was known to them
in the breaking of the bread.*
— Luke 24: 28–31, 35

CHAPTER THIRTEEN

GUIDELINES FROM HEBREWS FOR CONTEXTUALIZATION

Denis J. Green

Recent years have witnessed an increasing advocacy of a more culturally appropriate approach to Muslim evangelism. The adoption or adaptation of certain Muslim forms of worship by evangelists and the convert church has been proposed as a means not only of making Christianity more attractive to those yet to be converted, but also of giving to the church a form of genuine indigeneity.

Given widely different degrees of contextualization, how does one distinguish between true converts and merely deviant Muslims?

All such endeavors immediately raise the thorny problem of .i.syncretism;, a danger inherent in any attempt at contextual-izing pre-existing religio-cultural forms and beliefs. The point at issue becomes: Are the so-called "converts" truly Christian, or are they in fact merely a deviant sect of Islam? Must certain essential, non-negotiable precepts be accepted by Muslims to mark them as having moved from the camp of Islam to the camp of Christianity?

At issue are the divinity of Christ, the efficacy of his sacrificial death and the authority of Scripture.

The question before us is whether or not it is possible for Muslims to truly become Christians while retaining beliefs and practices which tend to reinforce a less than complete understanding of the basis of salvation and the nature of the Christian life.

For example, Muslims accept Jesus as a prophet; the Quran even acknowledges his sinlessness; but both his divinity and the concept of his substitutionary sacrifice are denied. Is it sufficient for converts to acknowledge Jesus as someone in the nature of the highest prophet, while not being required to acknowledge the divinity of Christ and to have understanding of how that relates to the efficacy of his sacrificial death before they can be regarded as Christians? And what are they to say about the position of Muhammad, whom they hold to be a true prophet of God?

The Christian Scriptures are acknowledged by Islam as being divine in origin, but the Quran is held to supersede them. Can the Quran have any place in the spiritual life of converts, or must they discard it altogether in order to be regarded as true Christians?

In addition to faith in God, Muslims are also required by the Quran to perform specified works in order to merit God's favor, so that in reality the works become a major criterion. Christianity, on the other hand, insists on faith as the sole ground of salvation, with works as its consequent product only. Further complicating the issue is the fact that three of the five major works required of Muslims (prayer, fasting and pilgrimage) are an integral part of their worship rituals. Can converts, therefore, retain or adapt such forms of worship and previous cultural customs in view of their close identification with building up merit before God in Muslim belief?

It has been said that the close similarity between Islam and its Jewish and Christian antecedents makes for easier contextualization and a smoother transition for the Muslim convert. The experience of the recipients of the Epistle to the Hebrews, however, might suggest just the opposite: that precisely in situations where a high degree of similarity exists, the danger of incomplete understanding and syncretism is correspondingly high.

This study therefore seeks to suggest some biblical guidelines for grappling with such issues, by relating the occasion, purpose and teaching of Hebrews to the process of contextualization and conversion from Islam to Christianity.

The Recipients and Purpose of the Epistle to the Hebrews

The Epistle to the Hebrews presents the student of Scripture with one of the most intriguing questions to occupy the minds of scholars over many centuries: namely, to whom was the epistle originally addressed and for what particular purpose? Although there have been arguments to the contrary, this paper proceeds on the assumption that the epistle should be treated as a unity and as having been written with a specific audience in mind.[1]

Over the past 100 years or so, New Testament scholarship has produced a wide variety of views on this topic. For a summary of the most prominent views, the reader may consult F.F. Bruce (1968-69), R.E. Glaze (1985), Donald Guthrie (1970), Everett F. Harrison (1971) and other recent introductions to New Testament studies.[2] To examine the respective merits of each view is well outside the scope of this paper. Rather, on the basis of such an examination already carried out,[3] I will proceed directly to present the hypothesis which I believe to be most plausible in light of the available evidence.

1. The general background of the readers was Jewish

Despite the existence of some factors in Hebrews which could be compatible with Gentile or mixed Gentile-Jewish recipients, the fact remains that all of these factors can also be adequately explained if the epistle is assumed to have been intended for a group of readers of purely Jewish background.

The converse is not as easily accommodated, however. To take one example, while we might agree that the general basis of the Old Testament held as much authority for Gentiles as for Jews, the emphasis placed by the author on the succession of Jesus in the priesthood of Melchizedek would hold little attraction for the Gentiles. If the purpose of the author was to warn his readers of the danger of paganism and unbelief, other Old Testament passages would have been more suitable.[4]

In brief, the author's emphasis on the levitical *cultus* and on the spiritual significance of the historical experiences of the people of Israel, his particular employment of the Old Testament in a manner reminiscent of the midrashic style,[5] and his assumption of a deep-rooted loyalty to those Scriptures on the part of his readers all find their most appropriate application in the context of an audience whose religious background was Judaism.

2. The specific background of the readers was a nonconformist Judaism

It cannot be denied that the subject matter of Hebrews displays similarities to the beliefs of the Qumran community in a number of areas. However, these similarities are insufficient to posit a direct relationship between Hebrews and former members of the community.

> The most that can be said..., is that the recipients of the epistle were probably Jewish believers in Jesus whose background was not so much the normative Judaism represented by rabbinical tradition as the nonconformist

Judaism of which the Essenes and the Qumran community are outstanding representatives, but not the only representatives.[6]

More certain is the connection between Alexandrian Hellenism and the epistle, as the study by Ronald Nash has shown.[7] Bruce has no doubts that the writer of the epistle was a Hellenist, and on this basis a similar religio-cultural context for his audience is to be favored.[8] Furthermore, there is evidence that a degree of nonconformism similar to that represented by the Essenes in Palestinian Judaism was also present in the Hellenistic Judaism of the Diaspora.

Hebrews gives us certain indications that the original readers were part of this nonconformist tradition. The attention given to proving the supremacy of Jesus over angels and other eschatological figures may indicate a tendency on the part of the readers to give undue prominence (while still falling short of actual worship) to those figures.

The residual attachment of the readers to such practices as ceremonial washings and the laying on of hands, and their apparent susceptibility to certain food regulations, also fit the type of nonconformism which was known to have existed, for example, in Rome.

3. The readers considered themselves to be Christians

Much discussion has been generated by the "apostasy passages" in Hebrews (6:4-8; 10:26-31) as to whether the readers were in fact already converted to Christianity. One possible interpretation of these passages is that Christians are being warned of the possibility of their falling away and losing their salvation. Another interpretation is that these people, while displaying many outward manifestations of Christianity, have never made an actual commitment to Christ and will move into a state of ever-increasing hardness of heart making true repentance impossible. A third alternative is that the author is putting up a hypothetical case of apostasy which has no direct relation to his readers.

This is not the place for the exegetical study required to evaluate the merits of these respective views. However, a brief comment on the nature of conversion and its relevance to our understanding of this epistle is in order.

Was the epistle written to the converted, to the not really converted, or to persons who were then at various points along the conversion road?

In my opinion most commentators on Hebrews proceed on the basis of an understanding of conversion as an essentially punctiliar event. This forces them to treat the readers as being in one of two categories: converted or not converted. However, an understanding of conversion as a process involving a progressive change of basic allegiances from "the world" (whether represented by pagan attitudes and lifestyle, another form of religious belief, or any other controlling worldview) to Christ allows for another alternative.

In that alternative view, the persons involved may at any point in time be placed on a continuum having as one extreme a point representing full and continuing allegiance to the world, and as the other a point representing full and continuing allegiance to Christ. Their progress along the continuum involves changes in the evaluative, affective and cognitive realms that make up their worldview, where increasingly the values adopted are those of Christ in place of those promoted by the world. But since such change depends on an exercise of the will of the individuals involved, it can be taking place in either direction on the continuum at any point in time.

My thinking about this process of conversion has been influenced to some degree by the model presented by Charles Kraft in *Christianity in Culture*, in which he sees conversion as a process that "consists of a large number of discrete decisions, many of which precede the point of conversion and lead up to it."[9]

GOD'S ACTIVITY ══════════════════════════════>

                 Wooing of the Regenerating Sanctifying Spirit

```
                  _____      Full
No                                               Alle-
Allegiance   :<D><D>< :<D><D> :<D><D> :<D><D>:   giance
to Christ         _____     to Christ

             Developing <--->Turning <--->Maturing
             awareness
```

HUMAN ACTIVITY <══════════════════════════>

The accompanying diagram is a modification of Kraft's model.[10] Each "D" represents a decision for or against commitment to Christ. The point of actual conversion, if such may be postulated, is known only to God, but would occur somewhere towards the end of the middle section of the continuum. Once that point has been passed, the convert can be expected to show clear signs of progression towards spiritual maturity. If such signs are not evident, there will be cause for doubt as to the authenticity of the conversion.

The ideal would be a steady movement towards full allegiance to Christ; the reality is more likely to involve "modes" of regression interspersed with "modes" of progression. And if those "modes" of regression persist, then we may envisage a time when the person has moved all the way back along the continuum to a point of full allegiance to the world.

This model of conversion gains a great deal of support from Hebrews and is hinted at by some commentators.[11] On the one hand, we gain the impression that the readers were regarded by both the author and themselves as being in the Christian camp: they had suffered persecution for their faith, had given sacrificial service to other Christians, had been well taught by former leaders and were expected to have reached a stage of spiritual maturity. On the other hand, it is difficult to deny that the author also contemplated a point where they might lose all that they had and fail to gain the salvation which was the object of their hope.

Hence, his use of the wilderness experiences of Israel as examples of those who failed to inherit the promised salvation and his repeated warnings that "we share in Christ, if only we hold our first confidence firm to the end" (3:14).

Like some Muslims now involved in the church, recipients of Hebrews were followers of Jesus in some way but were not yet living as Christ's disciples.

I submit that the recipients of Hebrews had progressed some distance in the conversion process. They were followers of Jesus in some way, but were certainly not living as his disciples. Now they were at a critical point: either they could go on to spiritual maturity and thus be assured of the hope of salvation, or they would find themselves regressing towards their former allegiances in Judaism, thereby facing the prospect of losing all that they had so far gained.

We may note that even "disciples" of Jesus are not immune from the possibility that the high demands of the gospel will cause a reversal of their allegiance to Christ (Jn. 6:66). And a persistent regression could have no other end than a permanent loss of the capacity to be "restored again unto repentance."

4. The readers were in danger of regressing for two reasons:

Persecution and immaturity threaten to reverse such persons' direction.

(a) *They were under pressures of persecution.* Formerly, they had successfully overcome such pressures (10:32-34), but now there was a threat of new and perhaps more severe persecution (10:35-36; 12:4). If we assume a date of composition for Hebrews in the early 60s A.D., we may reconstruct the situation as follows. The readers had endured earlier persecution, most likely at the hands of the Roman authorities and because they were Jews, rather than because of their specifically Christian stand. Now they faced persecution again, but this time it was primarily because of their connection with Christianity. In fact, in this situation to be known as a Jew rather than a Christian would be an advantage, since Jews still enjoyed official protection from the Roman state. Thus, as a means of escaping such persecution, and perhaps also under pressure from fellow Jews who were uniting against Rome, they were facing the strong temptation to renew official ties with Judaism.

(b) *They were spiritually immature.* Despite the considerable length of time that had elapsed since they first attached themselves to Christianity, they were still "babes in Christ" (5:12-13). They had not progressed beyond the first principles. Because of this condition, the author feared that they would not have the endurance required to withstand the imminent persecution and hold fast to the hope of salvation.

I submit that the primary reason for this lack of spiritual growth, which was fast turning to stagnation and even apathy (5:11), was the persistent clinging of the readers to certain beliefs and practices which they had brought into Christianity from their former brand of nonconformist Judaism. It has been suggested by some that they endeavored to retain just so much of their former religious practices as was necessary to allow them to remain under the larger umbrella of Judaism.[12] Thus, they continued to carry out ritual ablutions and the laying on of hands, observed certain food regulations, perhaps even worshiped at the synagogue, and participated in the festivals.

Dual allegiance worked havoc for the vacillating Hebrews; it can do so for Muslim-Christian counterparts today.

Now the crisis of persecution was forcing them to a position where such compromise was no longer possible. Either they must make a clear profession of allegiance to Christ by forsaking these former practices, or they could return to full identification with their fellow Jews and so escape the persecution. However, the author warns in the strongest terms that the latter choice would result in the virtual loss of all hope of salvation.

5. The Author's Challenge

To meet the situation just described, the author exhorted his readers that they not "neglect such a great salvation" or "throw away [their] confidence, which has a great reward," but rather "hold fast [their] confession of hope without wavering" (2:3; 10:35, 23; etc.). Throughout the epistle, there is a constant emphasis on the need for perseverance in attaining the goal of salvation. The means of maintaining such perseverance might be summarized as falling into two general categories:

(a) *Moving on to spiritual maturity.* For the readers of Hebrews, this meant leaving behind the elementary truths which brought them into Christianity and with which their former beliefs and practices were largely compatible, and establishing a deeper spiritual foundation for their faith. Central to this was the transition from a reliance on material rituals and regulations as a major sustenance of faith to a reliance on the spiritual ministry of Christ as the heavenly High Priest. It was only through him that they could be assured of access to God in order to "receive mercy and find grace in time of need" (4:16).

Along with increasing maturity, increasing identification with the wider Christian community is an indispensable part of the conversion process.

(b) *Strengthening ties with the wider Christian community.* This was to be demonstrated in two primary ways: by worshiping together with, and by serving fellow Christians (10:24-25). The readers had apparently become an ingrown group who, because of their distinctive religio-cultural background, had all but isolated themselves from other Christians in the vicinity. But it was time for them to make their true identity clear, to "go forth outside the camp." This would be most clearly demonstrated by a reaffirmation of their ties with the wider Christian community through joint worship and acknowledgement of the authority of its leaders (13:17).

Identifying themselves with the wider Christian community also meant a commitment to service in that context. The practice of hospitality and ministry to the needs of those imprisoned for the faith are given special emphasis by the author (13:1-3), perhaps because in both instances those being ministered to were most likely to be Christians outside of the immediate group of the readers. "Strangers" would be people not intimately known to the readers, perhaps even Gentiles, while the prisoners would be people who, unlike the readers, had already made their commitment to Christ clear and were suffering because of it.

The Relationship of Islam and Judaism

Shared roots and centuries of interaction account for significant similarities between Islam and Judaism, a fact that makes the Epistle to the Hebrews a highly relevant one for Muslims.

If the Epistle to the Hebrews is to provide any insights for contemporary Christianity, its most valid application will be to those people whose situation most nearly approximates that of the letter's original readers. Therefore, it is pertinent to compare the relationship between Judaism, as the conversion context of the Hebrews, and Islam, as the conversion context which is our particular focus.

Historical Interaction

As we shall see, the similarities between Judaism and Islam as two religious faiths are very significant. Consider, for example, the following three facts:

1. The interaction between Jews and Arabs stretches back for a long period prior to the lifetime of Muhammad, with numerous examples found in the Old Testament.[13] Assuming acceptance of the biblical evidence of their common ancestor, Abraham (a fact disputed by neither party), we should not find this too surprising. It would also be natural to assume some diffusion of religious concepts through these contacts.

2. There was no lack of opportunity for direct interaction between Judaism and Islam from the very earliest years of the latter's inception. The existence of a significant Jewish population in Arabia in the early 7th century A.D. is incontestable.

That Muhammad himself was in contact with Jews is quite clear from the contents of the Quran. Not only are there references to Jewish scholars (*ahbar*) and rabbis (*rabbani*) and to the "learned (*ulema*) of the children of Israel" (Sura 26:197), but there is a progressive growth in accuracy with regard to Old Testament stories and the incorporation of material which seems to have its origins in the Talmud, Midrash and Mishnah. Finally, there is the evidence of the Muslim practices related to prayer, fasting and worship, which were apparently adopted after the Jewish pattern initially, and then modified as a reaction to the Jewish rejection of Muhammad and his message.[14]

With regard to the type of Judaism with which Muhammad interacted, a variety of views have been promulgated, including orthodox Judaism,[15] a somewhat unorthodox variant influenced by Christian monastic piety,[16] and a late-surviving offshoot of the Qumran community.[17] Whatever the case, as Geiger points out, the silence of the Talmud concerning the Jews of Arabia can only be attributed to the fact that they were regarded as being of inferior status by comparison with those in Palestine and Babylon.[18]

3. The interaction between Islam and Judaism continued after the lifetime of Muhammad, particularly after the center of Muslim religious authority moved to Iraq. This was also a center of Jewish academia; the conversion of significant numbers of Jews resulted in a continuing interchange of ideas. "What Jews could never have achieved by proselytism, apostates managed to do by the imposition on Islam of a number of important Jewish ideas and institutions."[19]

We, however, are not primarily interested in the "how" and "why" of Islam coming to have so many similarities with Judaism. The fact is that the similarities are there and that in many ways the two faiths share a common outlook and spirit.

Similarities of Belief and Practice

Islam differs from Christianity in that, like Judaism, it is a religion of commandments rather than one of redemption through the atoning death of Jesus Christ.

The many areas of similarity should not surprise us when we recall that Muhammad viewed himself and his message as falling into a direct line of succession from the two earlier monotheistic faiths. But despite evidence in the Quran that Christianity, albeit probably an unorthodox or heretical form thereof, was also operating to influence Muhammad, there is a fundamental difference to be noted. The Christian faith is based on belief in the redemptive actions of Jesus Christ as Savior, and its acts of worship are merely symbolic of that fact. However,

> Islam, like Judaism, is a religion of commandments, in which the minute observance of ritual and ethical injunctions is intended to sanctify every moment of the believer's life and to make him continuously aware of his being but a servant of God.[20]

Such an outlook is consonant with the rigorously mono-theistic spirit of both Islam and Judaism. Just as the Jews of Jesus' day rejected the notion of the Godhead consisting of more than one person, so Islam also rejects the Christian doctrine of the Trinity as tritheism. The emphasis is on an awesome reverence for an entirely transcendent God.

A number of studies have shown the parallels between Islam (both in its Quranic formulation and in its subsequent development through the Hadith) and Judaism in a variety of areas. It would be impossible to cover them all here.[21] A few examples will suffice to illustrate the similarity of outlook and spirit shared by the two faiths.

1. Monotheism

As has already been mentioned, both faiths share a monotheistic outlook, shown most clearly in the basic creedal statement of each: "The Lord our God is one Lord" (Deut. 6:4); "He is God, one, God the alone" (Sura 112:1). The awkward construction of the Arabic here suggests that it may have been based directly on the Hebrew.[22]

2. Angels and Revelation

In both Islam and Judaism, high value is placed on angels as mediatorial agents in the revelation of God's Word. In Judaism, the Torah was revealed to Moses in this way; in Islam, the Quran was revealed to Muhammad under the supervision of Gabriel (Sura 2:97/91). Of the four archangels in Islam, two are unmistakably Jewish: Jibra'il and Mika'il.

3. Prophets

The fact that a significant number of the prominent Old Testament figures are recognized as prophets in the Quran is interesting in itself. What is of more interest is that many of these, such as Abraham, Lot, Noah, Aaron, David and Solomon are not categorized as prophets in the Bible, whereas they are so categorized in the later Jewish Aggada (folklore), which seems, therefore, to have been Muhammad's source for this idea.[23]

4. Eschatology

One of the main themes of the earliest suras of the Quran is that of the Day of Judgment. Because of the similarities with Christian apocryphal literature, it was assumed until recently that the latter was Muhammad's primary source for this material. However, the discovery of very similar material in the Dead Sea Scrolls raises the possibility that this type of apocalyptic writing was also circulating among the Jews of Arabia with whom Muhammad had his main contact. If Rabin's theory regarding the background of Arabian Jewry is correct, then the connection is already clear.

5. Community

Like Judaism, Islam makes no distinction between sacred and profane, religion and politics, private and public morals.

The concept of the *umma* in Islam and the theocratic community in Judaism are very similar. In both cases, a holistic view of human existence operates to regulate every aspect of life for those within the community. There is no separation of the sacred from the profane, religion from politics, private from public morals. The total conduct of life is determined by the dictates of God's will as it is contained in revealed scripture and the law developed therefrom.

6. Law

Both the initial formulation of Muslim law under Muhammad and its subsequent codification in what is now Iraq took place in an environment of constant interaction with Jews. Specific examples of the similarity between Muslim and Jewish law abound, but suffice it to note that the following general areas provide for fruitful comparison: the concept of ceremonial purity, with consequent dietary laws and regulations for determining "clean" and "unclean" states and ritual ablutions; obligatory duties and prescribed methods of worship, such as prayers, fasting and pilgrimage; and social laws regulating the life of the community, where correspondences can be seen particularly in areas such as provision for the disadvantaged (orphans and widows), marriage and laws of inheritance.

7. Messianism

In both Judaism and Islam one finds expectation of a messianic figure and an eventually united humanity experiencing justice, righteousness and peace.

Belief in a messianic figure (the Mahdi in Islam) who will bring a reign of perfect justice and righteousness on earth is another common feature. In Islam, this has special prominence amongst the Shi`ites. In both Islam and Judaism it is realized that there is a gulf between the ideal and the reality of the implementation of the principles of the Kingdom of God on earth. Therefore, both faiths share this common hope and expectation of a humanity united in the belief in the one and only God and experiencing the benefits of justice, righteousness and peace.

8. Priesthood

While Judaism has a designated priesthood with clearly defined duties, Islam acknowledges no office of priest or appointed mediator between man and God. However, as Samuel Zwemer has argued persuasively in *Heirs of the Prophets*,[24] this official dogma is contradicted in practice by the ascription of priestly functions to various categories of

Muslim leadership (*imam, qadi, khatib,* etc.). Such functions include: receiving converts into Islam and excommunicating apostates, presiding at public services and initiating the sacrifice and proper prayer ritual at the two great religious festivals, and participating in circumcision, marriage and funeral ceremonies.

Of equal significance is the ascription of intercessory powers to certain persons, most notably Muhammad himself, Husayn and the Hidden Imam in Shi`ite Islam, and the sheikhs, *walis* and *pirs* of Popular Islam. In the Islam of the masses, at least, these figures are looked to as a source of blessing, intercession before God, forgiveness and help of all kinds.

Implications for the Conversion of Muslims

The thesis of Crone and Cook[25] that in the early period Islam should more properly be called "Hagarism" and viewed as a sectarian Jewish messianic movement stretches the historical data (or lack of it) too far. Nevertheless, I submit that that less-than-orthodox Judaism in Northern Arabia was similar enough to the Islam developed under Muhammad, to make it valid for us to compare the process of conversion from Judaism to Christianity to that of conversion from Islam to Christianity.

In the Epistle to the Hebrews we have a document which is extremely relevant to this topic, and which to some degree provides needed guidelines in the quest to contextualize the gospel for Muslims.

"Stagnated contextualization," Hebrews reveals, may facilitate a transition to Christianity and yet operate as a barrier to a complete experience of Christ and his salvation.

I suggest that Hebrews gives us an insight into the possible consequences of what I might call "stagnated contextualization." By this I mean contextualization which has been employed as a means of facilitating the transition of Muslims from Islam to Christianity, but which then comes to operate as a barrier to their proceeding to a complete experience of Christ and his salvation. To illustrate this, let us return to the situation of the recipients of Hebrews.

Four faith deficiencies concerned the writer of Hebrews:

From the content of the epistle, it appears that the writer was concerned about the following deficiencies in the faith of his readers, which he proceeded to correct:

1) Incomplete acceptance of Jesus as the final and authoritative mediator of God's will;

1. A lack of complete acceptance of Jesus as the final and authoritative mediator of God's will, evidenced by their apparently continuing to attach a degree of significance to both angels (1:1-2:18) and Moses (3:1-6) which was in unhealthy competition with the status and role they assigned to Jesus.

2) Incomplete acceptance of the efficacy of Christ's sacrifice and his mediatorial powers;

2. A lack of complete acceptance of the efficacy of the sacrifice of Christ and the superiority of his mediatorial powers, evidenced by their apparently continuing to ascribe value to the levitical priesthood and sacrificial ritual (4:14-5:11; 7:1-10:39).

3) Incomplete acceptance of the concept of salvation by faith alone;

3. A lack of complete acceptance of the concept of salvation by faith alone, evidenced by their continued emphasis on ceremonial ablutions, the laying on of hands and certain dietary regulations (6:1-2; 9:10, 14; 13:9).

4) Withdrawal from the wider Christian community.

4. A withdrawal from the wider Christian community, apparently for two main reasons: (a) because of some perceived incompatibility with what was probably a Gentile Christian majority (perhaps implied by 13:17); (b) in order to avoid persecution (12:1ff.).

The result of all this was that the recipients of Hebrews were in serious danger of slipping back from whatever position they had reached in the process of conversion, and faced the prospect of ultimately losing the hope of salvation altogether.

Can we not envisage some of these very same issues arising in the context of Muslim evangelism and church planting? In our efforts to emphasize the similarities between Islam and Christianity as bridges to conversion and as a basis for contextualization of beliefs and rituals, the stage may be set for the eventual stagnation of the faith of the converts and their failure to reach spiritual maturity. Consider the following possibilities:

Stagnation of Muslim converts' faith can result from:
—continued ascription of revelatory authority to Muhammad
—continued dependence on rites and festivals
—continued reliance on forms of worship
—isolation from the wider Christian community.

1. A desire to ease the transition allows the continued use of the Quran as a source of devotional inspiration and teaching alongside of the Bible. The result is a continuing ascription of prophetic status and revelatory authority to Muhammad, instead of a complete transference of that status to Jesus and the Bible alone.

2. A desire to preserve the identification of the converts with their culture and community and to shield them from persecution allows continued participation in the Muslim rites and festivals, which, however, all have a close association in their minds with the concept of gaining merit before God.

Perhaps this is a case where the forms are not neutral and cannot be divorced from their attached meanings, at least not until after the convert church has been in existence for some considerable period. Continued use of these forms by the converts may make it extremely difficult for them to accept the sacrifice of Christ as all-sufficient.

3. A desire to contextualize the externals of Christianity through the use of forms of worship and religious piety with which the converts are familiar encourages the continued use and adaptation of forms of prayer, fasting, the observance of dietary regulations and ceremonial purity. But again, the identification of all of these items with the works necessary for favor with God in Islam could easily lead to a continued reliance upon them for salvation, rather than on faith alone.

4. A desire to shield converts from cultural incompatibility with other Christian groups in the vicinity leads to the formation of a separate homogeneous church. This, in combination with the factors mentioned above, may ultimately result in an isolated, culture-bound, immature, sectarian group which is unsure whether its true identity lies with Christianity or Islam.

"Props" can become "millstones." No doubt it will be objected that the scenario depicted here is overstated and that I have not done justice to the true objectives of true contextualization. Perhaps, but I am reminded of the fact that those who evangelized the recipients of Hebrews were certainly folk of the highest caliber (13:7), and the Holy Spirit had been active in their midst (6:4). The evangelists apparently felt comfortable with allowing their converts to retain certain beliefs and practices which were not wholly compatible with Christianity, expecting these things to fall away as spiritual maturity was reached. Yet the expected growth had not occurred (5:12-14); on the contrary, the Christian experience of the converts had stagnated (5:11).

They may have been followers of Jesus in some intellectual sense, but they were not disciples. The very things which had acted as "props" to ease them into a new faith had eventually become "millstones," inhibiting the onward progress of the conversion process and preventing them from having an effective witness to the non-Christians surrounding them.

Conclusion

Hebrews provides us with a strong warning regarding the potential danger of allowing, in the name of contextualization, the unplanned and prolonged retention of former religious beliefs and practices, unless accompanied by a clear reinterpretation of meaning along biblical lines. It also appears that at some point there is a need for converts to make a more complete identification with Christianity in distinction from the beliefs and practices of their former religion, if they are to have the full assurance of salvation and progress to spiritual maturity.

As much as anyone else, I am aware that for converts from Islam this may be an extremely difficult decision to make, fraught with potentially severe consequences. Furthermore, part of this identification may involve establishing closer ties with other groups of Christians in the vicinity, even though they may be from a different, even somewhat repugnant, religio-cultural background. Yet this is no different from the situation which faced the Hebrews.

On the basis of the above, it seems to me that attention should be given to at least five general principles:

1. Contextualization of existing religious beliefs and practices may undoubtedly serve an important role in facilitating the transition into Christianity.

The final goal is not just an indigenous church but a spiritually mature one.

2. Contextualization is not an end in itself, but a means to an end. The final goal is a spiritually mature church, not just an indigenous church. A point may be reached where certain contextualized beliefs and practices become an obstacle to further progress toward that goal. This is a particular danger for Muslim converts because of the high degree of similarity between many of the beliefs and practices of Islam and Christianity.

3. In such a case, those hindering beliefs and practices must either be further modified and corrected by systematic teaching, or be discarded and/or replaced by others.

4. In this process, a church in a particular religio-cultural context needs the insights and support of Christians from other religio-cultural contexts.

The Book of Hebrews shows converts from Islam the importance of preparing for the time when they also might need to make their own "agonizing reappraisal".

5. The reaction of the Muslim community must be noted. Do they really see the emulation of their practices as true piety, or just a cheap, and therefore unacceptable, imitation?

F.F. Bruce says with regard to the Hebrews,

> Not only for them, but for their fellow-Christians in many other places, the necessity of coming to terms with the Church's continued existence in history as a community completely separated from Judaism involved an "agonizing reappraisal."[26]

They must establish their full allegiance to Jesus Christ and validate their identity as his church.

So too, it is submitted, the Epistle to the Hebrews warns us that converts from Islam need to be prepared for the time when they also might be called upon to make their own "agonizing reappraisal" in order to establish their full allegiance to Jesus Christ and validate their identity as his church.

NOTES

1. Antony Snell, *New and Living Way: An Explanation of the Epistle to the Hebrews* (London: The Faith Press, 1959), 25; Donald A. Hagner, *Hebrews* , Good News Commentary (New York: Harper & Row, 1983), xxiii.

2. F.F. Bruce, "Recent Contributions to the Understanding of Hebrews," in *Expository Times* 80 (1968-69): 260-264; R.E. Glaze, "Introduction to Hebrews," in *The Theological Educator* 32 (1985): 20-37; Donald Guthrie, *New Testament Introduction* ,3rd ed. (rev.) (Downers Grove, IL: Inter-Varsity Press, 1970); Everett F. Harrison, *Introduction to the New Testament* , Rev. ed. (Grand Rapids: Eerdmans, 1971).

3. Denis J. Green, "The Addressees and Purpose of the Epistle to the Hebrews," (Unpublished paper, School of Theology, Fuller Theological Seminary).

4. Cf. William Manson, *The Epistle to the Hebrews: An Historical and Theological Reconsideration* , The Baird Lecture (London: Hodder & Stoughton, 1951).

5. Hagner, *Hebrews*, xiv.

6. F.F. Bruce, *The Epistle to the Hebrews* , NICNT (Grand Rapids: Eerdmans, 1964), xxix.

7. Ronald H. Nash, "The Notion of Mediator in Alexandrian Judaism and the Epistle to the Hebrews," in *Westminster Theological Journal* 40 (1977): 89-115.

8. Bruce, *The Epistle to the Hebrews*, 232.

9. Charles H. Kraft, *Christianity in Culture: A Study in Dynamic Biblical Theologizing in Cross-Cultural Perspective* (Maryknoll, NY: Orbis Books, 1979), 337.

10. Ibid., 338.

11. Hagner, *Hebrews*, 73.

12. Glaze, "Introduction," 28-29.

13. S.D. Goitein, *Jews and Arabs* , 3rd rev. ed. (New York: Schocken Books, 1974), 4; Philip K. Hitti, *History of the Arabs* , 7th ed. (London: MacMillan & Co. Ltd., 1961), 40-43.

14. See generally: W. Montgomery Watt, *Muhammad at Mecca* (Oxford: Clarendon Press, 1953); *Muhammad at Medina* (Oxford: Clarendon Press, 1956); Alfred Guillaume, "The Influence of Judaism on Islam," in *The Legacy of Israel* eds. Edwyn R. Bevan and Charles Singer (Oxford: Clarendon Press, 1927), 120-171; Charles Cutler

Torrey, *The Jewish Foundation of Islam* ,The Hilda Stroock Lectures, 1931 (New York: Jewish Institute of Religion Press, 1933); S.D. Goitein, *Studies in Islamic History and Institutions* (Leiden: E.J. Brill, 1968).

15. Torrey, *The Jewish Foundation*, 34-35.

16. Goitein, *Studies in Islamic History*, 57-58.

17. Chaim Rabin, *Qumran Studies* (London: Oxford University Press, 1957), 112-130.

18. Abraham Geiger, *Judaism and Islam* ,trans. F.M. Young (New York: KTAV Publishing House, 1970), 18. (Originally published as *Was hat Mohammed aus Judenthume Aufgenommen?*, Baden, 1833).

19. Erwin I.J. Rosenthal, *Judaism and Islam* (London: Thomas Yoseloff, 1961), 9.

20. Goitein, *Studies in Islamic History*, 20-21.

21. E.g., Guillaume, "The Influence of Judaism on Islam"; Julian Oberman, "Islamic Origins: A Study in Background and Foundation," in *The Arab Heritage*, ed. Nabih Amin Faris (Princeton: Princeton University Press, 1944), 58-120; Rosenthal, *Judaism and Islam*; Geiger, *Judaism and Islam*.

22. Hartwig Hirschfeld, *New Researches into the Composition and Exegesis of the Qoran*, Asiatic Monographs vol. III (London: Asiatic Society, 1902), 35.

23. Rosenthal, *Judaism and Islam*, 14.

24. Samuel M. Zwemer, *Heirs of the Prophets* (Chicago: Moody Bible Institute, 1946).

25. Patricia Crone and Michael Cook, *Hagarism: The Making of the Islamic World* (Cambridge: Cambridge University Press, 1977).

26. Bruce, *The Epistle to the Hebrews*, 255.

CHAPTER FOURTEEN

LESSONS LEARNED IN CONTEXTUALIZATION

Phil Parshall

Can anyone claim to have "learned contextualization?" We who are novice practitioners in the realm of applied Islamic contextualization, are in the stage of hypothesis and experimentation rather than that of confirmation and dogmatic pronouncement.

Yet small slivers of light are breaking forth and piercing the stygian darkness of the pre-dawn morning. Never before in 14 centuries of Muslim-Christian relations has there been such a mobilization of resources for the task of confronting the Sons of Ishmael with the liberating gospel of Jesus Christ. True, the Crusaders mobilized *en masse*, but it was with a sword of death, not a sword of Spirit and Life.

Can one imagine a mission executive stating that his society must consider immediately opening a Muslim front in their outreach because "Young people today seem only interested in going to Islamic countries"? As commendatory as this "new wave" is, I cannot help but ponder the potential contradictory influence of contemporary headlines vis-a-vis that of the Holy Spirit. Is all of this activity generated by a deep love for Christ and Muslims or have young people been seduced by a passing fad—a spotlight status—a romantic illusion? Only time will reveal whether we are in a pop or a classic mode. In the meantime we press on!

The contextualization issue is relevant in at least five areas of concern: This study will focus on five areas of relevance to the contextualization issue. Many of the anecdotes come from my personal involvement and observation. Included, however, are some secondhand accounts from reputable sources.

Theology, Lifestyle,
Finances, Critiquing
of Islam, Incarnated
Spirituality.

More than once I have been forced to resort to the use of pseudonyms in order to protect those ministering in sensitive situations—or to spare embarrassment to certain individuals. Obviously I will not be able to give more than cursory treatment to a number of the complex issues I raise. I refer the interested reader to my previous writings for further understanding of my missiological positions.

Theological Diversity

One time-honored and emotionally-preserved ethos of evangelicals is a high level of fidelity to non-essential theology and practice. How else could we ever have come to a place where opinions on pre-mid-post-millenialism become a test of whether one is an evangelical? Illustrations could go on ad infinitum. This propensity toward a sharp delineation of minutiae has affected the courage of innovators who otherwise would be eager to wade out into the sea of the unexplored. Probing, persistent questions relating to one's support base militate against an enthusiastic plunge into the unknown.

Lest I be misunderstood, I am unequivocally an evangelical. However, my reservation relates to people who are so dichotomistic in hermeneutics that they can only see theology in terms of sharply delineated black and white. Some of us have been forced to deal with third world cultures and non-Christian religions. We, at times, find ourselves awash in a sea of murky gray.

Even with total commitment to biblical faith, a contextualist is still extremely vulnerable to the surging waves of personal and institutional criticism. It was not easy for me to receive a mimeographed copy of a negative critique of my evangelistic methodology which ends up asking if I am not on a path which will lead to a denial of the work of the Cross. This was written by an esteemed friend who has spent many years ministering in a Muslim country. At least two churches dropped our support as a result of my views, though several others commenced giving to us.

I recall one sleepless night tossing and turning ensnared in a web of conflicting emotions towards a prominent person who had targeted my ministry as an example of unacceptable theological accommodation. Still, through it all, I am a total convert to contextualization. Without doubt, my writings and articulated thoughts are errant in numerous places and in need of correction. And so, in my more rational moments, I welcome the navigational correctives that keep the ship on course.

A few of the theological controversies in the contextualization debate are as follows:

Baptism

A prominent missiologist has been widely quoted as saying a close biblical equivalent to New Testament baptism would be to have a coffin in front of the church. A new convert would lie down in the coffin and then the lid would be closed and re-opened. The new believer would rise from the coffin, signifying death to the old life and resurrection to the new life in Christ. As far as I can ascertain, the coffin would not be filled with water.

No other postulate of mine has aroused the purists as much as my statement in *New Paths In Muslim Evangelism* that I would be interested in seeing experimentation done in the area of a functional substitute for baptism. The reason for my suggestion (not a dictum or even a conviction) relates to the Muslim view that baptism is the severing link with the Islamic community. Baptism has often been the seal of alienation and commencement of an extraction syndrome—thus, the appeal for a different type of initiatory rite that could be known more for its religious significance than for its negative sociological impact.

Known in Islamic cultures more for its negative sociological impact than for its positive religious significance, baptism needs to be interpreted to Muslims in a clear, biblical manner.

Perhaps the missiologist's proposal of a waterless coffin did not get wide enough exposure to provoke a counterattack. But my suggestion certainly managed to stir some of the saints to an impassioned defense of the baptistry. To me this is not worth a confrontation. The Bible clearly teaches *water* baptism and it is also a universal, historical practice of the church. Let us continue the sacrament in undiluted form and seek to interpret this ceremony to Muslims in a clear, biblical manner.

Homogeneity

Donald McGavran opened Pandora's box when he took a quietly practiced missiological strategy and went on to institutionalize it as a church growth principle. The flak has not abated nor are there signs of any real reconciliation between protagonists and antagonists.

There are many who feel a homogeneous convert church is the only practical way to bring Muslims to faith in Christ and at the same time see them remain within the general sociological boundaries of Islamic society. In most countries, Muslims view the Christian church as a foreign entity to be ridiculed, not respected. Its forms, procedures, creeds, architecture and articulation are totally alien.

To circumvent such antagonism, the formation of loosely structured, culturally relevant and biblically oriented convert fellowships has been the focus of a growing number of missionaries.

Although longer-term evaluation is necessary, some use of prostration, chanting and fasting seems to facilitate converts' transition to a Christian community.

As yet, it is impossible to give a thorough evaluation of the effort. But it is fair to say that initial reports have been favorable. Converts are appreciative of the opportunity to worship with others from an Islamic background. Biblical forms of prostration, chanting God's Word, fasting, and use of familiar words have all contributed to believers making a smooth transition to the new community. And, most importantly, in many of the researched fellowships, converts have remained as salt and light among their Muslim relatives and friends. They have not become the typical extracted, persecuted ones and twos that make exciting biography but are dead-ends as far as church growth potential is concerned.

The effort has just begun—but it is a worthy involvement.

Terminology

The names "Allah" and "Isa" are two of many linguistic forms that can help Christians reach Muslim friends.

Somewhat nervously, I sat in the home of missionaries in an ancient city of North Africa. Within a few minutes the "consultation" began with a fellow servant of Christ on the subject of proper terminology to use in Muslim evangelism. His pressing concern related to Christians using the quranic term "Isa" as the word for Jesus. My response was to ask why Christians use "Allah" for God throughout the Middle East and Indonesia. This is the quranic word for God and yet is fully accepted by all Arab Christians. Is not there an inconsistency to feel comfortable with the term "Allah" and yet be so antagonistic toward the term "Isa"?

Some Christians in Asia have forcefully opposed using "Allah" as the word for God. They can only think in terms of post-seventh-century Islamic linguistic forms. Historical research indicates not only that "Allah" was a common poetic word for God among Arabs in pre-Muhammad times, but that Arab Christians also used Allah as a biblical word in the centuries before Islam was launched.

Language usage is much more than a cognitive exercise of communication. Words are emotionally powerful. We must continue to probe for appropriate linguistic forms to reach both the hearts and the minds of our Muslim friends.

Fasting

Does the Bible allow for fasting in the prescribed Muslim form? Dogmatic answers abound. In North Africa the answer among missionaries has been consistently negative. Others, elsewhere, are not so sure.

In 1982 and 1985 I personally kept the Ramadan fast according to the prohibitions of Islam. According to my admittedly limited knowledge, I know of only one other missionary who has kept the entire fast. But missionaries from five different missions, who are working among Muslims in the Philippines, kept at least part of the 1986 Ramadan fast.

> Fasting along with Muslims has been for some missionaries a positive spiritual experience.

Our observations lead us to conclude that our Muslim neighbors have appreciated our following their fasting ritual. For a number of the missionaries, fasting has been a positive spiritual experience. To all, there has come a new appreciation of the discipline and rigor demanded by a month of daytime abstinence from food and water. It is my considered opinion that dogmatism and legalism is not called for. Rather there should be an open climate of freedom on the subject, unencumbered with any hypocritical value judgments toward either the doers or the abstainers.

Supernatural Experiences

Enter John Wimber, the intelligent, articulate advocate for hands-on healing. His books and tapes continue to cause a rippling effect among Christians around the world. After listening to some 20 hours of his teaching on tape, I conclude much of what he says has direct potential for good in our contextualized ministry. We are often dealing with Folk Muslims who are more interested in Elijah-type confrontations than in an academic exposition of the book of Romans. "Where is the God of the Bible?" they ask. "Show him, don't just declare him, and we will believe!"

> "Where," say Folk Muslims, "is the God of the Bible? Show him, don't just declare him."

What is our response? More talk about the lame man made to walk, the blind man made to see, the issue of blood healed, the demons exorcised...more talk, more exposition, more cognition...but no demonstrations, no signs, no healings.

Here is a challenge to faith: Is it not appropriate to pray for a reinstatement of Old and New Testament miracles, healings, visions, and dreams? Not for the purpose of self-aggrandizement or personal kingdom building, but purely for the glory of God to be revealed in the lives of Muslims.

To conclude this section, let me emphatically affirm the need for a careful, considered, mature risk-taking. Reading John F. Kennedy's *Profiles In Courage* makes one realize the cost of moving out into the unknown. It seems to me Christians should be in the front ranks of courageous innovation.

Lifestyle and Finances

Contextualized lifestyle

"At times it has been hard, not least because of resistance and skepticism of our colleagues. One fellow missionary is praying that we shall see the light and move. Discouraging, isn't it?"

This recently-received letter is from an extremely gracious and sensitive missionary wife. She and her husband have made the decision to "go national." They have adopted local Muslim dress and live in a very simple home completely surrounded by Muslims. Their neighbors accept them as one of their own, while at least some of their co-workers across town in the missionary compound direct devastating criticism at them.

Tension persists between many older missionaries' preference for Western-style compounds and many younger missionaries' more frequent choice of Muslim-style living quarters.

A basic cause of this type of alienation is the clash between the older and the newer breed of missionary. I am constantly amazed at the number of missionary compounds still intact throughout Africa and Asia. There, for decades, dedicated servants of Christ have found a relatively safe haven of Western style existence that many have felt essential to their emotional and physical well being. In these clustered communities, houses can be built to Western specifications, dogs are kept as pets, and even pork can be enjoyed.

The new missionary arrives and, in protest, insists on renting a small facility among Muslims. Almost invariably this leads to friction, with a result frequently being either that the new recruit capitulates or that he endures until his first furlough and then calls it quits. In this ongoing scenario the status quo is maintained.

I was saddened to observe how deeply the compound mentality can also affect nationals. In a small town heavily populated by Muslims, there is an excellent Christian hospital. A missionary leader decided to assist the national Christian staff in moving off the compound and into rented houses in various parts of the town. The purpose of this move was to diffuse the Christian witness out among Muslims. In a short time, the staff insisted that the mission acquire a large tract of land and allow them to purchase plots and build homes.

As I stood in the middle of the highway of that town, I saw the hospital on one side with all of the nationals' homes in an adjacent plot and on the other side of the road a sea of Muslim homes. Western mentality had been exported, accepted and applied. How sad!

But there are positive developments. In a paper delivered at SIM's "Consultation on Muslim Evangelism" held in January, 1987, in Monrovia, Liberia, John Miller stated,

> The example of a missionary who contextualizes his lifestyle will encourage converts to retain what is good or neutral in their cultural background. This will help the convert church to appear less foreign and may make it easier for other Muslims to give serious consideration to the Gospel...My wife has worn the black veil while visiting Arabs...Another lady missionary, in trying to make contacts to practice her Swahili, found that wearing the veil greatly facilitated her access to the people.

In the Southern Philippines, I met two Wycliffe American ladies living in a simple wood frame house at the home of the Muslim vice-mayor of the town. These young women had been warmly accepted into the household as family members. Their privacy was restricted to a small partitioned room on one side of the house. In another area of the Philippines a SEND International missionary has moved into a home with very poor Muslims, thus incarnating his faith in a lifestyle that would be impossible for most Westerners to consider.

There does need to be balance. In one Islamic country a very sharp missionary couple with small children took up residence in a tiny bamboo house in a village setting. Some of the Muslim neighbors felt the Westerners were a bit odd. They could not understand why Americans would deprive themselves in such an extreme manner.

Contextualized lifestyle must be cognizant of local norms, expectations, and preferences. Adaptations will vary greatly according to these considerations as well as health and emotional concerns.

Finances

And now to finances. The temptation in Muslim work is to become involved in some type of assistance ministry which requires significant monetary input. Missionaries see this as an expression of physical and spiritual concern for Muslims. It also is said to soften the ground for the proclamation of the gospel.

Many Muslims view externally-financed ministries, even of self-help programs, as unethical inducements toward proselytization.

On the other hand, Muslims frequently see ministries such as hospitals, schools, orphanages, self-help programs and agricultural projects as blatant, immoral, unethical inducements toward proselytization. They feel violated when they are forced to sit through a gospel indoctrination before receiving an out-patient checkup at the nearby Christian clinic. Whenever foreign money is introduced into the community by missionaries, Muslims feel intimidated. An example of this tension in a strong Muslim area was reported in a Christian newsletter:

> The Gospel work was going on smoothly. Souls were being saved and converts publicly identified themselves with Isa Almasih in water baptism. The clamor of the believers was for a place of worship because no house in the village was large enough to accommodate a Christian service. So the committee (of a foreign relief and development agency) decided to provide them with a church building.

> When the set of posts were completed, the lay leader was summoned by the local political head and there interrogated by him and one hundred Muslims. When he confessed he was a follower of Isa Almasih as taught in the Bible, he was requested to bring a translated Bible portion. Those who could read it said it is a good book, while the illiterate ones condemned it and confiscated all the copies. At intervals, words such as these were heard: "Let's shoot him...Let's cut off his head." Other sympathizers suggested releasing him with a stern warning to stop the spread of this new religion. The posts then could be utilized for a school building. The lay leader had to evacuate with his family to another town.

> At the point where external funds were utilized for the construction of a high profile building, Muslims began to direct severe opposition toward the small emerging group of converts. The result was the cessation of the work.

Consider carefully:
What will be the
long-term effects of
financial assistance?
This whole area of finance and assistance requires a great deal of prayerful consultation. It is possible to destroy, almost overnight, the careful ministry of years. I particularly recall our anxiety in one situation where a sister mission decided to set up a large agricultural project adjacent to an area where we had labored intensively over the past five years. We en-visioned the new believers in Christ immediately going to that large mission and requesting assistance and employment. This would have undercut all of our efforts for the converts to remain financially indigenous and in their pre-conversion employment.

As soon as we came to know of the mission's plans, we arranged for representation to ask their leadership to consider another location for their project. Unknown to us, they had already paid a non-refundable deposit on the property. Their mission committee met and decided to honor our request and in so doing lost a considerable amount of money. I will always remember this magnanimous act with a deep sense of gratitude.

In a number of my writings I have sought to propose creative alternatives to our past modus operandi in assisting Muslims financially. I will not repeat those suggestions here. However, I would urge all agencies and missions involved in Muslim ministry not just to take the easy road of distributing assistance whenever there is a need. We must carefully calculate and project the long-term effects of our help.

Critiquing of Islam

Quite unintentionally, a book which included a few sentences critical of Muhammad was introduced on the shelf of a Christian bookstore inside a hospital compound in a rural setting. A Muslim secured the book and roused the entire surrounding community to a feverish pitch of emotional opposition. Even though the hospital was the only adequate medical facility for many miles around, the Muslims made plans to burn it down. A military helicopter was sent to protect the compound. Only after a great volume of negotiation and conciliation were the Muslims pacified.

Due to the nature of Islamic belief and Muslim temperament, it behooves the Christian to exercise extreme caution in witness. Most of my missionary career I have felt I am sitting on top of the proverbial powder keg. One false move and I am in trouble.

Tough questions: How much can a Christian affirm when asked about Muhammad?

Is one obligated to point out Islam's inadequacies or is a positive witness for Christ sufficient?

So at this point the Christian is in conflict. Does he go for presence, proclamation or persuasion? How much can he affirm when constantly asked of his opinion of Muhammad? Are we obligated to point out the inadequacies of Islam or is a positive witness for Christ sufficient?

It has been somewhat amusing, and at times disconcerting, to be accused by some of being too harsh and by others of being overly sympathetic toward Islam. Perhaps I have been somewhat successful in finding a balance between the extremes. One person writes me as soon as he discovers something in my prayer letter which he considers derogatory toward Islam. Another friend said he was concerned that *Beyond The Mosque* was overly sympathetic to Muslims. But then he got to the last chapter and felt I had achieved parity!

Kenneth Cragg is often criticized by evangelicals for being soft on Muslims. Yet his recent book *Muhammad and the Christian* was negatively reviewed in the Islamic journal, *Arabia*. The Muslim reviewer was particularly displeased that Cragg was distressed over Islam's tendency toward violence.

Not only is Islamic theology a sensitive issue, but the Palestinian diaspora remains a question of burning significance. Throughout the Islamic world, most Muslims give at least verbal assent to the "Palestinian cause." To be critical of the Muslim position is to insure a negative response to one's attempts toward communication and friendship.

My understanding of the Muslim stand has been enhanced by the careful reading of Colin Chapman's *Whose Promised Land?* This excellent book succeeds in highlighting the biblical, quranic, historical and practical aspects of the ownership of the Holy Land. Both sides are given fair treatment.

In a more personal manner, I have been enriched by my friendship with Riad and Esdahar Kassis, Syrian Christians presently studying in the Alliance Biblical Seminary in Manila, Philippines. Riad is a strong Syrian nationalist who supports the Palestinian cause and yet a Christian who dearly loves our Lord. His insights on the terribly complex Jewish-Muslim-Christian controversy have been most helpful.

Some well-intentioned Christians have felt free to enter into publicized debates with Muslim orator par excellence, Ahmed Deedat. Deedat is an Indian now resident in South Africa who has made a study of certain aspects of Christianity. He delights to forcefully and eloquently point out supposed contraditions in biblical passages. His tapes and books are in great demand throughout the Muslim world.

John Gilchrist has authored several good responses to Deedat's attacks. To me this is a much more valid rebuttal to Deedat than taking him on in a debate hall filled with several thousand emotionally charged Muslims.

Without compromise, we can appreciate the good in Islam, affirm the theology which agrees with the Bible and unreservedly love the individual Muslim even though we may be distressed by aspects associated with his or her beliefs that we feel are wrong.

Incarnated Spirituality

This subject has been much on my mind as I have been researching and writing a book on this theme for the past two years. *The Dove and the Crescent: Reflections on Christian-Muslim Spirituality* will be an interaction between the spiritual beliefs and practices of the world's two largest monotheistic religions. It is my conviction that the mutual ethos of Islam and Christianity lie in the realm of the spirit. In Muslim thought, as much as in biblical theology, Allah is a spirit .

Do Muslims desire to be "spiritual"? Are they gripped with a sense of sin and guilt? Is God real to Muslims? What does a religion built on faith and works produce in the way of godly people? Why are there significant distinctions in religious practice between the Orthodox Saudi and the Sufi Bangladeshi? These are questions I am probing. I invite the input of others in this quest for a fuller understanding of Islamic spirituality.

My specific concern here is to explore issues relating to the goal of Christians effectively and dynamically incarnating godly lives within Muslim community. Followers of Islam must see a qualitative difference in the behavior of Christians before they will deem Christianity worthy of serious investigation. They must be convinced the rituals followed by Christians to assist them in knowing God are indeed superior to their own highly formalized and ritualized system of religious expression.

So, how are we doing? In seeking an answer to this question, I prepared a questionnaire on spirituality and sent it to 800 missionaries. Of those, 390 of them serving in 32 different countries with 37 mission societies responded. Forty-six percent of the respondents were under 40 years of age. Seventy-six percent of them are married. An equal number of men and women returned the form. The following are a few excerpts from the findings of the survey.

- The greatest spiritual struggle in life is in the area of having adequate devotions.

- The "least liked" aspect of being a Christian is the ongoing battle with sin.

- Eighty-seven percent spend less than 30 minutes in prayer on a daily basis. Twenty-seven percent of them pray under 10 minutes a day.

- Eighty-eight percent read the Bible less than 30 minutes daily.

- Only 23 percent stated Bible reading is always a joy to them.

- Thirty-two percent are frequently tense while 64 percent are tense on an infrequent basis.

- Seventy-one percent experience a problem with lust.

- On a monthly basis, 44 percent read one Christian book while 21 percent read none.

- Alcoholic beverages are imbibed by 26 percent while 20 percent have taken tranquilizers since becoming missionaries.

In a recent conversation with a well-known mission executive I was amazed at the intensely personal questions he asks each of his missionaries during private interviews. I queried as to the response he found in regard to time spent in personal devotions. He replied that the norm was between 15 and 30 minutes. This was a deep concern to the mission leader, particularly in light of the fact that most of these missionaries are ministering among Muslims.

Are missionaries in Islamic countries facing more sexual temptation than those working among other people? A young lady missionary met a married Muslim in a public market and commenced a relationship that only ceased when she was sent back to her home country. An American church leader in a Muslim setting succumbed to the temptation of an affair with a maid in his home. This led to his divorce and subsequent marriage to the Asian lady who is many years his junior. Loneliness led to two missionary women engaging in a lesbian relationship resulting in a great deal of trauma, both for them and for their mission leadership.

Satan attacks in areas of vulnerability. Loneliness, sexual drive, depression, moodiness and tiredness provide easy access to Satan's powerful influence on a man or woman of God. Mission societies must be more sensitive to the spiritual needs of their missionaries. This can be accomplished by prayer retreats, book reading facilities, inter-team counseling, tape lending libraries and adequate vacation breaks, as well as a constant emphasis (with accountability procedures) on personal devotions.

Has our technological age seduced us into thinking that contextualized methodology is more important than our spiritual encounter with our Lord?

One is gripped by reading the biographies of Jonathan Goforth, Hudson Taylor and Adoniram Judson. These men were permeated by spiritual priorities. Their lives were a penetrating reflection of their relationship with Christ. Perhaps our technological age has seduced us into thinking contextualized methodology is a more pressing area of emphasis than is our spiritual encounter with our Lord.

When the devout Muslim asks us if we pray five times a day, do we have an answer of spiritual equivalence? Are we somewhat embarrassed when requested to share details of our fasting belief and *practice*? Do we treat our Bible with the same respect the Muslim does his Quran? In sensitivity to the Muslim, can we assure him we do not eat pork or drink alcoholic beverages?

Perhaps we need to ponder deeply what it means to be "all things to all men" as we confront the issue of incarnated spirituality. Whatever else it means, the bottom line is that Muslims must experience Jesus when they experience us!

Whither Contextualization?

I am encouraged. Never before have missionaries to Islam been so sensitized to cross-cultural issues. Yet, we have just begun. Mission leadership must constantly, with gentleness, prod older field missionaries into dreaming new dreams and seeing new visions. Team seminars should struggle with localized issues regarding the implementation of contextualization. A few specifics of encouragement follow:

- Columbia Graduate School of Missions, Trinity Evangelical Divinity School, Wheaton Graduate School, Biola University and Fuller Theological Seminary have all offered credit courses on a contextualized approach to Muslim evangelism.

- The following mission societies of which I know are among those that have had some direct involvement in contextualized ministry to Muslims: International Christian Fellowship, Frontiers, SIM International, International Missions Incorporated, Assemblies of God, Navigators, Overseas Missionary Fellowship, SEND International, Youth With a Mission, Operation Mobilization and the Australian Baptist Missionary Society. Inclusion in this list does not indicate an official mission-wide policy nor even of total agreement within a specified field. It simply means individuals within these missions have made some definite move toward applied contextualization.

- The United Bible Societies have issued some very attractive and relevant biblical texts for vernacular Muslim audiences. One of the outstanding ones is the Muslim Bengali New Testament done in cooperation with Viggo Olsen in Bangladesh. This very attractive production has become the number one best seller of all books in Bangladesh.

- Other contextual literature has been marketed with local Muslim artwork and design. David Owen's Arabic harmony of the Gospels into one text is an outstanding example of linguistic and stylistic adaptation to Muslim thought. This harmony is framed in rhythmic and poetic form similar to that of the Quran.

- Frank Gray, overseas director of programming for Far East Broadcasting Company, has engaged in creative thought in regard to contextual radio broadcasts. He, along with others, may soon spearhead a significant new wave in mass media effectiveness.

- Zwemer Institute of Muslim Studies, under Robert Douglas, continues on the cutting edge of promoting Muslim evangelism.

- Fuller Theological Seminary has now initiated an M.A. and Ph.D. program under Dudley Woodberry and Dean Gilliland, with a concentration in Muslim Studies. This is a much-needed addition to formal training for Muslim ministry.

- And, most importantly, Muslims are actually accepting Christ and being baptized. Fellowships of believers are being formed in many Muslim countries.

Twenty-five years ago, my wife (of eight months at that time) and I took an overnight steamer journey from Dhaka to a lesbian relationship resulting in a great deal of trauma, both for them and for their mission leadership.

Satan attacks in areas of vulnerability. Loneliness, sexual drive, depression, moodiness and tiredness provide easy access to Satan's powerful influence on a man or woman of God. Mission societies must be more sensitive to the spiritual needs of their missionaries. This can be accomplished by prayer retreats, book reading facilities, inter-team counseling, tape lending libraries and adequate vacation breaks, as well as a constant emphasis (with accountability procedures) on personal devotions.

Has our technological age seduced us into thinking that contextualized methodology is more important than our spiritual encounter with our Lord?

One is gripped by reading the biographies of Jonathan Goforth, Hudson Taylor and Adoniram Judson. These men were permeated by spiritual priorities. Their lives were a penetrating reflection of their relationship with Christ. Perhaps our technological age has seduced us into thinking contextualized methodology is a more pressing area of emphasis than is our spiritual encounter with our Lord.

When the devout Muslim asks us if we pray five times a day, do we have an answer of spiritual equivalence? Are we somewhat embarrassed when requested to share details of our fasting belief and *practice*? Do we treat our Bible with the same respect the Muslim does his Quran? In sensitivity to the Muslim, can we assure him we do not eat pork or drink alcoholic beverages?

Perhaps we need to ponder deeply what it means to be "all things to all men" as we confront the issue of incarnated spirituality. Whatever else it means, the bottom line is that Muslims must experience Jesus when they experience us!

CHAPTER FIFTEEN

CONTEXTUALIZED WORSHIP AND WITNESS

Rafique Uddin

Here are salient observations of one who has worshiped God both as a Muslim and now as a Christian, who applies new meaning to Islamic forms of worship.

This chapter, written by a practitioner, not an academic, may lack some helpful theoretical framework. However, it offers the benefit of an insider's viewpoint, from a person who has had firsthand experience in practicing Islamic worship in both its original unaltered form, as a Muslim, and in its contextualized form, as a believer in Jesus Christ. Therefore, contextualization has not had to be devised; it has been culturally natural.

The subject will be viewed in this chapter from two perspectives:

The perspective of worship
The perspective of evangelism

Some examples of contextualized worship will be noted, along with the impact of such worship on the new believers in Christ as well as other Muslims.

First, however, here are some personal postulates that might help answer some of the queries and reservations which can be expected in such a presentation. The following are some of my personal postulates (which borrow heavily from my mentors):

1. Contextualization of the gospel is a means to an end and not an end in itself.

2. As such, contextualization is a process subject to continuous evaluation, reevaluation, adjustment and readjustment under changing circumstances.

3. We are saved by faith in Christ's redemptive power and not by virtue of anything we do, including the worship forms we use.

4. Worship is for expressing gratitude to God in Christ and also for communion with Him.

5. The New Testament does not advocate any definite form of worship which will fit Jew, Gentile and Muslim-Christian alike.

Worldwide, Christian worship forms are already beautifully diverse.

6. The currently prevalent forms of worship in Christian churches are many and varied, demonstrative of the possibility of diversity in Christian worship forms.

7. Faith in Christ demands changes which are aimed much more at meaning levels and much less at levels of external form.

8. As cultural beings, humans are basically ethnocentric. This ethnocentricity makes people think of their forms of worship as the only true and valid forms of worship. Contextualized forms of worship affirm the beauty of diversity.

Islam has always employed Judaistic and Christian teaching in its own worship.

9. Although contextualization at times can verge on syncretism, contextualization to Islamic cultures is not fraught with too many such dangers, since Islam is a post-Judaistic and post-Christian religion which has inculcated Judaistic and Christian teaching in its religious content and forms.

10. God can be praised, honored and worshipped by use of a variety of cultural forms. This is aptly demonstrated throughout the Bible.

With these few postulates, though the list could have been longer and more exhaustive, I now proceed to present the two perspectives.

The Perspective of Worship

Worship is to be rendered to God alone (Ex. 20:3; Deut. 5:7; 6:13; Mat. 4:10; Lk. 4:8; Acts 10:26; 14:15; Col. 2:18; Rev. 19:10; 22:8-9), and true worship is done in spirit and in truth (Jn. 4:23-24; I Co. 14:15; Phil. 3:3). Worship, in reality, is intense communion with God. The forms used in worship symbolize this communion between humans and their Creator.

These forms of worship (or of communion with God) are taught by one's culture. This teaching of forms of worship is

taught by members of one's family from childhood. Therefore, the forms used in communion with God become so in-
grained and integrated in the worldview of men and women
that any true communion with God becomes very difficult
without the use of these culturally acquired forms. Contextualized worship forms are, therefore, necessary to assure
true communion with God the Father and Jesus Christ, our
Lord.

As has already been pointed out, contextualization of the
forms of Christian worship to Islamic worship forms is not
heavily fraught with danger of syncretism. I make this statement from an insider's viewpoint. I am aware of the outsider's viewpoint from which it has been argued that it would
be dangerous to remain within or participate in Muslim
forms of worship. I am also aware of other points of view
from which are made recommendations for participation in
or continuation of the forms of Muslim worship. To argue
these different stands is not my purpose here.

In my current work I have suggested to many new and old
believers in Christ (from Muslim background) that we practice both the five daily times of worship and the annual one
month fast. I personally participate in these forms and recite
Bible portions in five daily prayers. In almost all cases, I have
found very positive response from the other first-generation
believers with whom I am acquainted. They indicate that they
are very happy that it is possible to use the old forms, sancti-
fying them in the name of Jesus Christ and using biblical
statements in the vernacular. Almost all feel happy and fulfilled worshiping God by means of these forms.

Many first-
generation
Christians feel that
growth in Christ is
easier if culture
shocks can be
mitigated through
retaining cultural
forms of worship.

To me and to many other first-generation believers in Christ
it is a necessity that we continue the Islamic forms of worship
but give Christian meanings to these forms. Growth in Christ
is much easier if culture shocks can be mitigated through retaining as much as possible of the cultural forms of worship.

In this matter of contextualization of worship forms, the
point that needs to be borne in mind is that Islam, though
claiming to be a complete code of life, is not at all monocultural; rather, it is multicultural. The Islamic religious practices one encounters from country to country, from region to
region, have countless variations. I have encountered some
Muslims we locally call Marifats, who have questioned the
saying of prayers five times a day. To them, I say that the
worship of God, which is taught by Jesus, is to be in spirit and
in truth. Many forms can be utilized in the worship of God.

The decision concerning the use of specific forms should not be based merely on a personal preference but rather on the impact these forms are apt to have on the majority of the local Muslims. This, then, brings forth the issue of the evangelistic perspective.

The Perspective of Evangelism

Choice of forms should be based not merely on personal preference but on the likely impact upon the majority of local Muslims.

Evangelism refers to the communication of the gospel—the good news. A news which is communicated as good must be good from the perspectives of both the communicator and, more importantly, the receiver. If a message is good from the viewpoint of the messenger but bad and destructive from the viewpoint of the receiver, the message cannot be termed good news.

In studying the book of Acts, we see that the gospel is good news not for the Jews only, but for the Gentiles, too. What about the Muslims? Is the gospel of Christ good news for the Muslims as well?

Muslims view cultural disruptions with suspicion. A gospel that rejects their forms of worship, therefore, is not seen as good news.

There is much talk these days about making the message receptor-oriented. Was the gospel receptor-oriented? Of course it was. Otherwise the Gentiles would be required to become Jews in order to be saved, or vice versa. But we see that Paul strongly advocates that the Jew can maintain a lot of Jewishness and yet have faith in the gospel of Christ and be saved. So also the Gentiles can retain a lot of Gentile practices and yet be saved. So, there is no doubt that the gospel is receptor-oriented. Cultural disruptions are viewed very suspiciously by Muslims. Change of worship forms constitutes cultural disruption, and to Muslims this is not good news.

After a Muslim becomes a believer in Jesus Christ, he has one of three options as far as the style of his worship and prayer is concerned:

1. He can stay within the frame of reference of Islamic worship, changing the inner values and meanings of the worship to fit his faith in Christ.

2. He can adopt the currently-in-vogue Christian worship forms and practices, thereby alienating himself from his erstwhile society and losing his witnessability to his relatives and friends.

3. He can create some new forms of worship depending on his personal temperament and exigencies, with resultant

alienation from his former sociological bonds, thereby also losing the ability to witness for Christ to the Muslim relatives and friends.

In view of the current unresponsiveness of Muslims to the gospel, should not all peripheral offenses be eliminated?

It needs mentioning, that in the current state of unresponsiveness of Muslims to the gospel, it is necessary that all peripheral offenses, though never that of the cross, be eliminated. Therefore, I believe the first option is the one that Muslim believers in Christ should be encouraged to follow.

Application of Worship and Results

In September, 1985, I gathered five believing couples, all of whom were former Muslims. I conducted a month-long training in the incarnational model of evangelism. We divided the training into three parts: cognitive, effective and experiential—knowing, being and doing.

The emphases of the first phase of training were on knowing and being. During the training we all prayed five times daily, using the forms of Islamic *salat* (or *namaz*). For the recitation from memory, we used different chapters of the Bible, such as the Psalms, the Sermon on the Mount, the Lord's Prayer and I Corinthians 13.

Many now offer the *salat* and fasting in the name of Christ.

The result was rather revolutionary. These believing couples saw that it was possible to reestablish the ruptured relationship with their families and thereby convince them that they are not renouncing God by becoming Christian; rather they have found God through Jesus Christ. They were able to convince their relatives and friends that they stand for everything that is good in Islam. The *salat* and fasting, if practiced with new understanding, can help in building a personal relationship with God. Of course, these should be offered in the name of Christ.

After the training, all of them returned to their homes in their respective villages. They started offering *salat* five times daily. They faced west as is customary for the Muslims of their country, since they have to face some direction, even though the direction does not influence the prayer. They performed all of the units at all of the appointed timings. This re-sulted in the couples' acceptance by their relatives and by their

They have been made aware—and must keep aware—that *salat* and fasting are not obligatory.

As Christians, they are saved by their faith in Christ, not by virtue of worship exercises.

But they consider their worship in such forms expressive of their thankfulness and praise to the heavenly Father and to Christ their Redeemer.

communities, as persons interested in God. Some of the couples entered the mosques while others did not.

Without going into all of the details here, I can say that there are three Imams of mosques who are now believers in Christ. In one area, during two years 1,200 to 1,500 have come to Christ.

All of these believers now have full understanding that God can be worshipped, honored and praised through multiple cultural forms, such as songs, dances, meditation and more importantly, through *salat*. They are aware that *salat* and fasting are not obligatory to them, as they are saved by their faith in Christ and not by virtue of *salat* and fasting. The *salat* and fasting are now expressions of their thankfulness and praises to the Father and to Jesus Christ the Redeemer.

I praise God that although cultural forms of worship have many inadequacies, yet God, because of his constant love, is willing to accept these and be glorified by them.

CHAPTER SIXTEEN

ISLAMIC AND CHRISTIAN ARCHITECTURE

Florence Antablin

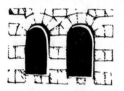

When the term "Islamic architecture" is used, some things come to mind immediately: minarets, domes, arcades, rich surface decorations, and so forth. These broad, popular associations are what we will be assuming when referring to Islamic architectural elements in this essay, without attempting to be more formal in our definition of terms. At times we will broaden our base even more, by using the term "indigenous" as well. Because the use of terms varies from place to place, definitive meanings must be provided in their local context by the people immediately affected. Only users and viewers can decide on the meanings for their architecture.[1]

This study, a brief exploratory introduction to a topic that is both timely and relevant to our Christian world mission, will rarely make value judgments as to the effectiveness of various architectural forms; rather it will be largely descriptive, that is, it will cite examples of Christian buildings which have incorporated so-called Islamic elements.

Muslims once raised the opposite question, seeking ways to use Christian architectural features in Islamic houses of worship.

In the early years of the Arab conquest, Islam came out of a desert culture into the Byzantine and Sassanian worlds with their highly developed architectural systems. The question the Muslims raised then might have been the reverse of ours. They may have asked, "How can we make use of all this *Christian* Byzantine and Sassanian architecture to serve our needs as a worshiping *Muslim* community?"

In Syria, the first country to be conquered, the existing three-aisle basilicas were a handy solution. Because their orientation was east-west, the Muslims closed up the western en-

trance and opened up doors on the north wall so that as they entered they would be facing Mecca, the south *qibla* wall towards which they directed their worship.[2]

The niches of Roman monuments and the apses of the altar-end of the churches provided a model for the smaller *mihrabs* which were placed into the *qibla* wall facing Mecca.

As for the minarets from which the call to prayer was given, they were probably first inspired by the square towers of the Syrian churches. The square form is seen in Syria, the Maghrib and Spain down to the present day.

The only piece of furniture in a congregational mosque is the pulpit (*minbar*, pronounced *mimbar*). It is interesting to note that this same word is also used for the pulpit in the churches of the Middle East today, and that the word currently used in synagogues is *al-menar*—also clearly relating to the Arabic word. These come from the root *nbr*, which means to elevate something, or raise the voice. In all three traditions the *minbar* elevates the person and/or provides a stand for the one who is reading scripture or giving a sermon.[3]

It was not again until the 16th century that Christian architecture seriously impacted Islamic forms. In Istanbul, Ottoman architecture experienced its greatest achievements and the great 6th century church of Justinian, the Hagia Sophia, served as the model. The favored architect of the Sultan, Koca Sinan, came up through the janissarie corps, and went on to clarify and perfect the central domed mosques: the Suleymania, the Ahmediye and his masterpiece, the Selimiye in Edirne. This domed mosque style was propagated to the farthest reaches of the Ottoman empire when-

ever an impressive building was called for. But in Istanbul the great model still stands— 1,000 years older than any of its impressive descendants— but hardly distinguishable from them because of added minarets.

Actually none of the architectural elements used in early Islam were new. But they were so thoroughly adopted and adapted to the needs of the Muslim community that, with time, they took on new "Islamic" meaning.[4] For example, the Dome of the Rock in Jerusalem is Byzantine in form and plan, and it was executed by Byzantine craftsmen. Yet this monument has become a universal symbol of Islam.

After the reconquering of Muslim lands, Christian buildings again incorporated Islamic architectural elements.

The adapting of architectural forms was reversed when Muslim lands were reconquered. The rich architectural inheritance left by the Moors in Spain and the Fatimids in Sicily was eagerly absorbed by the reestablished Christian kingdoms. As a result, the architecture in those areas has been significantly enriched with such elements as polychrome masonry, ribbed vaulting, lobed and interlocking arches, crenelated roofs, geometric window grills and plaster and tile work. Using Islamic architectural elements on Christian buildings posed no apparent problem in those situations.

One might ask about the ancient churches that somehow maintained their identity throughout the long centuries of Muslim dominations: Did they adopt "Muslim" architecture?

In the case of the Armenians, their great monuments, dating from the 6th century, show very little appropriation of Islamic elements—only the narrow band of relief on the Akh-tamar church at Lake Van (in the Abbasid style) and a small amount of stalactite ornamentation which was pervasive in the Islamic world after the 11th century.[5] Much later, however, in the 17th century, when Shah Abbas imported the population

of the Armenian town of Julfa to Isfahan, the churches that the Armenians built in New Julfa were vaulted in a manner similar to the Safavid structures of the time.[6] In general the Armenian Apostolic Church has continued down to the present day to build in its

to build in its traditional f orm—with the tall vertical volumes topped by a dome sheathed in a pointed roof and resting on a tall drum.

The Coptic Church of Egypt, which exists to the present day with about 8 million adherents, has followed a standard type of church plan consisting of a nave and side aisles covered with barrel vaulting and supported on piers. The chancel terminated in three apses covered with dome vaulting. However, of special interest to our topic is the fact that in upper Egypt a new church plan is seen. It is composed of wide short rows of domed bays whose aisles each terminated in apses. According to Krautheimer, this plan was obviously drawn from mosque plans.[7] This plan uses the Islamic hypostyle system which allows enlargement to take place at will by simply adding domed bays. Clarke comments on how attractive are the interiors of these churches.[8] Clarke also mentions that a little dome in the church of Der es Shuhada at Esna in upper Egypt is decorated with stalactite niches in the pendentives, a distinctly Islamic motif.[9]

On the southern shore of the island of Cyprus, the 15th century Greek monastery of Ayia Napa could easily be taken for a Muslim complex. It is complete with its inner courtyard surrounded by  pointed arcades, a domed pavilion in the center and a place for ablutions. The only distinctly Christian features are the cross on the church and the bell in the tower! The architecture itself is equally at home in either religious tradition. Examples of this kind can be found throughout the Middle East.

Buildings have sometimes been shared by both faiths. It is interesting to note that occasionally a building has been shared by both faiths. We hear of this happening in Syria immediately after the Arab conquest. Creswell writes:

> ...the Muslims, when they conquered a town in Syria, usually took one of the churches, and used it as a mosque or merely divided one of the churches if the town had surrendered without resistance. At Homs, for example, they took a fourth part of the Church of St. John. At Aleppo, according to Baladhuri, they took half the churches.[10]

Then again during the Crusaders' occupation of the Middle East, Ibn Jubayr writes of a place to the east of the city of Acre where there was a mosque:

> ...of which there remains in its former state only the *mihrab*, to the east of which the Franks have built their own *mihrab*: and the Muslims and the infidel assemble there, the one turning to his place of worship, the other to his. In the hands of the Christians its [the mosque's] venerableness is maintained, and God has preserved in it a place of prayer for the Muslims.[11]

Dudley Woodberry, while pastoring the church in Kabul, Afghanistan, recalls a similar situation outside the city. He went to visit a French scholar, S. de Beaurecueil, who was there working in a modest home for children. De Beaurecueil had built a little chapel with a *mihrab* facing Mecca and a niche facing Jerusalem for the Christians. Thus they were all able to pray together in the same room.[12]

In the Middle East, buildings were erected, surrendered and reclaimed throughout the centuries. For someone who, in

Beirut's quieter days frequently walked past the east end of the former Crusader Church of St. John (now the Mosque of Omari), it does not seem a bit unusual to see the triple apses of the 12th century Christian structure, topped off with a dome or a minaret! Unfortunately now, because of the war, no one is able to worship in this structure—neither facing east as the Crusaders did, nor facing across the three-aisled basilica to the south *qibla* wall as the Muslims did.

The opposite situation exists at the Anglican mission hospital in Peshawar. There the local congregation worships in an old Mughal monument. It is a great domed octagon in the pavilion style with its open *iwans* on the four main sides, and the chamfered corners have smaller *iwan* arches with similar arched balconies above them. The dome is raised on a drum of 16 blind niches in this classic Islamic structure—used now by a local Christian congregation.

Architectural styles of different regions and periods are frequently combined.

There was a great influx of Western building styles into Muslim lands during the period of the colonial empires. The Europeans usually built in the current styles of their homelands. Great cathedrals went up in all the large cities.

During the first half of the 19th century, neo-classical styles (Greek temple fronts, classical orders, etc.) predominated—as in William Carey's Serampore College. But the second half of the  century saw the neo-gothic style with the pointed arch take over. Missionary buildings often followed the same styles, but in a more modest way.

Now when the pointed arch returns to the Middle East and north India, it is coming home. First seen in the pre-Islamic Byzantine architecture of Syria,[13] it found its fullest use and development in the Islamic architecture of these lands. The British architect Christopher Wren has been quoted as saying that Gothic architecture is "Saracenic refined by the Christians."[14]   Art historian O. Grabar could not support this statement, but he does admit that Islamic architecture might have had a secondary impact on Gothic architecture in Europe.[15]   Be that as it may, it has been observed—and I believe correctly—that there is a certain affinity between local Middle East architecture and neo-gothic coming from Europe at this time.

Every major city can show an example of this church style. The Beirut Evangelical Church, dedicated in 1869, was a landmark example for many years in Lebanon. Unfortunately, its location, in a most vulnerable part of the city, made it one of the earliest casualties of the Lebanon War in the mid-1970s.

More recently, the Armenian Evangelical community has chosen this neo-gothic style for their Emmanuel Church in Aleppo and their church in Ras Beirut. It was important for Armenian Evangelicals to use a style that would identify them apart from the Apostolic Church from which most of them had come.

Neo-gothic hybrids are numerous throughout the Middle East, Northern India and present-day Pakistan. There is even a late 19th century mosque in this style: the Valide Mosque in the city of Aksaray in central Turkey!

When mission organizations and indigenous churches used local, traditional architecture, the results were often pleasing as well as functional. The early mission schools in Lebanon illustrate this with a regional style called the gallery style[16] which features arcades (with pointed arches) onto which all rooms opened. It was used effectively at the Abeih Seminary (forerunner of the American University of Beirut), the first Girard Institute building in Sidon, the American School for Girls and the Near East School of Theology in Beirut, to mention a few.

The British in North India and Pakistan made use of the Mughal style which was all about them there. Although it is not typical, St. John's College in Agra was a tour de force in this "Indo-Saracenic" style. Built by the Church Missionary Society of the Anglican Church, it is described as having:

> ...domes and pinnacles everywhere...besides looking partly like a Moorish castle, it flaunted its purpose with a marvelous insouciance by surmounting the whole Islamic pile of it with a gigantic Christian cross.[17]

Incongruous as it may seem, the Christian cross stands over many Islamic architectural design elements.

That highly visible cross must have been necessary to assure the viewers that it was indeed a Christian institution. For as late as 1861, when St. Stephen's was erected in Delhi, "...in a vaguely Mogul style, it was violently attacked as being unsuitable for Christian purposes."[18]

Nevertheless, numerous examples of hybrid styles—combining Mughal elements with other styles—are seen throughout the area, some of them apparently quite effective. An example is the church in Peshawar where the arches of the chancel are lobed in the Mughal manner, and the exterior incorporates little minarets in its façade.

Another church in the Punjab, the one at Shikohabad, uses the keel-shaped arch very effectively at the entrance gate, on the façade, and again in the sturdy bell tower. The cross is boldly displayed at these points also, as well as in the interior.

In Iran the local Anglican congregations have also used traditional forms successfully. The church in Shiraz is a fine example with its central dome raised high on a drum covered with a design in blue and beige tiles. The façade shows the traditional *iwan* portal with blue tiles filling the spandrils. A cross is predominantly displayed on the dome, as well as in the tile designs.

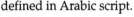

One of the decorative motifs that is uniquely Islamic, is the use of Arabic calligraphy. This powerfully effective device is used on a church in Isfahan in a large circular window. But instead of the usual names of God, the names of Christ are elegantly defined in Arabic script.

The National Evangelical Church in Homs, Syria, is another fine example of the use of indigenous forms. On the lower part of the exterior façade, one sees dark and light colored stone used on alternating rows of masonry—a device of Islamic building through the centuries. Then in the upper part of the façade, small coupled windows are outlined in white stone against the solid grey masonry. But the "over-door" is a showpiece of contrasting, beautifully shaped, interlocking vousoirs done in the style that dates from the Ayyubid period in Syria and Egypt.

More recently, the small chapel built by the Arab Evangelical congregation in the old town in Martah (Oman) was

Tasteful functionality as well as symbolism makes important statements.

built of concrete blocks laid on their sides. This created an open, screen-like wall so the air flowed through freely. The worshipers who sat on the floor, in true oriental fashion, were able to take full advantage of it—a natural form of air conditioning before the age of electric air conditioning!

Of course Westerners returned home from Eastern lands with exotic architectural innovations and ideas. So not only was the West indulging in revivals of its own historic styles, but it embraced the romantic oriental fantasies coming from the Near East. This architecture usually took the shape of garden pavilions and vacation castles in the 19th century and cinemas and restaurants in the 20th.

The Brighton Pavilion by John Nash illustrates this with a lavish array of exotic domes and minarets—and this as early as 1813.

Islamic elements found their way into more serious buildings of the period also. About the middle of the 19th century the small plain synagogues of Germany started employing the horseshoe arch of Western Islam.[19] It was simply used on the windows and portals. The large impressive city synagogues also began using this feature (and numerous others in a neo-Islamic style) at about the same time throughout Europe. This style was chosen to express their own identity against the background of church styles in use at the time. However, by the end of the century, the style disappeared as the Jewish community then chose the neo-Romanesque style.[20]

Another interesting example of the revival of Islamic architecture took place in North Africa in the last half of the 19th century and has been going strong into the 20th. It was called in some quarters *Arabisances* [21] and much of it was sponsored by the colonizing French. Some saw this as an attempt merely to patronize the indigenous traditions, but it seems to have become more than that. It was used quite effectively for large civic buildings as well as modest domestic architecture. It is characterized by arcades of round and horseshoe shaped arches, square towers topped with small domes, prominent eaves, crested roof lines and arched portals framed in rectangular spaces. Decoration was confined to windows, doors and cornices, thereby emphasizing the clean volumes defined by white plastered walls. It found its widest use in Algeria, but it is seen from Andalusia to Egypt. By mid-20th century it was eclipsed by the modern international style. Indeed, by the mid-20th century everything was being eclipsed by the modern style!

Designers of new mosques now are turning on a massive scale to a reappropriation of historic Islamic architectural forms and motifs.

This pervasive international style became the great common denominator in a building boom following World War II. No part of the civilized world was unaffected by it. This was especially true in the newly rich oil states in the gulf, where centuries-old building techniques were replaced by the most current building technologies on a scale unparalleled in the history of architecture. However, interestingly enough, not more than three decades into this era, these very countries were calling for a conscious reappropriation of historic Islamic architectural forms and motifs in contemporary architectural planning. This is now being implemented on a massive scale.

In regions where motifs have little symbolic significance in Muslim buildings, are they not equally insignificant in Christian buildings?

Oleg Grabar would suggest that the significance of these so-called Islamic motifs "...was minimal or merely cosmetic, that the contemporary world has made (this kind of) cultural discreteness obsolete..." This statement has a direct bearing on our topic. If these motifs have little, if any symbolic significance in Muslim buildings, then their use in Christian buildings would likely be equally insignificant. Again, if there is any particular meaning in the architectural statement, it would have to come from the local people in a particular region, and at a particular time.

It is interesting to note that when mosques are built in lands where Islam is a minority, architectural choices are made in ways similar to the ways Western countries made them. That is: 1. They adapt to the local styles (as in the Great Mosque of Xi'an in China, the early mosques of Kerala, South India, the Fatiha Jami near the agora in Athens, the Yaama Mosque in Niger, the Niomo and the Djenne mosques of Mali), or 2. They bring their home styles with them, (as seen in the Algerians' mosque in Paris with its Maghrib type square minaret or the pencil-slim Turkish ones in Munich). Sometimes there are surprising carry-overs, such as the Brazilian church styles brought back and used by the Nigerian Muslims when they returned to their homelands in Benin and Nigeria. The mosque builders of 19th century Singapore must have come by way of India as the Sultan Mosque there is a late Mughal style wedding cake!

Impressive mosques are now being built all over the world. These are a fascinating melange of traditional components (such as a highly visible dome or minaret) executed in a slick contemporary mode. The Islamic Center of Southern California, on the other hand, is a modern neoclassic structure that could pass for a Baptist Christian education building.[22]

Permission to build a Christian church is withheld in some lands (such as Saudi Arabia) and very difficult to obtain in others (such as Afghanistan and Egypt at the present time). However, a church was recently built in Kabul, Afghanistan.

It was a 49-foot-high A-frame contemporary structure built to attract the international community of that city. It had been dedicated in the spring of 1970 after almost endless negotiations with the government and much prayer and planning. Then after three years, government forces came in and completely demolished the building.

As J. Christy Wilson, the founding pastor of the congregation, writes:

> Government leadership was split into two factions. There were the hard-core Muslims who were determined to keep the country pure of non-Islamic influences. A second faction saw the value of close relations with Westerners... Sometimes the government would say one thing and then do another and vice versa. We were never quite sure what would happen.[23]

In a country largely hostile to a non-Islamic presence, would an architectural style choice make an important difference? The answer may never be known.

The former faction was obviously in control when in June of 1973 an expropriation notice was sent to the church board, and the next day the bulldozers began their assault on the building. The government responsible for the destruction was overthrown the very night they completed their work. The instability of that government, together with the fact that conversions to Christ were taking place in the institute for the blind, are seen as the major reasons for the opposition. Would a different architectural style have made a difference? That is a question that may never be answered. But the question certainly must be raised whenever church building is undertaken in a country with large segments of its people or government hostile to a non-Islamic presence in their land.

The degree of tolerance varies from place to place and time to time, depending on the political and religious climate. Missionary Harvey Staal recalls that all the churches in Iraq have had bell towers with permission to ring bells. Both the Kuwait and Bahrain National Evangelical churches have external crosses. The Bahrain one is prominently displayed on a modern tower. The Kuwait church received written permission to install and use a bell.

Historian H.A. Chakmakjian recalls that early Protestant Armenian churches did not show crosses, not because of intimidation, but probably because of the influence of the New England Protestantism which the missionaries represented. The Apostolic churches did use crosses. He also recalls that in the last years of the 19th century and the first of the 20th, the privilege of sounding church bells was granted and withheld, depending on the position of the sultan at the time, or the current political trends.

More recently, in Abu Dhabi, the Christians were given property by the government. They constructed a church with a free-standing cross that stood 30 feet high. It was reported that when the king of Saudi Arabia saw the prominent cross, he objected to it to his host. However, this did not prompt any adverse action. That property, nevertheless, became so valuable that it was deemed necessary for new property to be provided farther out from the city center.

Sometimes Christian architecture can be as innovative in Muslim lands as it dares to be any place else. The recently built Anglican church in Dubai is said to be built in the shape of a bishop's miter, with a stone communion table placed directly in the center under the high dome.

In the Tunisian seaside resort of Hammamet, the Roman Catholics have recently built a modest structure using the local building tradition of domes and barrel vaults. The ensemble is covered with unadorned white plaster. The street door is a typical traditional door with carving on its lintel and posts. A small decorative tile in the wall near the door, with the words "Eglise Catholique," is all that would distinguish this fine building from the structures on each side of it.

In the heart of the medina of Tangier, a Moorish-style white tower rises above a walled garden. Surrounded by rooftops of green glazed tiles, this little tower looks completely at home in a Moroccan city. It is the Church of England's St. Andrews Church and it occupies land donated by the Sultan Mulay Hassan from his own property in the late 19th century. Built in 1894, it was designed by a local architect (Alexander Cameron) who obviously understood the traditional Maghrib style well. The interior reflects the delicate charm of the Alhambra with a richly carved stucco chancel arch surrounded by the Lord's prayer in Arabic calligraphy. Paired columns, topped with Moorish capitals, support the cusped arches on each side of the main hall. Expert workmen were brought from Fez to execute the stucco carving as well as the fine wooden ceiling in the chancel. This building is a jewel—a superb example of the appropriate use of indigenous Moorish architecture.

The new Protestant church in Salala, Oman, features stepped arches over the door and windows, and contemporary drain spouts projecting from the flat roof—fresh interpretations (in sharply defined concrete and plaster) of age-old Middle Eastern motifs.

In Aleppo, Syria, a great new domed Orthodox church looks very much at home amid the other domed Islamic structures nearby.

The Protestant church of Muscat was dedicated in July of 1975 on land given by the sultan as a Christian *waqf*. It is next to a little Christian cemetery and an adjacent Roman Catholic church. Its contemporary style[24] blends well with the current building styles of the booming Arabian sultanate as well as with the nearby Catholic church. Both show beige exterior

walls with white plaster trim—a color statement that has been used for centuries in the Arabian peninsula.The Catholic church has incorporated Islamic features in a very current mode: the wide low dome and the keel-shaped broken arches of the windows, sharply defined in white plaster. Several young palm trees complete this attractive group.

In summary then, some observations can be made:

1. Originally Islam appropriated Byzantine and Sassanian architecture at the time of the conquest and again in the 16th century when Ottoman builders found their inspiration in Justinian's great 6th century church.

2. In the historical context, Islamic architecture has significantly affected Christian architecture only at the time of the reconquest of Sicily and Spain—and possibly during the Crusades.

3. With the colonial period and the modern missionary movement, Western missionaries, although they at times built in the styles of their homeland, often used regional, traditional styles and numerous combinations of these styles.

4. Contemporary international architecture has introduced a new pervasive common style all over the world. In the context of this modern style, some Middle East governments have been calling on their architects to revitalize traditional Islamic architectural forms and features, thereby creating an

environment where their use in Christian buildings would probably seem normative.

But a word of caution is in order: There are people in some Muslim lands that will always look suspiciously on any Christian presence in their land. Although this probably has nothing to do with whether or not Islamic architectural features are employed, this kind of situation calls for the most inconspicuous building style possible.

The message intended by an architectural statement is not always the message received. Real meanings must therefore be sought as diligently as possible.

5. By means of scale and style, architecture can project different messages. What this message should be will vary from place to place. Sometimes the message intended is not the message received by the larger community. To make sure this does not happen, a careful study of the local situation must be made. It is at this point that the option of using Islamic motifs must be thoroughly explored also. This is true both regarding the church community itself as well as the larger outside communities. For it is in the eyes of these users that the real meanings in architecture must be sought.

6. When Islamic features are used, they must not be applied in a superficial way like so many cliches. This calls for the finest designer that the community can obtain—someone with the skill and integrity to "reinvigorate the past at a deep level by transforming it into vigorous forms for the present."[25] No small task! But a very necessary one, considering that the alternative is a trivializing of traditional forms.

The adage, "Wherever a Muslim prays, that is a mosque," can be revised to apply to Christians too. The church is not the building; it is the people.

7. Lastly, do not underestimate the flexibility of a worshiping group. This brief study has shown that religious communities can adapt to all sorts of architectural spaces. The adage, "Wherever a Muslim prays, that is a mosque," can be revised to apply to Christians too. Let this fact serve as a reminder—particularly to those of us who are so concerned about architecture—that the real church is not the building but the people who gather in that building. Let our task then be to make sure that the architecture truly enhances the effectiveness of that worshiping Christian community—both to those within and to those without in the larger Muslim community.

NOTES

1. For a thorough discussion of meanings in Islamic architecture today see: O. Grabar, "Symbols and Signs in Islamic Architecture," in *Architecture and Community: Building in the Islamic World Today* (Millerton, NY: Aperture, 1983).

2. K. A. C. Creswell, *A Short Account of Early Muslim Architecture* (Beirut: Librairie du Liban, 1968), 7.

3. Samuel Zwemer, "The Pulpit in Islam," *The Moslem World* XXIII (1933), 217. For another point of view see: T. Burckhardt, *Art of Islam* (World of Islam Festival, 1976), 86, 91.

4. O. Grabar, *The Formation of Islamic Art* (New Haven, CN: Yale University Press, 1973), 207.

5. *Armenian Architecture* (Milan: Facolta de Architettura del Politechnico, 1981).

6. John Carswell, *New Julfa* (Oxford: Clarendon Press, 1968), 19.

7. R. Krautheimer, *Early Christian and Byzantine Architecture* (Penguin Books, 1975), 323-324.

8. S. Clarke, *Christian Antiquities in the Nile Valley* (Oxford: Clarendon Press, 1912), 120 (Plates XXXIII-V).

9. Ibid., 115.

10. Creswell, 7.

11. Ibn Jubayr, *The Travels of Ibn Jubayr*, trans. R. J. C. Broadhurst (London: Broadhurst, 1952), 318-319.

12. S. de Beaurecueil is famous for his work on al Ansari, the 11th century mystic of Herat.

13. Krautheimer, 262.

14. R. A. Jairazbhoy, "Influence of Islamic Architecture in Western Europe," *Arts and the Islamic World* I:1 (London: New Century Publishers, 1982-83), 25.

15. O. Grabar, "Art and Architecture," in *The Legacy of Islam*, ed. J. Schacht, 2nd ed. (Oxford: Oxford University Press, 1979).

16. F. Ragette, *Architecture in Lebanon* (New York: Caravan Books, 1980), 38.

17. Jan Morris, *Stones of Empire* (New York: Oxford Univ. Press, 1983), 31.

18. Ibid.

19. Hannelore Kunz, "Nineteenth Century Synagogues in the Neo-Islamic Style,"in *Eighth World Congress of Jewish Studies* (Jerusalem, 1982), 71-78.

20. The present synagogue in Beirut reflects this style and it still remains untouched by the present conflict.

21. G. Baudez and F. Beguin, "Arabisances," *Lotus International* 26 (Milan), (1980): 1. See also F. Beguin, *Arabisance* (Paris: Dunod, 1983).

22. For more on this see:

    M. F. Schmertz, "Conserving a Rich Architectural Heritage," *Architectural Record* (September 1983): 72ff.

    M. F. Schmertz, "The 1986 Winners of the Aga Khan Award for Architecture," *Architectural Record* (January 1987): 101ff.

    M. F. Schmertz, "Islamic Architecture and Rural Dwellings from Beijing to Kashi," *Architectural Record* (May 1982): 93ff.

    T. P. Kuttiammu, "The Mosques of Kerala," *Marj* (Bombay) 32, no. ii (1979): 85-89.

    C. De Benedetti, "Moschee d'Africa," *Domus* (Milan) 658 (February 1985): 30-37.

    Ihsan Fethi, "The Mosque Today," *Architecture in Continuity, Building in the Islamic World Today* (New York: Aperture, [1985]), 53-63.

    L. Akbarut, "The Role of Mosques in America," *The Minaret* (Croyden, UK: Minaret House), (November-December 1986): 12.

23. J. Christy Wilson, Jr., *Afganistan, the Forbidden Harvest* (Elgin, IL: David C. Cook Publishing, 1981), 59.

24. An international committee of lay experts was responsible for the design, but a local Muslim carpenter was hired to do the woodwork. When he learned that a cross was to be made for the interior, he insisted on donating both his labor and the lovely teakwood from which the cross was made.

25. W. J. R. Curtis, "The Aga Khan Award for 1985: 'Third-World Myths and First-World Fashions': a Critical View," *Architectural Record* (January 1987): 104.

SPIRITUAL EMPOWERING

Stay in the city until you are clothed with power from on high...Then... lifting up his hands he blessed them... And they returned to Jerusalem with great joy and were continually in the temple blessing God.
   — Luke 24: 49–50, 52–53

CHAPTER SEVENTEEN

THE PRACTICE OF EXORCISM AND HEALING

Vivienne Stacey

A few years ago I studied Paul's letter to the Romans in Urdu with a Muslim graduate of the al-Azhar University who had trained in Cairo for three years to become an orthodox religious teacher back in his own country. During our study of the Epistle's references to the Holy Spirit, the question of power and authority arose and the young man said he had power over nine kinds of snakes.

About three years later, he submitted himself to the Lord Jesus Christ and became his follower. He renounced demonic power and found spiritual power in his new relationship with God. He was publicly baptized in a nearby town. Despite opposition, he continues to live in his native village.

Perhaps it was the same teaching and a similar experience that led the profligate poet John Donne (1592-1631) to adopt a new seal after his conversion. He renounced his family seal and before his ordination (he later became Dean of St. Paul's Cathedral in London) took a new one which depicted Christ extended on an anchor. He had several copies of this seal made on bloodstone, which he gave to his intimate friends, notably Isaac Walton and George Herbert. Of the change of seal he wrote:

A sheaf of snakes used heretofore to be my seal,
The crest of our poor family.
Adopted in God's family, so our old coat lost,
Unto new arms I go.

Christians have underestimated the hold of folk religion. In minority situations, Christians have even adopted some of its practices.

It is interesting that in the early church very definite renunciation of the devil and all his works was required of the catechumen and became part of the baptismal service. Such a renunciation of the devil and his works is still part of some baptismal liturgies.

After spending over 32 years in the Muslim world I have come to the conclusion that Christians have underestimated the hold of folk religion. The church in minority situations is often hampered by folk religion, sometimes even adopting some of its practices. Christians in some places visit Muslim holy persons (*pirs* or *walis*) and go to makers of charms (*tawiz*) to purchase what may meet their special need.

Some authorities claim that 70 percent of the Muslims of the Indian sub-continent are involved in the practice of folk Islam.[1] This may be an underestimate. In recent years there have been definite evidences of more integration of the orthodox and the popular. For example, the well-patronized exhibition at the Badshahi Mosque in Lahore, Pakistan, appeals to the Sunni and Shia alike with its 27 relics of the Prophet of Islam and some of his closest associates. Muhammad's sandals, underwear and walking stick are venerated, along with Fatima's prayer mat. The sight of some dust from the battlefield of Karbala brings tears to the eyes of visitors who expect a blessing from such near contact with holy relics.

Dhikr, the constant repetition of Allah's names, links the orthodox to the magical.

The practice of *dhikr*, or constant repetition of Allah's names, also strengthens the bridge between what is orthodox and what may be magical. One example from a book giving guidance on the repetition of the 99 names of Allah is the use of the name Al-Halim, the Forbearing One.[2] "If one writes this Name on a piece of paper, and puts it where his seed is sown, no harm, disaster or calamity will befall his crop."

Inadequate renunciation may be a reason why some who leave Folk Islam return to it.

In a system in which form is as important if not more important than meaning, in which the exact detail must be correctly carried out or the meaning is rendered void, there may be a binding of the mind as well as of the will. Without doubt very many are involved with the occult and so the past and the occult must be totally renounced at baptism. Inadequate renunciation may be why some return to their former religion.

In reality we are contending with the powers of darkness and not just with people and concepts. If baptism is delayed or there is no baptism and teaching prior to it, the question will arise as to how and where the necessary renunciation of the devil and all his works will occur. Can one really say that Jesus Christ is Lord without first renouncing the devil? The bonds must be broken.

Power demonstrations are more effective when related to consistent teaching by members of a local body of Christ.

In view of a greater synthesis of folk religion with orthodox teaching and practice and the hold of the occult, there is need for more than intellectual persuasion and head knowledge. Theology has its place but teaching should be clinical, practical and event-oriented so that its relevance is apparent.

Power demonstrations related to consistent teaching are very convincing, especially when the teachers are members of a loving, spiritual community—the local body of Christ. Such a loving, extended spiritual family will draw in outsiders, as we have seen recently in one Muslim city where literally the lame walk, the deaf hear and the blind see (Lk. 7:22). Many Muslims come for teaching, and healing services are held for all regularly. Christ gave his own mandate to his church:

> The Spirit of the Lord is upon me, because he has anointed me to preach good news to the poor. He has sent me to proclaim release to the captives and recovering of sight to the blind, to set at liberty those who are oppressed, to proclaim the acceptable year of the Lord (Lk. 4:18-19 RSV).

I would like, therefore, to look at a small section of this mandate as it is fulfilled in the practice of exorcism of people and places and the practice of healing, together with some of the teaching which should be part of it.

The Exorcism of People

In a remote part of an Asian Muslim country, Muslims and nominal Christians have found new life in Christ. Some were delivered from demons and others were healed from various illnesses. The focus was not on "signs and wonders" but on preaching and teaching (Rom. 15:19). The national pastor leading this work only prayed for deliverance or healing when the Holy Spirit specifically guided him to do so, and it was always after one or more teaching sessions. Sometimes a family would stay with his extended family for four or five days to receive teaching and perhaps healing. This pastor had come with his wife and family to this remote area seven years prior to this writing, in response to a clear call from God. He worked mainly as a free-lance evangelist, attending a local congregation but not under the direct authority of any church.

The influence of the occult on both Muslim and Christian communities has been extensive.

About three years ago people began coming to him with requests for prayer for healing. Some principles may be illustrated by two case histories. It should be understood that the influence of the occult on both Muslim and Christian communities is extensive. This probably comes from an underlying animism, accretions from Hinduism, the prevailing faith before the arrival of Islam some centuries ago, and the deliberate practices of Islam (for example, constant repetition, incantation and mechanical reading which may themselves be used by demonic forces).

Case History 1. A Muslim father gave his very young daughter Farida (names have been changed in these factual accounts) a charm (*tawiz*) in an attempt to win her affection to himself and away from her divorced mother. After receiving the charm she sometimes had fits, spoke in unrecognizable words and called out for her father. During these abnormal times she spoke in a different, harsher voice and her appearance changed. Her face and tongue became long. Sometimes these fits lasted 24 hours.

When she became an adult she came to Inayat to request prayer for healing. Once when Inayat prayed she squirmed and then foamed at the mouth. Three men were unable to hold her still. Inayat prayed very much for her in private and also fasted. When he prayed with her, her mother said she had never come out of a fit so quickly before. The mother expressed her belief that God would heal her daughter.

Mother and daughter came regularly over a period of three months and also at any time that the girl had trouble. One morning she came complaining of pains in different parts of her body. She became blind and then dumb. After more prayer and the reading of Psalm 138, she was better and could see and speak. When she went to the local hospital to get a medical certificate to give to her employer to explain her absence (she works as a librarian), the psychiatrist was amazed at the improvement in her.

Farida gradually became better and better and began to read a small New Testament during the period between Christmas and Easter, asking questions from time to time. At the Good Friday service she testified to the Lord's healing. Through her testimony several nominal Christians became believers. She invited her Muslim cousins, the daughters of a religious teacher (*maulvi*), to meet Inayat and his wife to be prayed for.

When Inayat prays for Muslims, they are seldom healed instantly. Time is needed for teaching. But after the first prayers they receive a touch from the Lord which convinces them that they will be healed, and so they come regularly, sometimes from considerable distance and at much expense. They tell others of the power of prayer in the name of Jesus the Messiah.

The cousins report that they have seen changes in Farida's life. Farida asked Inayat for the blessing he had so that she could also pray for others. He told her to repent and believe. She said, "I have repented many times." Inayat counseled her to ask Jesus Christ to forgive her. She did so and for the first time received assurance of the forgiveness of sins, as did her younger sister. The cousins are now reading the New Testament.

Case History 2. Yakub, a nominal Christian, was afraid demons would kill him. He is now a landowner with a wife and three children. When he was a young athlete, a competitor had given him a charm in a potion to drink and he became ill. Over the years, he received some medical treatment, but then suspecting that he had been given a magic potion unawares, he had gone to various shrines and holy places to offer prayers for healing. His health improved and he married but soon became thin. His health deteriorated and soon he could not even work.

Finally, in the summer of 1986, demons took over at times and spoke through him, even "preaching" sometimes. One day they said, "If you don't get us cast out within two days we are going to break your neck." Yakub was extremely frightened and sent a request for help to Inayat. Inayat went to Yakub's village and found him uttering blasphemies. Inayat started to pray, grabbing his hair. Yakub vomited and then was better. Later, a service of worship and teaching (attended by many Muslims) was held in the church. All the village knew about Yakub's problems. A prayer and healing service followed and then another worship and preaching service in the evening was held, as well as the following morning.

Inayat and his wife invited Yakub to their home where he stayed for four days of prayer, teaching and fellowship. He stopped vomiting and set out for his village home. All the villagers, hearing that he was coming, turned out to welcome him, amazed and glad that he was still alive. They garlanded him and led him in procession back into the village, where he told them all what the Lord had done for him in giving salvation and how he was healed after 13 years of sickness.
During the next weeks Yakub spent several sessions in prayer and study of the Bible with other believers. Then a thanks-

giving service was held, attended by many Muslims and Christians. Various believers gave testimony to new life in Christ and Inayat preached. Many came for prayer and all claimed to be healed. There had been no emphasis on healing but this ministry was thrust upon them.

A team of 15 believers from Brethren, Roman Catholic, Pentecostal and Episcopal background has formed with Inayat as leader. The verse "By this shall all men know that you are my disciples, if you have love for one another" (Jn. 13:35), is being lived out. Inayat sometimes sends some team members to minister in one place and some in another as requests for ministry increase. All are lay volunteers. The team members stress that physical healing is not enough—it is only for this life. A healing of the soul is needed for this life and the next—the abundant life which Jesus gives (Jn. 10:10).

The emphasis is on team ministry. It is a ministering team itself under training with individuals learning from each other and from Inayat. There appears to be a need to go on having prayer times with some who have been healed. Inayat and his band seek to pray in the way that God guides them and not just because the patient requests prayer for healing. In these last few months the following facts have emerged:

1. Many more Muslims than before have come for healing and then, having been in some measure touched by the Holy Spirit to repent, have started to read the Bible.

2. The influence of believing cleaners in Muslim households is evident. Through their testimony their employers have come for help (compare this with the influence of the Israelite maid in the house of Naaman, the Syrian commander, as recorded in 2 Kgs. 5). Believing nurses also share with their patients. Thus the Good News is permeating society.

3. Everyone who receives spiritual blessing, whether literate or illiterate, is constrained by the Holy Spirit and commissioned by the team to pass it on and help others.

4. Inayat puts great emphasis in his teaching on God's word and God's promises. He questions those who come for healing. He asks, "Have you been to a medical doctor? Have you been to a religious holy man (pir)?" Before he prays for anyone he requires them to repudiate, take off and throw away any charms they might be wearing. He keeps a large urn for cast-off charms.

5. He teaches Muslims to pray for themselves using short prayers. For example:

Thanks be to God.
Praise be to God.
Lord, have mercy on me.
Lord, forgive my sins.

6. On the first Friday of each month, new believers from both Muslim and Christian communities come to a house-meeting for a service of praise, thanksgiving and teaching. Believers continue to live and witness in their Muslim homes, and Christians continue their previous church links.

Exorcism of people should be a *shared* ministry, based carefully on correct diagnosis and consistent teaching.

My own experiences and observations lead me to emphasize the following principles for the practice of exorcism in relation to people:

1. *Whenever possible, deliverance should be a shared ministry* with a team of two or three or more who are of one mind, who are walking in God's light and who believe that God has called them to help in this particular situation.

2. *Correct diagnosis is essential.* Some questions and tests as to whether a person is demonized are:

 a. What does the person think about his condition?

 b. Does he think he is possessed by an evil spirit or evil spirits?

 c. Does he want to be released?

 d. What has led other people to believe that he is demon possessed?

 e. How does the patient respond to counseling?

 f. How does he react when invited to join those around him in praising God?

 g. How does he react if he reads of or hears a portion of Scripture in which there is a mention of the blood of Christ, for example, 1 John 1:5-9?

 h. Do the spirits answer if commanded to do so in the name of Jesus?

3. *Consistent teaching is vital for the person and those around.* Exorcism is not an isolated act by one person. In fact, exorcism in isolation can be dangerous and does not bring glory to God (Lk. 11:24-26). If there is counseling and teaching both before and after, and if the act of exorcism is seen as part of the deliverance and healing of the whole person, then the gospel is proclaimed and many will be influenced spiritually.[3]

The Exorcism of Buildings

The Bible contains no record of the exorcism of a building. High places used for Baal worship were cast down and destroyed (2 Ch. 17:6). Land could be polluted (Jer. 3:2). In practice, however, I believe there is a strong case for cleansing a place or a building and then dedicating or rededicating it. One never knows what has taken place on that territory or in that building through the centuries. Too many buildings have been dedicated to the glory of God without the basic cleansing.

Christian workers, underestimating evil powers, have purchased "haunted" houses at very cheap prices when the local people have been afraid to buy them and to live in them. These Christians sometimes thought that dedication of such houses was adequate, but this was not the case. Through the years, guests and residents have been troubled. In some instances it has been observed by neighbors that evil spirits live in the houses occupied by believers in Christ. Surely this is a dishonor to Christ.

I spent my second Christmas in the Indian subcontinent, living in a former Moghul courthouse which still was not free from strange manifestations 50 years after its purchase by missionaries. In some countries workmen, thinking to protect themselves, seek to appease satanic forces by fixing a figurine at the highest point of the building. As the building rises, so does the mascot.

Would not a building built in the fear of demons require cleansing before dedication? I believe more Christians, both national and expatriate, would be more effective workers for Christ in the Muslim world if it were a general practice to cleanse and then dedicate every building, constructed or rented, in which they live or work.

Sometimes those who are not Christ's followers have more perception about what is happening in the unseen world and, when Christ's authority is used, they are challenged by it. I remember an Asian family who were living in an Arabian city. After moving to a new home in another section of the city, they had severe health problems for several months, whereas previously they and their children had kept very well. Finally, after discussion and prayer, several of us joined the husband and wife to form a team with the intention of cleansing and dedicating the home. In each room we:

1. Prayed in Christ's name for the casting out of any evil spirits and that they would remain bound in the appointed place for them until the judgment day, thereby troubling no one else in the future.

2. Praised God in song or with words of Scripture.

3. Prayed for the particular room and the people who would use the room and the activities for which it was designed—for example, the bedroom for sleeping and the dining room for eating.

In that particular home a Muslim neighbor visiting the next day commented on the change of atmosphere and the better health of the child. The Christian explained the service which had taken place and witnessed to the power of Jesus Christ.

Exorcism of buildings should be a Christ-exalting team ministry, characterized by simple obedience rather than publicity.

I have taken part in many such services in recent years, and I know that Christ's power has been made evident to Muslims as well as to Christians. Some crucial principles which emerge are:

1. The ministry is a team ministry exalting Christ in prayer and praise and through the use of Scripture.

2. Those participating must prepare themselves spiritually, and must be practicing and obedient followers of Jesus Christ.

3. It is not wise to talk unnecessarily about such ministry.

4. Obedience to Christ in the cleansing and dedication of buildings results in increasing fruitfulness and blessing.

One of the church's most ancient prayers of exorcism is as follows:

God, the Son of God, who by death destroyed death, and overcame him who had the power of death, beat down Satan quickly. Deliver this place (room, house, church) from all evil spirits; all vain imaginations, projections and all deceits of the evil one; and bid them harm no one but depart to the place appointed for them, there to remain for ever. God, incarnate God, who came to give peace, give peace.   Amen.

Years ago I learned the importance of commanding the evil powers to go "to the place appointed for them." On one occasion we failed to do this while cleansing a room. Our next-door neighbor was greatly scared by an inrush into his room and had a great awareness of evil powers rushing through. This happened, we discovered later, at the exact time that we had commanded in Christ's name the spirits to leave a certain room where they had been troubling guests. Ten years later I asked this man if he had ever had another similar frightening experience and he said he had not.

In October, 1986, I took part in the cleansing and dedication service for some new conference rooms. The service was very short and was based on the following hymn:

> For this purpose Christ was revealed
> To destroy all the works of the evil one,
> Christ in us has overcome,
> So with gladness we sing,
> And welcome his kingdom in.
>
> (two-part chorus - men and women)
> Men: Over sin He has conquered...
> Women: Hallelujah, He has conquered.
> Men: Over death victorious...
> Women: Hallelujah, victorious.
> Men: Over sickness He has triumphed.
> Women: Hallelujah, He has triumphed.
>
> All. JESUS REIGNS OVER ALL.
>
> In the name of Jesus we stand,
> By the power of his blood
> We now claim this ground.
> Satan has no authority here,
> Powers of darkness must flee,
> For Christ has the victory.[4]

Such services can take many forms, but the casting out of evil in Jesus' name, praise of God, prayer and the reading or reciting of Bible portions are essential ingredients.[5]

The Practice of Healing

In this brief space I cannot deal adequately with the vast subject of healing. I would like to approach the subject with emphasis on the sentence, "By his stripes you are healed" (Isa. 53:5 and 1 Pe. 2:24).

In some way beyond our understanding, Christ's sacrificial death can bring healing to every part of a person's being. Dietrich Bonhoeffer, the anti-Nazi German Lutheran pastor, chose to preach on this text on the day of his execution in prison in April, 1945. The doctor present at his execution said he had hardly ever seen a man die so entirely submissive to the will of God.[6] No doubt, Bonhoeffer saw death as the ultimate healing, for it meant to be with Christ in his glory.

Illness may have many causes. It is significant that Luke the physician, recognized Satan's hand in some illnesses and understood that healing could be miraculously given when Satan was rebuked, as in the case of Peter's mother-in-law (Lk. 4:38-39). Some illnesses are not so straightforward— there may be a satanic element but medicine and surgery may be required. Thus, everything should be done with prayer, for the Lord God is our healer.

It is good to let Muslims see Christians to be who they are. In a Muslim context, it is good if we can be seen to be who we are. Too often Christians misinterpret the verse about shutting one's door and praying in secret (Mt. 6:6). Daily chapel prayers for hospital staff and for patients, if they are able and willing to come, are a clear witness, even though this may not be the intention. A few minutes in public prayer for a patient and the relatives and staff before an operation or during informal visiting is generally much appreciated. If we fail to pray publicly and rely only on our lives and not our words to commend the gospel, then many will see our good works and conclude that we are acquiring merit for ourselves. We have to consider not only what we do but how others perceive us.

Christians who have spent their lives healing and teaching have made significant contributions to planting churches by their breaking down of barriers through love and service. We are all familiar with the work of medical missions over the last century in Africa, Asia and the Middle East.

The American Mission Hospital in Bahrain, founded by Samuel Zwemer, is not only a reminder of a ministry of healing and compassion but is a visible demonstration of love for Christ's sake. Here, in a materialistic society where host exploits guest and vice versa, an institution established before the discovery of oil in the Gulf is a symbol of another set of values. Its history gives credibility to its work today. Let us not ignore history.

The history of medical ministry gives credibility to Christian work. But it must be seen as only part of a holistic ministry.

However, just as some are tempted to see exorcism as an isolated act and not just part of the making of an individual whole in Christ, so there has been a tendency to isolate medical ministry and not to see it as part of service to the whole person in his total community. N. H. Antia, in an article in the *British Medical Journal* entitled "The Mandwa Experiment, an Alternative Strategy," described an experiment carried out between 1973 and 1983 in a rural area of the Indian state of Maharashtra. The purpose was to look at the health problems and explore ways in which the available medical technology could be applied.

The Mandwa experiment report noted that a few leaders in the community held political and economic control while the majority of the population of thirty thousand were poor. Most problems were related to maternal and child health, so a local woman, motivated to serve her neighbors, was chosen from each village and trained through weekly informal discussion groups. Most of the project staff were local people and were well accepted by the community. The project's health results were encouraging and were far above the national figures. However the Mandwa project had to leave the area and hand over its assets, partly because it was seen by the powerful local leaders and by some health professionals as a threat. N. H. Antia concludes:

> Sadly, even well-intentioned doctors see health as a problem rather than as a subsystem of the social, economic, and political structure of the country...The Mandwa experiment may either be seen as a failed community health project or as an experiment that shows that simple knowledge and technology can help poor people to overcome their fears and develop self-reliance. Before health can be improved appreciably, however, education, especially of women, must be developed and the political will generate to effect change.[7]

Where illiteracy, poverty and disease have been prevalent, an emphasis upon Christian community

development with attention to spiritual issues is refreshingly appropriate.

In recent years there has been a refreshing emphasis on Christian community development programs. For the last six years I have been linked to a small community development program as a consultant on spiritual issues and outreach. The team of ten, comprised of nationals and foreigners, men and women, works in a rural area where literacy is low and poverty and disease are prevalent. Evangelism is seen as the responsibility of each individual and the group together at special times such as Christmas and Easter.

The purposes of my visits have been to meet the team, see their work, lead them in spiritual retreat and guide their study and reading, as events in a process. It has been rewarding to see the influence they have had within the communities that have welcomed them. One of their objectives is the emergence of new congregations in villages where there are none. As Chris Sugden and Vinay Samuel have said:

> The scope of the Kingdom of God extends not just to the community of the King that consciously acknowledges Jesus as Lord, but is also seen in God's kingdom activity in the world beyond the church.[8]

In this wide context the practice of exorcism and healing can involve Christ's followers through that which we have inherited, seeking to transform, as appropriate, for example, Christian hospitals, through work with the local church, through work with the community and through work with the government. God's promise is shalom ("peace") in the sense of total well-being (See Ps. 85:8).

NOTES

1. M. Geijbels, "Aspects of Veneration of Saints in Islam, With Special Reference to Pakistan," *The Muslim World* (July 1978).

2. Shems Friedlander, *The Ninety-Nine Names of Allah* with al-Hajj Shaikh Muzaffereddin (New York: Harper and Row, 1978).

3. Vivienne Stacey, *Christ Supreme over Satan: Spiritual Warfare, Folk Religion and the Occult*. Ch. 2.

4. Graham Kendrick, *Songs of Faith* (n.d.), no. 364.

5. Stacey, *Christ Supreme*, Ch. 1.

6. Norman Hare, "Fresh Light on Bonhoeffer," *Church Times* (September 19, 1986).

7. N.H. Antia, "The Mandwa Experiment, an Alternative Strategy," *British Medical Journal* 292 (1986): 1181-1183.

8. Chris Sugden and Vinay Samuel, "Mobilizing for Wholistic Ministry," (unpublished, n.d.).

CHAPTER EIGHTEEN

BIBLICAL FOUNDATIONS OF PRAYING FOR MUSLIMS

Colin Chapman

Our aim in studying the Bible together is to sit together under the Word, so that all our thinking can be grounded in Scripture, and all our strategizing can be undergirded with theological reflection.

To connect the Bible and Islam we must: 1) Think biblically and theologically; 2) Try to understand the Muslim mind; 3) Reflect on the process of communication.

But how do we make connections between the Bible and Islam? How do we use our understanding of the words of Scripture in their original context and relate them to the world of Islam today? Three basic convictions underlie the attempt to make such connections in these studies:

1. If we are to get beyond the slogans, we need to get down to some hard study together, and try to *think biblically and theologically* about what we are doing. In getting to grips with the difficult questions, we will need all the resources not only of disciplines like anthropology, but also of biblical and theological scholarship.

    2. We need to take the trouble to *understand the mind of the Muslim*. This will mean understanding not only the total culture of Islam and folk Islam, but also understanding ideal Islam, Islam at its best. There is a sense in which we may need to know the Quran better than the Muslim does, not in order to find weapons to use in polemics, but simply in order to understand what it means to be a Muslim. I trust there is no need to defend or justify the study of the Quran and of other Muslim sources in this context.

    3. We need to *reflect on the process of communication*. Instead of making a false dichotomy between spiritual

warfare and subjects like cross-cultural communication, we have to wrestle both in thought and in prayer with questions about how to communicate the good news about Jesus. This will mean trying to read the Scriptures, as it were, with Islamic spectacles, and asking how they can address the Muslim mind and communicate the good news about Jesus.

The Lord's Prayer and the Fatihah

Here are the pattern prayers of the two faiths. Of course there will always be a gulf between the way we *actually* pray and the way we *ought* to pray. Our instinctive responses to sickness or misfortune of different kinds may bear little resemblance to the models we have been given; and in many cases, as the study of folk religion tells us, people often do not resort to any kind of genuine prayer, but to rituals of superstition and magic. But it can be valuable to compare the prayers which have been given to the two communities of faith—the one taught by Jesus to his disciples, and the other, as Muslims believe, revealed by direct inspiration from God to the Prophet.

Studying the two prayers side by side ought to remove the foreignness which we feel about prayer in Islam, and enable us to appreciate some of the common ground in Christian and Muslim spirituality. Thinking about Muslims at prayer may give us an opportunity to sit where they sit and to enter into something of their relationship with God. There is no place for polemics when we are on our knees! We want to see how far we can travel along the same road in worship and prayer before we come to the point where our paths diverge.

If we set the two prayers out side by side, we can see how some of the lines in the one correspond roughly to lines in the other:

Compare five themes in the two prayers—the Fatihah and the prayer Jesus taught.

The Prayer Jesus Taught	The Fatihah
Our Father in heaven	In the name of God the merciful Lord of mercy.
Your name be hallowed	Praise be to God the Lord of all being
Your kingdom come	the Merciful Lord of Mercy
Your will be done on earth as in heaven.	Master of the Day of Judgment. You alone we worship.

Give us this day
our daily bread.

To you alone we come for aid.

Forgive us our sins
as we forgive those
who sin against us.

Lead us not into temptation
but deliver us from evil

Guide us in the straight path
the path of those whom you
have blessed
not of those against whom
there is displeasure
nor of those who go astray.

For yours is the kingdom
the power
and the glory for ever.

What we want to do is to trace five different themes through the two prayers: our relationship with God, our worship of God, our need of mercy, our need of guidance and our need of deliverance.

1. Our Relationship with God

In the Lord's Prayer our relationship with God is that of children speaking to our Father ("Our Father..."). In the Fatihah it is the relationship of the servants speaking to their master. This is clear from the word that is used for "we worship" (*na'bud*), which also gives us the word "servant" or "slave" (*'abd*).

"To be the slave of Allah is the proudest boast of the Muslim, ...liberating from all other servitudes."
—Marmaduke Pickthall

We need to be careful, however, that we do not read into the master-servant relationship too much of the idea of servility and degradation. The Muslim counts it an honor to be a servant of God, for, as Marmaduke Pickthall says, "To be the slave of Allah is the proudest boast of the Muslim, bondage to Allah liberating from all other servitudes."[1]

This sense of both honor and grace which Muslims see in this relationship is summed up beautifully in a short Arabic saying/prayer: "It is enough of an honor to me that I should be your servant; it is enough of grace to me that you should be my Lord." (*yakfini sharafan an akuna laka 'abdan; yakfini ni'matan an takuna li rabban.*)

Having acknowledged what the master-servant relationship can be at its best, we must still say that it falls far short of the relationship which is offered to us through Jesus. The thinking of the Muslim at this point is close to that of the Prodigal Son, who in coming home works out what Kenneth Bailey calls a "face-saving plan:"[2] "make me as one of your hired servants..." (Lk. 15:19).

But the waiting Father can never be satisfied with that kind of relationship, since he wants even the prodigal to enjoy all the privileges and responsibilities of a son in the family. The wonder of the gospel is that Jesus, the only one who had the right to call God "Abba, Father" invited his disciples to enter into that same intimate relationship he enjoyed with the Father.

Whether we come as sons and daughters or as servants, our basic human needs drive us all to seek help from God our Creator. Thus the words "we come for aid" (nasta'in) in the Fatihah can be seen as roughly parallel to "Give us this day our daily bread." The Muslim is seeking from God everything that is implied in the word 'awn, which is defined in the dictionary as "help, aid, assistance, succor, relief, support, backing." The Lord's Prayer, similarly, encourages us to pray about our physical and material needs for the present and the immediate future.

So although we differ from Muslims to some extent in the way we understand our relationship with God the Creator, the basic needs which we bring to him as his creatures are exactly the same.

2. Our Worship of God

The idea of praying for the will of God to be done sounds strange to some Muslim ears.

The Fatihah expresses both praise ("Praise be to God...") and worship ("You alone we worship..."). In the words of A. Yusuf Ali, "In our spiritual contemplation the first words should be those of praise. If the praise is from our inmost being, it brings us into union with God's will."[3]

In the Lord's Prayer we worship God by praising him for all that he has revealed about himself (his name), by acknowledging his authority as king and by surrendering to his will. But our worship leads us into intercession, as we pray that his name will be honored on earth, his kingly rule acknowledged and his will done among all people here and now.

While the two prayers may have much in common in their spirit of worship, wherever there are differences in our perceptions of God and his ways, they are bound to affect our understanding of worship. Thus, for example, the idea of praying for the will of God to be done sounds strange to some Muslim ears. The popular Arabic expression "what God has willed" (*ma sha'a Allah*) suggests that all we can do is to accept what God has decreed.

But in the Lord's Prayer there is no place for the fatalism of popular religion (whether Muslim or Christian) which says "whatever will be will be." Our surrender to God is not a blind or passive surrender to decrees that are unalterable. So that when we pray "thy will be done" we are, in S.D. Gordon's memorable words, exploring the will of God, and aligning ourselves with it. We are surrendering ourselves to work with him in getting his will accomplished here on earth.

Both prayers acknowledge the sovereignty of God in his world. The Lord's Prayer speaks of God as king ("Your kingdom come... yours is the kingdom"), while the Fatihah speaks of God as "Lord of the worlds," or "Lord of all spheres of being" or "Lord of all being." It is worth noticing that confessions of the sovereignty of God in the Quran and the Bible sound remarkably similar: "Knowest thou not that it is Allah unto Whom belongeth the sovereignty of the heavens and the earth?" (2:107.) "The Lord has established his throne in heaven and his kingdom rules over all" (Ps. 103:19).

What is unique in the Bible, however, is the idea of the *coming* of the kingdom of God: "Say among the nations, 'The Lord reigns'...he comes to judge the earth" (Ps. 96:10-13). "The Lord will be king over the whole earth" (Zech. 14:9). "The time has come...the kingdom of God is near (is upon you, NEB)" (Mk. 1:15). "Some who are standing here will not taste death before they see the kingdom of God come with power" (Mk. 9:1). Biblical teaching about the kingdom of God does not simply remind us *that* God reigns; it goes on to tell us *how* he establishes his kingly rule.

The Quran tells us that God, who is the sovereign Lord of all creation seeks to establish his kingly rule in the world through the Islamic society living by its revealed law. But the Bible tells us that God has begun to establish his kingly rule in and through the person of Jesus and the community which he called into being. While, therefore, we share the same urge to praise and worship the one true God, we differ in our ideas of what God is like and how he works.

3. Our Need of Guidance

The similarity between the two prayers at this point emerges when we separate the words "Lead us..." in the Lord's Prayer from "not into temptation," and see that they express the same basic petition as "Guide us..." in the Fatihah. The idea of asking to be led in a straight path ought to be familiar to us, since the Psalmist has taught us to pray: "Lead me, O Lord, in your righteousness...make straight your way before me" (Ps.5:8).

But what is "the straight path," "the right path"? For Muslims it is the Path of Islam, the way of life revealed in the Quran and in the life of the Prophet. They are therefore praying "Guide us to and in the straight Way."[4]   This is the path of "those whom thou hast blessed," those who experience the blessing of God as members of the Islamic community.

If we ask who are the two categories of people referred to in the last two lines, one traditional interpretation is that "those against whom there is wrath" are the Jews, and "those who go astray" are Christians. There are, however, certain problems with this interpretation. In his introduction to the Fatihah, Pickthall writes:

> The fact that it has always, from the very earliest times, formed a part of Muslim worship, there being no record or remembrance of its introduction, or of public prayer without it, makes it clear that it was revealed before the fourth year of the Prophet's Mission (the tenth year before the Hijrah); because we know for certain that by that time regular congregational prayers were offered by the little group of Muslims in Mecca.

At such an early stage of the Prophet's ministry in Mecca, these phrases could hardly have referred to Jews and Christians, since he had not yet encountered opposition from them. In the context of Mecca around the year 613 AD, these phrases could refer only to pagan Arabs. It is true that the same terms are used in later Medinan suras, where they no doubt refer to Jews and Christians who opposed the Prophet (e.g., 5:60, 77). But Montgomery Watt suggests that this must have been "a new application to Medinan opponents of terms first applied to Meccan polytheists."[5]

NOTE: Since Muslims believe it is important for them to find out as far as possible the precise context in which verses of the Quran were first revealed (i.e., the occasions of revelation, *asbab il-nuzul*)...

Although Christians and Muslims are united in making a simple and straightforward request for guidance, we cannot avoid asking a further question: since this is the only explicit petition in the Fatihah, does it mean that guidance is *all* that we need? Does guidance convey the sum total of God's provision for humans in this world?

The Islamic diagnosis of the human condition can be summed up without too much over-simplification in two words: ignor-

...the situation of Mecca in the early days of the Prophet's ministry must shed some light on the identity of these groups of people whose example is not to be followed. In their original context they could hardly refer to Jews and Christians.

ance and weakness. Since humans are ignorant and forgetful, they need to be taught the truth and constantly reminded of it. And since they are basically weak (and *not* perverse), what they need is warning, admonition and encouragement to obey the law.

According to the Christian diagnosis, however, humans need something very much more radical than teaching, exhortation and example. And in the Lord's Prayer the request for guid-ance goes on to recognize the fact of temptation and trial, and reminds us of the reality of evil.

4. Our Need of Deliverance

Muslims and Christians alike sense a need for deliverance. They differ in awareness of kinds of evil to be delivered from—and of how God delivers.

Although the words "deliver us from evil" at first sight seem to have no obvious parallel in the Fatihah, the sentiment is clearly expressed in other verses of the Quran which are used regularly in prayer by Muslims—for example,

> Say: I seek refuge in the Lord of the Daybreak
> From the evil of that which he created;
> From the evil of the darkness when it is intense,
> And from the evil of malignant witchcraft,
> And from the evil of the envier when he envieth
> (103:1-5).

> Say: I seek refuge in the Lord of mankind,
> The King of mankind,
> The God of mankind,
> From the evil of the sneaking whisperer,
> Who whispereth in the hearts of mankind,
> Of the *jinn* and of mankind (104:1-6).

These are prayers for deliverance from different kinds of evil (e.g., "the evil of malignant witchcraft") and also from Satan himself ("the sneaking whisperer who whispereth in the hearts of mankind"). Similarly in the Lord's Prayer we are praying for deliverance from every kind of evil (if *tou ponerou* in the Greek is understood as neuter, as in the RSV), and from the Evil One (if it is taken as masculine, as in NEB, JB, TEV and NIV).

We are united, therefore, with Muslims in our desire to be guided and to be delivered from all that is evil. We both believe *that* we need to be delivered; but our paths may diverge when we try to identify particular kinds of evil; and we certainly go in different directions when we begin to ask *how* God provides a way of deliverance from the Evil One.

5. Our Need of Mercy

How do the two prayers deal with all that spoils our relationship with God? In the Lord's Prayer there is the petition "Forgive us our sins..." which reminds us constantly that confession should be a vital element in prayer. The Fatihah reminds us of the power and justice of God ("Master of the Day of Judgment"), but also reminds us of his compassion and mercy ("the Merciful, the Compassionate"). Muslims therefore hope or expect that God will be merciful on the Day of Judgment when they are called to account for their sins on the Day of Judgment. But we cannot help noticing that *confession* of sin is conspicuous by its absence in the Fatihah.

Conspicuously absent from the Fatihah is confession of sin.

The prayer "forgive us our sins" is found in the Quran (3:17), and it is interesting that the Arabic here is exactly the same as that used in the traditional version of the Lord's Prayer in Arabic (*faghfir lana dhunubana*). But it is surprising to us that in a prayer which is regarded by Muslims as expressing "the Essence of the Quran,"[6] or "the quintessence of Islamic doctrine,"[7] there is no suggestion that we need regularly to confess our sin.

If we are told that Christians suffer from an unhealthy and morbid preoccupation with sin, our reply is that we are simply praying here as Jesus taught us to pray. At the end of the day, however, what we are dealing with is two significantly different diagnoses of the human condition. And which of them is more realistic when we know ourselves and the state of the world?

While the Quran says much about mercy and compassion, the idea of forgiving others who wrong us boggles many Muslims' minds.

The Lord's Prayer also reminds us that we cannot think of our relationship with God in isolation from our relationship with people: "Forgive us our sins, as we forgive those who sin against us." Muslims are reminded of these horizontal relationships when they pray side by side and turn to greet those on their right and left at the end of their prayers. But it is not, I suspect, unfair to say that while the Quran has plenty to say about mercy and compassion, the idea that we have an obligation to forgive others who wrong us does not come so easily to the mind of the Muslim. I have heard of a Muslim who expressed sheer amazement when he heard that the Pope wanted to forgive the young Turk who had tried to murder him. And I know of a Muslim who once asked a Christian to recite the Lord's Prayer and interrupted after the line "as we forgive those who sin against us" with the words "Oh no! That's impossible!"

Is such a comparison of the two prayers anything more than an academic exercise? Perhaps I should lay my cards on the table and say that in my own prayer I sometimes say the Fatihah alongside the Lord's Prayer. When I do so, it provides a way of praying *for* and *with* the Muslim world.

So, for example, when I pray "to you alone we come for aid," I pray as a convinced monotheist coming to "the only true God..." (Jn. 17:3), and I pray for all the obvious material needs of Muslims all over the world—food, shelter, security, work, justice and so on. And with the words "Guide us in the straight path," my prayer is that Muslims will come to see Jesus, son of Mary, as the Way to the knowledge of God as Father.

If the Lord's Prayer is a pattern prayer, it lends itself to be used as a prayer for the House of Islam. As well as being a prayer recited on its own, it can be like a skeleton which needs to have flesh put on it through prayers which we express in our own words. Or, to change the metaphor, it is like scaffolding which enables us to build our prayers as the Spirit leads.

"Your name be hallowed" can be a way of asking that Muslims, who recite 99 beautiful names of God, will see how he is revealed supremely in his Son Jesus.

Thus when I pray that God's name may be hallowed in the House of Islam, I remember that Muslims often recite the 99 Beautiful Names of God, but I go on to pray that they will see how the name of God has been revealed supremely in the person of Jesus (Jn. 17:2). When I say "Thy kingdom come," I recognize that they know the kingly rule of God as a present reality, but pray that they will see how that kingdom has come in Jesus.

"Forgive us our sins" includes the sin of failing to love the Muslims.

When it comes to "Forgive us our sins," I have to say, "Forgive us our sins as a church for the way in which we have failed to love Muslims as neighbors and as people for whom Christ died, and failed to bear witness to him." But I also have to pray for and with all my fellow Christians in countries like Nigeria, the Sudan, Lebanon, Syria and Iran, who live much closer to Islam than I do, and find it hard to forgive those who are responsible for injustices against them.

One day, at the name of Jesus every knee will bow.

The prayer ends in worship, and has a strong eschatological thrust. "Yours is the kingdom" looks forward to the time when "the kingdom of the world has become the kingdom of our God and of his Christ, and he will reign for ever and ever" (Rev. 11:15). "Yours is the glory" reminds us of our hope that one day, at the name of Jesus every knee will bow, "in heaven and on earth and under the earth, and every tongue will confess that Jesus Christ is Lord to the glory of God the Father" (Phil. 2:10-11).

Prayer in the Church

If we think we know how to pray to the Father *in secret*, how should we pray *in the church*? The Introduction to the *Alternative Service Book of the Church of England* (1980) argues that "Christians are formed by the way in which they pray, and the way they choose to pray expresses what they are." So whatever our prejudices about the source of these words, I hope we would all agree that we need to give some thought to the question of how, as a church at prayer, we respond to the challenge of Islam. And what better place is there to start than the first recorded prayer of the early church in Acts 4?

1. Responding to Threats

As soon as Peter and John are released by the authorities after their first time in custody, they meet with the members of the Jerusalem church and pray together. The prayer begins with a long introduction which is full of theology. In addressing God they remember that he is the Creator (v. 24) and the Sovereign Lord of history, who carries out his purposes in spite of, and even sometimes through, the perversity of those who conspire to work against him (vv. 25-28).

The next line of the prayer sounds remarkably relevant to the situation faced by many Christians in the Muslim world today: "Now, Lord, consider their threats..." (v. 29). No doubt we all know of situations where Christians are conscious of pressures from Muslim authorities and from the society around them. They experience discrimination in their work, are questioned by the police and have their mail censored—simply because their Christian allegiance brings them under suspicion.

We are also aware of the revival of different kinds of fundamentalist Islam, and are apprehensive about the political implications of Islamization in many countries. Do they not say (or at least think) that Islam must rule, and that the whole world should come under the sway of Islam? When we feel threatened by all this, our feelings may be remarkably close to the feelings expressed in this prayer: "Now, Lord, consider their threats..." (v. 21).

There are, however, significant differences in our situations today which ought to caution us against using the language of "threats" too freely. In the first place, we need to be scrupulously honest and recognize that it simply is not true to say that Christians all over the world feel under threat from Muslims. Muslims in South Africa feel that they suffer unfair discrimination at the hands of a government which justifies apartheid on the basis of Christian dogma. The Muslims of Mindanao in the southern Philippines no doubt have good reason to protest about the way they have been treated by the predominantly Catholic majority and its government.

Two reasons not to exaggerate the "threat"of Islam: 1) In many places Muslims are the victims rather than the perpetrators of discrimination. 2) We must avoid the historic mistakes of Christendom based on ignorance, fear and hatred.

When we think of Muslims in Europe, once again it seems that it is *they* who feel themselves to be threatened. When I took a group of theological students to visit our local mosque in Bristol three years ago, the person who showed us around said at the end how much he appreciated visits of this kind. Pointing to the wire guards protecting all the windows of the mosque, he said, "At the very least it may mean one less stone thrown through our windows."

Although we know that many Muslim leaders see the Muslim presence in the West as an evangelistic opportunity, it is only fair to recognize that most Muslims in these communities do not feel that they are in a strong position to convert Europe to Islam. Rather they feel that their religion, their community and their whole way of life are threatened by the godless, materialistic society around them.

A second reason for caution in speaking about "the threat of Islam" is that we need to make sure that we do not repeat the mistakes of many Christians in the past. Albert Hourani, in an essay entitled "Europe and Islam," sums up the attitudes of Christendom to Islam in the Middle Ages with three words: ignorance, fear and hatred.[8] Norman Daniel, in his book *Islam and the West, the Making of an Image*,[9] argues that many of the stereotypes of Muslims and Islam in the minds of Westerners today can be traced back to the attitudes of Christian Europe from the 10th century onwards.

When, therefore, I read articles in Christian magazines like the one entitled "Islam in Britain!" (note the exclamation mark), the implication sometimes seems to be: "What is Islam doing in Christian Britain? These people have no right to be here!" This kind of reaction arises to some extent out of fear, sometimes even from a sense of panic.

Instead of this, perhaps we ought to be saying, "Now at last we have some idea of what it must have felt like for the Muslim world to be at the receiving end of Western colonialism and the Western missionary movement for two centuries or more!" We should also realize that it is impossible for us to understand the revival of Islam in recent years unless we recognize the extent to which it is the response of the Muslim world to the fact that they have been subject for so long to the threat of Christendom and the West.

2. Deciding What to Pray For

The prayer in Acts 4 strikes the delicate balance between what the church can do and what God alone can do.

If we now turn to the Jerusalem church and ask what exactly they prayed for in their situation, the RSV is the most helpful of the translations, since it recognizes the way the two main petitions are put together in one sentence:

> ...grant unto thy servants to speak thy word with all boldness [*parresias*], while thou stretchest out thy hand to heal, and signs and wonders are performed through the name of thy holy servant Jesus (vv. 29-30).

In responding to the threats of the authorities, the early church, instead of simply praying for protection, recognizes that there is something they can and should do, namely speak the word without fear. At the same time they recognize that their words may lack power and conviction unless God acts in his own sovereign way to demonstrate the truth of that word. One of the beautiful things about the prayer, therefore, is that they find the delicate balance between what *they* can do and what *God* alone can do: "grant unto *us* ...while *thou* ..."

And why are these petitions specially relevant for our praying about the Muslim world? In all the testimonies of Muslims who have become disciples of Jesus, there are three factors which recur again and again. In Bilquis Sheikh's *I Dared to Call Him Father* [10] we see all three side by side, and in every story I have heard there have been at least two out of the three:

(1) genuine love which shows itself in sacrificial caring;
(2) reading the Bible, especially one of the Gospels;
(3) some special demonstration of the power of God associated with the name of Jesus.

In this context I hesitate to use the word 'supernatural,' because it implies a false (and fundamentally pagan) distinction between what is 'natural' (and therefore works 'by itself') and what is 'supernatural' (i.e., above nature). What we are speaking of here is those special ways in which God breaks into a person's life in a totally unexpected way, revealing himself and his love and power—in and through the name of Jesus.

A "power encounter" is sometimes God's answer to the combination of social pressures, intellectual obstacles and spiritual forces that block Muslims' pathway to Christ.

Because of all the *social pressures* which make it hard for Muslims to think about joining a different community, all the *intellectual obstacles* which make it impossible to think of Jesus as anything more than a Prophet, and the *spiritual forces* which keep the mind and the heart so firmly closed, it seems that sometimes the only way for God to break into a person's life is through a clear demonstration of his power which is associated with the name of Jesus. Sometimes it is a healing; in other cases it is a vision of Jesus, or a dream. The important thing is that they see and experience the power of God in their lives, mediated through the person of Jesus.

These convictions find some support in a most unlikely source, namely in Ibn Hisham's recension of *The Life of Muhammad* by Ibn Ishaq (d. 767). This tells the story of how it was believed *Christianity* (not Islam!) first came to the area of Najran in the southwest of Arabia.[11] A Syrian Christian ascetic named Faymiyun, whom today we might call a "charismatic tentmaker," prayed for the sick that he encountered in his work and they were healed. When he and a disciple were traveling they were captured and sold in Najran where the people worshiped a palm tree. A "power encounter" was set up when the people of Najran said they would follow his faith if he cursed the palm tree and it was destroyed. After prayer, he did so in God's name, and they became Christians.

3. Adapting and Using the Prayer Today

If we now return from the 1st and 7th centuries to the 20th, the final question we might ask is this: Could we adapt this prayer of the early church in Acts 4? Is there any way of helping not only individual Christians, but also whole churches to pray regularly and corporately about their response to the challenge that faces them?

No doubt I ask such a question because I happen to be an Anglican and feel deeply grateful for the tradition of liturgical worship in which I have been raised. But even those who claim that they are most free in their form of worship, in practice tend to follow certain patterns and use some fixed expressions repeatedly. And perhaps believers from Muslim backgrounds might accept the idea of using some formal prayers of this kind more readily than we might imagine.

There is one further reason, however, for looking at the prayer in this light. The very fact that it has been recorded in Acts suggests that it was not simply a prayer uttered spontaneously on this occasion alone. "When they (i.e., the community of believers) heard this, they (i.e., the whole

congregation) raised their voices together in prayer to God..."
(4:24).

I doubt that Luke wants us to picture the whole congregation
spontaneously uttering exactly the same words in unison. It
makes more sense to imagine that one or more of the group
(and not necessarily Peter and John) expressed this kind of
response in prayer on the occasion of the release of the Apostles; and that as the community reflected on the situation and
prayed regularly in these terms, their prayer gradually took
shape as a kind of pattern prayer, expressing the way they
wanted to respond as a church to the opportunities and obstacles they faced.

The following, therefore, is a first attempt to adapt the prayer
and put it into a form brief enough to be memorized and used
regularly in public worship:

A prayer such as this is worth memorizing and repeating in unison during congregational worship.

> Sovereign Lord,
>   who wants all people to know you as the only true
>   God, forgive us for every failure in love and truth; and
>   enable us to speak your word with all boldness, while
>   you stretch out your hand to show your power,
>   through the name of your holy servant Jesus. Amen.

The second line brings together 1 Timothy 2:4 ("...God our
Savior, who wants all men to be saved...") and John 17:3
("...that they know you, the only true God, and Jesus Christ
whom you have sent."). A prayer for forgiveness is added,
since it is important that we acknowledge before God our
failure, as individuals and as a church, to love our Muslim
neighbors and bear witness to the truth.

If I am asked if there is any significance in the fact that the
"signs and wonders" have dropped out of the prayer, my answer is that it is partly for the sake of brevity, and partly because of the danger of trivializing signs and wonders through
constant repetition of the phrase. Christians who know
where the prayer comes from should have no difficulty in
reading into these lines of the prayer the same longings that
were first expressed by the Jerusalem church.

If the whole church, and especially those groups of Christians
who live in the Muslim world, were to be praying a prayer of
this kind regularly together, would it not have some effect
both on their witness and their expectation of what God
could do among them?

Prayer and Spiritual Warfare

Ephesians 6 is probably one of the first passages which comes to mind when we think of "spiritual warfare" or "power encounter." But does this passage have anything special to say to us if we study it in the context of our thinking and praying about Islam?

1. Our Concern to Locate the Powers of Evil

I frequently hear Christians asking questions like "Are there demonic powers in and behind Islam?" It is all too easy to see evidence of such powers in those aspects of Islam which we find most difficult or most sinister—whether it is the all-embracing system of belief and practice which cannot be questioned, or the close-knit nature of Islamic society which makes it impossible to opt out of the community, or the attitudes to political power based on the conviction that Islam must rule, or the alliance with occult powers in so much popular Islam.

Paul must have been all too aware of the "devil's schemes" and had his own ideas of how they were worked out in the Mediterranean world of the 1st century. But here in this letter he traces the power of evil back to its ultimate source—"the rulers...the authorities...the powers of this dark world... the spiritual forces of evil *in the heavenly realms*" (6:12). He knows that "the god of this age has blinded the minds of unbelievers..." (2 Co. 4:4), and presumably that he has used different means to blind them; but he does not try to locate the source of evil that we fight against in any political or religious system.

Paul might put it this way: "Our struggle is not against Islam ... but against the forces of evil in the heavenly realms."

When, therefore, I try to relate these words to the particular conflict in which we are engaged, I wonder if Paul might want to say this to us: "Our struggle (our *jihad!*) is not against Islam, against its social system or its system of beliefs, or against Muslims as people, but against the forces of evil in the heavenly realms..." So, if this is the thrust of Paul's emphasis here about the real source of evil, should we not be a little more cautious in the language we use about the powers of evil in Islam?

2. The Nature of our Weapons

Assuming that we have understood Paul's description of the nature of the conflict, what are the weapons needed by the individual Christian and by the church as a body as we seek to be involved in the conflict against the powers of evil and darkness?

The weapons that are described all relate to familiar themes in Paul's teaching about the Christian life. The belt of *truth* reminds us that if we want to be able to move in any direction without tripping up, we need to know all we can about the truth of God's revelation in Christ. The breastplate of *righteousness* means living with integrity, righteousness and a concern for justice in every area of life. The shoes represent "the *eagerness* to spread the gospel of peace" (JB), or "the *readiness* to announce the Good News of peace" (TEV). The shield of *faith* means trusting in all God's promises, while the helmet of *salvation* means enjoying increasing deliverance from the power of sin. Wielding the sword of the Spirit must mean knowing how to use the *word of God* in our life and witness.

Truth, integrity, eagerness, readiness, faith, enjoyment of | increasing deliverance from the power of sin, and ability to use God's Word effectively— all these interwoven with constant prayer —are essential in the spiritual battle.

And where does prayer fit in (verses 18-20)? It is obviously one of our weapons in the conflict, although it is not represented by a particular piece of the soldier's armor. We are to be praying constantly for all God's people who are engaged in the same conflict as we are.

What strikes me about all these weapons is that there is something incredibly down to earth about them all. There is no super-spirituality, no special charismatic gifts required to enable us to stand our ground in this battle—but simply faith, trust, holiness and boldness!

3. Our Concern for Effective Communication

Paul's general plea for prayer leads on to a much more specific request for prayer for himself:

> Pray also for me, that whenever I open my mouth, words (*logos*) may be given me so that I will fearlessly make known (*en parresia gnorisai*) the mystery of the gospel, for which I am an ambassador in chains. Pray that I may declare it fearlessly (*parresiasomai*), as I should (6:19-20).

If Paul is not going off at a tangent in making this request, his concern for effective communication of the gospel must be seen as part of his involvement in the great struggle against "the devil's schemes." He needs great wisdom to have the *right words* to articulate the good news, and much courage to overcome his fears and find a way through all the restrictions placed in his way.

Much of the energy and enthusiasm used in "praying against" Islam might yield greater results if applied to praying about the practical matters of communicating Christ effectively to Muslims.

I sometimes wonder what would happen if those who think simply in terms of "praying against" Islam were to turn their energy and enthusiasm into praying about all that goes to make up effective communication. It might mean, for example, thinking and praying about such mundane questions as whom to visit, when to tell stories and how to use graphics! And such a concern for communication leads us straight into the theme of rethinking and restating the gospel for the Muslim world.

NOTES

1. Mohammed Marmaduke Pickthall, *The Meaning of the Glorious Koran* (New York: The New American Library [Mentor Book], 1953), 35, n. 1.

2. Kenneth Bailey, *The Cross and the Prodigal* (St. Louis: Concordia Publishing House, 1973), 37.

3. A. Yusuf Ali, *The Holy Qur'an*, 2nd ed., n.p. (The Muslim Student Association of the United States and Canada, 1st ed., 1934), 14n.

4. Ibid., 15.

5. Montgomery W. Watt, *Companion to the Qur'an* (London: George Allen and Unwin Ltd., 1967), 14.

6. Pickthall, 31.

7. Watt, 13.

8. Albert Hourani, *Western Attitudes Towards Islam in Europe* (London: MacMillan, 1980), 1-18.

9. Norman Daniel, *Islam and the West: The Making of an Image* (Edinburgh: University Press, 1960).

10. Bilquis Sheikh with Richard H. Schneider, *I Dared Call Him Father* (Minneapolis: Jeremy Books, 1978).

11. Abd al-Malik Ibn Hisham, *The Life of Muhammad: [Ibn] Ishaq's Sirat Rasul Allah.*, trans. A. Guillaume (London: Oxford University Press, 1955), 14-16.

CHAPTER NINETEEN

THE EXPERIENCE OF PRAYING FOR MUSLIMS

J. Christy Wilson, Jr.

The planners of the Ziest conference rightly took the priority of prayer seriously. The theme of the gathering was Abraham's Prayer, "Oh that Ishmael might live under your blessing" (Gen. 17:18). The preliminary instructions sent to the participants requested all "to bathe the entire event in prayer"..."A significant part of the conference itself will be prayer for the Muslim world and each other."[1]

Prayer for Laborers

The greatest need in reaching the Muslim world is for leaders who are called, trained and sent out by God. When our Lord saw the multitudes scattered abroad and fainting like sheep without a shepherd, he called on his disciples to pray for workers. He said, "The harvest is plenteous but the laborers are few. Ask the Lord of the harvest, therefore, to thrust forth laborers into his harvest" (Mt. 9:36-38).

We must call on the God of the impossible to accomplish his revealed will. Bill Wilson of the Overseas Missionary Fellowship writes, "Missions is God at work. Either he is working in and through his people to accomplish his purposes, or nothing of eternal value is accomplished."[2] In Islam we are faced with an impossible task and an inadequate force where the laborers indeed are few. Therefore we must call on the God of the impossible to accomplish his revealed will. In our Lord stating that "this gospel of the Kingdom will be preached in all the world as a witness to all people groups (*ta ethne*)" (Mt. 24:14), we see that all of the Muslim world will surely eventually be evangelized. But prayer is the primary means for this to be done.

All of the Muslim world will surely be evangelized. But the primary means will be prayer.

Since my wife and I were forced out of Afghanistan in 1973, we have felt that our main calling in relation to that nation, as well as the whole Muslim world, is that of intercession. For this reason we have asked the Lord to raise up and send forth students into the needy places of the earth, especially to neglected Islamic peoples. We want to give glory to God for his faithfulness in hearing and answering prayer. Today 26 former Gordon-Conwell students, along with some spouses, are working in the Muslim world. Even though we were forced out of Kabul, one of these couples, along with their three children, is there serving the Lord at the present time. Another dedicated family is working with the Afghan refugees on the border. Furthermore, a husband and wife, both graduates of the seminary, are doing pioneer work in a Muslim country which previously has not had any missionaries.

Word has come this year from another seminary graduate. He left a position as professor of New Testament in a seminary in order to go with his wife, who is a medical doctor, to an unreached Muslim tribe. He writes as follows,

> On February 6 [1987], 21 sheiks from all over the country came to our house to discuss Islam and Christianity. Their spokesman was Sheik A.B. I answered all their questions from Scripture ONLY. The following week, Sheik A.B. came back, secretly, and repented and was born again. He began to preach Jesus in the mosques. Trouble aplenty... this week we took him to a neighboring city where he will remain in hiding for two months. What a lovely brother in Christ. This week the sheik at our neighboring town was also born again, as well as three other Muslims in the village. Baptism will be on Easter.[3]

This couple have combined medical work with evangelism. Within a year of starting their ministry with this unreached Muslim people group, they have planted a church of over 30 baptized believers!

My wife and I have prayed for the students by name time after time, asking the Lord to show them his best plan for their lives and to give them the will to obey his call. It has been a great joy to see God lead these men and women into the Muslim world as his witnesses. We praise him for his grace in hearing and answering.

Prayer is the answer for more needed missionaries and tentmakers to work among Muslims. It is also through interceding with God that Muslim nationals will be led to Christ and will become godly leaders in their own countries and people groups.

While Dr. William Miller, who is now a 94-year-old retired missionary in Philadelphia, was a student in seminary, he felt called of God to go to the Islamic world in eastern Iran near the border of Afghanistan. Before he left, he established a daily noon prayer meeting in his room for laborers. As a result, he got many to give their lives for missionary service through prayer even before he went in 1919 and spent 43 years in Iran. It was he who persuaded Dr. Philip Howard (father of Elisabeth Elliot of Auca Indian fame, as well as David Howard, the present general director of World Evangelical Fellowship) to go to Belgium. And through prayer and conversation, he got my parents to go as missionaries to the Muslims of Iran.

Prayer for Christian Students to Enroll in Universities in Muslim Countries

Christian students not only obtain degrees in other countries; they have an entreé to that culture—often with more freedom than their teachers.

Another great need is to pray for Christian students to enroll in universities where large numbers of Muslims are studying around the world. For example, while the situation was calm in Lebanon, I visited a Christian student at the American University of Beirut. He was meeting with another believer daily for prayer. He also was rooming with Muslim students from countries where missionaries were not allowed. While doing his four years of bachelor's degree work there, he led scores of other students to Christ, including many Muslims.

Not only can Christians obtain degrees in other countries, but they then can have an entree to that culture, since they are graduates of an indigenous university in that nation. Christian students also have much more freedom than do teachers. The reason for this is that authorities expect young people to have various ideas and therefore are not as strict on them as they are on those who hold positions of instruction.

While we were in Afghanistan, Russia sent 12 Communist students to enroll in Kabul University. They did not come for the academic standing but to be "tentmakers" for their ideology. It was not long before half of the Afghan students there claimed that they had become "Muslim Marxists." It did not seem to bother them that this was a contradiction of terms, since it is not possible to be a "theistic atheist." This was one of the main means the Soviet Union used to try to conquer that country.

Christians do not want to take over the world politically the way the Communists do. But we do want to complete Christ's commission in Islamic nations. Getting dedicated students to enroll in universities is an important way to accomplish this. Let us pray that many may be thrust forth by the Lord into these centers of learning.

Prayer against Principalities and Powers

In Kabul, Afghanistan, the local people have a tradition that when Satan was cast out of heaven he fell to earth there. The Scriptures speak of certain places where Satan's throne is (Rev. 2:13). Dennis Clark was one of the first Christians to go into Afghanistan as a tentmaker, entering that country as a businessman in 1945. During the two weeks he was in Kabul, even though he is a man of prayer, he said it was like having a dark cloud of evil over him all the time. His prayers did not seem to get through.

These experiences are borne out by Ephesians 6:10-18, where we are told that we are to take our stand against the devil's schemes:

> For our struggle is not against flesh and blood, but against the rulers, against the authorities, against the powers of this dark world and against the spiritual forces of evil in the heavenly realms.

We are then admonished to put on the full armor of God and to "pray in the Spirit on all occasions with all kinds of prayers and requests." Finally we are told to "be alert and always keep on praying for all the saints." Paul then concludes by requesting intercession on his behalf as he says, "Pray also for me, that whenever I open my mouth, words may be given me so that I will fearlessly make known the mystery of the gospel" (Eph. 6:19). Thus we see that the way we win battles against opposition to the evangelization of Muslim peoples is through intercession.

One of the great prayer warriors for Dennis Clark and for Afghanistan was Miss Flora Davidson, who was originally from Scotland. Flora lived in a two-story adobe house in Kohat, on the Northwest Frontier of British India, which is now Pakistan. In front of a window that looked out on the mountains of Afghanistan in the distance, she had a little bench. She would spend hours on her knees praying that God would open that country to the gospel. She said that the hands of Christ were not only pierced for us on the cross, but the knuckles must be bleeding and bruised because of knocking so long on the door of that closed country.

After years of prayer by Flora Davidson, Margaret Haines and others, Afghanistan opened to tentmakers.

Flora Davidson wrote a book entitled *The Hidden Highway*. In this she mentioned that so far the way into that land and into the hearts of the people there was hidden. However, she stated that the time would come when Christians would find the way to get into that country. The way turned out to be tentmaking. She also organized a prayer circle which was continued for many years by Margaret Haines of Philadelphia, who had worked with her as a missionary. It was because of this regular and prolonged intercession that God finally opened Afghanistan, enabling different ones to enter as tentmakers.

We met Flora Davidson after she was retired in Britain. She came to see us in the small hotel where we were staying in London. Before we had dinner together, she asked me to lead in prayer in Afghan Persian since she said she longed to hear it again. The other British guests in the restaurant did not know what to make of this as I carried out her request. She then told us that every afternoon for an hour, between 2:00 and 3:00 p.m., she prayed for nothing but Afghanistan.

The Primacy of the Ministry of Prayer

We got to Afghanistan in 1951, following others who had preceded us as early as 1948. Our service there became mainly a prayer ministry. With strict restrictions against proselytization, we nevertheless were free to engage in intercession. We sent a monthly prayer letter with requests for every day relating to the needs in that country. This was carried out by hand and mailed to Margaret Haines in Philadelphia, who duplicated it and sent it out as a labor of love to hundreds of prayer warriors who were asked to keep its contents confidential. Heaven alone will show all that was ac-complished through this.

Those of us who were teaching Afghan students in the government educational system would meet for prayer daily to remember those in our classes. Three-hour examinations gave marvelous opportunities to walk around praying for each of the students, that they one day would hear the gospel and respond and serve their Lord.

One of these for whom I prayed went abroad for further study. He belonged to the Royal Family of Afghanistan. I received a letter from him later on, telling how he had put his trust in the Lord Jesus Christ as his Savior, had joined an evangelical church and was teaching a young people's Sunday school class. He enclosed a check to help out with God's work in Afghanistan, stating he was so grateful for those who were witnesses for Christ in his country.

After graduating from university in the United States, he worked with an insurance company. Along with selling policies, he would also tell his clients about how they could get eternal life insurance. One lady objected. She phoned the head office asking why they had sent a minister to sell her insurance! The company, therefore, put him on the mat and told him he was not to mix religion with business. He answered that the reason he had stayed abroad was in order to have freedom of religion. If they did not grant him this, he would turn in his resignation. Even though he was one of the best salesmen, he left that insurance company voluntarily. He now has his own business, which God has blessed in a wonderful way. It is thrilling to see God's faithfulness in answering prayer.

Prayer and the Securing of Gospel Recording Messages

Prayer opened a way to record the gospel in 51 of Afghanistan's languages.

Two dedicated Christian women with Gospel Recordings Incorporated wrote to us in Afghanistan early in 1970. Miss Marlene Muhr from France and Miss Ann Sherwood from the United States wondered if they came to Afghanistan whether there would be an opportunity to record messages in the various languages. We prayed and invited them to come, saying that we would try to do this, but were not sure what would happen.

These two women, real prayer warriors, came and were in the country for four months. They cried to God, requesting that they be able to record messages in every language of the country. At that time, no one, including linguistic scholars, knew exactly how many different tongues were there.

In answer to prayer, representatives of every linguistic group in the nation were found. Many of these who helped with the various tongues were in the army since there was a universal draft. An Afghan Christian would go into the military camps and ask if any there had strange languages. When different ones were pointed out, he arranged for them to come to our home.

Marlene Muhr and Ann Sherwood had fixed one of the rooms as a recording studio by putting styrofoam all around the walls. They had top-grade Swiss recording equipment that would not make a sound starting or stopping. Since those who came were in the army, they had also learned one of the two major languages of the country besides the one they spoke as their mother tongue. We would serve them tea and cake, and tell them that we would like to record their language. Then, following the coaching of the two ladies, I would tell them phrase by phrase what we would like to have them say in their tongue. It took usually three hours to make a three minute message. We then played it back.

One of them said to me, "How does this little machine know my language?" He had never heard his own voice and had not seen a tape recorder before. He was actually preaching the gospel to himself and sounded like Billy Graham as he expounded it phrase by phrase. He then said to me, "This is the first time I have ever heard this, that God loves us and sent Jesus to be the Good Shepherd, and that he died for our sins and came alive again." He asked, "Why hasn't anyone told me this before?"

Because of praying that every language of the country would be secured, these women had 51 different tongues recorded before they left.[4] These were put on records and tapes, and now have been distributed to people from these various groups, not only in Afghanistan, but among the five million refugees who have been scattered by the Russian invasion in different parts of the world.

Prayer for Meeting Felt Needs

One of the great needs in Afghanistan was help for the blind. Many there have lost their sight because of high incidence of diseases such as trachoma, cataracts, smallpox, besides injuries, close intermarriage and infections that were left untreated. All that the blind could do was to beg or memorize the Quran in order to repeat it at various functions, like weddings and funerals, for which they were paid a small amount.

We prayed that God would open an opportunity to minister to these handicapped, and he did exceeding abundantly above what was asked. Two institutes for the blind were established, one in Kabul and the other 700 miles to the west in Herat. They were taught Braille in their own language for the first time. Many of these came to Christ and have become leaders of the Lord's work among their own people. Thus the institutes were closed, and we were put out of the country.

In a Muslim nation it is an unpardonable sin for anyone to leave that religion. We were given three days to leave after we had been there for 22 years. But when we had to leave Afghanistan in March of 1973, we prayed for the blind we were leaving and God gave us a wonderful promise concerning them. It is written in Isaiah 42:16:

> I will lead the blind by ways they have not known, along unfamiliar paths I will guide them; I will turn the darkness into light before them and make the rough places smooth. These are the things that I will do; I will not forsake them.

God has now allowed this work with the handicapped to be reopened under the Communist regime and thus has wonderfully fulfilled his promise to them.

A Prayer Power Encounter

When we went to Afghanistan as tentmakers, God heard prayer and enabled a house church to be started among the internationals there. Soon none of our homes proved large enough to take care of the ones who wanted to come to the services. Then we heard that President Eisenhower planned to come to Afghanistan on his Asian tour in 1959. A mosque had just been built in Washington for the Muslim diplomats there, and therefore, on a reciprocal basis, there was a need for a church building in Kabul for the Christian diplomats and others there.

After his election and before his inauguration, Eisenhower went to Dr. Edward Elson, whom he had known as a chaplain in the Army. He said that the job to which he had been elected was too big for him to do alone without God's help. He stated that he had never been baptized as a Christian, and therefore asked Dr. Elson to do this for him before his inauguration. Elson was happy to comply.

I therefore wrote to Dr. Elson, asking him to speak to the President about the possibility of requesting permission for a church building in Kabul. The President had attended the opening ceremony of the mosque in Washington and saw the need for a church building on a reciprocal basis for the Christian diplomats and others in Afghanistan. He graciously agreed, and spoke to King Zahir Shah during his visit to Kabul, requesting permission to be granted for a Christian church in that capital city.

The Afghan government eventually officially granted permission to build. Christians from all around the world helped with finances, plans, architecture and engineering. The building went up and was dedicated on Pentecost Sunday, May 17, 1970. It had a great ministry, especially to the hippies who at that time were pouring through that country. Many of them came to Çhrist and were baptized there. Dr. Dudley Woodberry also pastored this church during one of our home leaves and subsequently.

Mainly because Afghans were also becoming Christians, the Muslim government sent troops to tear down the wall between the main road and the church. It had become a focus of Christian work in that country. They said that they had government orders to destroy the church.

A member of the congregation, who was a German businessman, went to the mayor of Kabul, who had given the order, and told him that if his government touched that house of God, the Lord would overthrow his government. The mayor got angry and said that nothing of the kind would happen. But this proved to be a prophecy.

Since we, during those days, were forced to leave the country, we did what our Lord said and shook the dust off of our shoes at the airport before taking off. After our departure, the Prime Minister ordered the congregation to give the building to the government for destruction without compensation. The congregation, however, sent a letter stating that they could not give the church building to anyone since it did not belong to them. They mentioned that it had been dedicated to the Lord, and if the Afghan government took it and destroyed it, they would be answerable to God.

The very day the 227-year-old Afghan monarchy destroyed the country's only church building, that government was overthrown by a coup.

Bulldozers were brought in and that beautiful building was knocked down. When this happened, Christians all around the world were praying. Billy Graham, as well as other leaders, signed a statement of concern that the Afghan government was destroying the only church building on Afghan soil.

This turned out to be a real power encounter, as God answered prayer in an amazing way. The very day the building was completely destroyed, the government responsible was overthrown in a coup. It had been a monarchy for 227 years, but that night it became a republic. Afghan people are quick to see omens in events. Some said that Jesus Christ came down from heaven and overthrew the government because it had destroyed his church.

When an Afghan refugee family that we sponsored arrived in the States, the wife said that first of all she wanted to apologize for the terrible thing their government had done to the Christian church building. She added that ever since that happened, God had been judging their country. After the coup of 1973, there was a Communist overthrow of the republic in 1978, followed by the Russian invasion of that nation just after Christmas in 1979.

We are praying that after the Communists and the Muslims clash as they are doing in Afghanistan, that the Lord will force Russia to withdraw and that both of these nations will be evangelized.

"Ask of me, and I will give you the nations for your inheritance" (Psalm 2:8) includes Muslim people groups.

It was four and a half years after I first applied to teach English in Afghanistan that the Lord finally opened the way. As my wife and I were praying about the delay, we read Numbers 14:8, where Joshua and Caleb said, "If the Lord delights in us, he will bring us into this land...and will give it to us." He has fulfilled the first part in that he took us there for 22 years. We now believe that He will take us back in order to give the land for evangelization to Jesus Christ. This is further promised in Psalm 2:8: "Ask of me, and I will give you the nations for your inheritance, and the uttermost parts of the earth for your possession." This promise includes Muslim people groups.

Prayer and Muslim Evangelism

Andrew Murray was invited by Dwight L. Moody to come to the International Missionary Conference held in New York City in 1900. Since the Boer War was going on in South Africa, he did not feel that he should leave his people during the time of this emergency. Therefore he declined the invitation and remained at his church in Wellington.

Nevertheless, he did read the reports of the conference with great interest. In going over the messages and the program, he came to realize that there was a great omission. They had not dealt with the priority of prayer in missions. For this reason he wrote the book *Key to the Missionary Problem*.[5] In this book he deals with a call to prayer and contrition in relation to missions. He also proposed that the first week of the next year be set aside as a special time of prayer for missions. This was done in South Africa with thrilling results in the numbers who responded for missionary service.

Some Muslim Converts Witness Through Prayer

Ex-Muslim Bilquis Sheikh's prayers were a witness not only in their results but in their content.

When Madam Bilquis Sheikh came to Christ, her Muslim family members as well as friends came to realize that her prayers were being answered in an amazing way. For this reason, when they had problems, they would come to her and request that she pray for them. In the introduction to her prayer, she often would go through much of the Scripture thanking the Lord for his beautiful creation, for sending the prophets, for Jesus Christ and his death on the cross for our sins, for his resurrection and ascension to heaven, and for the fact that he had promised to hear us when we call on Him. She then would get to the request that the person had made. The Lord answered her intercession in wonderful ways. Thus her prayers were not only a witness in their results, but also in their content.

Another Muslim convert has become an effective evangelist among those in the Islamic faith. When they come to him with needs, he says the following:

> You do not believe that Jesus is the Son of God. However, I challenge you to pray to him and say that if you are the Son of God, hear and answer my prayer.

When this happens, many of them realize that there is power in Christ's name and different ones have come to accept Him as their Savior.

Founding of the Fellowship of Faith for Muslims

When Dr. Samuel Zwemer, who is probably history's greatest missionary to Muslims, spoke at the Keswick Convention in England, he chose to use the passage in Luke 5:4-7. He mentioned that Simon Peter's experience of toiling at fishing all night and taking nothing was like his experience in the Muslim world. He and other missionaries to Islamic areas had worked hard fishing all night and had taken almost nothing.

He went on to bring out that "nevertheless at thy word," we are to let down the net. He said that as we obey the Lord in taking the gospel to Muslims, the time would come when so many would be brought to Christ that just as the boats were filled with fish, so churches would be filled with converts from Islam. His message had a tremendous effect on the congregation. They afterwards came to him and asked what they could do. His answer was, "Pray."

This was the beginning of the prayer fellowship of faith for Muslims, which has continued from then to the present. They not only have distributed prayer requests for needs in the Muslim world, but also have held conferences of special intercession. When I was in the British Isles the summer of 1948, I attended a prayer time sponsored by this organization. Missionaries from all over the Muslim world each told of their areas for a half hour, and then they went to prayer for that area for 45 minutes. Thus the majority of the time was taken in intercession.

In 1965 hundreds of thousands of Indonesian Muslims became Christians.

Dr. Zwemer's prophecy came true with the Indonesian Revival in 1965 when hundreds of thousands of Muslims became Christians. Zwemer had already gone to be with the Lord in 1952, but the vision he had, as well as the prayer he started, resulted in churches in Indonesia being filled with Muslim converts. On one occasion when I was at a World Vision pastors' conference in Sumatra, I visited a church which was packed. Its pastor was a former Muslim leader who had also been to Mecca and had the title of Hajji. Thus in Indonesia, the greatest ingathering of Muslims to Christ in history has taken place through the revival there.

Christian Fasting Along with Prayer

Many Muslims put Christians to shame by the way they faithfully keep the month of fasting, or Ramadan. Of course, in the Islamic faith, it is an essential part of earning one's salvation.

Once in Afghanistan a senior missionary visited us. I introduced him to one of the new Muslims converts. The Afghan asked him about the Christian view of fasting. He replied that he had never fasted in his whole life. I was sorry to hear him say this because Scripture has a lot to say about Christians fasting.

Our Lord did not say "if you fast" but "when you fast".

In Matthew 6:17, our Lord did not say "If you fast," but rather "When you fast." Our Lord also himself fasted 40 days and nights before starting his ministry. And when our Lord was asked why his disciples did not fast, he answered that when the Bridegroom was taken away they would then fast (Mt. 9:15). This statement of Christ is repeated in Mark and Luke as well.

This was also the practice of the early church. For example, it was while the congregation in Antioch was fasting that the Holy Spirit spoke to them to send Barnabas and Saul on their first missionary journey. Following this, we also read that "When they had fasted and prayed, and laid their hands on them, they sent them away" (Ac. 13:3).

The Importance of Family Devotions in Muslim Nations

The Rev. William Sutherland spent over 40 years of faithful service in the area of India which is now northern Pakistan. After his retirement, I asked him what he felt had been his most effective ministry during his missionary service among Muslims. After thinking about this question, he gave a very surprising answer. He said, "Looking back over the years, I think my most effective ministry was the family devotions that we had in our home every morning, not only with our children but also with the help."

Because of those times, he said, he could point to pastors all over Pakistan who at one time worked with him and attended the morning times of prayer.

Having learned this from him, we invited our help in Afghanistan to join us every day in family devotions. It has been thrilling to see the way God has worked in the lives of those who met regularly, reading the Scriptures and joining in prayer in these gatherings.

The Powerful Witness of Answered Prayer in the Name of Christ

On one occasion, an Afghan friend came to me with his uncle who needed cataract operations in both eyes. They had just been to the government hospital and were told that a bed for him to have the operations would not be available for three more months.

My friend explained that this made it very difficult since his uncle came from the central highlands in the country which was a journey of several days. It therefore would be difficult for him to make a round trip to return in three months. On the other hand, it would be very hard for him to stay away from his family for three months.

He therefore asked if I knew the head of that government hospital. I told him I did. He then asked me kindly to write a note explaining the situation, asking whether it would not be possible to admit his uncle sooner. I answered that I did not have to write a note but would speak to the head of the hospital.

The friend then asked me what the name of the one in charge of that hospital was. I answered, "His name is the Lord Jesus Christ. He is the head of every hospital." I then said, "Let us talk to him now." Praying in their language, I explained the situation to the Lord and asked him to help this man. I then sent them back to the government hospital, but they were reluctant to go back since they had just been turned away. However, they agreed to try again.

Several hours later, my friend, all excited, returned to see me. He said, "You do know the head of that hospital!" He went on to explain that as soon as they returned, a patient was just being discharged and they admitted his uncle immediately, putting him in the bed which had just been vacated. I am convinced this friend is now a believer in Christ.

Conclusion

Dr. Charles Malik, who used to be President of the United Nations General Assembly, speaks about the revival that is taking place in Judaism with the establishment of the State of Israel, and the revival of Islam which is occurring through the resurgence of Muslim fundamentalism. He mentions that the revival really needed for the world is a Christian one. And he points out that the way to bring this about is through prayer. Let us faithfully pray that "the earth will be filled with a knowledge of the glory of the Lord as the waters cover the sea" (Hab. 2:14), and this will include the Muslim world.

NOTES

1. David Montague, "Project First-Born Monthly Update #1." (February 1987) unpublished.

2. Bill Wilson, "Praying For Your Missionary—The Why and How" (Robesonia, PA: Overseas Missionary Fellowship, n.d.).

3. From a letter received in spring, 1987.

4. Marlene Muhr, *Along Unfamiliar Paths...Proclaiming God's Light in Man's Night* (Pasadena, CA: Geddes Press, 1982).

5. Andrew Murray, *Key to the Missionary Problem* (Fort Washington, PA: Christian Literature Crusade, 1977).

RESOURCES FOR UNDERSTANDING

Then he opened their minds to understand the Scriptures, and said to them, 'Thus it is written...'
— Luke 24: 45–46

CHAPTER TWENTY

RESEARCH AND TRAINING CENTERS

Robert C. Douglas

Given the breadth, complexity and strategic position of the Muslim world, the variety of contexts in which Muslims are found, the number and diversity of Muslim cultures, the rich and unique resources embodied in non-Western believers, and the challenge of planting churches, only the most insensitive and presumptuous would dare to offer definitive proposals.

Hopefully, this presentation will contribute to a process. Hopefully, that process will take further shape and and move forward over the next several years. Reasonably productive results can be forthcoming only with extensive input from concerned parties. As peoples and locales vary, so any effort at research and training that leads to church planting must somehow accommodate to the situation.

I come to my topic not as a theologian, nor as a New Testament scholar, nor an Islamicist, nor an Arabist, nor an anthropologist. I am a pastor, a generalist, an ex-missionary, a trainer—an individual with limited experience, few successes, strong cultural biases, a diminishing list of certainties and yet a deepening confidence in those things about which I am certain. From time to time I undoubtedly fall victim to a tendency to think in traditional Western and sometimes academic terms. Clearly there are many ways of looking at a situation, many different starting points, many avenues of proceeding. Alone, each of us can do justice to only a few.

Assumptions

Several assumptions are at work in my presentation.
I assume:

—that the research and training of which I speak takes place within and strengthens a commitment to the truth and richness of the Gospel.

—that research and training are recognized as basic components in effective outreach to Muslims.

—that there is yet much to be done in these areas.

—that what is yet to be done can best be done by cooperative efforts between non-Western believers and Western believers. Such efforts must not be characterized by paternalistic attitudes, but by genuine respect and equality on the part of all parties.

—the value and necessity of cooperative efforts linking concerned churches and parachurch organizations—to avoid duplication and waste.

—the validity of a variety of approaches to research and training, to insure the flexibility and practicality appropriate to the various local/regional situations.

—the necessity of planning, carried out in an orderly, intentional way.

—that all people need preparation in order to function with the greatest effectiveness in a cross-cultural situation.

—that immersion in a Muslim context involves cross-cultural dynamics for almost all who undertake it.

—that research must include multitudes of dimensions of the Muslim world, Muslim life, thought, faith and ministry to Muslims.

—that research and training have a symbiotic relationship and that good training arises out of an accurate understanding of the task to be achieved and the realities of the setting.

—that while the gospel is in its essence supra-cultural, it must, to have its maximum impact, be contextualized.

—that since the message cannot be totally divorced from the messenger (though on occasion it seems to convert in spite of him or her), it is critical for the messenger to be appropriately trained.

—that the tasks of training and of research each require careful determination of goals and objectives.

—that good training embodies the behavioral and effective domains as well as the cognitive.

—that training deals with a multitude of issues which fall into at least the following categories:

> *Spiritual formation*—that process by which people consent to be transformed by the Holy Spirit, into the image of Christ by the exercise of spiritual discipline in the context of a Christian community.

> *Incarnational identification*—that process by which cross-cultural servants surrender certain of their own cultural distinctives, adapting to others from their host culture.

> *World transformation*—that process which is concerned with both the broad strategies and the specific field methods for bringing about conversion resulting in the planting of churches and the transformation of basic social institutions.

—that ultimately we are addressing issues involving a spiritual battle, and that while training for sensitivity to cultural dynamics is vital, there are ultimate theological and justice issues vis-a-vis Islam to be addressed, though skill in addressing these is rare and training to that end is even rarer.

In view of all of the above, I submit that there are no experts. Though many know something and a few know a great deal, no one is close to having it all together, as is witnessed by the paucity of our results. We all need each other.

Above all, of course, we need God, his providential action and the Spirit's convincing and equipping work from the work of evangelizing Muslims. Yet God has regularly chosen to work in partnership with people. Frequently those people used most dramatically of God have been more adequately prepared, formally or informally, for the tasks they undertook, and at the same time, more in touch with themselves and with God.

From this point forward I propose to do the following things:

1. Review where we are in the areas of research and training.

2. Note some of the broad, strategic realities impacting the development of a strategy.

3. Suggest a few models of getting on with the task.

4. Offer a modest proposal for moving on from where we are.

5. Note a couple of ingredients which are crucial to any forward moving process.

Where Are We?—Research

As noted earlier, we do not begin in a vacuum. Part of our task is to determine what has gone before and to seek to build on it, adding our contemporary adaptations. In 1978, our present topic was addressed at the Glen Eyrie Conference on Muslim Evangelization. Two separate presentations were made: one on research, a second on training.

"Research," says Roland Miller, is "an act of love designed as preparation for witness."

In the area of research, Dr. Roland Miller of Luther College, Regina, Canada, urged the establishment of a network of research centers. From Miller's perspective, research is "an act of love" designed "as preparation for witness." Dr. Miller argued for functional research into "living Muslim communities and significant modern Muslim developments." He stated that research ought to help identify peoples, cultural settings, receptivity, while drawing together an analysis of needs with a sense of possibilities. It was his concern that training apart from research "tends to a harmful superficiality", while research apart from training can become "ivory tower pedantry."

In a significant contribution, Dr. Miller listed research centers focusing on Islam. The basic entries of Dr. Miller's list follow:

1. *Pontificio Instituto di Studi Arabi*, Piazza S. Apollinare 49, Roma, Italy. Sponsor: Roman Catholic Church. Correspondent: Fr. M. L. Fitzgerald, Dir.

2. *Institute des Belles Lettres Arabes*, 12 Rue Jamaa El Haoua, Tunis, Tunisia. Sponsor: Roman Catholic White Fathers. Correspondent: Fr. Jean Fontaine.

3. *Dr. Marston Speight*, 39 Avenue Taha Hussein, Tunis, Tunisia. In continuity with the *Christian Center for North African Studies*, closed by Algerian government in 1969.

4. *Center for the Study of the Modern Arab World*, Université Saint-Joseph, B.P. 8664, Beirut, Lebanon. Sponsor: Roman Catholic Church, Jesuit Society. Correspondent: Fr. John J. Donohue, S.J., Dir.

5. *Near East School of Theology*, P.O. Box 7424, Beirut, Lebanon. Sponsor: interdenominational. Correspondent: Dr. K. E. Bailey.

6. *Islam in Africa Project*, (Church House), Room 611, Nairobi, Kenya. Sponsor: interdenominational. Correspondent: Dr. Peter Ipema.

7. *Christian Study Center*, 126-B Murree Road, Rawalpindi Cantt, Pakistan. Sponsor: interdenominational. Correspondent: H. Mintjes.

8. *Henry Martyn Institute of Islamic Studies*, St. Luke's Compound, Station Road, Hyderabad, A.P., India. Sponsor: interdenominational. Correspondent: Dr. Samuel Bhajjan, Dir.

9. *Dansalan Research Center*, Dansalan College, P.O. Box 5430, Iligan City 8801, Philippines. Sponsor: UCC-related Dansalan College. Correspondent:Dr.PeterC.Gowing,Dir.

10. *Duncan Black MacDonald Center for the Study of Islam and Christian/Muslim Relations*, Hartford Seminary Foundation, 55 Elizabeth St., Hartford, Conn.,USA. Sponsor: Hartford Sem. Foundation. Correspondent: Dr. Willem Bijlefeld, Dir.

Most, if not all, of the centers listed are more committed to a dialectical approach toward Islam than to the evangelization of Muslims. In 1978 no research center committed to Muslim evangelization was identified.

Several changes within Dr. Miller's list need to be noted.

- The Centre for the Study of Islam, Selly Oaks College, England, was not included because they did not respond to Dr. Miller's questionnaire. The Centre, however, was and is a center of research.

- The Centre d'Etudes, 5 Chemin des Glycines, Algiers, Algeria, also should have been included.

- Fr. André Demeersman is a contact at the Institute des Belles Lettres Arabes.

- Dr. Marston Speight is now assigned to the Office on Christian/Muslim Relation of the National Council of Churches at Hartford, Connecticut.

- Fr. John J. Donohue, S.J. is now in France.

- Dr. Kenneth E. Bailey is now at the Ecumenical Institute in Israel.

- Dr. Peter Ipema, now of Chicago, is retiring. The Islam in Africa Project continues to operate from its base in Nairobi under the direction of Dr. Johannes Haffkens.

- Upon the death of Dr. Peter Gowing, the Dansalan Research Center ceased to be.

- David Kerr is the newly appointed director of the Duncan Black MacDonald Center.

Known research centers at the time of this writing. In the nine years following Miller's Glen Eyrie report, only a few new research centers concerned with Muslim evangelization have come into existence. The Zwemer Institute of Muslim Studies (formerly Samuel Zwemer Institute) was inaugurated in February, 1979, as the outgrowth of the Glen Eyrie Conference's call for the creation of a North American Muslim Studies Institute. Warren Chastain has focused on various Muslim people groups, and more recently Sam Wilson has started researching the cities.

Subsequently other research centers concerned with evangelism have been created. The Gairdner Ministries of Great Britain carries on limited research on Central Asian Muslims. In the Philippines, Phil Parshall has established the Asian Research Center in Manila. Its focus is primarily on Muslims in the Philippines. The work of Patrick Johnston of World Evangelical Outreach and George Otis III of ISAACHAR touches on Muslim areas. Iman Santoso is beginning a center in Indonesia which, among other things, will be concerned with research on Indonesia's Muslims.

A host of varied publications address Islam and Muslim-Christian relations from time to time. Some are published by organizations whose identity suggests they are "Christian." Their materials represent "research"; whether the organizations are to be listed as research "centers" depends on one's definitions. It is also possible that a few of these groups do "training" of some kind. Listed below are some of the periodicals and publishers in question:

Secretariatus pro non Christians Vatican	BULLETIN	Quarterly	English/ French
Agenzia d'Informazione Islamica Rome, Italy	CESI	2 monthly	Arabic/ English
Christliche-Islamische White Fathers Frankfurt, W. Germany	CIBEDO DOKUMENTATION	Quarterly	German
Danish Missionary Society Copenhagen, Denmark	DANSK MISSIONSBLAD	Monthly	Danish
Pontificio Istituto de Studi Arabi Vatican	ENCOUNTER	Monthly	English
Comisión Episcopal de Relaciones Interconfesionales Madrid, Spain	ENCUENTRO	Monthly	Spanish
Islamic Culture Society Tokyo, Japan	ISLAMIC CULTURE FORUM	Yearly	English
Pontificio Istituto de Studi Arabi Vatican	ISLAMO-CHRISTIANA	Yearly	French
Evangelische Zentralstelle fur Weltanschauungsfragen Stuttgart, W. Germany	MATERIAL-DIENST	Monthly	German
Middle East Council of Churches Beirut, Lebanon	AL-MONTADA	Irregular	English
Missions Advanced Research and Communications Center California, USA	NEWSLETTER MARC	6 per year	English

Keston College Keston, U.K.	**RELIGION IN COMMUNIST LANDS**	Quarterly	English
World Evangelical Fellowship Guernsey, U.K.	**THEOLOGICAL NEWS**	Quarterly	English

It is further to be noted that the World Council of Churches' Commission on World Mission and Evangelism has organized a series of consultations on the role of study centers. Consultations were held in Sri Lanka (1967), Hong Kong (1971) and Singapore (1980).

Concerns of the study centers include investigation of "Religions and Culture" and "Christian Understanding and Theology of Other Religions." A directory of study centers was produced following the 1980 Singapore gathering.

To round out the beginnings of a research picture, it needs to be noted that research into various components of Islam and Muslim peoples is being done regularly by a variety of universities and government related agencies and private organizations. Some Christians are involved in these efforts and are doing good work.

The church, in its mission emphasis, can gain from "secular" efforts. However, it needs to be recognized that such research has different concerns from missions related research. This work can never replace specifically mission related research. There is a need for networks of believing people to be in touch with university based activities for the purpose of assessing what parts have implications for missions.

This past winter, Dr. Miller reiterated the need for research. He suggested the development of "a few good research centers," as opposed to a series of small, understaffed, under-equipped operations. He noted that past efforts at creating significant research centers have faltered for the most part. In his opinion, a variety of factors contributed to the faltering. He pointed to factors like nationalism, the perennial difficulty in securing funds for research, the geographical distance separating funding sources and research sites, and uncertainty as to what ought to be researched and for what purpose. As a consequence, he concluded, the church is faced with badly outdated materials and in too many cases with little interest in changing this sad state of affairs.

A problem beyond the scope of this study yet related to research is the question of circulation of usable information and "clues" to be pursued to enhance church planting among Muslims. Few vehicles for sharing exist. A real reticence to share often prevails. Questions of security are real, as are inclinations to parochialism. But that is another subject.

Where Are We?—Training

Training also received attention at the 1978 Glen Eyrie Conference. Ralph Winter called for "dozens, perhaps hundreds, of centers—focused on Islam—each representing the initiative of some particular group of Christians regionally or otherwise defined." I assume Winter had in mind training as well as research centers. The two components have always been basic to his outlook on world evangelization.

At Glen Eyrie, the task of specifically addressing training was left to Vivienne Stacey. At the core of her paper was a proposal for training done by "a small corps of specialists" based in five training centers, one each for Europe, Asia, Africa, the Americas and "Australasia." She envisioned each center's specialists conducting extension courses for missionaries and candidates, whether bivocational or not, supplemented by informational seminars for churches and students. She noted the need to train people at several levels—business and professional people, "professional missionaries," semi-literate and illiterate laborers and "those who suffer."

Besides pre-field training, Stacey also urged ongoing training once workers were in place among their target people. Interestingly, she did not anticipate the creation of any new structures to carry out this plan.

Ms. Stacey did not attempt to list existing structures which were doing training. Given the many levels at which training is possible—beginning with the local church, Bible school, theological institution, pastors' conferences and so forth, such a list would be most difficult to compile.

What do we know about training activities today? In view of the purpose statements of institutions listed by Dr. Miller, it is reasonable to assume that most of them were engaged in something they would call "training," a fact which again calls for definition of terms.

Obviously mission agencies, denominational and interdenominational, working solely among Muslims, were and are doing something to prepare their candidates prior to overseas departure. At the same time, we must recall there were (and are) few agencies of this kind.

Training centers created since the 1978 conference at Glen Eyrie.

Within four months of the conclusion of the Glen Eyrie Conference, in response to that conference, a new training center had been created, the Zwemer Institute. One, however, hardly constitutes a network. More recently, Gairdner Ministries in Great Britain, has come into being. A fraternal and cooperative relationship, including sharing of materials, characterizes the relationship between the Gairdner and Zwemer organizations.

The Assemblies of God now have started the Center for Ministry to Muslims in Minneapolis, Minnesota. This center spearheads Assemblies' training of missionaries to Muslims, while also mobilizing prayer.

A host of seminaries in the West have added regular courses on Islam/Ministry to Muslims to their curriculum since 1978. Among these are Dallas, Fuller, Wheaton, Asbury, Trinity, Concordia, Columbia Biblical and Western Conservative Baptist in the United States, and Trinity College, Bristol, in the United Kingdom. Likewise, Bible Colleges like All Nations in England and Columbia and Reformed in the United States have had courses on Islam for some time. While helpful, the programs of these institutions are not focused exclusively on the Muslim world and of necessity have to conform to the strictures of formal versus non-formal education.

A few training centers exist in Two-Thirds World areas. Included are the Henry Martyn Institute, India, and the Asian Research Center, Philippines. The Evangelical Seminary in Cairo and the Near East School of Theology in Beirut have Islamics programs. Note also needs to be taken of In Contact Ministries, London; Daystar in Nairobi; Jesus to the Muslims, Life Challenge, and Africa Centre for World Mission in South Africa; and Jesus to Muslims in Brazil. Inclusion in this list does not imply that all of the above focus training exclusively on Muslim work. No effort has been made to determine the level and kind of training offered or the constituency served.

New individual efforts are underway. One example is Ora Et Labora Christian Foundation (OELCF). Directed by Iman Santosa, OELCF, located in Indonesia, intends to stimulate vision and outreach of Christians to Muslims through production of materials, providing training and mobilizing prayer and workers.

The MARC division of World Vision International has compiled an extensive list of Christian workers who indicate some interest in Muslims. Though MARC classifies these people under the label "research," it is fair to assume some are involved in "training," a category MARC does not use.

Undoubtedly a number of national pastors and itinerant evangelists offer to their hearers some words of wisdom regarding reaching Muslims.

In the end, it is clear that a number of steps forward have occurred in the last decade. On the other hand, little has taken place by way of implementing the appeal voiced by Stacey. There still are gigantic gaps in providing the kind of world-encompassing training needed to carry the Kingdom forward among Muslim peoples.

Strategic Considerations

To develop a strategy, research and training centers, a great deal of interaction is needed about a multitude of factors influencing any strategy developed. We live in a world of realities that must be recognized and addressed. Some of the most obvious follow.

Regionalization

A major factor to be considered is the tendency toward regionalization—in the world in general as well as among evangelicals. Already a host of regional church-related organizations exist. Example: the Association of Evangelical Churches of Africa and Madagascar. Similar alignments of churches and missions characterize many other areas. And there is no indication of a lessening of this inclination.

Even within the Lausanne Committee for World Evangelization (LCWE), which has always viewed itself as a "movement" not a structure, steps are being taken to become structured. Ray Bakke has proposed that the LCWE organize itself into ten regions. Lausanne's leaders seem committed to "moving with the times" in organizing regionally. It is my understanding that LCWE leaders are looking seriously at Dr. Bakke's suggestions. If the "movement" is to become more structured, there are very good reasons to do it regionally. This inclination has definite implications for any strategy for developing training and research centers. My proposal grows out of Bakke's and parallels it.

The "regions" under consideration are:

1. North Pacific Rim...China, Japan, Korea, Taiwan
2. Association of Southeast Asian Nations
3. Oceania
4. The Subcontinent...Indo-Pak-Bangladesh, Nepal to Sri Lanka
5. Africa (the SubSahara, which could eventually be two regions)
6. Mediterranean World
7. East Block: Marxist Europe
8. West Europe
9. South or Latin America (eventually perhaps two regions)
10. North America

Interestingly this configuration conforms somewhat to the United Nations regional configuration of the world. It also somewhat parallels previously established affiliations of churches. With regard to the Muslim world specifically, Richard V. Weeks has divided Muslim peoples into nine areas. More ethno-linguistic/cultural in basis, his analysis gives undue consideration to Africa, while ignoring other parts of the world. His areas are:

1) Southwest Asia/Near or Middle East
2) Lower Nile Delta
3) The Maghreb—that is, the Mediterranean Coast of North Africa
4) The Sahel
5) The Northeast Ethiopic area/Horn of Africa
6) The East African Coast
7) Central Asia
8) The Indian subcontinent
9) Southeast Asia

Centers need to be thought about not only in relation to areas to be reached but also in relation to areas of resources. For example, though Latin America has few Muslims, comparatively speaking, it is a region stirring to life in cross-cultural missions, including concern for Muslims. And in East Asia, which has few Muslims, Korea nonetheless represents a tremendous pool of potential laborers for Muslim work.

In view of all of the above, it seems practical to think of regional centers in:

French Speaking West Africa
English Speaking West Africa

East Africa
The Middle East—possibly Cyprus
The Maghreb—possibly Southern Spain
Europe
Southeast Asia
India
Pakistan
East Asia
Latin America

It is certainly possible to combine some of those proposed regions. On the other hand, some of the considerations following may well dictate the division indicated.

Since movement toward regionalization is already occurring, it seems reasonable, whatever the final basis of "regions," to think that centers focusing on Muslim evangelization must somehow take seriously this phenomenon.

In the context of regionalization, other very practical items needing consideration are:

• **Political Realities**

—Which countries within a region would be tolerant of a center working toward the evangelization of Muslims?

—Is there sufficient accessibility to countries/communities where such a center would be permitted? Or would a center be limited to training only nationals from the host country?

—What kind of visibility should a center opt for in view of its political context?

• **Linguistic Considerations**

—Which languages characterize a region and to what extent?

—If a center is to serve a very extensive region, in what language must it function?

—How does the choice of particular language(s) affect the constituency to be served?

• **Access to Information and Opportunities**

—What sort of training resources are available in the form of schools, libraries and so forth, and where?

—What sort of opportunities exist for practical hands-on ministry experience as part of the learning process?

—How accessible is "outside" information to a given area?

• **Potential Workers**

—What sort of pools of potential workers exist in proximity to a potential center?

• **Attitudes of National Believers and Christian Leaders**

—Are there national churches in the region? What people groups do they represent?

—To what extent are national Christians open to and willing to encourage training for Muslim work?

—To what extent does disinterest, fear and/or opposition to Muslim work control local Christian thinking?

—To what extent should this be a consideration?

• **Levels of Training**

—What levels of training are needed where?

—How ought centers to respond to the need for various levels of training?

—Who will fill in the gaps left by decisions in this realm?

• **Funding**

—How will centers be funded?

—By whom will they be funded?

—At what level will they be funded?

• **Staffing**

—How will staff for centers be secured?

—What factors limit staffing?

—What background, experience and formal preparation ought staff to have?

• **"Strategic" Urban Settings**

—Should centers interface with Lausanne's urban emphasis, and if so, how?

—Where are the urban settings in proximity to Muslims that are "strategic" in view of Lausanne's world cities emphasis?

• **Training Objectives**

—What goals and objectives are to be considered valid and which goals vital?

—What levels, lengths, types and formats of training ought people to participate in?

Any training center, regional or otherwise, must be prepared to deal with a diverse constituency in terms of level of need. Purely theoretical/academic courses in the traditional mode will be of help to a small minority. Full-time workers in the fields of labor have different needs. Lay leaders have yet different needs. The average church member has still different needs. The young aspiring missionary has still different needs. The challenge is to strategize a way to equip as many as possible at all levels for work where God has placed them.

This means finding ways of making useful information available to people where they are, as well as inviting advanced-level students to grow. To do this might mean informal, low profile networks. It might mean a host of roving bands of practitioner instructors. It might mean area satellites. It might mean high visibility traditional schools, seminaries or institutes.

Criteria

Another area calling for major attention is the need to establish criteria defining what proper research and training are, and hence what adequate research and training centers would look like. At this stage in our development, research has to begin with the most basic information, such as identifying and networking people and resources useful to Muslim evangelization; and identifying and developing academic research which addresses themes and topics useful for Christian-Muslim interaction and determining what Muslim peoples exist—who, where and in what levels of social organization.

Frequently too little attention is given to specific training goals and objectives. Even more frequently, too little care is taken to correlate materials, methods and learning experiences with goals. The result often is labeled training but accomplishes little of what it proposes.

Due to regional differences, there needs to be room for variety in the exact specifications of both research and training. The training needed by Asians for work in North Africa will obviously have some different components and emphasis from training given North Americans who wish to evangelize Iranian immigrants in Los Angeles.

Some Models

What sort of models do we have for research and training efforts? There is always room for creative, from the ground up, first time ever, approaches. Sanctified genius can always give birth to such. What happens more often is that concerned people begin to analyze already existing efforts and work to adapt them to new situations.

Several models for enhancing the research and training tasks exist. These include:

1. The possibility of *building on existing programs and institutions*. Bible schools and colleges, seminaries and pastors' conferences already exist in many areas. Who knows how many? Who has some sense of which are doing outstanding work? A number of evangelistic and mission centers also exist. Again, who knows how many?

It is a relatively simple procedure to enrich existing programs by adding courses or seminars focusing on Islam and Muslim evangelization. This is what has happened repeatedly in North America. For example, in 1975, the School of World Mission at Fuller Seminary offered a year of Muslim emphasis. This "emphasis" consisted of three courses, one each quarter, two of which were taught by visiting professors. From that beginning, Fuller has now moved to the point of offering a Ph.D. degree in Intercultural Studies with a concentration in mission to Muslims. I hope more existing institutions will encourage one another to go forward in this matter. Each of us should become urgent advocates of such.

Concentration, mutual encouragement and networking are being found not only beneficial but imperative.

2. In those areas where institutions do not already exist, or cannot be interested in coming to grips with planting churches among Muslims, there is no recourse but to *begin something new*. In this case, the focus could and should be exclusively on Muslims! To do otherwise is to open the door to a dilution of resolution, due to the difficulty of the task. Missions history shows that agencies which sought relief from the difficulty of Muslim evangelization by working with other peoples, usually never got back to the original task. To assume that such would necessarily follow in a training context might not be

valid. But where there is the possibility of single-minded devotion to winning Muslims, why not seize it?

A model—certainly not the model—in this regard is the sequence of events leading to the creation of the Zwemer Institute of Muslim Studies (ZIMS), an event which, interestingly, parallels Fuller Seminary's movement toward a well-rounded program of Islamics—and helped it happen.

To understand the origins of ZIMS, one must recognize the early existence of several men and women who longed to see more productive extensive work in the Muslim world. What became Zwemer, then unnamed, was a dream in their hearts. From time to time, they encountered each other, shared and challenged one another—"networked." Fuller's Muslim emphasis year brought several together for a longer period of interaction.

An envisioned conference was roughed out on paper as a class assignment. Facilitating bodies were enlisted, one being the North American Lausanne Continuation Committee—interestingly a "regional" expression of the larger movement. World Vision International also played a significant role. With their assistance the Glen Eyrie Conference was held.

At the end of the Glen Eyrie gathering, the participants by consensus called for the creation of an independent institute focused solely on facilitating the evangelization of Muslims. Four months later, Zwemer Institute was born, its board made up initially of more than twenty conference participants.

A Proposal—On From Here

The Muslim Track of the Lausanne Movement clearly has among its goals "the establishment of research and training centers" for persons desiring to be equipped for church planting among Muslims. Part of that goal states that these centers should be located in "key regions—where such do not already exist." This being the case, let us accept the challenge. Let us work to implement this goal.

To that end, let me offer a proposal which is modest, specific and yet flexible in nature. I propose this meeting commit itself to a series of regional gatherings which would examine the needs, opportunities, focus and shape of regional training and research centers.

To do that most constructively, each consultation should be representative of its region's ethnicity, denominations, agencies, schools, ministry programs, and so forth, in so far as possible. Each consultation should also be in touch with representatives of Lausanne's various "working groups." A workable strategy with regard to Muslims must be holistic and thus take into account prayer, theology, communications and social concerns. Research and training must also be concerned with these dimensions.

A wide range of persons are needed in each of the consultations.

Further, each consultation should include a whole range of other persons vital to realistic efforts: local pastors, lay leaders, "doers," writers, fund-raisers, trainers and resource people who can draw upon anthropology, Islamics, research design, urban studies, and so forth.

The specific agendas of these regional gatherings should be determined by consultation with participants, not set by us at this time or by any outside group.

Funding for such gatherings should come from the regions involved rather than being financed from outside. There is a great need for national/regional churches to make the basic commitments of people, finances and facilities. This does not mean they should not seek outside assistance, but basic responsibility in these matters should be assumed regionally and not from outside.

A Key—Leadership

Focused leadership with untiring commitment is indispensable.

There are only two reasons why some variation on the process referred to above cannot be carried out. One is a lack of leadership. For regional research and training to become a reality, a dream must exist. We have that! Each of us has come here because we possess dreams about planting churches among unreached Muslim people groups.

A compilation of those dreams ought to encompass the whole Muslim world. Leadership is basic. The key is people who simply will not give up the dream. Leadership of this kind must have a single focus and untiring commitment to the task. The creation of major regional training activities will not come about if everyone gives it second, third or fourth priority while continuing "business as usual" in other areas. We are that leadership!

Leadership must not only be "possessed" by the vision, but must also be able to help others see where and how they fit into the realization of the dream. Good leadership always does that. The alternative is to fall victim to the "founder's syndrome" which will allow nothing more to happen than he/she can encircle with his/her arms! The result is strangulation and a fragmentation of effort at best—a death of the dream at worse. It also seems obvious to me that Westerners should not play that leadership role where national churches exist.

The word "center" might imply something static—acquiring a specific piece of property, a fixed location and fixed staff. An alternative word is "network." Network suggests people more than property; dynamic movement more than that which is static.

Whether a fixed location is appropriate or not, a network of people is basic to effective research and training—to determining what and how. The building and strengthening of networks stands at the heart of solving the "people" part of training. Books and buildings then can be strategic. People linked to people are the ingredients that can make new appropriate training really happen. Networking helps us break out of our parochialism, our survival mentality, the constraints of our own institutions.

The task is too big and too critical for any of us to "go it alone." Regional consultations can lead to the formulation and initial implementation of strategies for establishing research and training centers.

We at the Zwemer Institute, through the Muslim Track of the LCWE and in collaboration with its Strategy Working Group, are willing to commit our resources to networking, facilitating and coordinating the process of organizing regional consultations regarding Muslim research and training. We are willing to commit ourselves to:

1. Advocating the need to establish regional research and training centers.

2. Identifying key regional leaders who should be involved in planning for the development of regional research and training centers.

3. Planning regional consultations which would more precisely determine where and how to establish regional training and research centers.

4. Facilitating actual consultation interaction.

5. Developing plans for carrying forth the needed surveys to determine what already exists.

6. Providing training in research methods and planning upon request.

7. Developing training models for carrying out the task upon request.

8. When and if regional centers emerge, partnering with centers that invite us to do so in matters of research, training, materials development, publication and information brokering.

A Key—Cooperation

Real cooperation is a product of grace. It involves rising above the comfortable restrictions of personal, denominational and national prejudice.

Another basic ingredient is a spirit of cooperation. Such must prevail for efforts to succeed at the widest dimension within a region or even within a particular nation. "Cooperation" is rather like "church planting"—talk of it is far easier than doing it. Real cooperation occurs only as a product of grace. For it involves rising above the all too comfortable restrictions of personal, denominational and national prejudice.

For a rigidly sectarian or denominational spirit to dominate is to insure failure at worst and unnecessary and wasteful duplication at best. We all know that resources are too few and the task too large to allow this to occur. To fail to coordinate efforts and share information insures a delay in God's purposes being fully realized. He does seem to act in concert with his people, whether they choose to march straight into the land or wander for years.

So what is next? At this point, leadership, initiative and creativity are needed under the Lordship of Jesus with the prompting of the Spirit.

CHAPTER TWENTY ONE

ANNOTATED BIBLIOGRAPHY ON ISLAM

Warren G. Chastain

Compiling a bibliography is like eating nuts—it is difficult to know when to stop, and it is very much a matter of "taste." Two general criticisms of this collection are to be expected: "Why is *this* included?" and "Why is *that* omitted?" Both comments can be justified. But to justify my own procedure I must state that I did not just shake the nut-tree and gather whatever fell! Rather I walked around it carefully and selected nuts that appeared ripe for our consumer—the Christian worker who wants a bibliography that is more comprehensive than those that have been offered in the past, yet not locked in a thick shell of abstract scholarship. We hope that the shell can be opened easily to provide nourishment for the minds of hungry Christian witnesses.

In the past, mission agencies have sent out workers with minimal knowledge of and exposure to Islam. And many workers still go out hoping they will learn on the job but still unaware how to dig in and set up a study program for themselves. Islam has been to them like the macadamia nut: attractive, precious, but notoriously difficult to open with that hard, thick shell.

We hope that this bibliography will be a practical tool for the preparation of effective witnesses to Muslims.

This bibliography is limited to English language works which could be useful to Christian workers among Muslims. The books may be basic, but not necessarily simple; indeed, many of these works are primarily for avid students of Islam. We have sought, as careful scribes, to bring forth out of our treasure things new and old, works regularly cited by scholars as well as some lesser known books which are selected for some practical benefit.

This article updates the briefer but still useful article of Warren Webster, "A Selected Bibliography for Christian Workers" in *The Gospel and Islam* (available from MARC-WV), which is amplified by an article giving a methodology of research for almost any Islamic theme in Warren Chastain's "A Bibliography of Articles on Islam," available from EMIS, Box 794, Wheaton, IL 60187 and ZIMS, Box 365, Altadena, CA 91001.

Muslim, Christian, and secular titles are included, as well as some older apologetic materials difficult to find now, but which may become more relevant again as Muslims become more confrontational and as they make more contacts with Christian peoples.

Books will be listed below according to the following general outline used in *The Muslim World* "Survey of Periodicals" with some changes appropriate to this book's purpose.

Outline of Topics

1. General and Miscellaneous. Reference
2. Pre-Islamic Arabia. Muhammad. The Quran. Hadith.
3. Religious Instruction. The Mosque. Religious Duties and Devotional Life. Ethics and Customs. Folk Islam.
4. Theology. Movements and Sects. Shi'a. Philosophy. Sciences.
5. Sufism. Sufi orders. Saints. Mysticism.
6. Law. Politics. Socialism. Economics. Family & Women in Islam
7. Arabic. Other languages. Literature. Art. Culture. Education
8. Muslim Peoples: History, Anthropology, Islam in Modern History.
9. Christianity and Islam: Missions, the Message and Its Communication; Conversion; Apologetics; Approaches; Dialogue; Relations in General.

BIBLIOGRAPHY

1. General and Miscellaneous Works on Islam

Ali, Abdallah Yusuf.
  1929   *Fundamentals of Islam*. Geneva.   (Well-organized, clear Muslim
         statement.)

Ali, Maulana Muhammad
  1973   *The Religion of Islam*. Lahore: Ahmadiyya Anjuman Ishaat Islam.   (A
         systematic, modernistic statement of the Ahmadiyya position.   Highly
         recommended.)

Arberry, A. J., editor
  1969   *Religion in the Middle East*. London: CUP, 2 vols. 750 pp.   (The 2nd
         volume deals with Islam and is very useful for study of minorities like
         Zaydis, Ibadis, Druze, and Ahmadis.   A major section is given to relations
         between the three major religions.)

Cahen, Claude.
  1965   *Jean Sauvaget's Introduction to the History of the Muslim East*. Berkeley:
         University of California Press.   (A basic annotated bibliography for
         research.)

Cragg, Kenneth.
  1975   *The House of Islam*. Belmont, CA: Wadsworth Publishing Co.   2nd
         edition, 145pp.   (Excellent for getting students into a meaty introduction to
         Islam and primary sources.   Muslim leaders give an insider's view of
         Islam.)

Cragg, Kenneth and Marston Speight.
  1980   *Islam from Within*. Belmont, CA: Wadsworth.   (Judicious comments by
         the authors, plus use of key spokesperson for Islam give an "insider's
         view.")

Delval, Raymond. editor
  1984   *The Muslims in the World*. E.J. Brill, Plantijnstraat 2, 2321 JC, Leiden,
         Netherlands.   (The best large wall map in existence.   Shows concentrations
         of Sunni and Shi'a in all countries.   Includes an explanatory book with
         statistics.)

Ede, David. et al
  1983   *Guide to Islam*. G.K. Hall, 70 Lincoln St. Boston.   (A useful 261 page
         research tool with 2962 titles of books and articles carefully indexed.
         Annotated.)

al Faruki, Isma'il R. and Lois L. al Faruki.
  1986   *The Cultural Atlas of Islam*. NY: MacMillan.   (A major work by Muslim
         scholars covering a broad sweep of Islamic history, culture, and religion.
         Slights Shi'a and Sufis.   Exaggerates Muslim impact and serves as a
         corrective to the orientalist approach.   Not for beginners.)

Gaudefroy-Demonbynes, M.
   1954   *Muslim Institutions*. London. (Covers all aspects of Arab life and in a small compass delivers a massive amount of information on law, dogma, practices, etc.)

Geddes, Charles L.
   1973   *An Analytical Guide to the Bibliographies on Islam, Muhammad, and the Qur'an*. American Institute of Islamic Studies, Box 10191, Denver, CO 80210. (Detailed annotation of 213 bibliographies in western languages, Arabic, Persian, and Russian, 1658-1972.)

   1975   *Books in English on Islam, Muhammad, and the Qur'an: A Selected, Annotated Bibliography*. Denver: American Institute of Islamic Studies (A list of over 100 selected titles.)

Geijbels, M.
   1975   *An Introduction to Islam*. Christian Study Centre, 126B Murree Rd. Rawalpindi, Pakistan. (A valuable set of teaching materials in four parts by a Catholic scholar speaking from experience in a Muslim context.)

Gibb, Sir H.A.R.
   1953   *Mohammedanism: An Historical Survey*. 2nd ed. NY:OUP (A classic study by one the foremost scholars in the West. Profound and brief.)

   1982   *Studies on the Civilization of Islam*. Princeton, NJ.

Gibb, H.A.R. and J.H. Kramers, et al
   1953   *Shorter Encyclopedia of Islam*. Leiden: E.J. Brill. (Superb scholarship on the religious articles from the original *Encyclopaedia of Islam* with revisions.)

   1960   *The Encyclopedia of Islam New Edition*. Leiden: E.J. Brill. 6 volumes through "M" completed. (The best in contemporary scholarship. To be distinguished from E. J. Brill's *First Encyclopaedia of Islam*, 1913-1936, a 1987 reprint in 9 vols. 5164pp. with 9000 articles.)

Gilchrist, John.
   1986   *Muhammad and the Religion of Islam*. Jesus to the Muslims, Box 1804, Benoni, South Africa. (A 408p presentation of Islam from an evangelical who is heavily engaged in direct ministry. A second volume on how to handle controversial apologetic issues is in process—*The Christian Witness to the Muslim*. Very useful for apologetic ministry.)

Glasse, Cyril.
   1988   *The Concise Encyclopedia of Islam*. Atlantic Highlands, NJ: Humanities Press. 416 pp. (An American Muslim writes for the general reader. Includes chronology, dynastic chart, flow chart of the hajj, the divine names/titles of Muhammad.)

Graham, William A. and Marilyn R. Waldman.
   1983   *Islam-Fiche, Readings from Islamic Primary Sources*. From IDC, Poststrasse 14, 6300 Zug, Switzerland. (This is a new kind of anthology for studying and teaching Islamic civilization. These series of selected

microfiche collections would make an excellent means for Christian schools to make available to its students critical primary and secondary source materials, and thus build a stronger Islamic study program.)

Grimwood-Jones, Diana and Derek Hopwood (eds.)
1979   *The Middle East and Islam: A Bibliographical Introduction.* Zug, Switz.: Inter Documentation. (A collection of bibliographies, many heavily annotated.)

Hodgson, Marshal G.S.
1974   *The Venture of Islam.* 3 vols. Chicago: Univ. of Chicago Press (Profound and massive. Brilliant interpretative study that places Islam in the context of world civilization. For advanced students.)

Holt, P.M. et al., (Eds.)
1970   *The Cambridge History of Islam.* CUP. 2 vols: 815 and 966 pp. CUP. (Authoritative, but non-interpretative and tedious in parts. Good on religion, culture, etc.)

Hughes, T.P.
1895   *The Dictionary of Islam.* Islamic Book Publishers, Box 20210, Safat, Kuwait; or from FFM, 205 Yonge St. Toronto. (A Christian work that is appreciated by Muslims. Old but gold. A standby for missionaries.)

Jeffrey, Arthur.
1962   *A Reader on Islam.* 'S-Gravenhage: Mouton & Co. (Gives passages from standard Arabic writings showing the beliefs and practices of Muslims. An extensive anthology.)

Lammens, H.
1929   *Islam, Beliefs and Institutions.* London: Frank Cass. 256 pp. (A Catholic scholar provides a superior sweep of Islam as a religion. May be unpalatable to Muslim scholars.)

Littlefield, David N.
1975   *The Islamic Near East and North Africa: Annotated Guide to Books in English for the Non-Specialist.* Littleton, CO.

Maududi, Abul A'la.
1973   *Towards Understanding Islam.* From ATP, 10900 W. Washington St. Indianapolis, IN 46231 (A foremost conservative Muslim scholar whose works have influenced thinkers across the whole Muslim world.)

1978   *Fundamentals of Islam.* 3rd edition, 263pp. From Islamic Publications, 13-E Shahalam Market, Lahore.

Mitchell, Richard P. and David Schoenback.
1980   *An Annotated Bibliography on the Modern History of the Near East.* Ann Arbor, Mich.: Center for Near Eastern and North African Studies. (An essay for students and non-specialist readers.)

Nasr, Seyyed Hossain.
   1966   *Ideals and Realities of Islam*. London: George Allen & Unwin. (An influential Muslim thinker deeply conversant with modern western thought provides an interpretation of Islam.)

Rahman, Fazlur.
   1979   *Islam*. 2nd ed., Univ. of Chicago Press, 283pp. (An in-depth modernistic interpretation of Islam by one of the foremost Muslim scholars. Beginners will miss many of the issues Rahman debates.)

Robinson, Francis.
   1982   *Atlas of the Islamic World since 1500*. NY: Facts on File. (May be compared with another excellent historical atlas by William Brice (ed.), *An Historical Atlas of Islam*. Leiden: E.J. Brill, 1981.)

Ruthven, Malise.
   1984   *Islam in the World*. NY:OUP, 400pp. (A fascinating, original and interpretative introduction.)

Said, Edward W.
   1978   *Orientalism*. NY: Pantheon. (An Arab Christian literary scholar criticizes the attitudes and methods of western journalism and scholarship dealing with the Arab world.)

Saliba, Maurice.
   1981   *Index Libanicus*. Jounieh, Lebanon: Paulist Press, 510pp. (An immense bibliography of books and articles from 650 periodicals with 5,359 titles covering the Levant from 1515 to 1979.)

Schuon, Frithjof.
   1976   *Understanding Islam*. London: D.M. Matheson. (A convert to Sufi Islam providing one of the best works in English on the meaning of Islam for a scholar.)

Sell, Edward.
   1920   *The Faith of Islam*. 4th ed., London. (A well-organized, useful presentation of Islam.)

Simon, Reeva.
   1978   *The Modern Middle East: A Guide to Research Tools in the Social Sciences*. Boulder: Westview. (This can be used as a "modern Sauvaget".)

Watt, W. Montgomery.
   1968   *What is Islam?*. London: Longmans. (A summary of how a noted Christian scholar evaluates Islam.)

2. A. Pre-Islamic Arabia and Muhammad

Andrae, Tor.
   1960   *Muhammad, The Man and His Faith*. NY: Harper & Row. 194pp. (Highly recommended sympathetic biography placing Muhammad in a religious and psychological continuity with the Arab worldview of the time. Stresses influence of Monophysites.)

Anees, Munawar A. and Alea N. Athar.
1986   *Guide to Sira and Hadith Literature in Western Languages.* London:
Mansell. 404pp. (2,996 entries covering early 16th century to 1985.
Annotated.)

Bell, Richard.
1968   *The Origin of Islam in its Christian Environment.* London: Frank Cass
(Reprint of 1926 edition), 224pp. (Links Muhammad's ideas to Christianity,
not a fashionable view in contemporary Islamic studies.)

Cragg, Kenneth.
1971   *The Event of the Qur'an: Islam in its Scripture.* London: Allen & Unwin.
(Cragg gets into the mind of the Quran and studies it in its pagan context.)

1973   *The Mind of the Qur'an.* London: Allen & Unwin. 209pp. (Companion
to above volume. Studies three classic commentators.)

Gabrieli, Francesco.
1968   *Muhammad and the Conquests of Islam.* NY: McGraw. (An Italian
scholar writes the best survey of conquests in English. Objective, solid
scholarship. Very readable and well illustrated)

Guillaume, A. (translator)
1955   *The Life of Muhammad.* (An early full-length biography by Ibn Ishaq in
the 8th century, and radically edited later by Ibn Hisham. Gives a more
authentic flavor than contemporary hagiography.)

Haykal, Muhammad Husayn.
1976   *The Life of Muhammad.* Indianapolis: ATP. 841pp. 8th ed. (A modernistic
biography by a noted Egyptian author. Theological in tone and one of the
most influential biographies ever written.)

Muir, Sir William.
1894   *The Life of Mahomet from Original Sources.* London. 3rd ed., 536 pp.
("Longest, most faithful resume of the sources on the life of Muhammad
in English"-Ede.)

Rodinson, Maxime.
1971   *Mohammed.* Revised edition trans. by Anne Carter. NY: Viking Penguin.
xx, 361pp. (French scholar of Semitic languages with long experience in
the Middle East who sees Muhammad as having experienced real sensory
phenomena, but interprets it rationalistically. Well written.)

Watt, W. Montgomery.
1961   *Muhammad, Prophet and Statesman.* London: OUP. 250pp. (A sympathetic modern biography that stresses economic forces and Muhammad's
skills in forging tribal relationships. Abridges his *Muhammad at Mecca*
and *Muhammad at Medina.* Leans over backwards to apologize for moral
failures in Muhammad.)

2. B. The Koran and the Traditions (Hadith)

Ali, A. Yusuf.
    1946   *The Holy Qur'an*. Indianapolis, IN: ATP. 1915pp. (An English/Arabic version with English commentary on every verse. One of the most used versions by a noted Muslim scholar, which could become even more of a standard since it has been used as the basis for computer database covering the entire text—see *QURANBASE* below.)

Ali, S.V. Mir Ahmed.
    1964   *The Holy Qur'an*. Karachi: Muhammad Khaleel Shirazi. (Useful for comparison as a Shi'a version as against the Yusuf Ali version which presents a Sunni view.)

Arberry, A.J.
    1955   *The Koran Interpreted*. London:OUP. (Considered to be the finest rendition of the flavor of the original in English. Its position as a standard was enhanced by the recent publication of a complete concordance to the Koran using Arberry as the basic text.)

Baljon, J.M.S.
    1961   *Modern Muslim Koran Interpretation (1800-1960)*. Leiden: Brill. 135 pp. (Examines modern exegesis, methods of interpretation, and major issues. The introduction treats important exegetes, their lives and work).

Basetti-Sani, Giulio. O.F.M.
    1977   *The Koran in the Light of Christ*. 223pp. Franciscan Herald Press, 1434 W. 34 St, Chicago, IL 60609. (The biographer of Massignon rejects the skepticism of Maracci, Caetani, and Lammens and calls for a new view of the role of Islam in the history of salvation.)

Bell, Richard.
    1953   *Introduction to the Qur'an*. Edinburgh. x, 190pp. (An essential tool for study of technical issues related to the development of the Qur'an. He has developed a major theory to account for the disorder of the Qur'an. Revised by Watt—see below.)

Burton, John.
    1977   *The Collection of the Qur'an*. London: CUP. 273pp. (Technical.)

Cragg, Kenneth.
    1970   *The Event of the Qur'an*. London: Allen & Unwin. 208pp. (A more readable and less technical introduction than Bell's.)

    1973   *The Mind of the Qur'an*. London: Allen & Unwin. 209pp. (Deals with the significance of the Qur'an for both the Muslim and non-Muslim. The recitation and interpretive sciences explained as well as a look at how the Qur'an is relevant in a secular, pluralistic world.)

    1985   *The Pen and the Faith*. London: Allen & Unwin. (Analysis of contemporary quranic exegetes.)

Gatje, Helmut.   Translated and edited by Alford T. Welch.
   1976   *The Qur'an and Its Exegesis: Selected Texts with Classical and Modern Muslim Interpretations.*   Berkeley: Univ. of California Press. 313 pp.   (This unique work is very useful for comparing Muslim and Christian concepts such as revelation, Muhammad, God, angels, eschatology, angels, and other topics like dogmatics, exegesis of Shiites, mystics, and moderns.   Uses key texts from selected commentators.)

Geiger, Abraham
   1970   *Judaism and Islam.*   NY: KTAV Publishing House 170pp.   (A pioneering work of 1832 that concludes that Jewish and other sources were used by Muhammad through oral communication.   Influential.)

Goldsack, William.
   1923   *Selections from Muhammadan Traditions.*   Madras: Christian Literature Society.   (Uses *hadith* drawn from the 6 *sahih* books plus a few minor authorities.   Traditions are grouped by topics to make them easier to study, and removal of the *isnad*   saves time.)

Graham, William A.
   1976   *Divine Word and Prophetic Word in Early Islam: A Reconsideration of Sources, with Special Reference o the Divine Saying or Hadith Qudsi.*   The Hague: Mouton, 266 pp.   (Rejects common idea that there was a clear distinction from early Islam between the prophet's teaching and revelation.   New light on the Muslim concept of revelation.)

Guillaume, A.
   1924   *The Traditions of Islam.*   Oxford. 182pp.   ("An Introduction to the Study of the Hadith Literature" that builds on Goldhizer's epochal studies.   Gives Muslim criticisms of traditions and a chapter on Jewish and Christian borrowings.)

Islamic Computing Centre.
   1986   *Computerised Hadith.*   From ICC, 73, St Thomas Rd.   London N4 2QJ, UK.   (Some 10,000 sayings taken from the six major hadith collections are conveniently codified for easy retrieval, available on IBM/PC/XT or compatibles with a minimum memory of 512K of RAM and 10 megabytes of disc storage.)

Izutsu, Toshihiko
   1964   *God and Man in the Koran.*   Tokyo: Institute of Cultural and Linguistic Studies.   (A semantic study of the Quranic worldview.)

   1966   *Ethico-Religious Concepts in the Qur'an.*   Rev. ed. Montreal: McGill. 284pp.   Orig. pub. as *The Structure of Religious Terms in the Koran.* 1959.   (The transformation of key ethical ideas such as faith, unbelief, good, bad, hypocrisy, etc. in the Quran.)

Jeffrey, Arthur.
   1928   *The Foreign Vocabulary of the Qur'an.*   Baroda: Oriental Institute. 311 pp.   (A dictionary and indexes of loan words.   Contains a critical bibliography of works that analyze the teaching and content of the Qur'an.)

1937   *Materials for the History of the Text of the Qur'an.* Leiden: Brill. 609 pp. ("A listing of the known differences distinguishing some 28 codices of the Qur'an." Introduction discusses variant readings problem. Technical.)

1952   *The Qur'an as Scripture.* NY: Russell Moore. 103pp. ("The nature of the sacred book, prophecy, inspiration, the relation of the Qur'an to earlier scriptures, and the textual history of the Qur'an are subjects of this important study.")

Juynboll, G.H.A.
1969   *The Authenticity of the Tradition Literature: Discussions in Modern Egypt.* Leiden: Brill. 171pp. (Modern Muslim scholars in debate among themselves are studied to bring out major issues regarding the hadith in a unique work.)

Kassis, Hanna E.
1983   *A Concordance of the Qur'an.* Berkeley: Univ of California Press. xxxv, 1444pp. (The most complete concordance of the Qur'an in English; based on Arberry. It has a major section on Allah including all terms related to the divine name.)

Katsch, Abraham
1954   *Judaism in Islam.* NY: New York University Press. (Jewish parallels with Suras 2 and 3 and their commentaries.)

Khan, M.M. translator
1979   *The Translation of the Meanings of Sahih al-Bukhari*   4th ed., 9 vols. Kazi Publications. (The classic authority made available in English.)

O'Shaughnessy, Thomas. S.J.
1948   *The Koranic Concept of the .Word of God.* Rome: Pontificio Instituto Biblico. (Jesus as the Word of God in the Koran.)

1953   *The Development of the Meaning of Spirit in the Koran.* Rome and Chicago: Loyola Univ. Press. 75pp. (The term "ruh" shows gnostic influences in the Koran. Jewish and Christian influences considered.)

1969   *Muhammad's Thoughts on Death: A Study of Qur'anic Data.* Leiden: Brill. 90pp.

QURANBASE
n.d.   Arabic Software & Computers, Inc. has produced a database containing the entire Quranic text from Yusuf Ali's translation. "The database includes a series of data query commands for quickly searching through the text. (One) can quickly find a ... group of verses by entering a simple command. *QURANBASE* locates verses by subject and by key word as well." $295 from ASCI, 725 Deep Valley Dr., Palos Verdes, CA 90274.

Rahbar, Daud
1960   *God of Justice: A Study of the Ethical Doctrine of the Qur'an.* Leiden: Brill. 446pp. (Not a comprehensive study of the ethical system of the Quran, but a focus on the problem of man's free-will and God's predestination. Seeks to prove that people's actions are not pre-determined by God.)

Rahman, Fazlur.
1980   *Major Themes of the Qur'an.* Chicago: Bibliotheca Islamica. 180 pp. ("A brilliant, original examination of the contents of the Qur'an that diverges significantly from previous studies, both Muslim and Western." Rahman studies basic ideas of God, man, evil, Satan, prophethood, revelation and eschatology.)

Raisanen, Heibbi
1972   *The Idea of Divine Hardening: A Comparative Study of the Notion of Divine Hardening, Leading Astray and Inciting to Evil in the Bible and the Qur'an.* Helsinki: Finnish Exegetical Society. 108pp. (The problem of predestination studied exegetically. The "negative predestination" is explained by the "bitter experience of the Mecca opposition." Western writings on the subject surveyed.)

Robson, James. (Translator)
1975   *Mishkat-ul-masabih.* 2 vols. Lahore: Sh. Muh. Ashraf. ("This translation of al-Baghawi's collection of hadith brings to the English reader all of the authentic traditions found in the classical Sunni manuals, except the isnads." Excellent introduction and translation. 1453pp.)

Sale, George and E.M. Wherry.
1975   *A Comprehensive Commentary on the Koran.* NY: AMS Press. (A reprint of an 1896 four-volume work.)

Sherif, Faruq.
1985   *A Guide to the Contents of the Qur'an.* Atlantic Highlands, NJ: Humanities Press. 180 pp. (A compendium of themes arranged systematically without comment, but giving sum of the verses. Indexed.)

Siddiqui, A.H. (Trans.)
1976   *Sahih Muslim.* vol. I-IV. Indianapolis: MSA Islamic Book Service. (This 1600 page set is a classic on the words and deeds of Muhammad as narrated by his companions. Available in hard-back at $12 a volume.)

Stanton, H.U.W.
1969   *The Teaching of the Qur'an.* NY: Biblo & Tannen. (Provides a topical index to passages on essential themes, but does not write out the verses cited. A useful study tool. Another useful tool which can be used in conjunction with this is Don Rickard's *A Religious Topical Index of the Qur'an* which when published should greatly benefit students.)

al-Tabari, Abu Ja'far Muhammad b. Jarir.
1987   *Commentary on the Qur'an or Tafsir.* Vol 1 (of 5), NY: Oxford. 546 pp. Abridged and translated by John Cooper, W.F. Madelung, and Alan Jones, et al. ("This edition of the most famous commentary on the Qur'an, abridged from 30 to 5 volumes and including the full text of the Qur'an in Arabic and English, is the first translation of a work considered second only to the Qur'an itself in importance as a sacred Islamic text.")

Tisdall, W. St. Clair.
1901   *The Sources of Islam.* 1973 reprint from Amarko Book Agency, B-42 Amar Colony, New Delhi 110024, India.

Torrey, C. C.
    1933 *The Jewish Foundation of Islam.* NY: Jewish Institute of Religion Press. (Influential study presenting evidence for Jewish elements in Islam.)

Watt, W. Montgomery.
    1967 *Companion to the Qur'an.* London: Allen & Unwin. Gives background information on each chapter; brief but enlightening. Arberry is basic text, but keyed to other translations.)

    1970 *Bell's Introduction to the Qur'an.* Edinburgh Univ. Press. Watt is more sympathetic to Islam than Bell, and more readable. He includes a table for converting the Fluegel to Egyptian verse numbers. Two new chapters have been added on the Qur'an and both Muslim and western scholarship.)

Wensinck, A.J.
    1927 *A Handbook of Early Mohammedan Tradition.* Leiden: Brill. 268 pp. ("An English concordance of the traditions in the collections of al-Bukhari, Muslim, Abu Da'ud, al-Tirmidhi, al-Nasa'i, Ibn Maja, al-Darimi, and Malik b. Anas."-Ede.)

3. Religious Instruction. Mosque. Duties & Devotional Life. Ethics. Customs. Folk Islam. Sociology of Islam

Calverley, E.E.
    1957 *Worship in Islam.* London: Luzac. Rev. ed. (Great detail on Muslim daily prayers. Translates much from al-Ghazali.)

Cragg, Kenneth.
    1985 *The Call of the Minaret .* Maryknoll, NY: Orbis. 2nd edition, revised and enlarged, 358pp. (Outstanding classic. "An account of the spiritual tradition of Islam so sensitive as to inspire Muslims themselves.")

Donaldson, D.W.
    1963 *Studies in Muslim Ethics.* London: SPCK ("The only comprehensive treatment of the subject in English." Deals with ethical theories of philosophers, mystics, the Qur'an, hadith, and modern trends.)

Fakhry, Majid.
    1970 *A History of Islamic Philosophy.* NY: Columbia, 427 pp. (Misleading title since it deals heavily with theology and mysticism, also politics and social affairs. Covers early theological controversies and modern trends.)

von Grunebaum, G.E.
    1976 *Mohammedan Festivals.* London: Curzon Press. 107pp. (Deals with the meanings of major holy days, the hajj, ramadan, Muharram 10, with a section on prayer, veneration of Muhammad and saints.)

Guellooz, E. and A. Frikha.
    1978 *Pilgrimage to Mecca.* London: East-West. (A major work with photographs.)

Levy, Reuben.
    1957 *The Social Structure of Islam.* London: CUP. 536pp. (Sociological development of institutions and changes in societies penetrated by Islam.)

MacDonald, D.B.
   1912   *The Religious Attitude and Life in Islam.* Chicago. ("MacDonald set himself
           to lay bare the real context of the religious perceptions of the greater mass of
           Muslims, and he succeeds in showing the inner nature of their religion as no
           treatise on theology...can do. This book is one of the fundamental works in
           the entire field of Islamic studies.")

Padwick, Constance
   1961   *Muslim Devotions.* London. (Noted collection of actual prayers and
           devotional materials Muslims use.)

Quasem, Muhammad Abul.
   1983   *Salvation of the Soul and Islamic Devotions.* London: Kegan, Paul Interna-
           tional. 289 pp. (What are Muslim ideas about salvation and how one seeks it.)

Roberts, Robert.
   1925   *The Social Laws of the Qoran.* London. (A short work but useful for its
           summary of what the Koran teaches about marriage, divorce, slavery,
           inheritance, criminal law, food laws, and commerce.)

Wagtendonk, K.
   1968   *Fasting in the Koran.* Leiden: Brill. 154pp. (A basic study on the subject
           with an exegetical analysis of Koranic texts, and the historical background
           of the origin of Ramadan.)

Wensinck. A.J.
   1925   *Arabic New Year and the Feast of Tabernacles* Amsterdam. 41 pp. (Technical
           study of Ramadan as a modification of the pre-Islamic New Year's rites. He
           traces parallels between Ramadan and Feast of Tabernacles.)

Zwemer, S.M.
   1920   *The Influence of Animism on Islam.* NY: MacMillan. 246pp. (Zwemer did
           extensive authoritative research on folk Islam. His chapter on "The Aqiqa
           Sacrifice" can be very useful.)

   1939   *Studies in Popular Islam.* NY: MacMillan. (Completes his studies in
           common beliefs and practices. Zwemer often brings out materials useful
           for witnessing.)

4. Theology. Movements. Sects. Shi'a. Philosophy. Sciences

Ahmad, Bashir-ud-Din Mahmud.
   1980   *Invitation to Ahmadiyyat.* London: Routledge and Kegan, Paul.

al-Amin, Hassan.
   1970   *Islamic Shi'ite Encyclopaedia.* Beirut: Slim Press. 3 vols. (An excellent
           source of information about Shi'ite themes. Arrangement difficult to use.)

Cragg, Kenneth
   1965   *Counsels in Contemporary Islam.* Edinburgh. ("Offers a full bibliography
           of modern Muslim writing and a review of the major themes and move-
           ments of its inner debate.")

Donaldson, Dwight M.
   1933   *The Shi'ite Religion*. London: Luzac. (An ex-missionary to Persia presents a general introduction; stress on Persia and Iraq.)

Ghani, Cyrus.
   1987   *Iran and the West: A Critical Bibliography*. NY: Methuen. 967pp. (A massive work containing over 4,200 annotated entries on studies covering Iran from ancient times to the present.)

Goldhizer, Ignaz.
   1981   *Introduction to Islamic Theology and Law*. Princeton Univ. Press. 302pp. (This reprint of an older work is valuable because of Goldhizer's massive erudition.)

von Grunebaum, G.E. editor.
   1971   *Theology and Law in Islam*. Wiesbaden: Otto Harrasowitz. (Contains articles by J. Schacht, M.W. Watt, Fazlur Rahman, et al.)

Lewis, Bernard.
   1940   *The Origins of Isma'ilism*. Cambridge: W. Heffer. (A condensed scholarly doctoral thesis that illuminates the intricate links of this group.)

MacDonald, D.B.
   1903   *Development of Muslim Theology, Jurisprudence, and Constitutional Theory*. NY: Scribners. 386 pp. (Basic concepts, problems, and history of Muslim law. Dated but useful, especially for the three short creeds of al-Ash'ari, al-Ghazali, and al-Nasafi.)

Makarim, Sami Nasib.
   1974   *The Druze Faith*. Delmar, NY: Caravan. 153 pp. (A Druze examines history and beliefs from within.)

Nadwi, Abul Hasan Ali.
   1974   *Qadianism-A Critical Study*. From New Era, Box 8139 Ann Arbor, MI 48107. 139 pp. (A Muslim critique of the Qadian Ahmadiyya sect.)

Pelly, Lewis.
   1879   *The Miracle Play of Hasan and Husain*. (2 vols). London: Gregg International Publishers. (The 37 scenes of the Hasan and Husain passion plays in English with the historical background. Reprinted in 1970.)

Sachedina, Abdulaziz A.
   ___   *Islamic Messianism: The Idea of the Mahdi in Twelver Shi'ism*. Albany, NY: State Univ of NY Press. (Traces the development of the Mahdi concept, compares it to Judeo-Christian ideas of the Messiah, and links it with the experience of Shi'ite Muslims relating to political regimes.)

Smith, Jane Idleman and Yvonne Y. Haddad.
   1981   *The Islamic Understanding of Death and Resurrection*. Albany, NY: State Univ. of NY Press. 262 pp. (Shows the eschatological views of classical and modern Islam with chapters on"The Special Case of Women and Children in the Afterlife," and "The Cult of Saints.")

al-Tabataba'i, Muhammad Husayn.
   1975   *Shi'ite Islam.* Albany, NY: SUNY Press. 253pp. (Useful compendium by a member of the main branch, the "Ithna Ashari" of the Shi'ah.)

Watt, W. Montgomery.
   1973   *The Formative Period of Islamic Thought.* Edinburgh. 424 pp. ("The most detailed and comprehensive treatment of the development of early Islamic thought <632-945> that exists in the English language"-Ede.)

Wensinck, A.J.
   1962   *The Muslim Creed: Its Genesis and Historical Development.* London: Cass. 304 pp. ("A classic study on early theological developments in Sunni Islam" with an analysis of early creeds.)

Wolfson, H.A.
   1976   *The Philosophy of the Kalam.* Cambridge: Harvard Univ. Press. 779 pp. ("A monumental work that systematically examines with great care the origin, structure, and diversity of six central teachings of Islamic theology:divine attributes, Qur'an, creation, atomism, causality and the freewill problem.")

Yarshater, Ehsan. (Ed.)
   1983   *Encyclopaedia Iranica.* NY: Methuen. (Now in its 3rd volume, this will be the most authoritative research tool and reference source from prehistory to the present. Gives best treatment to Iranian Islam than any other reference work.)

5. Sufism, Saints, Mysticism

Abun-Nasr, Jamil.
   1965   *The Tijaniyya, A Sufi Order in the Modern World.* NY: OUP 204pp. (The history, doctrines, and role of this order in Northwest Africa.)

Arberry, Arthur.
   1950   *Sufism.* London. George Allen & Unwin. (Probably the best English history. Simple, clear, but rich.)

Burckhardt, Titus.
   1959   *An Introduction to Sufi Doctrine.* Lahore: Mohd Ashraf. 155 pp. (A study of select Sufi doctrines stressing intuitive insight and the teaching of Ibn al'Arabi.)

Lings, Martin.
   1981   *What is Sufism?* London: Unwin Paperbacks, 139pp. ("A brief introduction to Sufism that tries to explain and interpret it from the 'inside'.")

Nicholson, Reynold. A.
   1921   *Studies in Islamic Mysticism.* Cambridge: CUP (A classic study.)

   1975   *The Mystics of Islam.* London: Routledge & Kegan, Paul. Reprint of 1921 edition. (A classic.)

Schimmel, A.
  1975 *Mystical Dimensions of Islam.* Chapel Hill: Univ. of North Carolina Press.
        506 pp. ("The most comprehensive historical treatment of Islamic mysticism
        in English...from origins to the 19th century.")

Smith, Margaret.
  1985 *Rabi'a the Mystic and Her Fellow Saints in Islam.* 2nd ed. Cambridge: CUP.
        256 pp. (A reissue of the 1928 classic with a valuable introduction by
        Prof. A. Schimmel on mysticism, Sufism, and the role of women in the
        Muslim world.)

  1931 *Studies in Early Mysticism in the Near and Middle East.* NY: MacMillan.
        (She shows the links with Christian practice in arguing for Christian
        sources to Sufism.)

  1954 *The Sufi Path of Love.* London: Luzac. (A highly regarded short anthology
        from original sources and key interpreters. Explores the nature and doctrines
        of Sufism with an excellent bibliography.)

Subhan, Bishop John.
  1938 *Sufism, its Saints and Shrines.* Lucknow Publishing House. (He "gives a
        veritable catalogue of the mystic orders of India, where this phenomenon
        took a deep hold...and continues to be significant.)

Trimingham. J.S.
  1971 *The Sufi Orders in Islam.* Oxford. 333pp. (It lists all Sufi orders with useful
        information on the organizational structures.)

Watt, W. Montgomery.
  1953 *The Faith and Practice of al-Ghazali.* London: George Allen & Unwin.
        (Watt links the depths of the philosophical mind with the mystical heart
        of this epochal figure.)

6. Law, Politics, Socialism, Economics, Family & Woman in Islam

A. Law, Politics, Social Affairs and Public Life.

Anderson, J.N.D.
  1976 *Law Reform in the Muslim World.* London. (A brief survey of how
        Muslims are handling change of some modern major legal issues.)

Chapman, Colin.
  1983 *Whose Promised Land?* Herts, UK: Lion. 253 pp. (A biblical and critical
        study of claims that Israel has divine rights to the land of Palestine.)

Chacour, Elias.
  1984 *Blood Brother.* Grand Rapids: Chosen Books. 224 pp. (A Palestinian
        Christian seeks reconciliation between Jews and Arabs.)

Coulson, N.J.
  1964 *A History of Muslim Law.* Edinburgh. 264 pp. (Recommended for the first
        reading on Islamic law).

Ibrahim, Ahmad, et al. (Compilers).
 1985   *Readings on Islam in Southeast Asia.* Singapore: Institute of Southeast Asian Studies. 407 pp. (49 articles on early and colonial Islam; post-independence politics, the institutionalization of Islam, socio-cultural settings, and perspectives on modernization.)

Schacht, J.
 1964   *An Introduction to Islamic Law.* Oxford: Clarendon. ("A work of established scholarship by an expert in the field."-Cragg.)

B. Women and the Family in Islam.

Abdul-Rauf, Muhammad.
 1979   *The Islamic View of Women and the Family.* NY: Robert Speller and Sons.

Beck, Lois and Nikki Keddie (Editors).
 1978   *Women in the Muslim World.* Cambridge: Harvard. 698pp. (36 essays on Middle East, China, etc.)

Esposito, John.
 ___   *Women in Muslim Family Law.* From New Era, Box 8139 Ann Arbor, MI 48107. 155 pp.

Fernea, Elizabeth W.
 1975   *A Street in Marrakech: A Personal Encounter with the Lives of Moroccan Women.* Garden City, NY: Anchor.

Fernea, Elizabeth W. and Basima Qattan Bezirgan (Editors).
 1977   *Middle Eastern Women Speak.* Austin: Univ. of Texas Press. (A collection of personal sketches, spanning 13 centuries which gives superb insights into the diversity of the experiences of Muslim women.)

Gulick, John and Margaret Gulick.
 1974   *Annotated Bibliography of Sources Concerned with Women in the Modern Muslim Middle East.* Princeton Univ. Press. 26pp. (Almost 200 annotated entries.)

al-Qazzaz, Ayad.
 1977   *Women in the Middle East and North Africa: An Annotated Bibliography.* Austin: Univ. of Texas. 178 pp. (Lengthy annotations.)

Raccagni, Michelle.
 1978   *The Modern Arab Woman: A Bibliography.* From New Era, Box 8139 Ann Arbor, MI. 262 pp.

7. Literature, Art, Culture and Education

Bosworth, C.E. and Joseph Schacht.
 1979   *The Legacy of Islam.* 2nd ed. Oxford: Clarendon. ("Contributions by leading scholars on aspects of Muslim civilization.")

Burckhardt, Titus.
 1976   *Art of Islam.* World of Islam Festival Trust, Kent, UK: Westerham Press. 204 pp.

Creswell, Sir K.A.C.
  1960 *Bibliography of the Architecture, Arts, and Crafts of Islam to 1st January 1960.* Cairo: American Univ. in Cairo Press. (A massive work by a scholar who gave almost 50 years to study Muslim culture. Almost 16,000 entries.)

  1973 *A Bibliography of the Architecture, Arts, and Crafts of Islam Supplement, January 1960 to January 1972.* (Like the first volume, weak on China and S.E. Asia.)

Haddad, Yvonne, Byron Haines and Ellison Findly, eds.
  1984 *The Islamic Impact.* Syracuse Univ. Press. 249pp. (Ten essays covering contemporary problems.)

Pearson, J.D. et al.
  1984 *A Bibliography of the Architecture, Arts, and Crafts of Islam by Sir K.A.C. Creswell, C.B.E., Second Supplement, January 1972 to December 1980.* 578 pp. (Corrects former omissions on China and S.E. Asia.)

Kritzeck, James. (Editor)
  1966 *Anthology of Islamic Literature.* NY: Mentor. ("Translations of selections from the Arabic, Persian, and Turkish literary traditions from the rise of Islam to the modern era.")

  1970 *Modern Islamic Literature.* (A broad selection of writings, including poetry, from 1800 to the 1960s.)

Savory, R.M. (Editor)
  1979 *Introduction to Islamic Civilization.* NY: CUP. 204 pp. (18 essays by leading scholars widely dealing with broad aspects of Islamic civilization.)

8. Muslim Peoples. History. Anthropology. Islam in Modern History

Ahmad, Aziz
  1964 *Islamic Culture in Its Indian Environment.* Oxford.

Binder, Leonard (Ed.)
  1976 *The Study of the Middle East.* NY: John Wiley.

Clarke, Peter B.
  1982 *West Africa and Islam.* London: Edward Arnold. (Best on West Africa.)

Donohue, John J. and John L. Esposito. (Eds.)
  1982 *Islam in Transition.* NY: OUP. 322 pp. (A source book of 57 Muslim spokesmen on Islam, the modern state, social change, with case studies of Egypt, Pakistan, and Iran.)

Esposito, John L., ed.
  1983 *Voices of Resurgent Islam.* NY: OUP. 294pp. (Key spokesman for modern Islam and Western scholars study problems of Islamic identity and resurgence.)

Friedmann, Yohanan. (Ed.)
  1984 *Islam in Asia.* Vol. 1. Boulder, CO: Westview. (Helpful articles by experts on South Asia.)

Geddes, Charles L.
   1972   *An Analytical Guide to the Bibliographies on Modern Egypt and the Sudan.*
   Denver: American Institute of Islamic Studies. 78 pp. (An annotated list of
   books and articles since 1789.)

Geertz, Clifford.
   1968   *Islam Observed.* New Haven. (A sensitive comparison of the forms of Islam
   in Morocco and Indonesia.)

Gellner, Ernest.
   1969   *Saints of the Atlas.* London. Weidenfeld & Nicholson. 317 pp. (An anthro-
   pological study of Berber tribal government led by hereditary saints. An
   invaluable account of popular practices and the role of the saint and Sufi
   lodges.)

Gilliland, Dean
   1986   *African Religion Meets Islam.* Lanham, MD: University Press. 241pp.
   (Scholar with missionary experience analyzes dynamics of interaction of
   Traditional Religions, Islam and Christianity.)

Gibb, H.A.R.
   1947   *Modern Trends in Islam.* Univ. of Chicago Press. (Dated but still useful for
   broad view and comparisons.)

Indian Council on Social Science Research.
   1983   *Select Bibliography on Indian Muslims.* From Library, Osmania University,
   Indian Council on Social Science Research, Hyderabad, 500 007, India.
   (Covers all areas of Indian Muslim life. 4428 entries.)

Israeli, Raphaeli and A.H. Johns,(Editors).
   1984   *Islam in Asia: South East and East Asia.* Vol. 2 Boulder, CO: Westview.
   (Articles by specialists on various countries and problems.)

Jennings, George J.
   1983   *A Middle East Consultant Views Middle Eastern Culture and Personality.*
   103 pp. (A mission leader provides socio-anthropological material useful
   to Westerners working among Muslims.)

   1986   *Welcome into the Middle East.* From Middle East Missions Research,
   P.O. Box 632, Le Mars, Iowa 51031.

Kettani, Dr. M.A. (Ed.)
   1986   *Muslim Minorities in the World Today.* London: Mansell. (Useful to find
   out who are the important minorities, their location, and their problems.)

Lewis, Bernard.
   1964   *The Arabs in History.* 3rd ed. London: Hutchinson. (Short interpretative
   survey. Excellent study.)

Patai, Raphael.
   1976   *The Arab Mind.* NY: Scribners. 376 pp. (Much used study, helpful to explore
   Arab values.)

Pullapilly, Cyriac K. (Ed.)
  1980   *Islam in the Contemporary World*. Notre Dame, IN: Cross Roads Books.
       (Articles on various Muslim countries with some short, but perceptive
       discussions of major Muslim minorities.)

Smith, W, Cantwell.
  1967   *Islam in Modern History*. Princeton Univ. Press. (Dated, but an important
       analysis of the Muslim experience in the modern era and the sense of crisis it
       engenders.)

Stoddard, Phillip H. et al.
  1981   *Change and the Muslim World*. Syracuse Univ. Press. 187 pp.   (Short
       articles by specialists on various Muslim countries.)

Voll, John Obert.
  1982   *Islam: Continuity and Change in the Modern World*.   Boulder, CO:
       Westview Press. 397 pp. (Covers the broad sweep of Islam from the 18th
       century to the present, studying four types of Islam.)

Weekes, Richard V. (Ed.)
  1984   *Muslim Peoples: A World Ethnographic Survey*. 2 vol. 2nd edition.
       Westwood, CN: Greenwood Press. 953 pp. (The best survey in existence.
       Deals with 190 peoples, providing a useful bibliography for each.)

9. Christianity and Islam. Missions. The Message and its Communication. Conversion. Apologetics. Approaches. Relations

Abdul-Haqq, Abdiyah A.
  1980   *Sharing Your Faith with a Muslim*. Minneapolis: Bethany Press. 189 pp.
       (Not a manual for witnesses as the title might imply, but an excellent grap-
       pling with the major issues of the Bible, the person of Christ, and salvation.)

Addison, James T.
  1942   *The Christian Approach to the Muslim*. New York. 365 pp. (A historical sur-
       vey of missions to Islam from the beginning with a country by country study.)

Aziz-us-Samad. U.
  1976   *A Comparative Study of Christianity and Islam*. From New Era . Box 8139,
       Ann Arbor, MI 48107. 188pp. (Islam as the revival and true religion of Jesus.)

Bailey, Kenneth E.
  1973   *The Cross and the Prodigal*. St. Louis, MO: Concordia. 134 pp. (Gives an
       example from Luke 15 on how to present Christian truth through narrative.
       Useful for learning to witness apart from propositional "plans of salvation.")

  1976   *God is ... Dialogues on the Nature of God for Young People*. From Youth
       Club Program, 700 Dewberry Rd. Monroeville, PA 15146. 278 pp. (Use of
       parables and dialogue to present truth to an average Muslim.)

Bentley-Taylor, David
  1967   *The Weathercock's Reward: Christian Progress in Muslim Java*. London:
       OMF. (Deals with the history of reaching Javanese and Madurese
       to the 1960s.)

Browne, L.E.
1955   *The Quickening .Word*. Cambridge: W. Heffner. (Some key theological issues answered.)

Bucaille, Maurice.
1978   *The Bible, the Qur'an, and Science*. From American Trust Publications, 7216 S. Madison Ave. Indianapolis, IN 46227. 253 pp. (A French convert to Islam tries to prove that the Qur'an anticipates modern science and is therefore a divine revelation, superior to Scriptures. Widely heralded in Muslim circles as a definitive proof of Islam.)

Christensen, Jens.
1977   *The Practical Approach to Muslims*. NAM (An extended discussion of controversial issues pertinent to missions by an experienced church leader in Pakistan. Specially prepared for Christian workers.)

Clark, Dennis
1977   *Jesus Christ, His Life and Teaching*. From David C. Cook 850 N. Grove, Elgin, IL 60120 320 pp. (A useful biography of Christ to give to Muslims.)

Committee of Evangelical Missionaries to Islam.
1960   *Report of the Conference of Missionaries to Islam*. 261 Mary Street, Hackensack, NJ. 07601. (A series of conferences from 1960 to 1968 issued reports containing useful articles for workers in various ministries. Reports issued every two years.)

Cooper, Anne. (compiler)
1985   *Ishmael My Brother: A Biblical Course on Islam*. Bromley, Herts, Kent: STL Books. 217 pp. (A good survey for beginners in Muslim work.)

Cragg, Kenneth.
1958   *Sandals at the Mosque*. (A defense and development of his Christian perspective in *The Call of the Minaret*.)

1984   *Muhammad and the Christian*. London: Darton, Longmans, and Todd. (An erudite Christian view of Muhammad.)

1985   *Jesus and the Muslim*. London: George Allen & Unwin. 315 pp. (Compares portrayal of Jesus in the Koran, Traditions, and the Scriptures on a deeper level.)

Deedat, Ahmed.
1980   *Is the Bible God's Word*. From Islamic Propagation Centre, 47 Madressa Arcade, Durban 4001, South Africa. 64 pp. (Deedat distributes a series of anti-Christian polemical material in books, tracts and cassettes.)

Dretke, James P.
1979   *A Christian Approach to Muslims*. Pasadena, CA: William Carey Library. 261 pp. (Practical study from former director of "Islam in Africa"project.)

Elder, J.
1978   *Biblical Approach to the Muslim*. Houston: LIT International. (A simple self study course for witnesses by an experienced missionary.)

Fellowship of Faith for Muslims.
___   *Literature Resource Pool.* (FFM has a repository of tracts, booklets, books, radio scripts and other materials useful for Muslim ministries.)

Finlay, Matt. H.
1968   *Face the Facts, Questions and Answers Concerning the Christian Faith.* Bombay: Gospel Literature Service. (A small useful book, inoffensive to Muslims, but which answers typical Muslim problem areas.)

Gilchrist, John.
1986   *Christianity and Islam Series.* From Jesus to the Muslims, P.O. Box 1804, Benoni 1500, South Africa. (A very useful set of studies, 27 to 35 pages long, on controversial issues). The titles are: *An Analytical Study of the Cross and the Hijrah.Nuzul-i-Isa: The Second Coming of Jesus Christ.Al-Masihu-Isa: The Glory of Jesus the Messiah.The Uniqueness of Jesus in the Qur'an and the Bible. The Titles of Jesus in the Qur'an and the Bible. Millat-al-Ibrahim: The True Faith of Abraham.The Love of God in the Qur'an and the Bible.The Temple, the Ka'aba, and the Christ.*

1979   *Qur'an and Bible Series.* (A set of short essays which can be used with Muslims.) Titles include: *The Crucifixion of Christ: A Fact, not Fiction. What indeed was the Sign of Jonah? The Textual History of the Qur'an and the Bible. Christ in Islam and Christianity. Is Muhammad Foretold in the Bible? Origins and Sources of the Gospel of Barnabas.*

1984   *Evidences for the Collection of the Qur'an.* 24pp.

1988   *The Christian Witness to the Muslim.* Jesus to the Muslims, Box 1804, Benoni 1500, RSA. (Fruit of Gilchrist's long experience in apologetics with Muslims.)

Hahn, Ernest.
n.d.   *Man, Sin, and Salvation Series.* From FFM, 205 Yonge St. Toronto MB5 IN2. (Booklets on key issues.)

___   *Jesus in Islam: A Christian View.* From FFM.

Harris, G.K.
1957   *How to Lead Muslims to Christ.* London: CIM (Now Overseas Missionary Fellowship.) (An old China hand gives tips on apologetic issues.)

Jadeed, Iskander.
n.d.   *Sin and Atonement in Islam and Christianity.* From Centre for Young Adults, P.O. Box 354, CH-4019 Basel, Switzerland. 48 pp. (Jadeed has several essays in various languages useful for his style of presentation.) Other titles include:
Did God Appear in the Flesh? 48 pp.
God and Christ 48 pp.
Person of Christ in the Gospel and the Quran. 72pp.
How Do We Pray? 40 pp.
Infallibility of the Torah and the Gospel. 64 pp.
The Cross in the Gospel and the Quran. 50 pp.

Jomier, J.
1964 *The Bible and the Koran.* NY: Desclee Co. 120 pp. (Useful to verify Scriptures to Muslims.)

1974 *Jesus, The Life of the Messiah.* 228 pp. From Christian Literature Society Box 501, Park Town, Madras 60003, India. (Biography for Muslims.)

Jones, L. Bevan.
1964 *Christianity Explained to Muslims.* rev. ed. 173pp. Reprinted by ELD, 3, R.N. Mukherjee Rd., Calcutta, 700 001, India. (A classic for answering Muslim objections. Also good for use with Ahmadiyya.)

Joseph, John.
1983 *Muslim Christian Relations and Inter-Christian Rivalries in the Middle East.* Albany, NY: SUNY.

Kateregga, B.D. and D.W. Shenk.
1980 *Islam and Christianity.* From Uzima Press, Box 48127, Nairobi, Kenya. 182 pp. ("A Muslim and a Christian in dialogue" in 24 chapters. Each presents his beliefs which is followed by the other's response.)

Koelle, S.W.
1889 *Mohammed and Mohammedanism Critically Considered.* London. (Older style, condemnatory apologetics. Useful information.)

Lenning, Larry.
1980 *Blessing in Mosque and Mission.* Pasadena, CA: William Carey Library. 156 pp. (Builds a conceptual bridge to the Muslim mind by use of *baraka*.)

Levonian, Loutfi.
1940 *Studies in the Relationship between Christianity and Islam.* London. (Believes the basic difference between the two religions lies in their concepts of "spirit.")

Madany, Bassam M.
1981 *Sharing God's Word with a Muslim.* From Back to God Hour, 6555 W. College Dr. Palos Heights, IL 60463. 92 pp. (A broadcaster with over 20 years experience shares a "Biblical way of teaching the Christian faith to Muslims.")

Marsh, Charles R.
1975 *Share Your Faith with a Muslim.* Chicago: Moody. 96 pp. (Practical suggestions for witnessing from a worker in Africa for some 45 years). Also from STL, 9, London Rd., Bromley, Kent, UK.

Massey, Kundan L.
1980 *Tide of the Supernatural.* From CCC Box 1576, San Bernardino, CA 92402. 184 pp. ("A call to love for the Muslim world." Based on extensive experience in Pakistan and the Middle East, Massey presents keys for ministry through personal experiences.)

Matheny, Tim.
1981 *Reaching the Arabs: A Felt Need Approach.* Pasadena, CA: William Carey Library. 244 pp. (Points out cultural themes, social structures, and basic human needs as potential tools for effective witness.)

McCurry, Don. (Ed.)
1979 *The Gospel and Islam: A 1978 Compendium.* Monrovia: MARC. 638 pp. (A compilation of articles written by 43 authors on Islamic themes.)

McDowell, Josh and John Gilchrist.
1983 *The Islam Debate.* From CCC,Box 1576, San Bernardino, CA 92414. (An example of a formal debate against Ahmed Deedat.)

Miller, William.
1976 *A Christian's Response to Islam.* Nutley, NJ: Presbyterian and Reformed Pub. Co. Also STL Books, Kent, UK. (Practical helps from a missionary with over 50 years experience in Iran and N. America.)

NAM. (now Arab World Ministries)
1976 *Reaching Muslims Today.* From STL Box 48, Bromley, Kent, UK or AWM, Box 96, Upper Darby, PA 19082. 63 pp. (Tool for anyone wanting basic information for ministry to Muslims.)

Nazir-Ali, Michael.
1984 *Islam: A Christian Perspective.* Exeter, UK: Paternoster. 185 pp. (Excellent broad sweep of contemporary issues such as the Christian mission to Islam, fundamentalism, Islamic culture, Muhammad.)

Nehls, Gerhard.
1980 *Christians Answer Muslims.* From Life Challenge, Box 273, Claremont 7735, South Africa. 148 pp. (Answers criticisms of the Bible and key Christian doctrines.)

n.d. *Christians Ask Muslims.* Cape Town: Life Challenge. 142 pp. (Discusses contradictions in the Qur'an, its collection and sources, the numerology of 19, ethics, and the claims of Muhammad.)

n.d. *The Great Commission, You and the Muslims.* 113 pp. (Strategies and hints on how to be a better witness with a survey of history and teachings of Islam.)

Parrinder, Geoffrey.
1977 *Jesus in the Qur'an.* NY: OUP. 187 pp. (Covers all references.)

Parshall, Phil.
1975 *The Fortress and the Fire.* (Deals with chief social and religious hindrances to Muslim reception of Christ.)

1980 *New Paths in Muslim Evangelism.* Grand Rapids: Baker. 280 pp. (Contextualization, its principles, application, and potential, in a Muslim context.)

1983 *Bridges to Islam.* Grand Rapids: Baker. 163 pp. (Deals with Folk Islam,Sufism, mysticism, and how to use "bridges" within them to present the Gospel.)

1985   *Beyond the Mosque.* Grand Rapids: Baker. 256 pp. (Promotes a deeper Christian understanding of the Muslim "ummah" and how a Christian community might take shape without extracting converts from their culture.)

Pfander, C.G.
1910   *The Mizanu'l Haqq ('Balance of Truth').* From the Centre for Young Adults, CH-4019 Basel, P.O. Box 354, Switzerland. 370 pp. (Tisdall's revision of the 1835 Persian classic apologetic work which provoked "the Great Controversy" of the 19th century. Pfander, in 3 parts, seeks to prove the Bible is uncorrupted, and unabrogated; that the major Christian doctrines are true; and challenges the claims made for Muhammad and the Quran.)

Register, Ray G. Jr.
1979   *Dialogue and Interfaith Witness with Muslims.* Kingsport, TN: Moody Press.

Rice, W.A.
1910   *Crusaders of the Twentieth Century.* London: CMS. (The most extensive practical witnessing tool ever written for missionaries to Muslims. Despite its unfortunate title, it is a gold mine of practical helps covering almost every area of ministry and apologetics. About 560 pages, with a detailed table of contents. Needs updating in certain areas.)

Richter, J.
1910   *A History of Protestant Missions in the Near East.* Edinburgh. (Useful for gaining background of mission strategies, policies, and results in a context of traditional churches.)

Riggs, Henry H. (Ed.)
1938   *Near East Council Inquiry on the Evangelization of Moslems.* Beirut. (New workers will find the deliberations of former generations of missionaries surprisingly contemporary and insightful.)

Robson, James.
1929   *Christ in Islam.* London: John Murray.

Samartha, S.J. and J.B. Taylor, (Editors)
1977   *Christian-Muslim Dialogue.* Geneva: WCC. 167 pp. (Papers presented at the Broumana Consultation, July 1977.)

Schlorff, Samuel P.
1981   *Discipleship in Islamic Society.* From FFM or AWM, Box 96, Upper Darby, PA 19082. 77 pp. (Sections on discipleship qualities in convert churches, obstacles in the Muslim worldview, and positive doctrine in an Islamic context.)

1984   *The Missionary Use of the Qur'an: An Historical and Theological Study of the Contextualization of the Gospel.* (A Westminster seminary thesis that grapples with a fundamental issue all missionaries must face: the use of the Quran in Christian witness. Anticipated publication by William Carey Library.)

Shumaker, C. Richard (Ed.)
1974 *Media in Islamic Culture.* Wheaton, IL: Evangelical Literature Overseas. (Media specialists wrestle with the communication problems of the Gospel in Muslim contexts. Valuable resource materials.)

Slomp, Jan.
1974 *Pseudo-Barnabas in the Context of Muslim-Christian Apologetics.* Hyderabad: Henry Martyn Institute.

1981 *The Gospel in Dispute.* (From author, Postbus 203, 3830 AE Leusden, Netherlands.) 48 pp.

Spenser, H.
1956 *Islam and the Gospel of God.* From FFM or ISPCK, P.O. Box 1585, Kashmere Gate, Delhi 110006, India. 122 pp. (Shows disparity of meaning when Christians and Muslims use the same terms. This grows out of the divergent conceptions of God.)

Stacey, Vivienne.
n.d. *Practical Lessons for Evangelism among Muslims.* Wiesbaden, Germany: Orientdienst. 27 pp. (Short, practical tool for witnessing, with a special attention to ministry among women.)

Steele, Francis R.
1981 *Not in Vain: The Story of the North African Mission.* Pasadena, CA: William Carey. (History of a mission with a century of experience working among Muslims.)

Sweetman, J. Windrow.
1947 *Islam and Christian Theology: A Study of Theological Ideas in the Two Religions.* 4 vols. London: Lutterworth. (Survey of theological and philosophical development in Islam in relation to Christianity. FFM has a brief abridgement.)

Syrjanen, Seppo.
1987 *In Search of Meaning and Identity: Conversion to Christianity in Pakistani Muslim Culture.* Vammala, Finland: The Finnish Society for Missiology and Ecumenics. 247 pp. (A scholarly research project using 36 Pakistani converts as informants and giving reasons why Christianity is not attractive to Pakistanis.)

Thomsen, Mark. et al.
1986 *God and Jesus: Theological Reflections for Christian-Muslim Dialog.* From DWMIC, American Lutheran Church, 422 S. 5th St. Minneapolis, MN 55415. 94 pp. (A task force deals with problems like how to witness to a trinitarian faith to Muslims. Is our purpose dialog or conversion? And "What mission stance and strategy have integrity in witnessing...?)

Tisdale, W. St. Clair.
1980 *Christian Reply to Muslim Objections.* From Light of Life, P.O. Box 13, A-9503, Villach, Austria. (A reprint of the excellent , "A Manual of the Leading Mohammedan Objections to Christianity.")

Vander Werff, Lyle L.
  1977   *Christian Mission to Muslims: The Record.* Pasadena, CA: William Carey.
         366 pp. (A survey of "Anglican and Reformed Approaches in India and
         the Near East, 1800-1938." Evaluations and bibliographies of Tisdale,
         Gairdner, and Zwemer.)

Watt, W. Montgomery.
  1983   *Islam and Christianity Today.* London: Routledge & Kegan, Paul. 157 pp.

Wilson, J. Christy.
  1950   *The Christian Message to Islam.* NY: Fleming Revell. 189 pp. ("This is a book
         of methods of approach to Islam." Stresses "speaking the truth in love.")

Willis, A.T.
  1977   *Indonesian Revival: Why Two Million Came to Christ.* Pasadena, CA:
         William Carey. 263 pp. (Deals with some of the social, political, and
         religious factors in the turning of masses of Javanese to Christ.)

Wismer, Don.
  1977   *The Islamic Jesus: An Annotated Bibliography of Sources in English and
         French.* NY: Garland Publishers. 305 pp. (Annotated listing of 726 entries.)

Ye'or, Bat.
  1984   *The Dhimmi: Jews and Christians under Islam.* Fairleigh Dickenson.
         (Shows Muslim relations with minorities.)

Zwemer, Samuel.
  1912   *The Moslem Christ.* London: Oliphants. 198 pp. (Excellent treatment of
         Islamic sources on Jesus and how to preach Christ.)

INDEX